A SPECIES
OF ETERNITY

JOSEPH KASTNER

A SPECIES OF ETERNITY

ALFRED · A · KNOPF

NEW YORK

1977

Library of Congress Cataloging in Publication Data
Kastner, Joseph [date].   A species of eternity.   Bibliography: p.
Includes index.
1. Naturalists—United States—Biography.   I. Title.
QH26.K3R   500.92′2 [B]   77-74983
ISBN: 0-394-49033-9

Manufactured in the United States of America
First Edition

Portions of this book originally appeared in *Horticulture*
and *Smithsonian* magazines.

Grateful acknowledgment is made to the following for
permission to reprint previously published material:

The University of Illinois Press: for excerpts from
Lewis and Clark, Pioneering Naturalists, by Paul Russell Cutright.
Copyright © 1969 by the Trustees of the University of Illinois.

The University of North Carolina Press: for excerpts from
Doctor Alexander Garden of Charles Town, by Edmund Berkeley
and Dorothy Smith Berkeley (University of North Carolina Press, 1969),
by permission of the publisher.

Since this page cannot legibly accommodate all permissions,
acknowledgments to reproduce illustrations appear on page 335.

FOR BARBARA

CONTENTS

AUTHOR'S NOTE *xii*

INTRODUCTION *xiii*

ONE *THE MASTER OF COLDENGHAM* 3

TWO *AN ADAM AND HIS APOSTLE* 26

THREE *THE CURIOUS QUAKER* 40

FOUR *THE FRUSTRATED PHYSICIAN* 68

FIVE *PUC PUGGY IN XANADU* 79

SIX *PRESIDENT OF THE WEST* 113

SEVEN *THE NATURAL SHOWMAN* 143

EIGHT *A PEDDLER OF BIRDS* 159

NINE *A CHAOS OF KNOWLEDGE* 193

TEN *THE AMERICAN WOODSMAN* 207

ELEVEN *THE GULLIBLE GENIUS* 240

TWELVE *THE INNOCENT TRAVELER* 254

THIRTEEN *THE CLOSET BOTANISTS* 284

FOURTEEN *THE LAST ADVENTURE* 305

FIFTEEN *A SPECIES OF ETERNITY* 318

BIBLIOGRAPHIC NOTES *325*

ACKNOWLEDGMENTS *333*

ILLUSTRATION CREDITS *335*

INDEX *337*

Inserts of color pictures follow pages 48 and 224.

ILLUSTRATIONS

Page

4   Cadwallader Colden, portrait after one by Matthew Pratt

11   Drawings by John Banister: *Gillenia trifoliata, Dodecatheon meadia*

13   Plants shipped by John Lawson

15   A sketch of the burning of John Lawson, by Franz Louis Michel

19   Skunk cabbage by Mark Catesby

23   Jane Colden's flower drawings

28–9   Drawings of Lapland by Linnaeus

33   Linnaeus in Lapland dress

50   Peter Collinson, portrait attributed to Gainsborough

61   Grouse by George Edwards

65   Tipitiwichet or Venus's-flytrap by William Bartram

74–5   Mud Iguana or *Siren lacertina*

92–3   Alligators by William Bartram

96   Wattoolla or great Savannah crane by William Bartram

100   Frontispiece of Bartram's *Travels*

101   Rattlesnake and water moccasin by William Bartram

109   William Bartram, portrait by Charles Willson Peale

115   Pages from André Michaux's journal

126   Bones of the Megalonyx

131   Mountain goat and pronghorn

134   Grizzly treeing an explorer

137   Mountain quail and Louisiana tanager by Charles Willson Peale

140   *Erigeron compositus*

147   *The Artist in His Museum* by Charles Willson Peale
152   Mastodon skeleton by Titian Peale
164   Alexander Wilson, portrait by Rembrandt Peale
      Owl by Alexander Wilson
167   Canada jay by Alexander Wilson
184   Carolina parakeet by Alexander Wilson
194   Heath hen by Alexander Wilson
197   Sheepshead and other fish by Samuel Latham Mitchill
201   The Elgin Gardens
209   Grebes by John James Audubon
213   Birds' eggs by John James Audubon
215   Portraits of James Berthoud and his wife by John James Audubon
222   Female grackle by John James Audubon
226   Audubon's portfolio; Audubon finding his drawings destroyed
227   Winter wren by John James Audubon for Hannah Rathbone
230   Audubon's self-portrait as the American Woodsman
234   Wilson's Mississippi kite and Audubon's copy
242   Audubon's mythical devil fish drawn by Constantine Samuel Rafinesque
244   Constantine Samuel Rafinesque, portrait by Thomas Birch
249   Caricature by Rafinesque
258   James Fenimore Cooper's absent-minded naturalist, Obed Battius
265   Prairie iris or *Ixia coelestina* by William Bartram
271   Indian horseman by Titian Peale
273   Frontispiece of Thomas Say's *American Entomology* by Charles Le Sueur
276   Nuttall's long-billed curlew and ruff with Audubon's notations
281   Photographic portrait of Thomas Nuttall
292   Asa Gray in his study
298   Southwestern cactuses
300   Saguaro cactus
301   John Cleves Symmes, portrait by John James Audubon
303   *Shortia galacifolia*
309   Say's chipmunk by John James Audubon
315   Photographic portraits of John James and Lucy Audubon

CHAPTER FIFTEEN: A portfolio of namesakes

COLOR INSERTS

Bison by Mark Catesby
"Parrot of Paradise" by Mark Catesby
Magnolia warbler by William Bartram
Seed vessel of the calocasia by William Bartram
The Exhumation of the Mastodon by Charles Willson Peale
Parrot fish by Mark Catesby
Great yellow bream by William Bartram

Woodpeckers by Alexander Wilson
Songbirds by Alexander Wilson
Water birds by Alexander Wilson
White-headed or bald eagle by Alexander Wilson
Black-billed cuckoo by John James Audubon
Bush-tailed wood rat by John James Audubon
Jaguar by John Wodehouse Audubon
Common loon and common puffin by John James Audubon
Blue jay, belted kingfisher, winter hawk (red shouldered) by John James
  Audubon
Snowy owl by John James Audubon

AUTHOR'S NOTE

This book contains many quotations from the writings, letters and journals of its subjects. For both reasons of space and readability, it has been necessary to cut some of them severely. The use of the conventional three-dot elision (. . .) throughout would have made reading difficult and pockmarked the pages. In most instances, therefore, elisions have not been indicated. Having decided upon this treatment, I have tried to be as conscientious as possible in preserving the writer's meaning and context. Also, in most cases, spelling and punctuation have been changed to conform to modern usage.

INTRODUCTION

Columbus had told them that the trees and plants in his new-found world were as unlike Europe's as night is to day. Still, people in the Old World were always being surprised by reports from America of spiders as big as cats and birds as small as fingernails, squirrels that flew and frogs that whistled, of plants so blessed that they could cure almost any sickness and of others so strange that their discoverers were afraid to describe them, lest they be called fools or liars. The stories and their proofs came from the adventurous travelers and settlers who, hunting for the New World's plants and animals, wandered purposefully through wildernesses too thick with trees for sunlight ever to reach the ground, across meadows whose flowers, crushed underfoot, clouded the air with fragrance, along streams where shad danced in the springtime waters.

They had other affairs to attend to—politics, medicine, farming, teaching or tending store—but as if driven by some enchantment they went throughout the unmapped country filling bags with seeds, boxes with birds and bottles with carefully killed insects. These they sent across the Atlantic to delighted—and demanding—naturalists who always wanted more and more. Distance, disasters, even war could not stop the traffic. Americans forested the parks of rich Europeans with sugar maples and hemlocks, filled collectors' cabinets with mockingbirds and rattlesnakes, enlivened their gardens with fly-eating tipitiwichets and early blooming skunk cabbages.

The Europeans in their turn sent back books, money, encouragement and, most welcome, intellectual companionship. Friendships grew up across the ocean between men who had never met and who knew each other only through the letters they wrote and the specimens they exchanged. Even in America, men wrote to each other for years before they met, but their common interests shaped a community of naturalists that, like the established international circle of scientists in Europe, became a binding intellectual force in their new world.

Their science was a matter of the heart as well as the mind, a way to express their feeling for their land and their countrymen's unabashed pride in it.

The men who appear in this book are known today for their contributions to science, art and literature. But they have a special, peculiarly appropriate hold on the world's memory. They have gained what one of them happily called "a species of eternity," for their names are now borne by the subjects of their science—the flowers, birds, even frogs that they found, classified and brought into the world of naturalists.

A SPECIES
OF ETERNITY

CHAPTER ONE

THE MASTER
OF COLDENGHAM

❦ ❦ ❦ ❦ ❦ IN THE LATE SUMMER OF 1754, ALEXANDER GARDEN, A YOUNG Scottish doctor for whom an elegant white flower was later to be named, traveled north from Charleston to escape the oppressive heat and revive his failing health. Reaching New York, he went by boat up the Hudson River to the landing at Newburgh, then rode west to an extraordinary place called Coldengham, where at the edge of endless forests Cadwallader Colden, the powerful senior councilor of the province, had cut out for himself a self-contained realm. He had built a stone house, filled it with his children, his books, his instruments and his genteel Chippendale furniture, and there, running away from what he called "the dunghill of men's passions," lived as a scientist and philosopher.

The fledgling doctor and the elderly politician—Garden was twenty-three and Colden sixty-five—quickly came to enjoy the exchanges of their lively, learned minds, absorbed most of all in discussions of botany, which both had studied at the University of Edinburgh. As they walked about, they were joined by Colden's daughter Jane, whose knowledge of plants surprised the visitor. The young doctor's delight in their botanizing was capped by a new arrival: John Bartram, a Quaker farmer, had been hunting for plants in the nearby Catskill Mountains and dropped by to see his friend Colden.

The image of this encounter in the gardens at Coldengham persists across the years as if history had stopped, like a frame frozen in a movie, to emphasize a passing moment. Alexander Garden sensed its meaning. "How grateful was such a meeting to me," he wrote in an ecstatic letter to a naturalist in Sweden. "And how unusual in this part of the world. What congratulations and salutations passed between us."

The letter was addressed to a professor at the University of Uppsala who was already well acquainted with Garden's new friends. He had, in fact, helped publish Colden's pioneering catalog of American plants and had dubbed him

Cadwallader Colden was a formidable man in all of his many pursuits. He looked it in this portrait, a copy from one originally done by Matthew Pratt.

"*Summus perfectus*" in botany. And, having received many American plants from Bartram, he had called him "the greatest natural botanist in the world." In the exacting realm of science, these were no idle compliments. They came from a colossus of the age, Carl Linnaeus, whose genius and awesome industry had brought order out of the centuries-old confusion of natural history and helped make it the preeminent science of his century—and an intellectual glue that held men in all civilized countries together.

Mention Linnaeus today and you summon up an archaic figure, master of a dusty discipline called nomenclature, compiler of endless Latin lists, a man who is memorialized in bird and botany clubs. But in the eighteenth century he stood as flesh-and-blood force, charming men into agreeing with him, outraging them with what they considered his lewd analogies, and commanding from most of them an almost reverent obedience to his revolutionary systems. Sitting in his study at Uppsala, writing and revising his universal works of classification, Linnaeus decided how plants and animals should be named and where they should be placed in nature's order, interrupting his massive work to pick over the bales and boxes that kept coming in from all corners of the earth —seeds from Jesuit priests who had talked their way into the forbidden cities of China, shrubs dug up by ships' captains idled at the ports of Africa, snakes from missionaries inching up the dark-hung Amazon, shells from doctors who

were to die on the malarial shores of Surinam. No specimens were more gratefully received than those from the new Western world, where plants that
Europe had never heard of grew and where animals never imagined lived. And
no correspondents were more useful to Linnaeus than the men who met that
September day in Cadwallader Colden's garden.

They could hardly be more different—the ambitious philosopher-politician
of Coldengham, the plain-mannered Quaker farmer of Kingsessing Creek and
the scrupulous doctor of Charleston—but they were moved by the same purpose. Though they served the Old World, and were admired by it, they served
the New World even more. They helped to bring together an extraordinary
community of American naturalists, and to usher in the age of the adventurer-
naturalists who made their way boldly and patiently over the continent, crossing and recrossing one another's paths within each generation and from one
generation to the next as they searched out, described and displayed the plants
and animals of America. The naturalists were united by a love of nature, of
knowledge and of their land. They were spurred by the curiosity that always
impels scientists and artists. They were goaded by the need to refute a group of
vociferous Europeans who, in one of science's stranger aberrations, scorned all
nature in America as an inferior creation. And the Americans marveled, all
of them, at the beauty and diversity around them.

There were, as one of the first reporters of this world wrote, "a thousand
different kinds of birds and beasts of the forest which have never been known
neither in shape nor name neither among the Latins nor Greeks nor any other
nations of the world," and they lived in a wilderness which early-comers found
"daunting, terrible, cloathed with infinite thick woods." It was in this daunting
wilderness, a dozen miles in from the Hudson, that Cadwallader Colden had
built Coldengham. "I have made a small spot of the world which when I first
entered upon it was the habitation of wolves and bears," he wrote a friend, where,
as men of his time liked to say, he could look down on the busy vain world below. Those who knew Colden must have laughed at such ivory-tower stuff—they
knew that from him it was nonsense. One of the most hyperactive men in the
colonies, busier than most and as vain as any, Colden lived with gusto in the
world of affairs and left it only when it wouldn't do things his way. From early
in the century until the Revolution, in front of the scenes or behind them, he had
a hand in governing New York. Meanwhile, he gained a fortune in American
land, and a European reputation as the best scientific thinker in the New World.

Colden was a transplanted version of the brilliant phenomenon of his
time called the "virtuoso," the cultivated, interested layman who, at his
best, came to know a great deal about a subject (or several of them), followed
it with pleasure and diligence and often added valued facts and conclusions to

the body of knowledge. A true virtuoso, a man of serious intention and accomplishment, Colden excelled in many fields. Botany, in fact, was just one of his pastimes. He had studied it at the university and in medical school—plants were prime *materia medica* and physicians had to recognize them and their uses in order to prescribe them. Before setting out for Philadelphia in 1710, he stopped, as botanists made a practice of doing, at James Petiver's apothecary shop in London, and promised to send Petiver some plants from America. Setting himself up as a merchant more than a physician, he found that Philadelphia suffered either from shortages or gluts. Too much flour, he complained, not enough linen or nails: "Rum is ye only thing that brings ready money." Going back home, he raised a company of volunteers to help put down the Jacobite rebellion, took himself a wife and, venturing into the virtuoso's world, wrote a paper on animal sweating which was praised by Sir Edmund Halley, known now for the comet that bears his name.

In 1716, he sailed to Philadelphia again and this time stuck to medicine. He found a good friend in William Penn's agent, James Logan. He and Logan were Scotsmen of the same mold, eager for worldly success but longing to retreat into the world of the intellect. Another of their small company in the colonies was the governor of New York, Robert Hunter, who met Colden through Logan and, to Logan's dismay, lured him to New York in 1718 where he gave him lucrative government jobs, including the post of surveyor-general.

In this position, Colden supervised the land grants by which the king paid off his favorites and through which speculators made shady fortunes. Efficient and fair-minded, Colden straightened out the system, which had become a scandalous shambles, and shrewdly but honestly picked up some forty thousand acres for himself. At this point, he ceased to be a practicing physician, though he was a good one, and embarked on his career as the most durable political figure in colonial New York and a pivot of intellectual life in the colonies. A short man with little physical presence and hardly any charm, he was sharp-tongued and thin-skinned, cool-minded but often capricious. Friends admired him but were wary of him. Enemies could scarcely contain their venomous feelings for him. Though he grasped political power and held it through half a century, popularity always eluded him.

What really mattered to Colden was his own mind—wide-ranging, daring, unresting. He exercised it mostly in his interludes at Coldengham, where he would go intermittently when politics turned against him. Though he never did send the promised plants to Petiver, he collected flowers and shrubs as he traveled about the province. He was officially commissioned to write a natural history of New York, but in London the auditor-general subtracted the modest appropriation from the budget, and Colden, in a huff, refused to proceed. The confused state of the science frustrated him. "I understood only the rudiments of botany," he explained, "and I found so much difficulty in applying it to the many unknown plants that I met with everywhere that I was quite discouraged." Then, in a box of books that came to Coldengham around 1742, Colden received a volume that was stirring Europe: Linnaeus's *Genera Plantarum*, which set forth the basis for a sensible system of plant classification. "Your books gave me so much new light," Colden later wrote Linnaeus, "that I resolved again to try what could be done." He set his agile mind to mastering the new system and applying it to America's flora.

Browsing through the woods and cleared fields at Coldengham, exploring its deep forests and mountain valleys, he collected scores of plants native to his little domain. In the room where he kept his books, his microscopes, his instruments and his endless stock of quill pens, he matched his plants to Linnaeus's descriptions and found a proper place for each. There were many he could not find in the *Genera* and he classified them himself, often very shrewdly. Drawing up a list of 141 local plants, he analyzed them by the Linnaean system and, through intermediaries in Europe, got his exposition to Linnaeus himself. The Swede was so taken with this skillful and innovative American that he published the catalog as *Plantae Coldenghamiae*. The first complete work of its kind done by an American—"a truly wonderful performance," a later American botanist, Asa Gray, called it—it made a landmark impression on European scientists. And it gave confidence to American naturalists who appreciated the honor given by Linnaeus in publishing the book and in stamping Colden with the epithet "*Summus perfectus*."

THE JOINING OF THE SWEDISH COLOSSUS AND THE PROvincial botanist did not come about as directly as this account may make it seem. In fact, there is no really straightforward way of telling about the advance of natural history in America. The naturalists kept coming upon each other again and again, in person or in their work, as they moved through the land and through the decades, overlapping, adding and subtracting, clearing up and confusing. Trying to track their progress is sometimes like trying to untangle the patterns that sandpipers leave as they double back and forth across each other on a wave-whipped beach.

By the time Cadwallader Colden received the Linnaean light, there had been two centuries of collecting by often misguided naturalists in the New World, and of classifying by easily misled Old World scientists who tried to cram shiploads of new species into their unwieldy and inadequate systems. All this had built up a considerable body of uncertain information about nature in the Western Hemisphere. The first to bring back a description was, of course, Columbus, who owed a debt to America's birds: faced with failure and mutiny in the last days of his first voyage, he set his final course by following the autumn flocks of migrating birds making their landfall. Columbus found in his new world that "all the trees are unlike ours as day is to night and so are the fruits and so are the plants."

From then on, reporter after reporter wondered at the improbable novelties of America. A friend of Columbus's, Gonzalo Fernández de Oviedo y Valdés, who started as pageboy to Queen Isabella and rose to become a colonial governor, published a widely translated *Natural History of the West Indies* in which he described "spiders of a marveylous biggenesse, her bodye as bygge as a sparrow. Vypers leape in the ayre to assayle men. Adders so redde that in the nyght they appeare like burnynge coales. Byrdes so lytle that the whole body is no bigger than the toppe of the biggest finger of a man's hand. Manye toades so big that the bones of sum of them appere to bee the bones of cattes." And he told of their vocalizing: "Summe of them synge pleasantly. Summe also whistle. They are noyous by the great multitude."

From Virginia, Alexander Whitaker, a minister, wrote of the strange "possown," a beast which "will let forth her young out of her bellies and take them up into her bellies again," and of "a squirrel which will flie from tree to tree 20 or 30 paces in one flight." King James, entranced by an earlier gift of two alligators, now coveted a flying squirrel. William Strachey, whose account of the hurricane he encountered off Bermuda set the scene for Shakespeare's *Tempest*, reported that vines "climbing to the toppes of the highest trees" bore grapes which made wine as good as any from France.

Virginia was the source of two new plants of all-encompassing medicinal virtues. One was uppowoc, called tobacco by the fumbling English translators, which was useful for head pains, kidney stones, blisters, toothache and bad breath. It was so highly regarded as a preventive of the plague that students at Eton were instructed in the correct way to use their pipes and to inhale, and had to carry pipe and tobacco in their schoolbags. They were whipped if they did not smoke regularly. Even more valued were the roots and bark of the sassafras tree, which, besides doing everything tobacco could do, also relieved "griefes of the breast and evil of the joyntes," according to Thomas Hariot, "and comforteth the liver and stomach." The woods of Virginia were being stripped of the trees until a vessel arrived in London with two tons of bark, glutting the market.

The early-comers found a new bird, the wild turkey, that could "runne as swift as a greyhound," and grew "exceeding fat, sweet and fleshy from feeding on wild strawberries." William Wood was among the first of generations of naturalists to be awed by the flights of passenger pigeons: "an airy regiment, seeing neither beginning nor ending the length and breadth of these millions of millions." And in no time at all, these birds were on their way to becoming endangered species. John Josselyn reported in the 1670s that, because of overhunting, " 'tis very rare to meet a wild turkie in the woods" and that passenger pigeons "are much diminished, the English taking them with nets."

Josselyn, an enthusiastic observer, set down a compendium of New England wonders, including "snakes three yards long with a sharp horn on their taile, squnk with so strong a scent there is no abiding of it." His new world was full of unexpected perils. When he plucked a "pineapple" from a tree in Massachusetts, a horde of wasps charged out to give him a grievously "swolen lipe." (In Paris, the nests of paper wasps were in great demand, considered more precious than pearls.) Josselyn was wary of the porcupine, "a very angry creature and dangerous, shooting a whole shower of quills at their enemies." But he found gentler marvels: "a thousand flowers never seen in England and each of a more masculine virtue than the same species at home." One early herbalist stopped to muse over the "sea-star fish." Men knew as a matter of faith that God had a purpose for everything He created but William Hughes could imagine none for this star-shaped sea creature. "Doubtless it is good for something," he concluded, giving up the effort to understand, "there being nothing made in vain."

Out west, the French priest Marquette found a bright and lovely land where many-colored parakeets flew through forests of tall canes. He heard "great numbers of wild cattle bellowing." The explorer La Salle added that "the number of bison is almost beyond belief. I have seen twelve hundred killed in eight days by a single band of savages." Europeans complained that there were no nightingales in the New World, but some spoke well of a bird that could imitate any song it heard and whose Indian name "*artamoke*" lent itself readily to translation as "mocker."

There were, however, complaints from visitors who found America a frigid place. At the latitudes of England and France, where they expected the mild climate of their homelands, they found instead long winters so fiercely cold that whole rivers and lakes froze over. Others, hoping from early reports to come upon sunny palm groves inhabited by gracious natives, were greeted instead by gloomy forests and inhospitable Indians. The wilderness overwhelmed the newcomers, the snakes scared them, the insects beleaguered them. From their disgruntled accounts, some of the most eminent European scholars and scientists fashioned a picture of America as a miserable land where the sun scarcely shone and all life was degenerate. (A later chapter will tell how the wiles of Benjamin Franklin and the logic of Thomas Jefferson were recruited to knock this foolishness out of European heads.)

The first American settler to try to bring some sense out of the confusion of

real and dreamed-up wonders—in fact, the New World's first resident naturalist—was a young clergyman named John Banister, who in the late seventeenth
century became the protégé of two admirable British patrons of botany, the
Temple Coffee House Botany Club and the Bishop of London. The Club was
a group of some forty Londoners who met Friday evenings at the Rainbow
Inn at Temple Bar to share the latest news in natural history and arrange ways
of advancing its study. The Bishop of London, Henry Compton, was an unusually fortunate member. When he took over his post, he also took over the
bishop's estate at Fulham, which boasted one of the grandest gardens in all
England. An Elizabethan predecessor named Grindal had started it and Compton
expanded it with exotic plants from everywhere. His missionaries felt it prudent
to send plants to their superior, and travelers were rewarded so lavishly for
their contributions that Compton became known as "the Maecenas of botany."
A stubborn anti-papist, he was exiled to Fulham by the Catholic James II, but
found this a kind of blessing since it gave him more time for his garden.

In his official capacity as Bishop of London, Compton was responsible for
filling church positions in the colonies, and in John Banister, who had published
an excellent folio on English plants, he saw a way to take care of his needs both
as bishop and botanist. When a chaplain's job opened in Virginia, Compton assigned Banister to it and the Coffee House Club added its support. Arriving in
Virginia in 1678, Banister, like so many other naturalists newly come to America,
was all but overcome by "a new world of plants, so strange and monstrouse that
I am affraide that they may be thought chameras to be found nowhere but in
his brain that drew them."

An adventurous man, curious about all nature and touched by a romantic
delight in it, Banister was painstaking and vivid in telling of the things he encountered. The passenger pigeons astonished him into Biblical phrases: "They
darken the sky, the wind of their wings is like the rushing of waters." He belittled the beaver's industry. There was always one beaver "the Indians call
perecue, ye overseer of ye gange whose care it is to see his hands mind their
work which is falling of saplings, walking with them and biting and lashing
forward with his tayl those that do not keep up and bear their equal weight."
The "pascimmon," he noted, was "a sort of fruit between the plum and medlar,
pleasant enough when rotten but green it is of exceeding harsh taste which draws
the mouth into a purse." Banister promoted the undying myth about the rattlesnake which "hath a kind of fascination in its eyes with which it does constrain
in some creatures to make themselves a prey unto it. I have been told that they
have accidentally seen a squirrel running down a tree and up a little way and
down again, all the while crying out and trembling, where at the foot of the
tree they beheld the snake lye gaping with its eyes fixed on the squirrel which
at length tho with a great deal of reluctancy run full into its mouth."

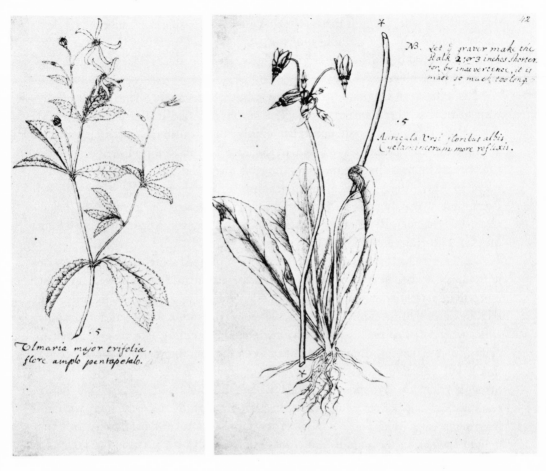

John Banister made delicate drawings of the plants he gathered. At left is the Gillenia
trifoliata *or bowman's-root; at right the* Dodecatheon meadia *or shooting star.*

America to Banister was a land of happy plenty. "In the spring of the year,
herrings come up into many of our runs and fords in such abundance that it is
impossible to ride through without treading on them. Our shad leap and dance."
In his fourteen years in Virginia, he sent back to Compton and the Club 340
species of plants, a hundred insects and the best natural history reports yet received from the colonies. Some of his information was practical. Tobacco growers,
he reported, sent their best leaf to England and Holland but "that which is dark
and not fit for the market, we sell to Irish and west countrymen." Watermelons
were "a very pleasant and innocent fruit. I have eaten near half a score in an
afternoon." Curious about the way flies flew, he conducted experiments that revealed the function of their halteres: "under each wing a small flexible apex with
which they poise their body and keep it in equilibrium, as the dancer on the rope

does with his pole, for pull these off and their flight is short and unsteady." And he was amused by the gullible bullfrog: "I have seen our frogs in an evening (perhaps mistaking them for fireflies) take in little live coals as greedily as chickens peck up corn."

His patrons in England, gratified by what Banister sent them, could hardly wait to receive "the many discoveries of North America in the next shipping." John Ray, the best British naturalist of his time, called Banister a "botanist of the first order," and leaned heavily on him for his comprehensive *Historia Plantarum*. Banister had begun compiling his own "Natural History of Virginia" when in May, 1692, he went on a trading and exploring trip with William Byrd, first of that famous Virginian family. He was walking through the brush along the Roanoke River when a woodsman in the party, apparently mistaking him for a deer, fired and killed him.

Banister's "Natural History" was never completed, which is a pity because it promised to be, like the work of so many naturalists that followed him, far more than a treatise on plants and animals. When, in a report of a collecting trip, he notes that he came upon a "rivulet conveyed into a small vault of craggie rocks where its fall makes a dead-hollow sound something like that of a kettle-drum," and of having dinner beside "an open arch of rough stone where grows this small but rare kind of hart's tongue," and of going home at day's end through "rich low grounds abounded with a kind of wild balm which being trampled by our horse as we rode through it mightily refreshed us with its fragrant scent"—then John Banister's matter-of-fact record brightens with the delight he took in the sounds and sights and smells of his pristine world.

❦ ❦ ❦ ❦ ❦ AMONG THE MEN WHO MOURNED BANISTER WAS JOHN LAWSON, who came to America a few years after Banister's death. "Had not the ingenious Mr. Banister (the greatest virtuoso we ever had on this continent) been unfortunately taken out of this world," said Lawson, "he would have given the best account of the plants of America." Lawson was in a good position to judge, for he himself was on the way to becoming the New World's leading naturalist. He gave a suggestion of what he might do in *A New Voyage to Carolina*, published in London in 1709.

The book begins as if the author were about to launch a swashbuckling novel.

In the year 1700 [reads his opening sentence] when people flock'd from all parts of the Christian world to see the solemnity of the grand jubilee at Rome, my intention at that time being to travel, I accidentally met with a gentleman who had been abroad and was very well acquainted with the ways of living in both Indies; of whom, having made enquiry concerning them, he assured me that Carolina was the best country I could go to; and that there then lay a ship in the Thames in which I might have my passage. I laid hold on this opportunity and was not long on board before we fell down the river.

What followed this adventurous beginning was a sensible, observant account of the resources and inhabitants of the Carolinas. Once there, Lawson quickly became a man of substance as surveyor general, a boundary commissioner, a land developer and a negotiator with the Indians, for whom he had an uncommon sympathy and understanding. His *New Voyage to Carolina* was actually written as a piece of real estate promotion to interest settlers and land speculators. But

In 1710, John Lawson sent off a half-dozen carefully pressed plants for James Petiver's huge shambles of a collection. Today they are filed in the British Museum.

it is filled with information on natural history. "The possum is found nowhere but in America," he wrote; "he is the wonder of all the land animals. The male's pizzle is placed retrograde and in time of coition turning tail to tail. If a cat has nine lives, this creature surely has nineteen for if you break every bone in the skin and mash their skull leaving them for dead, you may come an hour after and they will be gone quite away. Their flesh is very white and well tasted but their ugly faces put me out of conceit with that fare.

"The raccoon," he goes on, "is the drunkenest creature living, if he can get any liquor that is sweet and strong." The eagle, a cowardly bird whose "nest stinks most offensively," is an "excellent artist at stealing young pigs which prey he carries alive to his nest, at which time the poor pig makes such a noise overhead that strangers have thought there were flying sows and pigs in that country." And Lawson was among the first to fall under the spell of that dulcet mimic of the Western world, the mockingbird. They are, he wrote, "about as big as a Throstle in England. They sing with the greatest diversity of notes that is possible for a bird to change to. They will sing with us tame in cages yet I never take any because I have their company as much of the time as if tame. They often sit upon our chimneys in summer and sing the whole evening and most part of the night."

He had great praise for "Indian corn or maiz, the most useful grain in the world, the most nourishing grain for a man to subsist on without any other victuals. It refuses no ground except the barren sands, besides the stalks bruised and boiled make a very pleasant beer." There were, however, plants to be wary of—"jamestown [Jimson] weed, excellent for curing burns but taken inwardly brings on a sort of drunken madness."

All the while he was making his land deals and preparing his book, Lawson was collecting plants and animals and shipping them to England. He had his own sponsor, less exalted than Banister's bishop but just as important. This was James Petiver, the London apothecary. As young Colden was to do a few years later, Lawson called on Petiver before leaving England and promised to send him specimens from whatever part of the world he landed in. Unlike Colden, Lawson kept his promise. Shortly after he arrived in Carolina, he sent word he was ready to start shipping animals, plants, sea shells and butterflies. Petiver promptly sent him brown paper for wrapping plants, widemouthed bottles for keeping insects, pins for butterflies and detailed instructions on how to pack and ship things.

This Petiver was a testy, omnivorous virtuoso, a member of the Temple Bar Club, who garnered from his many correspondents what was probably the largest, most variegated and certainly most disorganized botanical and zoological collection of his time. He already had a web of collectors in the colonies. He received lizards, scorpions and an Indian queen's petticoat made of moss from

Hannah Williams of Charleston; dried plants from Joseph Lord, a Charleston preacher; glowworms from Benjamin Brilliant, an apothecary of Boston; butter-flies from Hezekiah Usher, a pious New England land speculator. He corre-sponded regularly with the Massachusetts theologian Cotton Mather, who informed him of his experiments in hybridizing Indian corn, a pioneering work in plant breeding. But even so, Petiver felt let down by this New World network. Robert Steevens of Goose Creek, South Carolina, stopped sending specimens because he thought Petiver's pay of five shillings for a quart jar of insects, snakes, frogs or fireflies was too little. Daniel Henchman, dismissed from Harvard for stealing a silver spoon, went to the Carolinas with Petiver's en-couragement but sent back only promises and tall tales. Petiver equipped a Maryland-bound young Englishman, whom he called "Isaak the butterfly boy," with "a quire of brown paper, insect box, pins, a small vial half filled with spirits in which to drown flies, beetles, caterpillars, a book for butterflies and moths, a paper bag or two to put all ripe seeds, fruits and berries, also shells." On the same voyage went another Petiver protégé, Dr. David Krieg of Riga. But the butterfly boy never sent anything to his patron and Dr. Krieg went back to Riga.

John Lawson was a solace in Petiver's vale of disappointments. He industri-

The Indians who captured John Lawson bound him, along with his slave and his employer Baron von Graffenried, before burning him at the stake. This contemporary sketch was made by Franz Louis Michel.

ously continued to ship things to Petiver's shop on Aldersgate Street where they disappeared into the apothecary's great jumble. Yet in the British Museum, where Petiver's collections rest today, there are thirty specimens labeled, in Petiver's hand, "Lawson's Virginia trees." Lawson himself was ambitious to be more than a collector. He had a grand scheme to do what Banister had started to do: write a complete natural history of the region he had come to know so well. But he was stopped, as Banister was, by death in the wilderness. Out exploring and botanizing in the back country, he was captured by Tuscarora Indians rampaging against white settlers. They accused Lawson of stealing Indian land and, as a witness told it, "they stuck him full of fine small splinters of torch-wood like hog's bristles and so set them gradually afire."

Petiver, Bishop Compton and their fellows of the Temple Bar Club persisted in their attempts to settle a naturalist in the colonies. The bishop ordained a young botanist named Hugh Jones and gave him a post as chaplain to the governor of Maryland. But Jones died after a few frustrating years. The real bonanza for British naturalists was a man who went over to America on his own, without sponsors or any intentions of working seriously in natural history.

❦ ❦ ❦ ❦ ❦ MARK CATESBY DEVELOPED A SOUND KNOWLEDGE OF NATURAL science through his friendship with the eminent John Ray. Accompanying his sister to Virginia in 1712 when she came to join her new husband, Catesby stayed on as a guest of the second William Byrd, son of John Banister's companion on his fatal last trip. A plantation owner of wide culture who read the Bible in Hebrew every morning before breakfast, always dressed in silks and ate off fine china plates, Byrd was a slipshod virtuoso who sent some plants, animals and a good deal of scientific misinformation to England. With Byrd's encouragement, Catesby traveled through the Carolinas and the Caribbean, gathering seeds and plants for Bishop Compton's gardens and drawing the covetous attention of James Petiver.

When Catesby went home in 1719, he found a dozen patrons eager to finance his return to the colonies. Back in Charleston in 1722, he started what Banister and Lawson could never bring off: a comprehensive natural history of the Southern colonies. He roamed west up the Savannah River and south into the untouched territory of Georgia and Florida, traveling on foot, loaded with boxes and bottles, paints and papers, relying usually on Indians for food and shelter. It was wearying and sometimes risky work.

> An odd accident happened last February [he wrote a friend]. A negro woman, making my bed a few minutes after I was out of it, cried out: "a rattlesnake!" We being drinking tea in the next room, surprised with the

vehemence of the wench's bawling, went to see the cause and found a rattlesnake actually between the sheets in the very place where I lay, full of ire, biting at everything that approached him. Probably it crept in for warmth in the night, but how long I had the company of the charming bedfellow, I am not able to say.

During his four years of travel, he made drawings and paintings on the spot. In designing the plants, he wrote, "I always did them while just gathered and the animals, particularly the birds, I painted them while alive." His shipments to England were so filled with fascinating things that the distinguished scientists of England got into unseemly wrangles over who was to get what. This sent Catesby into a rare temper. "It can't be expected I should send collections to every one of my subscribers," he complained. "I'll do the best of my abilities nor can I say or do more." As his specimens found their way into gardens and collections in Paris, Leiden and Danzig, Catesby gave Europe a fuller and more accurate picture of American flora and fauna than anyone else had up to that time.

In 1726, he went home to stay and set about putting down what he had seen and learned during his twenty years in the New World into *The Natural History of Carolina, Florida, and the Bahama Islands*. He had to do it mostly on his own. Now that he was no longer sending them shrubs or bird skins or stuffed fish, his fickle patrons turned away from the man they had once fought over. Catesby had to make his own engravings and color the plates himself. The finished work displayed 171 plants and 113 birds, along with animals, insects and fish.

The first volume of his *Natural History*, published in 1731, established Catesby as the first real ornithologist of America. He made detailed drawings of birds and methodical observations of their habits and migrations. In a time when respected naturalists believed that birds in winter hibernated in caves or under water or flew high out of the atmosphere, Catesby gave evidence that they migrated in a perfectly sensible manner for sensible reasons: to get to warm places where there was food. A self-taught artist, he tried to give his subjects a feeling of life and action. "As I was not born a painter, I hope some faults in perspective and other niceties may be more readily excused," he wrote apologetically, "for I humbly conceive plants and other things done in a flat, though exact manner may serve the purpose of natural history better in some measure than in a bold and painter-like way." They very simplicity of his style enhances Catesby's paintings. In their studied use of indigenous plants as backgrounds for his birds and animals, they anticipate the later work of Alexander Wilson and John James Audubon—and their charm is exceeded by neither.

The *Natural History* was received as a "noble work," bought by the Queens of England and Sweden, by dozens of British peers, by Continental noblemen and, in America, by six colonial governors. Catesby thus became the first naturalist of America to attract wide attention from Americans. Back home in London, he became a joining force in American natural history, corresponding with naturalists like General James Oglethorpe, the founder of Georgia; Dr. William Bull of Charleston; John Custis and John Clayton in Virginia; Bartram in Pennsylvania; Colden in New York. He told them what their colonial neighbors were doing and in this roundabout way helped tighten the new community of natural scientists.

It had members now, by the 1740s, in all the colonies—doctors, planters, merchants, preachers, public officials, ships' captains—almost all enlisted one way or another by English virtuosos to provide them with seeds, plants and animals. Cadwallader Colden, once he had his Linnaeus in hand, found himself enmeshed in this pleasant business, especially after he came to know Peter Collinson, the busiest botanical go-between of his time. He had, Colden wrote a friend, "begun a correspondence with a gentleman who is curious in several branches of the natural history of America. I am told he has the most compleat garden of American plants that is in Great Britain." This, he added snobbishly, "is the more extraordinary by his being a merchant (a mercer) who seldom apply themselves to any study that no way tends to advance their cash." Among many plants that the master of Coldengham sent the mercer of London were a prickly pear, the leaf of a pitcher plant and a skunk cabbage. Collinson particularly appreciated the last, because it bloomed so early.

Through Collinson, Colden sent his collections and descriptions of Coldengham plants to the esteemed Johann Friedrich Gronovius of Leiden. The Dutch botanist, Collinson reported, was "in raptures" cataloguing the plants and passing his catalog on to Linnaeus. After *Plantae Coldenghamiae* was published, Linnaeus congratulated Colden on his mastery of botany and the Linnaean system: "You taste a pleasure but few know. You have a secret to beguile a lonesome way and shorten a long journey which only botanists know." Colden was flattered by the attentions of such renowned men, but humility was not part of his character and he answered Linnaeus's compliments by picking flaws in his system. With surprising intuition for a botanist of such short and narrow experience, he found contradictions which troubled Linnaeus himself. But the colonial observed the amenities. In a letter to Gronovius that criticized the way Linnaeus classified Indian corn, he added, "I send with this a curious and new invention for warming a room with a small fire more effectually than can be done by a large fire in the common method. It may be particularly useful to you and Dr. Linnaeus by preserving your health while it warms your studies. It is the invention of Mr. Benjamin Franklin of Philadelphia, the printer, a very ingenious man." It was, however, not the Franklin stove but Colden's con-

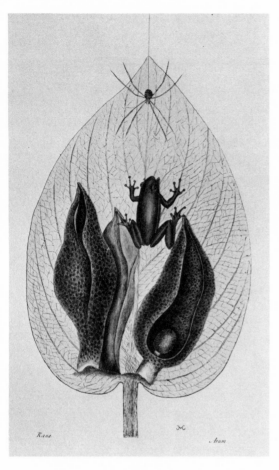

Rana   ✕   *Arum*

The New World's skunk cabbage was prized by English gardeners because it came up so early in the spring. Catesby drew this one as a backdrop for a tree frog.

tribution to his botanical work that warmed Linnaeus into giving the name *Coldenia* to a wild heliotrope.

His interest in botany introduced Colden into that international circle of natural scientists which was the eighteenth century's most pervasive and influential intellectual group. Its members were found all the way from Siberia to South America, and by their incessant correspondence, they kept information and ideas moving through all the civilized world. John Amman, the English physician working in St. Petersburg, might send a report on Russian rhubarb to Johann Jakob Dillenius, the German botanist working in England, who would pass the information on to Albrecht von Haller, the argumentative plant physiologist of Göttingen, who would inform Isaac Lawson, the physician general of the British army in Flanders, who would tell it to one of the de Jussieu brothers in Paris, who might suggest to Sir Hans Sloane in London that he pass the information on to Patrick Browne in Jamaica. Inevitably, Peter Collinson would hear of it and so Cadwallader Colden would hear what Dr. Amman had reported on. The world of the eighteenth century, a historian has remarked, was a small place and every prominent person knew all the others. Naturalists who never laid eyes on each other became intimate friends by virtue of the long and faithful letters they wrote to each other, year in and year out, until death ended their exchanges.

Before the emergence of Franklin, no American was so well known in this circle as Colden. The plants he sent were gratefully received and his discussions of the new classifications were listened to with respect. Since botany was so much concerned with medicine, Europeans were impressed when Colden cited instances where pokeweed had mitigated the pains of cancer. He recommended witch hazel as a remedy for blindness—it had helped him—and introduced the "root of accaise" as a softener of corns.

Some European scholars were already familiar with Colden, not as a botanist but as an authority on American Indians. As surveyor general of New York, Colden constantly had to deal with the Indians whose lands were being taken by the English. In 1724, he wrote *The History of the Five Indian Nations*, the first authoritative work in English on American aborigines. In England, the first printing of five hundred copies was quickly sold out and the work remained a standard for decades.

For his *History* Colden borrowed heavily from published French sources but he added much firsthand information and showed a compassion, surprising in a hard-headed colonial official, for the usually maligned subjects of his book. They "are a poor barbarous people, bred under the darkest ignorance," he wrote. "Yet a bright and noble genius shines through these black clouds. None of the greatest Roman heroes have discovered a greater love to their country or a greater contempt of death when liberty came in competition. They greatly sully those noble virtues by that cruel passion, revenge. But what alas have we Christians done to make them better? Instead of virtues we have only taught them vices." Colden was adopted into a Mohawk tribe, and an old sachem gave him his own name, Cayenderongue, explaining that with it went "all the acts of valor" the sachem had performed.

But the biggest stir Colden made in the international circle of scientists resulted from his sortie into Newtonian physics. Every virtuoso of the time felt he had to read and understand the *Principia*. Colden was not content with that. In an essay called *An Explication of the First Causes of Action in Matter*, he set out to do what even Sir Isaac himself never felt equal to doing: explain why gravitation works. The nub of Colden's theory, which is not easily explained, much less condensed, was that the force of gravitation in the solar system was exerted by the ether, which drew planets inward toward the sun.

This force was counteracted by the sun's light, which pushed the planets outward away from the sun. The *Explication* was a tortured and fuzzy piece of theorizing based less on observation and mathematics than on intellectual speculation, which Colden sometimes held superior as a scientific method to a conventional amassing of facts.

Colden considered this theory to be the high achievement of his mind, but the reasoning of his *Explication* baffled his admirers while his stubborn dedication to it embarrassed them. James Logan, his old Philadelphia friend, was puzzled by it: "It must necessarily have some further meaning in it than the language itself imparts." John Bartram "could not read it with the necessary attention till after harvest," but even then he "apprehended he should find it out of his reach." Franklin simply said it would take a lot of his time and attention, and tactfully put off any comment.

None of this discouraged Colden. He sent copies of the work to friends in London, where it was published. Peter Collinson enthusiastically circulated this among his friends in England and on the Continent. Most were uncomprehending or noncommittal. A few were hostile, annoyed at what they considered colonial presumption, an attempt to outdo their demigod Newton. It was, however, a measure of the respect in which Colden was held that some of the finest contemporary scientists took pains to consider the work, if only to criticize it. The Swiss mathematician Leonhard Euler found it full of "ingenious reflections, but also of absurdities." The greatest unkindness was committed by a German named Abraham Gotthelf Kästner, who went to considerable trouble to translate Colden's knotty work into German, then picked it apart, point by point, to show how wrong it was. Still the work continued to be read. Years later, when the famous French naturalist Buffon lost his copy, he asked Thomas Jefferson to get him one. Jefferson, finding his own misplaced, had to borrow another through Francis Hopkinson, the patriot poet.

A stubborn man in science, Colden was even more persevering in politics, and far more successful. Shortly after coming to New York, he was made a member of the Council, which ran the colony. By dint of staying alive and in office, he became the senior councilor and lieutenant governor. As royal governors came and went, sometimes serving just long enough to enrich themselves through land grants, Colden became a continuing thread of authority and policy in the province. An ardent supporter of the king's strict rights, he opposed the local merchants who wanted more home rule and freedom to trade. In the seesaw of provincial politics, Colden was frequently out of favor. Then he would petulantly leave what he called "the troublesome broils" of public affairs, and go off to Coldengham to philosophize. But as soon as a new regime sought him out, he was back happily in the broils, running New York. A half-dozen times, in the interludes between one royal governor's departure and another's tardy arrival, he ruled the province as lieutenant governor. Eventually even his opponents supported his farseeing proposals to guard the borders with a flexible chain of small forts. In the wars against the French and Indians, he gave commands to Sir William Johnson, the frontier fighter, and laid out campaigns for Sir Jeffrey Amherst.

At the center of almost everything intellectual and scientific in the colonies, Colden gained his place as the first of America's home-grown materialist philosophers by arguing against the new idealism. As a doctor, he published a *Treatise on Wounds and Fever* which was consulted by physicians for decades. He suggested a useful way of printing by stereotype and proposed that a canal be dug to connect the Hudson River and the Great Lakes. Theorizing in meteorology, he knocked down the accepted theory about waterspouts: that they were formed by sea water sucked up into the clouds. If this were so, Colden pointed out, the skies would rain salt water, which they were never known to do. Colden suggested that a waterspout might be formed from a cloud by a kind of whirling effect in the atmosphere—which later meteorologists proved to be the case.

All the while, Colden kept up his correspondence with the international circle of naturalists, and to this circle, in 1755, he introduced one of the most beguiling botanists of the time, his daughter Jane. Like the rest of Colden's ten children, Jane was educated by the tutors he installed at Coldengham and by Colden himself, who paid considerable attention to his children's minds. Jane and her hunchbacked brother David responded most to his attentions. David carried on Colden's work in physics, doing research in electricity which was admired by Franklin and several French scientists. Jane was chosen to carry on for her father in natural history. He explained why in a letter to Gronovius in Leiden.

> Now in the 68th year of my life [he wrote], my eyes so far fail me that I cannot with sufficient accuracy examine the parts of fruitification nor can I bear the fatigue which accompanies botanical researches. I thought that botany is an amusement which may be made agreeable for the ladies who are often at a loss to fill up their time. Their natural curiosity and the pleasure they take in the beauty and variety of dress seem to fit them for it. I have a daughter who has an inclination to reading and a curiosity for natural philosophy. I took the pains to explain Linnaeus's system and put it in English for her use. She is now grown very fond of the study and understands in some degree Linnaeus's characters.

Colden enclosed some descriptions of plants Jane had found, along with prints she had made on a simple press of her own devising. Several of them, Colden thought, were new to botanists.

Jane made impressions of more than three hundred plants, traded drawings and information with John Bartram's son, William, and swapped seeds with Dr. Garden. On the way home from that happy meeting at Coldengham, Dr. Garden had found an unfamiliar plant and he asked Jane if it was a new species. No, she replied; it was No. 153 in her catalog. He sent her some exotic seeds he had received from Dr. Monsey, a British doctor acting as physician to the Prince Royal of Russia, who had gotten them in Moscow from a correspondent in Africa. There were certainly very few ladies anywhere in the world in Jane's fortunate position: having a father who, in provincial isolation, could translate a complex system into plain English for his daughter, then guide her into it and, to cap it all, spread news of her accomplishment among the world's most distinguished scientists.

The advent of the first lady Linnaean sent a twitter of excitement through the international circle. Colden sent samples of Jane's work to Collinson, who responded that his "ingenious daughter" was "the only lady that I have yet heard

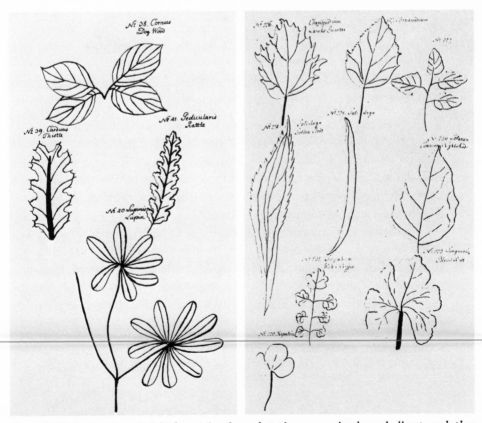

Jane Colden's drawings had little art in them, but they were simple and direct, and they clearly identified the plants that grew wild around Coldengham.

of that is the professor of the Linnaean system." Collinson passed on word to Linnaeus, who, he reported, was "not a little proud" of it. Garden sent a sample of Jane's *Hypericum* No. 153 to Dr. Robert Whytt, at Edinburgh University. Dr. Whytt informed Garden's famous teacher Dr. Alston, who sent his compliments to Jane. Jane's hand-drawn volume, *The Flora of New York*, with 340 illustrations she had made, was bought by the president of the Royal Society and wound up in the British Museum. A London virtuoso proposed to Linnaeus that he give an American filipendula the name *Fibrurea coldenella* after his lady disciple. This brought a shocked objection from one of Jane's aunts. "What!" she exclaimed. "Name a weed after a Christian woman!"

For all her talents, Jane was a modest young woman and, in fact, her achievement was modest. Her drawings were not detailed, her descriptions barely adequate. She had many other things besides botany to keep her busy. She supervised Coldengham's vegetable gardens and made its cheese, which a visitor pronounced "the best I ever ate in America." She read the latest books, shopped for the family and waited for a suitable husband. But men may have found this backwoods bluestocking too formidable and she herself was apparently very choosey. Her newlywed younger sister gently scolded Jane for this in a letter to the family describing the kind of life better suited to a young lady than hunting for weeds and sending them to old men in Scotland.

"We were to have a frolick of fish and lobsters," she wrote, reporting on a picnic at the estate of one of Jane's rejected suitors whom she calls "the Majour."

> There was 20 of us in company, 10 ladies and 10 gentlemen. The first thing we did was to prepare dinner of fine black fish and lobsters where we had in perfection for the poor fish was jumping after their guts and scales were off and the lobsters crawling in the boiling pot. We then sat down upon the green grass and din'd most daintily, music playing all the time. The Majour gave all the company a hearty invitation to his seat where we were entertained with wine and punch in great plenty, the Majour himself as gay as any young man and never stopped from dancing for several hours together. Tell sister Jennie that I wish she could have seen him. He has a pleasant place and a good house, nothing wanting but a mistress to take care of it. But, methinks I hear you say, what a deal you write about Jane's admirer.

Jane never took up with the Majour. When she was thirty-five, she married a 40-year-old widower, Dr. William Farquhar. The one glimpse of her wedded life shows that it was a loving one.

> My dear Mr. Farquhar is confined to his chair [she wrote her sister Kate]. I will not tell papa how he got his hurt but I will tell you and will

excuse your laughing at the manner it was done. I came into the part
where he was with (as he afterward told me) a mighty demure face to remove which he took me up in his arms and, turning suddenly round with
me, wrenched the sinews of his thighs. I little thought it would get so bad
as it is now and I fear he will not soon get well of it. O Kate, you feel for
every little sickness or pain he had in a manner you knew nothing of before.

And so, with the demure Linnaean giving herself over to domesticity and
her impulsive husband, botany lost a second Colden.

CHAPTER TWO

AN ADAM
AND HIS APOSTLE

❦ ❦ ❦ ❦ ❦ THE LETTER, WITH ITS EARNEST ENGLISH, CAME TO COLDENG-ham the way most letters came to Cadwallader Colden—or John Bartram or Alexander Garden or any of the others in the American community of natural-ists: through Benjamin Franklin. As postmaster in Philadelphia, Franklin was the most reliable conduit in the colonies. Better yet, he could give his col-leagues in science free postage, no small matter for the prolific correspondents of those days.

The letter, Franklin explained, had been left at his post office by "a Swedish gentleman, a professor of botany lately arrived." His name was Pehr (or Peter) Kalm and the credentials he presented were impressive, marking him as the most finished naturalist yet to visit the New World. But what would recommend him far more to Americans was his sponsor, and Kalm was careful to mention him right off.

"Dear Sir," began Kalm's note to Colden, "I have here the honor to send you the letters of Mr. Linnaeus which he did leave to me the last year when I went from Sweden. I can't enough express the kind love and great esteem he has for you. I have just had the advantage to be by Mr. Linnaeus about 2 years time and was loved of him as was his own child." Then, escaping to the language in which he was more at home, he concluded: "Ignoscas, quaeso, Vir Nobilissime, si minus bene lingua vestra vernacula utar. . . ."

He dipped back to English for a postscript. "I should be most obliged if you could procure for me some seeds of the kind of Acer whereof the Indians make a sort of sugar."

The favor asked was all too familiar by now to American botanists, ac-customed to such by-the-way requests from Europeans. But the introduction of Linnaeus's name was an event. A letter from him would open a scientist's door anywhere in the civilized world as surely, say, as one from Sir Isaac Newton would have a few decades earlier or one from Albert Einstein a couple of centuries later. In Kalm, American naturalists could meet for the first time a man who had studied under Linnaeus. He could tell them, from firsthand knowledge, all about the sage of Uppsala, who, barely a dozen years before, had published his first works on natural history, and stood now, almost unchallenged, as the shaper and arbiter of that science.

CARL LINNAEUS, BORN IN 1707 TO A SWEDISH CLERGYMAN, HAD botany thrust upon him. His father taught Carl the names of flowers almost as soon as he could talk. An uncle with a whimsical approach grew a round raised garden in which flowers were planted like food set on a table and shrubs stood behind like dinner guests. At college, young Linnaeus quickly capitalized on his knowledge of botany and his talent for attracting the support of useful men. First it was a bilious one-eyed professor named Stobaeus, who gave Linnaeus access to his library and his own knowledge. Then it was a venerable teacher named Celsius, who overheard Linnaeus discoursing on plants and was so impressed that he became his patron and introduced him to the eminent Professor Rudbeck, at Uppsala, who is remembered by a flower that Linnaeus years later named for him—the *Rudbeckia* or black-eyed Susan.

Linnaeus became Rudbeck's favored pupil and gained a reputation at the university by the lively language of his thesis on plant fertilization, which described flowers as perfumed bridal beds where bridegrooms embraced their beloveds. By badgering university and government officials, he got a grant to explore the harsh and little-known regions of Lapland.

As an exploring botanist, Linnaeus was the prototype for the intrepid adventurer-naturalist who roamed the wilds of America: a man ready to plunge into the dangers and uncertainties of the wilderness and just as ready afterward to dramatize the hardships and perils he faced—and his own courage in surmounting them. In his journal Linnaeus quickly put himself on center stage by portraying himself as setting out "in a light coat of linsey woolsey cloth lined with red shalloon, leather breeches, a round wig, a green leather cap and a pair of half boots. A small leather bag contained one shirt, two pairs of false sleeves, two half shirts, an inkstand, pen case, microscope and spying glass."

The trip, which began in May, 1732, took Linnaeus on a shambling horse through, as he wrote, "desolate forests and sandy heaths, the Lapland Alps, the shores of the Arctic oceans." He was shot at by a trigger-happy hunter, shared a hut one night with sixteen naked Lapp deer herders, and "had more than enough of hunger, thirst, sweat, cold rain, snow, ice, rocks and the language

Linnaeus recorded his trip through Lapland in a set of child-like drawings. They showed (from above, clockwise) an owl, the arctic sun rising over the regions he visited, a curiously constructed skin boat, Linnaeus taking a rest, a harnessed reindeer and a sketch of the Andromeda plant illustrating his allegorical comparison of the plant with its mythical namesake.

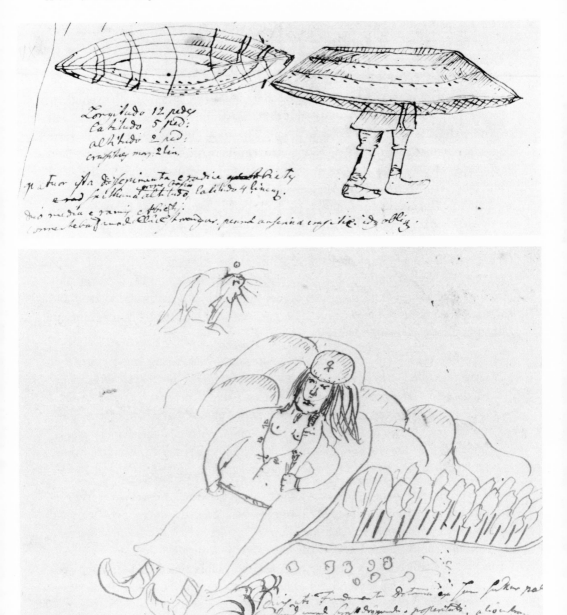

of the Lapps." He found dozens of new plants and minerals while gathering data on the habits of the nomads. Back home, where he later published his report, *Flora Lapponica*, he was received not just as a scientist, but as a kind of Columbus back from a dark world.

On his way now to success as a teacher, he fell in love with the daughter of a wealthy doctor, who would permit a marriage only if Linnaeus got himself a physician's degree and a good practice. The most desirable medical degrees could be obtained in Holland, so Linnaeus went there, quickly got his degree and just as quickly, through his charm and talents, found important men to befriend him. One was Hermann Boerhaave of Leiden, the most revered teacher of medicine in Europe and a botanist so dedicated to nature that, Linnaeus said, he tipped his hat to every elder tree he passed in a tribute to its medicinal virtues. Boerhaave, impressed by Linnaeus's personality and ideas, introduced him to George Clifford, an immensely rich banker and director of the East India Company. A hypochondriac horticulturist, Clifford found in Linnaeus a physician to tend his real and imagined ailments as well as a naturalist to tend and catalog his gardens at Hartecamp. The gardens were unbelievably magnificent. When he first saw them, Linnaeus wrote:

> My eyes were ravished on the instant by so many masterpieces of nature, aided by art, menageries full of tigers, monkeys, wild dogs, Indian deer and goats, American falcons, parrots, peacocks, swans, American crossbills, greenhouses full of so many plants that a son of the north must feel bewitched, treasures from Asia, Africa's misshapen plants, carnivorous flowers, the charming inhabitants of America, orchids, yams, calabash trees. I felt completely enraptured.

At Hartecamp (where Kaiser Wilhelm went after the First World War to live out his exile from Germany), Linnaeus was treated—in his own words—"like a prince of botany, a coach and four at his service, the best circumstance any mortal could hope for." With the Dutch naturalist Johann Friedrich Gronovius, he worked on a catalog of American plants that had been sent over by a Virginian, John Clayton. His Dutch friends helped him publish the first of his many works, the *Systema Naturae* and *Fundamenta Botanica*.

In *Systema Naturae*, Linnaeus set forth a coherent and serviceable way of classifying all living things. This had been a preoccupation of natural scientists since the days of Aristotle, but the systems they devised were all unsatisfactory. The worthy ones were unwieldy, the simple ones almost frivolous. Some classifiers divided all animals into domestic and wild or started with what they considered the noblest animals, the lion and the eagle, and worked downward. Plants were pushed roughly into categories such as trees and shrubs, according to size. The best of the systems had limited use, and as the number of known plants increased the systems grew more and more cumbersome. When explorers and travelers began sending back specimens from the edges of the expanding world, as Asia, Africa and the Americas began to swamp Europe with exotic samples that were as bewildering in their resemblance to European plants as in their strangeness, the whole structure of natural history seemed ready to surrender.

Linnaeus solved the problem with one of those extraordinary leaps that genius makes across the gaps of science: by establishing a simple consistent way of describing and classifying plants; and by establishing and rigidly enforcing an economical way of naming plants and animals. His botanical system was based on characteristics that almost all plants have, their sexual characteristics. The number of the flower's stamens, the male organs, and of its pistils, the female organs, largely determined the class and order to which the plant belonged. One stamen was the class Monandria, two stamens the class Diandria and on up to Triandria, Tetrandria and so on. The number of pistils determined the order to which the plant belonged: one pistil Monogynia, two pistils Digynia and so on. Thus a plant like the canna, which has one stamen, is in the class Monandria. Since the canna also has one pistil, it is the order Monogynia. It is classified, therefore, as Monandria Monogynia. Sea blite has one stamen, putting it in Monandria, and two pistils, putting it in Digynia. Thus it is classified as Monandria Digynia. Lilac, with two stamens and one pistil, is Diandria Monogynia.

Having thus categorized plants in large groups, the classes and orders, Linnaeus set about identifying them more closely and giving them firm, usable names. He took to heart the classical precept of the Greek botanist Isodorus: "If you do not know the names, the knowledge of things is wasted." Linnaeus set up the binomial, or two-name, system. It provided that all plants should be known by two words. The first would distinguish the genus, a group smaller than a class or order, whose members shared some generality of structure. For example, it could be the structure of the flower or fruit. The second name would refer to some special recognizable characteristic—shape of leaves, taste or habitat, for example—and would define the species.

The binomial approach was brilliant and economical. In pre-Linnaean language, a common ground cherry was called "physalis amno ramosissime ramis angulosis glabris foliis dentoserratis," which meant that it was a bladder-fruited annual, many-branched with angled branches and smooth, deeply toothed leaves. Linnaeus brusquely set aside most of the description, picking out the words "physalis angulata," which described the two unique characteristics: the bladder fruit and the angled leaves. A botanist coming upon the plant would, by counting the five stamens and one pistil, find the proper class (Pentandria) and order (Monogynia). Then, noting the bladderlike fruit and angled leaf—Eureka!—the genus *Physalis* and species *angulata*.

The binomial idea, in itself, was not new, as folk names of many plants show: watercress, sweet marjoram, horse-weed. But these are loose terms and vary with locality—one country's horse-weed is another's butterweed. By Linnaeus's binomial system, it is everywhere and always *Erigeron canadensis*. Linnaeus went to the heart of the problem of nomenclature by discarding inessentials and providing standards. He had an instinct for recognizing what was truly characteristic, a patience for examining and reexamining details, a brilliance in choosing names and a firmness of mind that enforced his rulings.

Others had anticipated Linnaeus's approach; he fused and extended their diverse findings and conclusions. His method was invaluable to science at the time, the best tool yet devised for a natural historian. It imposed an orderly system and was adaptable for the amateur as well as the professional. A Cadwallader Colden or anyone with a copy of Linnaeus and a growing plant could quickly become a botanist. Natural history became the most widely and readily mastered of all sciences. Novices collecting in nearby woods and fields felt free to send their finds to more knowing naturalists, who were happy to get the specimens and to welcome useful recruits into the ever-enlarging natural history community. Learned naturalists, receiving specimens from newly explored lands, loyally sent them on to their peers in other countries, creating an ever-tighter international circle of natural scientists. They strengthened the great intellectual impulse of the eighteenth century, the age of the Enlightenment and of the encyclopedists who tried to bring together everything men had learned and present it in a disciplined fashion. Man's knowledge and consciousness of his world was increasing at an almost unmanageable rate. The Enlightenment's purpose was to put the discoveries in their proper places, to make knowledge accessible to everyone. It was the first real age of popularization, and Linnaeus did more to popularize science than anyone had ever done before—or has done since.

Linnaeus was to develop and extend his system throughout the natural sciences for a quarter of a century, but his work in Holland, when he was barely thirty, set the foundation for it. He did not exaggerate too much when, in one of several autobiographies, he later wrote (he was given to writing about himself in the third person) that "within the three years he was in Holland he had discovered more new things and reformed botany more than anyone before his time had been able to do in his entire life." His Dutch friends begged him to stay in Holland. France offered him citizenship and a handsome stipend if he would work in Paris. He made a triumphant tour of England, winning skeptics there to his system.

After he returned from Lapland, Linnaeus was painted in the attire he wore on the journey. His leather bag held clothes, inkstand, pens, microscope and spy glass.

But he wanted to get back to his fiancée, who was growing impatient with her absent suitor. Returning to Sweden, he married, made friends at the court, became physician and confidant to Queen Ulrika, who fancied herself a botanist, and joined the faculty at the University of Uppsala, where students packed the classrooms and stood out in the hallways to hear his lectures. Eventually, scientists, famous poets and philosophers—Thomas Gray, Goethe, Rousseau— also became devout Linnaeans.

Precise and painstaking in his work, Linnaeus could be colorful and poetic in his writings. His sexual approach to botany was anything but clinical. When he described the andromeda plant, he mused about the mythological maiden Andromeda, whom the poets

> represented as a Virgin of the most exquisite and unrivaled charms; but these charms remain in perfection only so long as she retains her virgin purity, which is also applicable to the plant. This plant is always fixed on some little turfy hillock in the midst of swamps, as Andromeda herself was chained to a rock in the sea. Dragons and venomous serpents surround her, as toads and other reptiles frequent the abode of her vegetable proto- type; and when they pair in the spring, throw mud and water over its leaves and branches. As the distressed virgin cast down her blushing face through excessive affliction, so does the rosy-colored flower hang its head, growing paler and paler till it withers away.

In discussing the classification Diandria, he referred to the two stamens as "two husbands in the same marriage." In the complicated case of marigold that carries sterile florets in its disk and fertile florets in the petals, he used the term "Confederate Males with Necessary Polygamy," and went on to say that "the beds of the married occupy the disk and those of the concubines the circum- ference, the married females are barren and the concubines fertile." Such uninhibited botany offended some of Linnaeus's colleagues, who denounced the sexual system not for its scientific limitations but for its bad taste, In Russia, it was officially banned as "lewd and licentious." The eminent Dr. Johann Siegesbeck of St. Petersburg declared that such "loathsome harlotry as several males to one female would not have been permitted in the vegetable kingdom by the Creator."

Linnaeus brushed aside such carping just as he did the complaints of botanists who accused him of renaming almost everything on earth according to his own tastes. But he did just that: no plant or animal really had a name in science until Linnaeus either gave one or approved one. Everybody waited on him. He acted as if he, like Adam, had the Lord's mandate to name His crea- tions. Sitting in the study on his estate at Hammarby, enjoying his title as Count von Linné, listening to the tinkling of glass bells he hung in the trees, kept company by a pet raccoon named Szub sent him from America and a parrot who would issue the call for dinner, "Twelve o'clock, Mr. Carl," he accepted plants, animals and homage from everywhere.

Every Wednesday and Saturday, he forsook his study for expeditions into the countryside, taking with him "some two hundred pupils who collected plants and insects, made observations, shot birds and, after having botanized from seven o'clock in the morning until nine o'clock in the evening, returned through the city to his garden, their teacher walking at their head, with flowers in their hats, with drums and trumpets and shouts of *Vivat Linnaeus!*" This was the poet Linnaeus evoking a scene that could have come from some medieval tapestry, fragrant with unscented flowers and woven with unheard music.

He had given up more arduous exploring and traveling now that he had his pupils and admirers to do it for him. In a few brief lines to an English friend, he described his far-flung network of collectors and apostles:

> My pupil Sparrmann is just gone to visit the Cape of Good Hope. Another of my scholars, Thunberg, is to accompany the Dutch embassy to Japan. The younger Gmelin still remains in Persia. My friend Falk is in Tartary. Mutis is making splendid botanical discoveries in Mexico. Koenig has found many new things in Tranquebar. Professor Früs Rottböll of Copenhagen is publishing the plants found in the Surinam by Rolander. The Arabian discoveries of Forksall will soon be sent to the press at Copenhagen.

And Peter Kalm was on his way to Coldengham.

🌱 🌱 🌱 🌱 🌱 HE SEEMS TO HAVE BEEN LINNAEUS'S MOST PRIZED PUPIL. When Linnaeus went to Russia in 1744 at the invitation of the Czarina, he took Kalm along. When the Swedish Royal Academy was looking for a botanist to search America for plants that could be useful in Sweden, Linnaeus recommended Kalm, which settled the matter. En route to America, Kalm stopped in England, where he got advice from Catesby, and arrived in Philadelphia in late summer of 1748. Like John Banister and so many other naturalists, he was all but overcome by the New World. On a first casual walk ashore, he wrote, "Whenever I looked on the ground I found everywhere such plants as I had never seen before. I was seized with a terror at the thought of learning so many new and unknown parts of natural history."

He quickly shook off his fears. With a sharp eye, a beautifully trained mind and an unending curiosity, he pried into everything and peppered his American friends with questions. Where, he asked Colden, did American cockroaches come from? (The West Indies, said Colden.) What good was sassafras? he asked Bartram. (It eased sore feet, said John.) Why did herring unfailingly come back to spawn in certain places? he asked Franklin. (Because they were born there, replied Ben.)

Kalm had a practical mind. Pokeweed berries provide a rich purple dye and its young sprouts make delicious greens, he discovered, but eating the old leaves can cause fatal dysentery. He grew rhapsodic about the sweet-bay tree: "The whole air is filled with their sweet and pleasant scent. It is agreeable beyond description to travel in the woods, especially at night." He added that the wood is used by carpenters to make planes and that the berries, steeped in rum, cure consumption. He admired the straight tall trunk of the sweet gum and, describing the prickly cones that drop from its branches, added, apropos of nothing at all, that "it is not particularly pleasant to dance barefooted under these trees." He went out of his way to mention the shrub that "the Swedish call spoon tree and the English call laurel," which Linnaeus, "because of the particular friendship and kindness with which he had honored me, has been pleased to call *Kalmia latifolia.*"

Kalm gave a gruesome description of a plant unique to America. When a person touches it, "blisters arise in great numbers and make the sick person look as if he were affected by leprosy. Their eyes are sometimes shut up for days by the swelling." Kalm was wary of poison ivy, but a companion, though warned, went on heedlessly collecting the plants until, after some time, "his hands swelled and he felt a violent pain and itching." Kalm was probably the first to set down what generations of Americans have learned this same painful way about immunity to poison ivy and poison sumac. "Though a person may be secure against the power of this poison for a while, yet in the course of time he may be affected by it."

To Kalm, America was a noisy new world: "Thousands of frogs croaked all night long in the marshes and brooks. The locusts, as soon as their wings were dry, began their song which is almost sufficient to make one deaf when traveling through the woods. The tree toads are very clamorous in the evening and drown the singing of the birds." As for bullfrogs: "They croak so loud that two people talking by the side of a pond cannot understand each other. It seems as if they had a captain among them, for when he begins to croak all the others follow; and when he stops the others are all silent. In the night, you may hear them although you are near a mile and a half off."

He was struck by the abundance of fruit in America; blackberries grow as common as thistles in Sweden "and have a very agreeable taste." Farmers were astonishingly casual about their orchards; when "our leaders leaped over the hedge and gathered some agreeable fruit, the owners were so little concerned that they did not even look at us. The country people in Sweden guarded their turnips more carefully than the people here do their most exquisite fruits."

Already, two centuries ago, Americans were concerned about man's mistreatment of nature, appalled at how the country's wildlife was being wasted. A 90-year-old man told Kalm that when he was young a hunter could "shoot eighty ducks in a morning but at present you frequently wait in vain for a single one. In spring the people steal eggs, mothers and young indifferently because no regulations are made to the contrary." And if any rules had been made, Kalm added, "the spirit of freedom which prevails in the country would not suffer them to be obeyed." Years before, "the bays, rivers and brooks" were so full of fish that fishermen "at one draught caught as many as a horse was able to carry home. But at present they often work in vain all night long."

After several months on the eastern coast, Kalm set out northward on the real business of the trip: to find cold-climate plants that would be useful to Swedish farmers. He went up to Coldengham, but, Colden wrote to Linnaeus, Kalm "was so industrious I could not persuade him to stay above one night in my house." Canoeing up the Hudson, Kalm was wide-eyed at the sturgeon, "all day long, leaping high up into the air." Then the cultivated Swede confronted the primeval wilderness, trudging through the forests, exhausted by heat, plagued "with mosquitoes, gnats, and wood lice. Our fear of snakes and especially of the Indians made the night's rest very uncertain and insecure. We heard great trees fall of themselves in the night, though it was so calm that not a leaf stirred. They made a dreadful cracking sound. We did not venture to make a fire for fear the Indians should find us out and kill us. We heard several of their dogs barking in the woods, which added to our uneasiness." Actually, they learned later, there was a scalping party out. It missed the travelers by only one night.

At Quebec, he cataloged the hardy fruit trees and amassed information from the Marquis de la Glissonière, a French virtuoso who was vice-governor-general of Canada and gave a standing order to his scouts and missionary priests to write reports on the plants and animals of the country they went through. Kalm noted in passing that Catholic Canada was grateful to the Pope for classing the beaver as part fish so it could be eaten on fast days. He himself thought it inedible. On the trip back south, Kalm found "the long autumn nights terrifying in this vast wilderness. May God be with us!"

Back safely in Philadelphia, he continued to mine his American friends for information. Franklin told him how he had learned about the migrating habits of herring. When he was a boy, he and his father were puzzled that in the spring the fish always ran up one particular stream, ignoring an almost identical stream close by. Taking up some herring eggs, they transplanted them to the neglected stream. The herring hatched and went out to sea. Next spring—and every spring thereafter—schools of herring came up the new stream. When Kalm remarked that blackbirds foraged a great deal of corn before it could be harvested, Franklin told him how New England farmers had learned about the balance of nature. Blackbirds had so devastated crops there that bounty hunters were hired to kill them off. The farmers were delighted until they found that, without blackbirds to eat them, worms had infested their fields and were devouring their hay. "The people," Kalm wrote, "repented of their enmity to the corn thieves" realizing that since they kept the worms down "they were entitled to some reward for their trouble."

When the winter grew so cold that Kalm's ink froze in his inkwell, Franklin lent him one of his "newly invented Pennsylvania fireplaces," which Kalm pronounced excellent both for heating his room and warming his chocolate. Kalm told Franklin about the theory that the Norsemen had visited America before anybody else, which was news to Franklin, and Franklin in turn told Kalm that the Indians had sold Rhode Island to the English for a pair of spectacles.

Bartram was an unending source of information. The plantain, he told Kalm, was known as the "Englishman's foot" to the Indians because they found it grew wherever the white man walked and nowhere else. Kalm had had the usual disagreeable experience of eating an unripe persimmon, but Bartram told him that a tolerably good wine could be made from the mature fruit. Bartram explained the uses of a local truffle, described stalactites he had found in a cavern, analyzed the construction of wasps' nests, instructed Kalm in how to root white cedar (stick a shoot in swampy soil) and lectured him on the natural habitats of American trees. He talked about the strange, almost perfectly round holes that were found in rock formations, and theorized—correctly —that they were made by the grinding action of pebbles propelled round and round by rain and melting ice.

Cadwallader Colden advised Kalm that skunk cabbage was a good remedy for scurvy and told him a story about the fierce, tenacious habits of American snakes. As Kalm reported it, a workman had interrupted a blacksnake in the act of mating, and the snake chased after the meddler, coiled around his leg, pulled him to the ground and did not let go until it was cut into pieces.

In America, Kalm stayed for the most part at the Swedish colony of Raccoon (now called Swedesboro) in southern New Jersey. Since he had studied first to be a clergyman, he often took over the pulpit for the colony's ailing preacher. From Raccoon he traveled up to Niagara Falls and his published description of that wonder was one of the earliest done by a European: "The effect is awful, tremendous, enough to make the hair stand on end."

Though Kalm used his American friends, they also found him exceedingly helpful. He brought a disciplined eye to natural history and saw things they had not noticed. He explained the Linnaean system to them as only a trained student could, sharpening their own understanding of American resources. Kalm has "so much more knowledge on botany and in natural history than anyone in this country can pretend to," Colden wrote to Linnaeus when Kalm left for home in 1751, "and he has been so industrious and has undergone such great difficulties in traveling through a great part of this vast forest and risked such dangers to his person from its savage inhabitants that his zeal in the pursuit of knowledge cannot be sufficiently applauded." Along with his compliment, Kalm carried back to Sweden hundreds of plants he had found in America and also a wife—the young widow of the sickly preacher of Raccoon, who had died the previous winter.

Linnaeus was delighted to see his disciple. Though ill, he "rose from his bed and forgot his troubles." Of the plants Kalm brought back, ninety were new to Europeans. He failed, however, in his original mission: to find plants that would be useful in Sweden. Virtually nothing he took back could be profitably grown by Swedish farmers. His journey did profit his own career. He went on to live a long and prosperous life as a clergyman and professor, and his book, *Travels in North America*, was widely and eagerly read.

But he disappointed his friends in America. For years Bartram grumped that the ungrateful Kalm never sent him a copy of his *Travels*. And when Cadwallader Colden heard Kalm's version of his blacksnake story he was so distressed by the exaggerations that he had his son David write a correction and circulate it among the colonial naturalists. Franklin, on reading it, issued another of his many maxims. "It is dangerous," said Ben, "conversing with these strangers that keep journals."

CHAPTER THREE

THE CURIOUS QUAKER

⸙ ⸙ ⸙ ⸙ ⸙ PETER KALM COULD ASK JOHN BARTRAM ENDLESS QUESTIONS and get patient answers because Bartram was what the eighteenth century admiringly called "a curious man": not an odd man but an inquiring one. Bartram, who asked himself more questions than anyone else did and traveled all over the unexplored land to find his own answers, used that word himself in a letter to Cadwallader Colden in the summer of 1743. "This journey may afford us a fine opportunity of many curious observations," he wrote his friend as he set out on a trip which took him over the Endless Mountains, past the Licking Place, through the Dismal Vale and across the Impenetrable Mountains to the Aquanishuonigy, the country of the Confederate Indians.

These were names set down on the map which Lewis Evans, Bartram's companion, made of the regions they went through. "The third of July," Bartram wrote in his account of their journey from Philadelphia up through Pennsylvania to Lake Ontario, "I set out from my house on the Schuylkill River. We ascended the Flying Hill, so called from the great number of wild turkeys that used to fly from them to the plains." They came by Tulpehocken Hill, "so called from the Indian word signifying a tortoise, unto which the natives of the country have conceived it bears some similitude." Riding up a steep and stony ridge, he was warned "by a well-known alarm to keep our distance from an enraged rattlesnake that had put himself in a coiled posture of defense within a dozen yards of our path." With his attention to specific detail, Bartram recalled that after they had "punished his rage by striking him dead, we took notice that while provoked he contracted the muscles of the scales so as to appear very bright and shining but after the mortal stroke his splendor became very much diminished."

They traveled on to "the last great ridge which is composed chiefly of large gravel as big as pigeons' eggs, through a grove of white pine very lofty and so close that the sun could hardly shine through," then up a hill composed of "white clay under a shallow surface" where he saw fossil "impressions of shells in the loose stones." They settled one night at a spot where there was "an Indian cabin that we took the liberty to remove knowing they usually leave behind them a good stock of fleas." But it rained and "the wet deprived me of my rest that I had taken so much pains to secure against the vermin."

On the way, they stopped to pick up two more members of the party: a frontier mystic named Conrad Weiser and an Indian chief named Shickellamy. These two would conduct the main business of the journey—negotiations designed to prevent a threatened border war between settlers and Indians. They were an interesting team. Weiser, son of immigrants from the Palatinate states of Germany, had been adopted as a boy by a Mohawk chief and, living with him, had gained an understanding of Indian dialects and psyches that made him invaluable as a negotiator and peacemaker for the colonists. A shrewd but sometimes unworldly man, he had lived for years as a celibate monk in a Lutheran cult led by a bogus abbot named Beissel. Though he came back into secular life, he still carried with him a strangeness that the Indians appreciated and trusted. They named him Tarachwagon, or "he who holds up the heavens."

Shickellamy was a French Canadian who, captured as a child by the Oneidas, had grown up to become a chief. He and Weiser had worked together before in dealing with the Indians and were sent out this time by Cadwallader Colden's old friend James Logan, who more or less ran Pennsylvania. Weiser would do the main negotiating. Shickellamy's presence and prestige would protect the party. "We would not but derive a confidence from the company of a chief," wrote Bartram. Lewis Evans, a surveyor, was to map the territory, a special need because of the incursions of the French from Canada. Bartram, whose good sense and knowledge of natural history recommended him to Logan, would be on hand to give counsel and make observations on the character and resources of the region.

The party complete, Bartram's narrative went on with the lilt of a nursery rhyme: "Riding over a hazel plain we met eight Shawanese Indians going to Wiomick," and they all sat down under a shady oak. After a squaw had kindled a fire to light their pipes, "Weiser acquainted them with our business. They were so well pleased that they gave us the Yohay, a particular Indian expression of approbation which is very difficult for a white man to imitate well."

They rode on, along

> a fine bottom full of great wild nettles, up a hill covered with spruce, oak spruce, laurel, opulus, yew with ginseng and ataliashum in abundance over boggy rotten places to an old beaver dam, by very thick and tall timber of beech, chestnut, linden, ash, great magnolia, sugar birch, sugar

maple, poplar, spruce, with ginseng and maidenhair, the soil black on the surface and brown underneath, roots and moss perpetually shaded, constantly rotting and rendering the earth loose and spongy; this tempts an abundance of yellow wasps to breed which were very troublesome to us. We lodged in a bottom, producing ginseng, sarsaparilla, mediola, maidenhair, darallia, panax, mitela, christophoriana with white, red and blue berries. We had a fine warm night and one of the Indians sung in a solemn harmonious manner very different from the common Indian tune, from whence I conjectured it to be a hymn to the Great Spirit. In the morning I asked the interpreter what the Indian meant by it but he did not hear him and I believe none of the company heard him but myself who wake with a little noise, rarely sleeping sound abroad.

They passed through a "great white pine, spruce swamp full of old trees lying on the ground or leaning against live ones. They stood so thick that we concluded it almost impossible to shoot a man at 100 yards distance. A bullet must hit one before it could fly 100 yards in the most open part." Hurrying, they sent a messenger ahead with a string of wampum to Onondaga, "to acquaint them with our coming that they might send messengers to the several nations to hasten their deputies to meet them for this town serves the Five Nations as Baden does the thirteen cantons of Switzerland."

He paused in his narrative to debunk an Indian legend:

We perceived a hill where the Indians say Indian corn, tobacco and squashes were found on the following occasion: an Indian whose wife had eloped came hither to hunt, he espied a young squaw and inquiring where she came from he received for answer that she came from heaven to provide sustenance for the poor Indians and if he came to that place twelve months after he should find food there. He came accordingly and found corn squashes and tobacco which were propagated and spread through the country and this silly story is religiously held for truth among them.

After pushing through a "miserable thicket" and woods where the trees grew so close "it seems almost as if the sun never shone on the ground since the Creation," they reached the town of Onondaga.

The chiefs [Bartram wrote] were already assembled to receive us with a grave cheerful complaisance. At night soon after we were laid down to sleep we were entertained by a comical fellow. He had on a clumsy vizard of wood colored black with a nose four or five inches long, round the eyes circles of bright brass, long tresses of buffalo hair. He would sometimes hold up his head and make a hideous noise like the braying of an ass. I asked Conrad Weiser who lay next the alley what noise that was? and Shickellamy, who I supposed thought me somewhat scared, called out "Lye still, John." I never heard him speak so much plain English before.

While Weiser and Shickellamy stayed to negotiate with the chiefs, Bartram and Evans went on to Oswego, on Lake Ontario. His reflections on observing the lake show how far Bartram's inquiring mind had carried him. Reminded of something he had read in Newton, he commented that "these lakes are said to have a kind of flux and reflux. The water of the lake Ontario is considerably diminished and has lost ground a great number of years. Whether this effect is common to all the waters of the earth, according to a conjecture of the great Sir Isaac Newton, or to the removal of some great obstruction or to the gradual wearing away of the falls, I do not know." From this geophysical speculation he went on to anthropology, discussing the early landings in America by Danes and Norwegians, or even, he thought, Egyptians or Carthaginians. Suggesting that there was a land link between America and Asia, he later mentioned a story he had been told about an Indian woman "well known by a person in Canada" who "after an interval of many years" was "met again by the same traveller in Chinese Tartary."

Weiser and Shickellamy got their treaty, and after an exchange of wampum and speeches, the party set out for home. The traveling was pleasant: "the gooseberries being now ripened, we were every now and then tempted to break off a bough and divert ourselves with picking them, though on horseback. The great green grasshopper began to sing (catedidist)."

Bartram pressed on—and so wore out his horse that at Weiser's farm "she stretched herself at full length and rose no more for 24 hours." He hurried home on a borrowed horse. He knew he really had no business going on the trip when he did. Summer was not the time for a farmer to leave his crops. What had moved him to go when Logan proposed the trip was his curiosity, just as it had, a dozen years earlier, nudged him into the study of botany.

John Bartram was born in 1699. His father, having fallen out with his fellow Quakers, moved to North Carolina where he was killed by the Indians, apparently in the same uprising that killed John Lawson. Young John Bartram, left behind in Pennsylvania with his grandparents, had only rudimentary schooling before he then turned farmer. Settling at Kingsessing Creek, several miles down the Schuylkill from Philadelphia, he drained his wet riverfront meadows, rotated his crops, and got almost twice as much hay and grain from his acres as neighboring farmers did. He enlarged his house with huge stones he cut in a novel way, while his second wife enlarged his family. Of their nine children, seven survived, an extraordinary number in those days— and a tribute, in part, to John's skill as a country doctor. His knowledge of Indian cures kept him busy treating his neighbors, and his study of medicinal plants led him inevitably into botany.

There is a lovely legend about how the unlettered farmer turned himself into "the greatest natural botanist in the world." It was told by J. Hector St. John Crèvecoeur, who visited Bartram, and in his classic *Letters from an American Farmer* set down a story he said Bartram had told him.

> One day [said Bartram] I was very busy holding my plow (for thee seeist that I am but a simple plowman) and being weary I ran under the shade of a tree to repose myself. I cast my eyes on a daisy, I plucked it mechanically and viewed it with more curiosity than common country farmers are wont to do; and observing therein many distinct parts, some perpendicular, some horizontal. What a shame, said my mind, that thee shouldst have employed so many years in tilling the earth and destroy-ing so many flowers and plants without being acquainted with their struc-tures and uses! This seeming inspiration suddenly awakened my curiosity for these were not thoughts to which I had been accustomed.

The story holds as much truth as any allegory does. Actually, on another occasion, Bartram wrote that he had, "since ten years old, a great inclination to plants and knew all that I once observed by sights though not their proper names, having no person nor books to instruct me." In any case, at some time before 1730, Bartram went into Philadelphia where he bought some botany books and a Latin grammar, then found a schoolteacher who taught him basic Latin. In this efficient way the simple plowman launched himself into a life which was to take him into the far wildernesses of the New World and into the Old World's circle of scientists. It would make him the century's most important contributor of American plants to Europe's gardens and herb-ariums. It would also make him a prime force in the intellectual movements of the colonies and a natural philosopher who, through his writings—and those of his son—was to exert a deep influence on a whole school of Romantic writers in England.

As a botanist, Bartram started out with local excursions, collecting plants for a garden he laid out along his creek. His interest and skill soon caught the attention of the learned men of Philadelphia, who were ready to encourage plain men with good ideas.

A venerable physician named Christopher Witt, who wasted his classical education and fine mind in promoting astrology and necromancy, took Bartram into his library and his garden in Germantown, one of the first botanical gardens in America. Witt lent Bartram books and offered him guidance in botany and magic making. Bartram gratefully accepted the former, but, he wrote a friend, "when we are upon the topic of astrology, magic and mystic divinity, I am apt to be a little troublesome by inquiring into the foundation and reasonableness of these notions."

James Logan, who also tutored Bartram, was quite another matter. He had come to Pennsylvania in 1699 as secretary to William Penn and stayed on as his agent and viceroy. For all his plain-living philosophy, Penn was always in need of money—he was simultaneously philanthropic and extravagant and was always being bilked by his agents. While straightening out Penn's tangled finances in Pennsylvania, Logan built a fortune of his own through dealings in land and furs. At Conestoga, west of Philadelphia, he set up a trading post and contrived a type of sturdy wagon that lumbered into Philadelphia laden with bear, muskrat, lynx and mink pelts for the eager markets of Europe. For five decades, Logan ran the politics of Pennsylvania while, like his friend Cadwallader Colden, fostering the spread of knowledge in the New World. "Books are my disease," he confessed and, in his mansion at Stenton, he amassed the finest library in America. A serious botanist, he conducted a pioneering inquiry into the sexuality of plants. Observing on a tassel of corn "an adventitious dust lodged like dew from the air," he guessed that the dust was pollen and that the tassels were tubes through which the pollen traveled to fertilize the seeds. To verify this guess, he undertook a brilliantly simple experiment. Working in his garden, he cut the tassels from some stalks of corn and let them grow on others. On the plants where tassels were removed, no kernels developed. Where they remained, kernels formed. His discoveries about fertilization were published by the Royal Society of London.

A learned and snobbish man, Logan appreciated raw talent. When a glazier named Thomas Godfrey conceived the idea for a novel navigational instrument while puttying a window at Stenton, Logan led him into mathematics, lent him a copy of Newton's *Principia*—he had the first copy in the colonies— and helped the glazier build his widely used double reflecting sea quadrant. When Logan learned of John Bartram's interest in botany, he introduced him to the microscope, lecturing him on the stamens and pistils of the thorny mallow, the convolvulus, succory and motherwort. He lent his protégé the standard books of English botany: Culpeper's *English Physician*, Turner's *Herbal* and Parkinson's *Earthly Paradise*. Some years later, when he acquired the first edition of Linnaeus's *Systema Naturae*, Logan recommended it to Bartram as "curious and worth thy notice." To Linnaeus himself, who had been greatly impressed by Logan's corn-tassel experiment, he recommended Bartram in the highest terms: "If God grants him life and his narrow circumstances do not hinder," he prophesied, "you may look for great things from him."

Through Logan, Bartram met the educated men of the city and through them found his true vocation. It is hard to say just how soon it was after picking that legendary daisy that Bartram, the novice naturalist, set out to become Bartram, the professional collector. As so often in accounts of American natural history, a discursion is required, this time to tell about another helpful Philadelphian, less august than James Logan but more endearing.

Joseph Breintnall was, as his friend Benjamin Franklin told it, "a copier of deeds for the scriveners, good natur'd, friendly, a great lover of poetry, reading all he would meet with and writing some that was tolerable; very ingenious in many little nick nackeries." Breintnall worked in Franklin's stationers' shop, contributed to his *Busybody Papers* and also served as sheriff of Philadelphia and secretary of the Library Company, the city's first public library. He conducted experiments on the heat of the sun's rays, and left a melodramatic report on what it was like to be victim of a rattlesnake. "I am bit with a rattlesnake and there lies my murderer," began his agonized chronicle. Having killed it, he threw it on his threshold and quickly wrapped a freshly killed chicken around the wounded hand, where "immediately he swelled, grew black and stunk." After burning the snake, Breintnall covered his hand with plaster, soaked it with vinegar and finally cut it with a razor. All summer long he suffered a surrealist ordeal. Snake spots covered his arm. His dreams had always been pleasant, but "now I dreamed of horrid places and very often of rolling among old logs. Sometimes I was a white oak cut in pieces; and frequently my feet would be growing into two hickories." Finally, "in the fall my arm swelled, gather'd and burst. So away went the poison spots and all. Heaven be thanked for ridding me of such a cursed adversary."

In the course of some business dealings, Breintnall came in touch with Peter Collinson, the botanizing London merchant. Collinson had been trying for years to find a reliable man who would send him American plants and seeds. It was, as it had been for James Petiver, a frustrating search. Collinson explained:

> My business brought me acquainted with persons that were natives of Carolinas, Virginia, Maryland, Pennsylvania and New England. My love for new and rare plants put me often soliciting their acquaintance for seeds or plants. I used much importunity to very little purpose. What was common with them but rare with us they did not think worth send-

ing. I obtained but few seeds or plants; neither money nor friendship would tempt them. At last some more artful than the rest contrived to get rid of my importunities by recommending a person whose business it should be to gather seeds, and send over plants. Accordingly John Bartram was recommended as a very proper person for that purpose, being a native of Pennsylvania with numerous family.

Joseph Breintnall was the artful contriver who recommended Bartram. No go-between ever brought off a more satisfying match, nor had there ever been a pair who worked more effectively for botany's benefit than John Bartram, the collector, and Peter Collinson, the disperser.

At the start, Collinson proposed to pay Bartram £5 5s. for each box of plants. Able now to earn money while indulging his hobby, Bartram promptly began to fill boxes and send them to London. Opening his first shipments in 1734, Collinson could scarcely believe his good fortune. Bartram had sent witch hazel, sugar maple, bittersweet, white cedar, wild and swamp honeysuckle, hemlock, river birch, beech, mayflower, rosebay, cucumber tree, mountain laurel, buttonbush, arrowwood, steeplebush, false alder, staggerbush, sand myrtle, white osier. Shipment followed shipment. When the Londoner received a rare *Dodecatheon* or shooting star (John Banister had sent Bishop Compton one years before, but it had died in the bishop's garden), Collinson really knew what a treasure he had in Bartram. "I can't enough admire thy industry and curiosity in descending to so many minute rarities what commonly escape the observation of most but such a prying eye as thine," he wrote.

By 1736, Collinson was so sure of his new collector that he gathered a group of English gardeners willing to pay an annual fee to share in what Bartram sent. All eagerness, Bartram took time off from spring planting to journey to the Rattlesnake Mountains and in the fall, he went up the Schuylkill into the Blue Mountains. He usually went alone (though his son William later accompanied him), riding on horseback. Most of his roads were simply well-traveled trails, and from these he would go off on Indian paths. "Solitary and difficult traveling," he wrote, "climbing over mountains and precipices amongst the rattlesnakes and often obliged to follow the track or path of wild beasts for my guide through these desolate and gloomy thickets."

He rode slowly, bulky leather bags sagging with plants slapping at his horse's flanks, his eyes moving from ground to treetops, his lean body sliding from his seat when he spotted an interesting flower or a seedpod he didn't recognize, hauling out a book to check on it—but soon knowing far more than any book could tell him. He took in everything as he went—the direction of the wind, the changing of the weather, the force of streams and the taste of their water, the steepness of inclines, the feel and color of the soil, the presence of shells and fossils, seeing everything and missing nothing. He never found anything on a second visit to a place, he boasted, that he had not seen the first time. On overnight trips, he would stop at settlers' huts, crowding with a family into a shack "hardly enough for a hen roost" and so thick with vermin he could scarcely sleep; or at the mansions of Virginia aristocrats, welcomed as an interesting caller; or at an Indian village, being introduced to Indian food which at first he "thought poor entertainment but learned not to despise." He observed the way Indians built their huts, treated their wives, gave their speeches and even how they behaved when drunk. Whereas an Englishman "will fall asleep for the most part," he noted, "an Indian falls to dancing, running and shouting."

Bartram dutifully tried to fit his collecting trips into his farmer's schedule. He preferred to go out in the fall, when his hay was all in, his crops harvested, his main chores done. Out in the countryside, meanwhile, seeds had ripened and plants, now half dormant, could be safely dug. Everything was crammed into his saddlebags and boxes—slips, roots, dried flowers, seeds, chunks of boggy sod from which might sprout Lord knows what kind of strange plants. His clients in Europe mostly wanted woody plants—trees, shrubs—or seeds of perennials. The growing season of American annuals often did not match the seasons in Europe and the plants would not produce seeds.

Home with his haul, Bartram set samples in the garden he had built between his house and the creek. It was laid out not to impress visitors but to provide a natural habitat for the plants—boggy spots for skunk cabbage and pitcher plants, ample room on the border for oaks, sheltered spots for magnolias and sweet bay. Visitors who came to see Bartram's famous garden would, almost without exception, be disappointed at its lack of elegance. "His garden is a perfect portraiture of himself," Alexander Garden told Colden. "Here you meet with a row of rare plants almost covered over with weeds, here with a beautiful shrub, even luxuriant amongst briars, and in another corner an elegant and lofty tree lost in a common thicket. Every den is an arbor, every run of water a canal and every small level spot a parterre where he nurses up some of his idol flowers and cultivates his darling productions."

Inside his house, Bartram built cupboards near the fireplace where he could slowly dry the seeds he saved. Some plants were dried, pressed between heavy paper and labeled. Those ready for shipping were wrapped in damp moss and put into heavy boxes, layer upon careful layer. Every conceivable wrapping and receptacle was used: glass jars filled with camphor to discourage mice, tortoise-shell snuffboxes varnished to seal out the air, old linen to fold around grasses. Nuts were waxed to preserve them. Insects and small animals were embalmed, crammed into jars filled with rum.

Buffalo were still seen in eastern America when Mark Catesby was traveling in the Carolina back country. He painted this one standing under a bristly locust tree.

When he was only sixteen, William Bartram painted a magnolia warbler for Peter Collinson, his father's friend, who wrote a note at the top: "Not in Catesby fr Pensilvania."

Frutex Lauri folio pendulo, fructu
tricocco Semine nigro Splendente.

Red Wood.

Psitticus Paradisis.
The Parrot of Paradise

This "Parrot of Paradise" is a tribute more to Catesby's art than to his ornithology. The painting
is rich and elegant but no one is sure what the bird is.

William Bartram drew this mainly to show "a seed vessel of the calocasia," or American lotus, and "a large land snail." He wound up with a scene that, in its disparate and dreamlike details, seems almost surrealist. It was sent to his patron, Dr. John Fothergill, perhaps to be given to the Dutchess of Portland.

fig 5.

In his painting The Exhumation of the Mastodon, *Charles Willson Peale celebrated his great dig for fossil bones. The huge wheel, turned by a man walking inside, brings up buckets to bail out the pit. Peale stands at the far right with his family and the drawing of a mammoth bone. Alexander Wilson (who wasn't really there) is shown with arms crossed, at left.*

The parrot fish was one of several fish Catesby painted for his Natural History. *He had trouble getting its colors right because they faded so quickly once out of water.*

The great yellow bream evoked a rapturous description from William Bartram in his Travels. *"A warrior in a gilded coat of mail," he called the fish.*

Then the boxes and jars were put aboard sailing ships whose captains might well leave cases of hard-found shrubs out on deck to be killed by salt water or stowed in damp holds to be infected by molds. Rats and mice sometimes found the well-packed cases a dry and comfortable place to nest and the tender slips a welcome change in diet, in which case whole shipments of plants would be chewed to death. Or a sailor, coming upon jars of snakes or beetles preserved in liquor, would throw out the specimens and drink the preservative.

The constant wars between the European countries, declared or undeclared, left cargo ships at the mercy of warships; shipments destined for England might be taken by French or Spanish frigates, while shipments addressed to France would be captured by the English. Or marauding privateers would simply loot a ship and throw the plants overboard. Bartram, as time went on, would get around such hazards by putting on Collinson's shipment the alternate address of Antoine de Jussieu at the royal gardens in Paris. Though the French "are what is commonly called our enemies," he explained, "yet if they make proper use of what I have labored for, let them enjoy it with the blessing of God." Such was the prestige of the international circle of naturalists that French captains, if they captured the boat, would honor the address and deliver the box to Paris. And such was the loyalty of the circle that, when hostilities abated, de Jussieu would transship the botanical booty to London—usually after picking out some specimens for himself.

Bartram came on the botanical scene at a time when Europe was avid for new plants. Before 1560, the historian Gregor Kraus has estimated, virtually the only plants grown in Europe were natives. In the next half-century, with a growth of interest in gardening, new plants arrived from the eastern Mediterranean as gardeners sought out flowers and shrubs of the classical and Biblical world. Then plants began to come in from regions whose climates roughly matched those of Europe: South Africa and eastern North America. Not until the late eighteenth century was Australia exploited. Of the eight thousand species of flora that grew in eastern North America, only a half-dozen were known to Europe before 1600. During the next half-century, perhaps fifty of these species were introduced into Europe. The botanical traffic picked up as the early collectors like Banister and Lawson began their shipments, and when Bartram began collecting in 1734 about three hundred North American species were known in Europe. By the time the American Revolution halted the traffic, that number had doubled. Bartram was responsible for about half of the increase. In short, over four decades he had introduced a full one-quarter of the six hundred American plants known then in Europe—to say nothing of the hundreds of already known but desirable plants he had sent over to satisfy gardeners' demands.

Over the years, Bartram acquired many correspondents and customers, but

Peter Collinson was more responsible than any other man for introducing American plants to Europe's botanists and gardeners. This portrait is attributed to Gainsborough.

none were so important to him, professionally and personally, as the man to whom the deviser of knickknackeries had introduced him. Peter Collinson was a Quaker brought up to love gardening almost as an article of faith. The founder of the Society of Friends, George Fox, had urged gardening on his followers as a way whereby, through knowledge of nature, they could better know God's ways and purpose. Botany also proved a convenient intellectual outlet for Quakers, who, refusing to swear allegiance to the crown, were barred from Oxford and Cambridge—perhaps no great deprivation considering the academic stuffiness there.

A warm and obliging man with a genius for promoting the talents and interests of others, Collinson generously shared the plants and seeds sent him from overseas with fellow naturalists in England and on the Continent. Soon he found himself as involved in getting and giving away plants as in buying and selling woolens and silks. "This business of procuring foreign seeds," he wrote, "brought on me no little trouble to carry on such correspondence, keeping accounts, receiving and paying money, attendance at the customs house to procure delivery of the seeds and then dispersing the boxes to their proper owners. After I had supplied persons with seeds the next was 'Pray sir, in what manner must I sow them?' This creates more trouble yet to encourage planting. I never refuse anyone and they were not a few."

"Not a few" is superb understatement. It was an age of letter writers.

Both businessmen and learned men were kept inordinately busy with their mail, but surely no one kept up such a voluminous, constant, wide and devoted correspondence as Collinson. His mail went to Sweden, Switzerland, Holland, South Africa, Italy, Paris, Boston, Manila, Leipzig, Charleston, Kingston, Philadelphia—bills of lading, lists of seeds, instructions to sea captains, botanical identifications, letters of introduction, recommendation of books, expositions on the political troubles in England, news of how his garden was growing, medical advice, coaxings, complaints at not having heard from his correspondents, righteous replies to their complaints that they hadn't heard from him. The letters flowed out and the replies came back to require more replies, all written with quill pen in English or in Latin, with a hurried man's disrespect for the rules of capitalization and punctuation.

He gave and sought help lavishly. He kept Benjamin Franklin informed of the latest European experiments with electricity, urged the American to continue his own experiments and sent him needed apparatus. Then he helped introduce Franklin's paper on his kite-flying adventures to the world of science through the Royal Society. An authority on Franklin's scientific achievements has called Collinson "the most important single person in Franklin's career."

Collinson wrote regularly to Linnaeus, sending him plants, introducing naturalists to him, scolding him. "You have not sent me the least specimen of either fossil, animal or vegetable," he wrote. "It is a general complaint that Dr. Linnaeus receives all and returns nothing." When he read Linnaeus's *Genera Plantarum*, he asked him to send two copies, "one for John Bartram, the other for Dr. Colden." He worried about his friends. When Kalm ventured into the Americas, Collinson admitted: "I was afraid of some wild Indians doing him a mischief"—which, as we have seen, they almost did.

The letters between Collinson and John Bartram ran on for more than thirty years, chronicling the growth of a business arrangement into a warm, intimate friendship that endured distance, lost letters, business disagreements, brotherly bickering and the fact that the two men never, at any time in their lives, saw or spoke to each other. The letters are full of argument and affection: Bartram sounding hurt that he hadn't heard from Collinson for months and Collinson complaining that friend John doesn't understand how much time it takes to keep up correspondence; Collinson impatient for shipments and Bartram listing the troubles he has had collecting; Bartram sympathizing over the death of Collinson's wife, Collinson worrying over the futures of Bartram's wandering sons—a persevering, efficient exchange by slow ship across an endless ocean between the farmer on the banks of the Kingsessing and the mercer on the wharves of the Thames.

The earliest letter still extant is a rambling affair "writ," Collinson explains, "a bit now and then as business permits" to "My good friend John Bartram" on January 20, 1735. Acknowledging his pleasure at "thy curious entertaining letter of November 6th," it goes quickly on to a reminder: "please to remember those Solomon Seals that escaped thee last year" and to some requests for

> the great and small hellebore, great rarities here, spotted martagons, blazing star, a root or two, and any of the lady's slippers, a root of the aristolochia, ground cypress, your wild senna, a pretty plant, mountain goat's rue. Pray what is your sarsaparilla? Send a root or two of Joseph Breintnall's snakeroot, a root or two of the glassy leaves that bears little blue flowers, that's good against the obstruction of the bowels. I don't expect or desire them but as they happen to be found accidentally, and what is not to be met with one year may be another. I have [sent] some hard-shelled almonds of my own growth. The almond makes a fine pie. They must first be coddled over a gentle fire and then put in crust.

After signing, "thy real friend, P. Collinson," he could not resist the inevitable postscript, requests for "a quantity of seed of the birch or black beech, a good root of the Swallow-wort, the pretty shrub called red root, the cotton weed or life everlasting, seed of the perannual pea that grows by the river, this year, or next, or next after, as it happens. Pray send me a walking cane of the Cane-wood."

This letter crossed one from Bartram. Only three days later, Collinson wrote again: "I am very sensible of the great pains and many tiresome steps to collect so many rare plants scattered at a distance. In some measure to show my gratitude I have sent thee a small token; a calico gown for thy wife." He also sent heavy paper.

> When thee observes a curious plant in flower or gathers a seed of a plant, gather branches or sprigs with their flowers on and with their seed vessels fully formed; for by these two characteristics the genus is known. Spread them between the sheets of brown paper laying the stems straight and leaves smooth and regular, put a moderate weight on. In a week or two being pretty well dried, convey them into the whited brown paper. I further propose thy own improvement in the knowledge of plants; thou shall send me duplicates, I will get them named by our most knowing botanists and then return them again which improve thee more than books.

Something pleasant had happened on the voyage, he notes: "The warmth of the ship and want of air had occasioned the skunkweed to put forth two fine blossoms, very beautiful; it is of the *Arum* genus."

Barely two weeks later, the merchant was back with another grateful letter mentioning half a dozen shipments: "Though I am vastly hurried in business yet the many instances of thy regard for us obliges me to steal time to say something further. I have done with thine of the 9th of September, have received thine of November 18th, December 1st and the 9th and 10th. The box of insects was prettily put up." Collinson seemed worried that Bartram would burn himself out. "Pray rest a little from thy labors," he said, but couldn't help asking for "all the sorts of Lady's Slippers thee happens to meet with," and could he send some branches of red and white cedar to clear up the confusion about them? Meanwhile, Collinson was sending Bartram a real rarity: seeds of the China aster "sent per the Jesuits from China to France; from thence to us."

At the same time, Collinson was spreading the word of his new collector and informed Bartram that he had given some seeds to Lord Petre, "a universal lover of plants," who agreed to put up ten guineas a year to keep Bartram going. This was a coup. Robert James, the eighth Lord Petre, was the premier Catholic peer of England. His father had achieved a kind of minor immortality by cutting a bit of hair off the head of his kinswoman Arabella Fermor and inspiring Alexander Pope to write *The Rape of the Lock*. Robert was not given to such pranks. A virtuoso gifted in natural history and mathematics, who was already a patron of Mark Catesby, he had magnificent gardens in Essex where he grew plants from all over the world. Collinson was rapturous in describing them to Bartram several years later, when Bartram's own contributions were growing there: "Trees and shrubs, about ten thousand Americans mixed with about 20,000 Europeans and some Asians. When I walk amongst them one cannot help thinking he is in North American thickets."

With Lord Petre as a subscriber, Collinson seemed to have little trouble rounding up others. One of them was Charles Lennox, Duke of Richmond and grandson of Charles II, as eminent a peer as Petre, though less lavish in his patronage. He contributed only five guineas a year. His interest in natural history had led to an implausibly romantic married life. Wed, when young, to the daughter of the Earl of Cadogan (it was a family arrangement, made, in part, to settle a gambling debt), he left his bride immediately after the ceremony to pursue his education. Half a dozen years later, polishing off his studies on the grand tour of Europe, he happened to meet his wife in Holland. The two discovered that they shared a deep interest in gardening and botany. Thus brought together, they fell in love with each other, and back at his great house in England they settled down to the joys of life amid their flowers, birds and greenhouses—and also to its sorrows. One year, Collinson informed Bartram, the Richmonds "had 40,000 young pines destroyed by a plague of cockchafers."

A Bartram subscriber knew exactly what he would get for his five guineas: a box containing seeds of 105 trees and shrubs, each one specified by Bartram. He even included seeds of poison ivy and poison oak, plants which fortunately did not naturalize in Europe, though they are still grown as curiosities in some botanical gardens there.

Having established Bartram in business, Collinson began flooding him with advice and instructions. From his tall counting stool, he made proposals that John Bartram, riding through primeval forests, must have found pretty far-fetched. "It will be necessary," wrote Collinson, "to take a servant with thee, and two horses for yourselves and a spare one to carry linen, provisions and other necessities." Meanwhile, he asked Bartram to please stop sending

> tulip cones, swamp laurel cones, hickory, black walnut, sassafras, dog-wood, sweet gum, white oak acorns, swamp Spanish oak, red cedar berries; but all other sorts of acorns, firs, pines, black gum or black haw, Judas tree, persimmon, cherries, hop tree, Benjamin or allspice; all the sorts of ash sugar tree, wild roses, black beech or hornbeam; all sorts of flowering and berry-bearing shrubs, honey locust, lime tree, arrow-wood, guelder rose. If thee observes any sort of fresh water or river shell fish, send me two or three of each sort, or land snails. My inclination and fondness to natural productions of all kinds is agreeable for the old proverb: Like the parson's barn, refuses nothing.

He balanced flattery with faultfinding: "I can't enough admire thy industry and curiosity in descending to so many minute rarities"; but the butterflies in the last shipment "are a little torn. I will revive a little thy memory with our manner of catching them. We put sticks in the handle of our nets two, three or four feet long. We watch till they settle on a leaf, then we apply both nets together, the one close under, and with agility clap the other over. We lay them on the next smooth ground and give the body a pretty smart squeeze between the finger and the thumb until we hear the ribs crack."

Encouraged now by the assurance of customers and cash, Bartram in 1738 was ready for his longest trip, a 1,200-mile trek down into Virginia. Collinson had been in correspondence with several wealthy planters there, and while he was pleased to give Bartram introductions to them, he was apprehensive over the impression his farmer friend might make. "One thing I do insist," he told Bartram, "that thou not appear to disgrace thyself or me; these Virginians are a very gentle, well-dressed people and look perhaps more at a man's outside than his inside. For these and other reasons, pray go very lean, neat and handsomely dressed." Meanwhile, Collinson notified John Custis of Williamsburg: "Don't be surprised if a downright plain country man should come. You'll not look at the man but his mind for my sake."

John Custis—whose name is familiar to us because his widowed daughter-in-law Martha married George Washington—had one of the finest gardens in the colonies. Years before, he had sent Collinson some mountain cowslip and that led to a busy swapping between them. Collinson need not have worried about the impression Bartram would make. "He is the most taking facetious man I have ever met with," Custis reported to Collinson after Bartram's visit. "And never was so much delighted with a stranger in all my life." Bartram went on to Westover to visit William Byrd II, Catesby's patron.

Collinson was discovering unsuspected sides of his plant collector. Bartram was not only a reliable correspondent but a man of dignity and social grace, not only a diligent collector but a thoughtful scientist. Collinson read some of Bartram's remarks on rattlesnakes to the Royal Society and he reported to him. "Thee has their thanks for it, desiring thee to continue." Because Bartram had apologized for his unfinished writing style, Collinson reassured him: "Thy style is much beyond what one might expect from a man of thy education." Irritated when Bartram kept asking for more and more books, Collinson admonished him: "Remember Solomon's advice, in reading of books there is no end." To which Bartram replied tartly, "I take thy advice about books very kindly, although I love reading such dearly." And, throwing the Bible back at his friend, he went on: "I believe if Solomon had loved women less and books more, he would have been a wiser and happier man."

Collinson felt it necessary from time to time to put Bartram down. "Thee thinks thyself not amply rewarded?" he asked impatiently. "If thou canst not afford to go on with this business, tell us so and it will be at an end." His friend was not easily subdued. "Thee supposes me to spend five or six weeks in collections for you," Bartram replied. "I spend more than twice that time annually besides my neglect of business at home in fallowing harvest and seed time." It took him two weeks to gather a few willow-leafed acorns, trying to get them before the squirrels and hogs did. "You are not sensible of a fourth part of the pains I take to oblige you." But the letter softened. "My kind and generous friend, my hearty thanks for thy care and pains and many good offices. If thee find any expressions in my letter a little out of the way, thee will not take it in the wrong sense. I love plain dealing." And he later thanked Collinson for some money that "came in the very nick of time when I wanted to pay the mortgage interest."

Collinson's letters are a catalog of what he called "pleasure and pain." Bartram had sent preserved butterflies and live beetles in the same box, and the beetles had devoured the butterflies. "Pray next time divide the precious from the vile," advised Peter, drown the beetles in rum. But he glowed over what happened with a box of turtle eggs that came in the shipment. "I took off the lid and saw a little head just above the ground and saw the ground move in a place or two. In three or four hours, eight tortoises were hatched. It was well worth observing how artfully they disengaged themselves from the shell and then with their forefeet scratched their eyes open. They have had many visitors, such a thing never happening I dare say in England before."

And when he received a collection of wasps along with Bartram's report on the way they built their nests and cared for their young, Collinson launched into a homily on "the unlimited power and wisdom of the great author of all things. Great is thy pleasure that at the same time thee are obliging thy friend, thee art improving thyself in the knowledge of nature."

Bartram had indeed improved his knowledge of nature. Famous men consulted him and he himself was reaching out for recognition. "If I can without much loss of time, oblige Linnaeus or Gronovius at thine or their request I am willing to do so," he wrote Collinson. "I perceive they are curious and ingenious botanists." In Philadelphia, the center of American culture, Franklin became his friend and sponsor, raising money to free Bartram from some farm chores and let him spend more time on science. The subsidy never amounted to much but Franklin did get Bartram a free membership in the Philadelphia Library Company. When, in 1743, Franklin formed the American Philosophical Society, Bartram was one of the nine founding members.

Having started a correspondence with Cadwallader Colden, Collinson tried to bring him and Bartram together. "If an ingenious man and a great teacher unto nature named John Bartram of Pennsylvania should wait on you, please to give him what information you can." Bartram, Peter wrote, was "a wonderfully natural genius considering his education and that he is an husbandman." When he met Colden in 1742, Bartram was impressed: "He hath the greatest knowledge in botany of any I have discoursed with." Colden was equally impressed. "It is very extraordinary," he wrote Gronovius, "that a man of the lowest education without the advantages of any kind of learning should have such a taste for knowledge and acquire so great a share of it."

The lack of learning did hamper Bartram. His correspondents in Europe would sometimes intersperse their letters with explanations in Latin, the language into which educated men automatically lapsed. Gronovius, in a letter expressing his pleasure at a shipment of rocks and fossils from Bartram, wrote: "I give you the following scheme: *Transeundum nunc est ad tales lapides, qui simulcram animalis. . . ."* Flattered but frustrated, Bartram asked Gronovius, "Please to write all thy further observation in English. Latin is troublesome to me." Gronovius suggested Bartram send the Latin to Colden for translation, which was done, and the doctor kindly provided a translation: "We must now pass to such stones as have a resemblance of some animal. . . ."

Colden and Bartram settled into an easy friendship, trading information about plants, medicines and favorite collecting spots. Bartram told Colden where he could find a snakeroot he had been hunting for, and Colden directed Bartram to some red cedars Collinson had ordered. Soon the farmer of Kingsessing and the squire of Coldengham were joined as central figures in the natural history community of colonial America. Colden, the scientist, could help bring order out of the field findings Bartram had made. Bartram, the unexcelled collector, could close gaps in Colden's information. He could also introduce Colden to two Virginians who had been pursuing their independent ways in natural history. He had become aware of them, of course, through Collinson.

One was John Mitchell of Urbana, student of the eminent Dr. Alston of Edinburgh. An aloof, unlikable man, Mitchell was in some ways the most astute scientific researcher in the colonies. By his own observations, he upset the accepted theories about how the opossum, a unique American beast which fascinated Europeans, bore its young. It had been believed that the young were delivered from the mammary glands inside the pouch. Mitchell, painstakingly watching the birth process, found that, as with all mammals, the young gestated in the womb and, after delivery, made their way into the pouch, where they suckled.

Mitchell botanized through the Virginia mountains, and, devising his own system of classification, he boldly recommended it to Linnaeus, who found it "very difficult to make out." Then, acknowledging the American's work, Linnaeus named a bright-fruited little woodland creeper after him—*Mitchella repens*, the partridgeberry.

In 1746, Mitchell sailed for England with a thousand American plants. His ship, which also carried plants Colden was sending Linnaeus, was looted by a Spanish privateer and Mitchell arrived empty-handed. His most notable work in England was a map he drew of the British and French settlements in America. Its purpose was more political than geographic: an attempt to defend and enlarge British territorial claims. Nevertheless it was the best map of its day and has in fact been called "the most important map in American history." George III kept it in front of him when he agreed to peace terms with the Americans in 1783, and it was actually used to settle a boundary dispute as late as 1932.

The only Virginia botanist that Mitchell had anything to do with was John

Clayton of Gloucester County. There is a confusion of Claytons involved in American natural history. A missionary doctor named John Clayton came to Virginia in 1684, encouraged apparently by Bishop Compton. He made a particular study of Indian medicine—"nature is their great apothecary," he said —and was friendly with John Banister. Returning to England after two years, ·he conducted the first successful efforts to manufacture gas from coal and wound up as the dean of Kildare. He was only distant kin to the second John Clayton, who came to Virginia around 1715, and settled into a long and prosperous life as farmer and clerk of Gloucester County. He was friend to Custis and Byrd and became acquainted with Byrd's protégé Mark Catesby. Stirred to an interest in botany, perhaps by Catesby, Clayton progressed so remarkably that, after returning to England, Catesby introduced him by mail to Isaac Lawson. A wealthy Scottish virtuoso who was serving as physician general to the British army in Flanders, Lawson had helped pay for the publication of Linnaeus's first books. Thus the colonial clerk entered the international circle of naturalists. Collinson, as was to be expected, learned of him and informed Bartram, who told Colden. Thus Clayton came into the American circle of naturalists.

Clayton was, in fact, sending plants to England before Bartram was. A witch hazel he sent to Catesby astonished English gardeners by being in bloom when it arrived just before Christmas. Through Catesby, Clayton sent some plants to Gronovius, who grumbled that Catesby kept too many for himself, but on examining the batch exulted, "Oho, how curious they are." When Clayton sent him a catalog of Virginian plants, fruits and trees, Gronovius proposed to publish it as a book. By nagging Linnaeus mercilessly for assistance and bribing him with promises of "most elegant" American plants, Gronovius arranged Clayton's modest catalog according to the young Swede's new system. Clayton's *Flora Virginica* was the first Linnaean book based on New World material and in its revised edition is a work still consulted by botanists today. Linnaeus later gave Clayton the same kind of accolade he had given Mitchell. He named an American plant after him, the charming spring beauty, *Claytonia virginica*.

Bartram and Clayton corresponded for some twenty years before they finally met in 1760. Through Bartram, the Virginian became a member of the American Philosophical Society. This gained him a highly useful perquisite of membership in the naturalist circle. Franklin let him send his papers and plants through the mails post-free.

Clayton was a foppish man, but nature had touched him with an honest piety. He could not look into a flower, a friend said of him, "without seeing the display of infinite power and contrivances and thus he thought it impossible for a botanist to be an atheist."

John Bartram shared this devout belief. He saw "the immediate finger of God" in the simplest facts of nature: the way flowers opened in the morning and shut up at night; the way sensitive plants shut out the rain until their flowers were fertilized; the way in which weed seeds might lie in the ground for years before coming up, while seeds of useful grains sprout the first year; the way nature maintained its balance—all this manifested "a portion of universal intellect diffused in all life."

"Oh," he exclaimed, "the wisdom of divine providence!" And in the skies: "Orbs beyond orbs, without number, suns beyond suns, systems beyond systems, how can we look on these without amazement, most humble adoration. Esteeming ourselves, with all our wisdom, but as one of the smallest atoms of dust praising the living God, the great I am."

In these expressions, Bartram revealed himself as a man bred by the Age of Reason, as much a disciple of the Enlightenment as any *philosophe* in Paris or logician in England. He lived in that world-changing era when man could free himself to think and speak and use his talents as he himself wished, not as others desired him to do. "Dare to know," commanded Immanuel Kant and, from the celestial speculations of Isaac Newton to the earthy explorations of John Bartram, men followed this precept. The first lessons of the Enlightenment, learned from Newton, were frightening. Man was no longer the center of his universe but a minuscule piece in an infinite mechanism created by a God who was unconcerned with him as a special creation. The chasm that opened between this new self-estimate and the old belief that men were God's chosen creatures made men humble about their ignorance. In one of the profound philosophic analogies derived from nature, Newton described himself as simply standing on the shores of the great undiscovered ocean of truth picking up the smoother pebbles and shells.

The Enlightenment gave a religious base to natural history. Looking for some comfort, for some new way to approach an inattentive God, men turned to nature as a manifestation of divine purpose. John Bartram took as his creed Pope's dictum: "Slave to no sect, who takes no private road,/But looks through Nature up to Nature's God."

By early belief, he was a Quaker, a prominent but troublesome member of the Darby Meeting. Leaning toward deism, he expressed views that the Friends found distasteful. "Living in love and innocency," he declared, "we may die in hope. Then if we don't go to heaven I believe we shan't go to hell." Even more heretical was Bartram's denial of the divinity of Christ. A committee of Friends called on him and labored "in the spirit of meekness" to turn him away from this blasphemy. When Bartram still insisted that "although Christ was endowed with the power of God, he was no more than man," the Darby Meeting finally disowned him.

In some secular matters, Bartram was a true and orthodox Quaker. He opposed slavery and set free a slave who had been brought up in the Bartram family. But he departed from the Friends' teachings when it came to Indians. Although he respected many Indians as individuals, he had an abiding distrust of them in general. He was repelled by Indian savagery, by the fact that they had killed his father—and, as much as anything, because their hostility kept him from traveling freely wherever and whenever he wanted to. "In our most peaceable times," he once recalled, "as I was walking in a path an Indian man met me and pulled off my hat in a great passion and chewed it all round—I suppose to show me that they would eat me if I came in that country again." There was only one way, he declared, to keep Indians in hand: "Bang them stoutly."

In the 1740s, with both himself and his century in their middle years, John Bartram was at home in many worlds: that of the farm, where he prospered, and the wilderness, which he came to know as well as his hay meadows; among the Indians, though one had chewed his hat, and the cultured citizens of Philadelphia, who esteemed him as a scientist; among the settlers of the backwoods; among the virtuosos of Europe, who waited eagerly to see and hear what new plants he had found.

His prestige in Europe, enhanced by the tireless Peter Collinson, was increased in 1751 when the account of the trip he took with Weiser and Shickellamy was belatedly published in London as *Observations on the Inhabitants, Climate. Soil, Rivers, Productions, Animals and Other Matters Worthy of Note, Made by Mr. John Bartram in His Travels from Pennsylvania to Onondaga, Oswego and the Lake Ontario in Canada.* The printer botched facts and spellings and made some patronizing remarks about the author, explaining that because Bartram lacked a literary education his writing style was not what it should be. Bartram gave such criticism the back of his hand. "Good grammar and good spelling may please these that are more taken with a superficial flourish than real truth," he snorted.

After his journey to Onondaga, Bartram was kept close to home by the wars against the Indians and the French. The Catskills became a favorite hunting ground, "the greatest variety of uncommon trees and shrubs I ever saw in such a compass of ground." He went there in 1753 to gather seeds of the balm of Gilead tree, the balsam fir which English gardeners believed to be the tree that grew on Mount Gilead in the Holy Land and prompted Jeremiah's bitter question "Is there no balm in Gilead?" Seeds of the tree were hard to come by. The cones are covered with a sticky balm until the seeds ripen. Then the cones scatter the seeds beyond practical garnering. For only a few days, as the cones dry on the trees and the seeds are ripe, a collector can gather them—if he gets to them before the birds and squirrels.

Collinson had nagged Bartram for seeds and Bartram set out, though he suffered from the ague, on a troubling trip. He stumbled on a rattlesnake, which almost struck him. He had to chop down whole trees, and all he had to send Collinson in the end was a "hatful of cones." It would not have mattered if he had got bushels of them. The seeds germinated poorly in England and the few

Philos. Trans. Vol. XLVIII. TAB. XV. p. 499.

John Bartram supplied birds to the noted British nature artist George Edwards, who used a ruffed grouse as the model for this drawing in his Gleanings of Natural History.

that sprouted grew into spindly trees not worth the bother. With Bartram, for the first time on such an outing, was his 14-year-old son William. The boy was already showing a bent for natural history. "Botany and drawing are his darling delight," John noted.

The troubles that kept Bartram from traveling at home were compounded by sad news from abroad. Collinson's wife had died, and the reserve that Bartram usually showed broke down. "Her dear sweet bosom is cold," John wrote his friend. "Her tender heart is motionless; her dear arms are no more extended to embrace her beloved." Two clients—the Duke of Richmond and the Prince of Wales—lost their lives, John Mitchell reported to Bartram, through their devotion to botany "by being out in their gardens in very bad weather. The Prince of Wales contracted a cold by standing in the wet to see some trees planted, which brought on a pleurisy." Had he not been so concerned about his trees, he—and not George III—would have been King of England.

The American plant collectors, led by Bartram, were helping to change the face of Europe's gardens. The stylized, outrageously clipped designs that had been the fashion were being discarded for more natural effects. "America," declared Catesby, "has furnished Europe with a greater variety of trees than has been procured from all the other parts of the world for more than a thousand years past." Bartram's own circle of clients and correspondents had grown enormously. He was a prime source of plants for Philip Miller, "the accurate Miller," the most famous professional gardener and nurseryman of his day and author of the *Gardener's Dictionary*, which ran through eight editions. Miller helped spread the gospel of gardening among the prosperous middle class, now enjoying an avocation limited once to royalty and aristocracy. Gardening became a fiercely competitive pastime. The skilled landscape designers of their time—notable among them a Scotsman known as Capability Brown, who lorded it over the realm's real lords—were as sought after by nobility and wealth as painters and sculptors had been in Renaissance Italy. This was fine for the business of men like Bartram, who was now very much aware of his own worth. When Miller proffered his help and his patronage, Bartram replied with some proud name-dropping. He already had Miller's *Gardener's Dictionary*, "sent me by Lord Petre," and Linnaeus's works, "which Dr. Gronovius, my good friend, hath sent me." At Miller's request, Bartram drew up a list of plants "that are most troublesome in our pastures and fields." He started with "the stinking yellow linaria," the familiar butter-and-eggs, and ran through a litany all too familiar to today's gardeners: "saponaria, dandelion, docks, chickweed, purslane, sorrel. . . ."

Just keeping up with the people Collinson referred to him was work enough for Bartram. Catesby, then finishing his *Natural History* with the help of an interest-free loan from the generous Collinson, asked Bartram for information about "a monkfish having a hood like a friar's cowl" and about the "whipper Will, sometimes Whip Will's Widow, by which names it is called —as the bird clinketh, the fool thinketh." Dr. Johann Jakob Dillenius repaid Bartram for some seeds by instructing him in his specialty, mosses. Until then, Bartram "took no particular notices of mosses but looked upon them as a cow looks at a pair of new barn doors." Now he was making "good progress," he said, "in that very curious vegetation." The only American plants that bear his name today are mosses of the genus *Bartramia*.

The correspondent Bartram seemed proudest to know was the renowned Sir Hans Sloane, successor to Isaac Newton as head of the Royal Society and author of a *Natural History of Jamaica*. Written after Sloane had spent two years on that island as a physician, this book was full of observed fact rather than reputed marvels, the most sensible work at the time on the natural history of the New World. In England, Sloane became the country's most highly regarded physician, attending Samuel Pepys and Queen Anne in their last illnesses and serving as court physician to George II. He helped found the Temple Coffee House Botany Club, devised a recipe for chocolate which is still sold today as Cadbury's Milk Chocolate, entertained such celebrities as Voltaire and Handel (who blotted Sloane's precious notebook with a hot buttered muffin) and presided over the shells, corals, crystals, insects, butterflies, bird skins, dried plants and assorted artifacts which filled the 110-foot-long gallery of his house— a collection that became the nucleus of the British Museum.

At the suggestion of Collinson, Bartram sent Sir Hans "some petrified representations of sea shells" and some Indian stone tools. Sir Hans returned the favor by sending Bartram his *Natural History* and asking for some seeds and plants. Bartram delightedly sent them, and when Sloane offered Bartram five guineas as a gift, Bartram asked instead for a "silver cup as big and good as thee can get for that sum." It came inscribed, "The Gift of S. Hans Sloane to his Fr. John Bartram." For all his Quaker ways, John Bartram was something of a show-off. He wrote Sloane that he was "well pleased that thy name is engraved upon it large so that when my friends drink out of it they may see who was my benefactor."

Despite these distractions, the exchanges with Collinson never flagged, nor did their querulous tone. "When I read in thy letter," John wrote Peter, " 'What didst mean to send me so large a box of seeds? It makes much trouble to part it,' I reflected what pains I had taken to collect those seeds, all to put my friend to trouble!" Peter could be just as irritable. "If my friend John Bartram knew better my affairs, my many engagements and incumbrances, he would wonder that I do so well as I do. To serve him I often neglect my own business." But when he did not hear from John for a full half year, he was softer in his reproaches. "I have a sprig in flower of the Kalmia in water and it stares me in the face all the while I am writing; saying or seeming to say 'As you are so fond of me, tell my friend John Bartram who sent me to send more to keep me company.' "

Bartram could be excused for not writing. At this time—1760—he was again off to a new place, the Deep South, where he visited Alexander Garden. "I have been lately in the woods for two hours with John," Garden reported to Collinson, "and have shown him most of our new things, with which he seems almost ravished of his senses and lost in astonishment." In an area that Garden had combed, Bartram's sharp eyes found a shrub the doctor had never noticed. He fitted himself pleasantly into the cultivated society of Charleston and was pleased with the company of its women, one of whom, Martha Logan, is remembered by botanists as John Bartram's "fascinated widow." A wellborn woman of the colony, Mrs. Logan started a plant nursery which quickly became a prime source for Charleston's extensive gardens. "The elderly widow spares no pains to oblige me," Bartram wrote Collinson. This brought a mocking reply from Collinson: "I plainly see thou knowest how to fascinate the longing widow." Mrs. Logan kept up a steady exchange with Bartram, and in one year three silk bags full of seeds made the round trip between Charleston and Philadelphia. Crowing like an old rooster, Bartram informed Collinson, "I received a lovely parcel of seeds and cuttings from Mistress Logan, my fascinated widow." What's more, he added, she paid the postage.

Bartram was scarcely back from Carolina than he was, he told Collinson, "all in a flame to go to Pittsburgh and down the Ohio," and prepared to go "if the barbarous Indians don't hinder me and if I die a martyr to Botany, God's will be done." He went west at the invitation of Colonel Henry Bouquet, who, by defeating the French at Fort Duquesne, the scene of Braddock's disaster, had secured the western frontier for the English. Some time before, Bouquet had sent Bartram some plants, writing: "I thought it might be agreeable to you to know what nature produces in these wildernesses." Now he escorted his new friend down the Ohio.

As if in haste to go everywhere before age stopped him, Bartram in 1762 journeyed to the Carolinas. Along the way, he found the tipitiwichet or Venus's-flytrap, whose movements encouraged him in his belief that plants had feelings and volition—and brought many Europeans into agreeing with him. On receiving the plant, Collinson burst out, "O botany! delightfulest of all sciences. There is no end of thy gratifications." He sent Linnaeus a tipitiwichet leaf: "Only to him would I spare such a jewel."

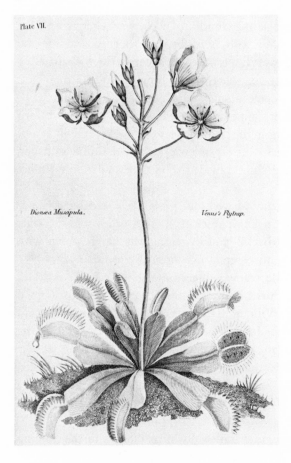

Plate VII.

Dionæa Muscipula.   *Venus's Flytrap.*

Europeans marveled at the tipitiwichet or Venus's-flytrap that Bartram found. Its characteristics led Bartram to conclude that plants had will and understanding of their own.

"*Miraculum natura!*" the great classifier exclaimed. "I never met with so wonderful a phenomenon." When he came to describe the plant, he used the phrase "*Miraculum natura.*"

With the French and Indian Wars ended in 1763, the frontiers were safe all the way to the Mississippi and the British had taken over Florida. Bartram could not wait to explore the region. "The variety of plants and flowers in our southwestern continent is beyond expression, the very palace garden of old Madam Flora," he wrote Collinson.

But he needed money to pay for himself and a companion—and "I can't be expected to be able to perform such a task many years hence," he told Collinson in 1764. "I must yield to the infirmities of age or death." Finally, with the help of Franklin, who was now in England representing the colonies, Collinson got Bartram an appointment as King's Botanist, with a salary of fifty pounds a year and a commission to range over Georgia and Florida.

Bouquet, now a general, was sailing south to take over as governor in Florida and urged Bartram to come with him. It was short notice for the aging collector, but he dropped everything else to accept. He dispatched a note to his son William, now twenty-six, who had set himself up as a merchant in North Carolina, telling him to come along. John reached Charleston weak from seasickness and, rashly, went immediately off with Dr. Garden to see the summer plants. He stayed so long in the midday heat that he became ill again. "To think a wise man should have so little prudence," scolded Collinson when he heard of it and, with a resigned sigh, added, "What cannot be cured must be endured for I see no remedy."

Nothing stopped Bartram. By day he was out with Dr. Garden, stopping to dig in a worn-out rice field for "a fine parcel of spotted lillies whose petals grew half upright and part turned back," and by night was on the town with the doctor, "exceedingly diverted with complaisant agreeable company."

William arrived, and the two Bartrams explored along the Altamaha River in Georgia, discovering "several curious shrubs, one bearing beautiful good fruit," the Franklin tree, which William a few years later would seek out and literally save from extinction. John was almost wide-eyed at what he was seeing: an oak measuring "105 feet diameter in the spreading of the boughs, two kinds of ash, a rare tupeloe with large red acid fruit called limes which is used for punch, a very odd catalapa with pods round as an acorn." The ague hit him so badly that he could hardly stand, but "I took a purge of Glauber's salt which works well."

The first part of their trip over, they sailed down to Florida to the landing on the St. John's River. Bartram described his journey in *A Description of East Florida with a Journal Kept by John Bartram of Philadelphia*, which was published in 1767 in London. It is the fullest of his works, the only one written with an eye to publication and perhaps to the criticism of friends that he had always been too laconic in his writing, never telling all he saw and learned. The account starts: "December the 19th, 1765, set out from St. Augustine early in the morning, the ground being covered with a white hoar frost. I, my son William, Mr. Yates and Mr. Davis embarked in a battoe. Mr. Davis was not only to conduct us but to hunt venison for us and his negroes to row and cook for us all, the governor bearing our expenses." Bartram had never traveled in such style but now, of course, he was King's Botanist. On the river shore, he found a "pretty evergreen which produces nuts as big as acorns and good to eat"—the tallow nut. They poked at an animal nest and "a large rat ran out and up a very high sapling with a young one hanging to its tail" ; these were wood rats. The naturalists pulled some honey from a hollow tree and ate it Indian style, poured over the pulp of sour wild oranges—"a relishing morsel."

Pushing up the unexplored waterway, "we came to a creek, up which we rowed a mile, in 4 and 6 foot water and 30 yards broad, of the color of the sea, smelled like bilge water, tasting sweetish and loathsome, warm and very clear, the spring-head is about 30 yards broad, and boils up from the bottom like a pot. What a surprising fountain must it be, to furnish such a stream."

John was introduced to a wilderness delicacy. "Our hunter killed a large he-bear supposed to weigh 400 pounds. Two of us had never eaten an ounce of bear's meat before, but we found it to our surprise to be very mild and sweet, above all four-footed creatures, except venison. His fat, though I loathed the sight of it at first, was incomparably milder than hog's lard and near as sweet as oil of olives."

They ran into muggy weather. "The mosquitoes were very troublesome last night. The flies blowed our meat, the ticks creeping and lizards running about our tent." They cut down three "tall palm or cabbage trees," taking out the heart of the top bud "which cuts as white and tender as a turnip; it eats pleasant and much more mild than a cabbage." With an elderly man's concern for his stomach, he added, "I never eat half so much cabbage at a time and it agreed the best with me of any I ever eat. This situation pleased me so much we called it Bartram's Bluff."

And so John Bartram, King's Botanist, in the last half of his seventh decade, with no complaints about his digestion, content in the company of his son, continued his last journey. "Fine warm morning," he wrote in his journal. "Birds singing, fish jumping and turkeys gobbling."

CHAPTER FOUR

THE FRUSTRATED PHYSICIAN

❦ ❦ ❦ ❦ ❦ TO HEAR HIM TELL IT, ALEXANDER GARDEN'S LIFE WAS ONE long floral frustration. While in Florida, Bartram got a letter from his friend. "Think that I am here," the doctor wrote, "confined to the sandy streets of Charleston where the ox, where the ass, and where men as stupid as either fill up the vacant space while you range the green fields of Florida where the bountiful hand of nature has spread every beautiful and fair plant and flower." Try as he would to get out and botanize, Garden never seemed able to leave Charleston, chained there by circumstance and, even more, by his own success. He had come to America in 1751, with no money and a poor constitution. When he sent his complaint to Bartram, barely a dozen years later, he was so busy and prosperous a doctor and so eminent a citizen that he could not take time off to pursue what he called "the demon" of natural history. One thing after another stopped him—his practice, his health, his love life, an epidemic, the Indians. . . .

It was doubly disappointing because the New World, when he came to it, seemed such a promising place for him to indulge his demon. He was a young man then—only twenty-one—but he knew what he wanted and how to get it. Born in 1730 to a needy minister in Scotland, he was given a progressive education at a school run by William Rose, an unorthodox master who refused to flog his students—and prompted Samuel Johnson's classic comment on the fate of unflogged pupils: "What they gain at one end, they lose at the other."

Apprenticed to a physician at the age of fourteen, Garden served as a surgeon's first mate in the navy before beginning the serious study of medicine at the University of Edinburgh. There he learned his botany under the famous Dr. Charles Alston, who had himself studied under the even more famous Dr. Boerhaave, Linnaeus's patron in Leiden. When he came to South Carolina as assistant to a physician in a town near Charleston, Garden was out botanizing almost before he had settled into medicine, sending back to Edinburgh an Indian pink which, he said, had virtue as a worm medicine. A kindred naturalist of the city, Dr. William Bull, who was one of Collinson's correspondents, lent Garden Linnaeus's books and a copy of Clayton's *Flora Virginica*. Garden had never read Linnaeus at Edinburgh. For all his rare qualities as a teacher, Dr. Alston was outraged by the sexual system and prissily refused to admit Linnaeus into his classes. As it was to so many other colonial naturalists, Linnaeus was a revelation to Garden. "For one whole summer scarcely a week passed away without my reperusing it with greatest attention," he wrote. "Botany never was placed before in so clear a light."

Whenever he had the time, Garden gathered plants, studied their structure and classified them according to the Linnaean method. He tempted British doctors and naturalists with offers of plants if they would keep him in touch with what was going on at home and pass the word around that there was a worthy collector in Carolina. Though his studies had given Garden a classical approach to natural history, he was also an ingenious kitchen scientist. One day coming home with a large whelk shell, he put it on his table. "To my surprise," he wrote, "I saw the shell moving about but taking it up hastily could see nothing in it. Upon laying it down it began to move again. I could yet observe nothing as far as I could look with my eye. I then applied a hot iron to its axis, which immediately forced out one of the ugliest creatures that ever I beheld and in appearance bigger than the shell in which it had contracted itself." Thus, with his hot poker, the doctor made the acquaintance of the hermit crab.

The humid Carolina summers enervated Garden, and in 1754 he made his trip north to Coldengham where he had the meeting with John Bartram he so happily described to Linnaeus. All aglow, he made his way back south slowly, relishing the new friends and region. At Philadelphia, he visited John Bartram in his garden and met Benjamin Franklin, who of course admitted him to the chosen group of scientists permitted free postage.

No sooner was he back in Carolina than he sent seeds to the Coldens: magnolia, indigo, button snakeroot, catalpa, dahoon holly, swamp palmetto— along with notes on the use of agaric of oak in amputations and a discussion of Franklin's sensational paper on lightning and electricity. Shortly, he took over the considerable practice of Dr. John Lining, a botanically inclined physician of Charleston, and at the age of twenty-five, only three years in the colony, Garden was a citizen of standing. Reaching out into the international scientific circle, he wrote pointed letters to Linnaeus and Gronovius. "We have many plants wild in the more southern parts of North America which cannot bear the climate of the northern provinces," where Bartram and Colden concentrated. He would be pleased to send plants, whatever they wished. "I am preparing to make war on the vegetable kingdom," he declared grandly, "and to submit the lofty honors of the forests to the rule and authority of botanic science."

Meanwhile he got around to answering a letter he had received months before from a Londoner named John Ellis, who, like Collinson, was a merchant-virtuoso and was to serve for Garden, as Collinson did for Bartram, as emissary, agent, promoter, confidant and enduring friend. An authority on corals, Ellis insisted, against the general opinion of the day, that they were animals, not plants.

In the first of the hundreds of letters he was to write Ellis over the next quarter century, Garden was modest about his talents: he was "so young a beginner and at such a distance from the proper helps of either men or books; there is scarce one here that knows a cabbage stock from a common dock but when dressed in his plate, by his palate." Still he spoke knowingly about botanical systems, told of his friendship with such eminent colonials as Colden, Bartram and Franklin, and of his correspondents in Europe. Garden's modesty did not go very deep, nor should it have. He was a skillful and critical scientist, patient, precise and proud. He defended his conclusions against the views of the world's most authoritative scientists, and though he often sought recognition in humble words, he would accept it only on his own terms.

In his first shipment to Ellis, Garden sent a hundred kinds of seeds, some butterflies and a king crab's tail. Soon he was writing widely to naturalists in England, gaining their favor by sending seeds and shells and promises of more. Natural history was not a business for him as it was for Bartram. He never accepted any money for his specimens and bore the considerable expense of packing and shipping himself.

Suddenly, in 1755, Garden's burgeoning correspondence languished. He explained why in apologizing to Colden for being half a year late in answering a letter. "My excuse was love. A kind of animal botanizing occupied my thoughts and time." The cause of his animal botanizing was the 16-year-old daughter of a Huguenot merchant who favored the tall, level-eyed, prospering young doctor. Where the love-stricken Garden found time both to work and to woo is hard to see. The people of Charleston were very demanding of their doctors—"preferring a slavish attendance to any other qualifications," Garden said. "The most pitiable slave must be as regularly seen and attended as the governor. From seven in the morning until nine at night I cannot call half an hour my own." And with the "hours spent attending the fair, I had few supernumerary hours to devote to botany."

The hours may have seemed supernumerary, but Garden had not been trifling with science. He sent more than a hundred rooted trees and shrubs off to Ellis. When his brother-in-law sailed for England a few months later, he entrusted him with a marvelously diverse batch of fish, shells, starfish, limpets and bracket fungi.

"This night I expect to be matrimonized," he wrote Ellis at Christmas time, and settled into a happy marriage. Still he missed the company of other naturalists. A project to start a botanical garden was launched with great to-do but faltered. Garden was consulted by Charleston landscapers and his taste showed in the beauty and grace of the city's garden. This was rewarding but it wasn't science. Dr. Bull, an expert botanist, went off into politics. Dr. Lining, whose practice Garden now owned, had given up botany to undertake an extraordinary medical study of the effect of weather upon people. For a solid year, he recorded every physical fact about himself, setting down day by day his weight, pulse, temperature, the amounts of food and liquid he took in and the amounts of his excretions, including his perspiration. All the while, he took equally meticulous readings of the weather: temperature, barometric pressure, winds, rainfall. Though his statistics were authoritative and as firsthand as statistics could be, they never provided any links between meteorology and metabolism. Garden found such diversion discouraging: "I have often wondered how there should be a country abounding with almost every sort of plant and almost every species of the animal kind and yet that it should not have pleased God to raise up one botanist."

A glorious chance came to explore a region where no one had ever botanized: an official expedition was going across the Appalachians to the tributaries of the Mississippi. The governor assigned Garden as physician, promising all the time he needed for botanizing, plus an artist to draw what he found. Just when they were getting into the mountains, a new governor arrived in Charleston and called the whole expedition back. "Good God," wrote Garden bitterly. "My prospect of glutting my very soul was instantly blasted. With what pleasure did I bear the sun's scorching beams, the cold ground for my pillow and the uncomfortable dreariness of rain. Our promised Elysium vanished!" Garden's disappointment was real, but he had plainly already adopted the habits of the American collectors who dwelt endlessly on their hardships to impress their European counterparts—snug in their walled gardens and greenhouses—with the enormous effort that went into getting all those tiny seeds and shriveled shoots.

His correspondents did not have to be talked into appreciating Garden. He was not only eager and expert in collecting specimens but very careful in describing and cataloging them, telling where and in what habitat they were found. This was a blessing to the European naturalists, who too often got seeds in such a jumble that they never knew what they were until the seeds came up—and sometimes not even then. When a shipment came from Garden, it would be accompanied with the kind of catalog reproduced by Edmund and Dorothy Smith Berkeley in their invaluable biography *Dr. Alexander Garden of Charles Town*. This is a 1760 excerpt from

> A list of seeds shipped on board Capt. Strahan of the *Union* for London. *Packt in tallow*: Halesia, Pavia, Loblolly Bay, Laurus Baccis purp, Azalea, Castanea Pumila, Pinus, Hammamelis, Magnolia Palust, Black Jack Oak; *Packt in Myrtle Wax*: Various kinds of acorns from the Cherokees, ditto, Loblolly Bay, Halesia, Pavia, Castanea Pumila, Magnolia Palust. Magnolia Altiss, Carolina Kidney bean Tree. Granadilla-Cassine or Yappon, Convolvul. fol. hast., Ditto fol. Tring. Sagit. Nov. Genus; *Packt in Bees Wax & Tallow*: Magnolia Palust, Callicarpia Stewartia, Corallodendron. *Packt in Paper*: Aralia Arborescens, Cornus Mas, Liriodrendron, 2 parcels, Gleditsia, Calla, Button Snakeroot, Euonymos, Jessamy, Purple berried Bay, Blue Spike N. Genus, Palmetto Royal, Red Cedar berries, Halesia a large parcel, Swamp Palmetto, Supple Jack, Ptelea, Cypress nuts a large parcel . . .

With the added note: "The Box directed in case of Capture au Monsieur Du Hamel De Monceau Intendant de Marine à Paris."

With carefully numbered lists would go further explanations:

> 21 A very beautiful shrub, its fruit hangs in bunches and when green smells like English hops. 27 Frutex formossissima—Decandria Monogynia —it has flowers like an orange blossom in spikes—a new genus 28 Mr. Catesby's Stewartia—a most beautiful shrub. There are some seeds of all the antidotes yet known or used by the Indians or whites on the continent for a rattlesnake bite: they are Nos. 9, 24, 41, 71, 75, 16. I made very particular enquiry among the different nations of Indians as it was my particular desire to learn all their indigenous physic, being persuaded that from the meanest things, useful hints may be gathered.

His descriptions of plants were based on dissection and the use of a microscope that Ellis had sent him.

> *Cal.* Perianth of 4 lanceolate, acute, spreading permanent leaves, shorter than the Corolla. *Cor.* Petals 4, horizontally spreading, deciduous oval lanceolate with convoluted points; the upper side variegated with spots. Nectaries 4, one on the upper side of each petal in the form of a hollow, callous, gaping tubercle bearing honey and fringed with innumerable long, thread-shaped, twisted converging bristles.

He would taste the plant to confirm what his eyes told him. "I find rather the flavor of tobacco than of gentian," he wrote of one specimen, "for though I took but a very small piece, it produced nearly the same kind of nausea that tobacco usually does."

His diligence was sometimes poorly rewarded. In one month in 1757, nineteen of twenty-one ships that sailed from Charleston to England were taken by the French. But Ellis could report that some of Garden's shipments had been received by a French botanist to whom they had been alternately addressed, and would be sent over to London when feasible.

For a while, Garden concentrated on finding new sources of dyes, then in great demand in England. His experiments with the prickly pear were direct. He fed the pears to his slave's children and examined their urine. Sure enough, it had "a lively red color." He then had a young nursing mother eat half a dozen pears and "upon taking some of her milk in a teacup and putting it by for some hours, the cream had a reddish lustre." Nothing practical, however, came of this or of his finding a red flower from which the Indians extracted a durable dye. The Indians would not bring him a fresh plant because they believed that if the whites knew about it, it "immediately lost its wonted virtue."

His interest in dyes as well as plants drew him to a remarkable Carolina lady who was also interested in both, though she was usually too busy for botany. At the age of sixteen, Eliza Lucas was left in charge of the family plantations outside Charleston. Her father, who had gone off to become governor of Antigua, sent her some indigo seeds and instructed her to grow them. Other Carolina planters were skeptical: they had tried indigo, but it hadn't matured properly. Eliza discovered that they had simply not planted the seeds early enough, and triumphantly produced a good crop. She generously gave seed and advice to other planters, and the first indigo shipment to England sold out immediately. Trying to break the French near monopoly of the dyestuff, the British government offered a bounty to the colonial growers. Indigo became a hugely profitable commodity, contributing more than anything else to the Carolinas' prosperity and the fortunes of planters.

After long spinsterhood, Eliza married a widower named Charles Pinckney, who had been scandalously attentive to her during the illness of his wife. An astute plant collector, she was a better botanical companion for Garden than the men of Charleston, and the friendship survived a sharp difference in politics. Garden remained loyal to the King throughout the Revolution. Eliza was a patriot, as were her two famous sons—Charles, an aide to Washington, who helped draft the Constitution; and Thomas, who became governor of the state. When Eliza died, in 1793, President Washington served as a pallbearer.

By the 1760s, Garden was acknowledged as the leading doctor of Charleston and one of the finest in all the colonies. During a disastrous epidemic of smallpox, he led the city's doctors in a prodigious effort, inoculating 2,800 people, a third of the population, in less than two weeks. The inoculations, by

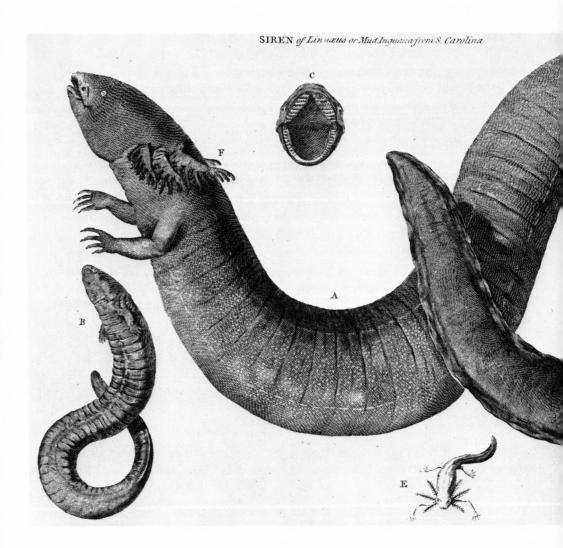

SIREN *of Linnæus or Mud Inguana from S. Carolina*

a method less effective than the one Jenner was later to introduce, cut down the mortality, but even then more than seven hundred of the city's inhabitants—almost one in ten—died.

Meanwhile a very pleasant thing happened to him. He got a letter from Linnaeus—finally. The doctor's first letter to Sweden, written in 1754, was never answered—no reflection on Garden, because Linnaeus had become a notoriously poor correspondent. In a second letter, in 1758, Garden had been lavish in his compliments to Linnaeus, "whose learning," he wrote, "has received its last polish from genius" and whose critics see "their futile reasonings fall harmless to the ground, like the dart of Priam from the shield of Pyrrhus." Moving from the

Alexander Garden discovered this curious amphibian, the mud iguana or Siren lacertina. *In his description he remarked that it sang plaintively, "almost like a young duck."*

fulsome to the matter-of-fact, he pointed out that Linnaeus's system did have its "disputable, inconvenient or faulty parts"—but, after all, nobody is perfect. This letter did bring a reply a year later. In it, Linnaeus disagreed about a plant Garden had described as a new genus. No, said Linnaeus, it was a *Swertia*, an established genus. But it couldn't be a *Swertia*, Garden insisted. It didn't look like one and, moreover, didn't taste like one. As it turned out, Linnaeus was partly wrong, and so was Garden. It was, as Garden thought, a new plant. But it was also a *Swertia*, though not the one Linnaeus believed it was.

Now that Linnaeus seemed ready to answer his letters, Garden began plying him with fish, sending specimens so well preserved and identified that they are still readily recognizable in the Linnaean collections today. There were some, however, that got away. Garden had intended to include a rockfish but had to be content simply with a description. "I never had but only one to examine," he explained to Linnaeus, "and the company who permitted me to make out the description insisted on their having the pleasure of eating it." Garden's fish were of utmost importance to Linnaeus. At least forty of them were noted in the definitive edition of his *Systema Naturae.*

Having sent Linnaeus fish, lizards, tortoises, an alligator and more than a dozen snakes, the last especially valuable to Linnaeus in classifying American reptiles, Garden topped it all with his most spectacular zoological find: an amphibian, shaped like a lizard, with two small front legs and equipped with both gills and lungs. "Head snake-like" went Garden's thorough description, "face snub-nosed, eyes pale yellow, blue underneath, the roof of the mouth filled with many small sharp teeth. It sings with a plaintive voice almost like a young duck."

Garden was sure it was a new genus somewhere between lizards and moray eels. English scientists dismissed his contention: it was simply the larval stage of some lizard, they concluded. Linnaeus at first agreed with this, but Garden urged that it could not be a larva because it made a noise, which no larva was known to do. Won over, Linnaeus added a brand-new class of amphibians for it, Sirenidae, and named Garden's find *Siren lacertina*, which is somewhat more impressive than the common name given it: mud iguana. Later, Garden added another strange creature to his amphibian finds. It was three feet long, looked like a snake, yet had four two-toed feet. It is now called the two-toed congo eel.

Along with his work in botany, zoology and medicine, Garden was busy in Charleston's civic and cultural activities and led a full social life. Benjamin Franklin visited Garden and never forgot his hospitality. When General Bouquet, Bartram's guide, was dispatched to Charleston to arm the city against threatened Indian raids, Franklin told him to look up Garden. "I pity you for the hot summer you must undergo in Charleston," Ben wrote Bouquet. "I do all I can for your relief by recommending you an ingenious physician of my acquaintance who knows the rule of making a cool weak refreshing punch not inferior to the nectar of the gods."

Through all this, Garden was, as he complained, "oppressed by the fatiguing, worrying uninterrupted constancy of business." The time he spent in the pursuit of natural history, "the demon of which constantly agitates me of myself," was "necessarily stolen from the usual hours of sleep." His youthful eagerness for science turned sometimes into weary self-pity touched with jealousy. When he learned that Bartram had been appointed King's Botanist, he wrote: "Surely John is a worthy man but yet to give the title of king's botanist to a man who can scarcely spell, much less make out characters of any one genus of plants, appears rather hyperbolical."

Having proved himself as a naturalist, Garden assumed one of the prerequisites that collectors took to themselves: the right to name plants. Here the ultimate authority rested with Linnaeus, who liked to reward someone who had helped him or natural science by bestowing his name on a new species. Other naturalists disputed the Swedish savant's power or wanted to share it. Confusions, contradictions and controversies over nomenclature multiplied as unfamiliar plants poured into Europe, often in such bad condition that identification was difficult, or carrying misleading descriptions, or accompanied by strained attempts to prove that the plant in question was really a new one.

Garden threw himself eagerly into the nomenclature game. His first involvement came after his visit to Coldengham, when Jane Colden proposed to give the name "gardenia" to a plant he had found on the way home. It turned out not to be a new species and the name was disallowed. Some time later, he picked a quarrel with Linnaeus over a so-called bignonia. It wasn't a bignonia at all, Garden asserted, but a new kind of jessamy. Since it was new, he would like it named Ellisiana, after his good friend. This was disallowed when it turned out that the plant (now called the evening trumpet flower) really belonged to the Logania family, named for Colden and Bartram's Philadelphia friend.

Next Garden proposed that a new genus of loblolly bay he found be called Gordonia, after his old teacher James Gordon. Here again, he said, Linnaeus had misnamed the plant. There followed a confused wrangle and a farcical ending. Linnaeus was finally judged wrong and Garden right, and the plant was named *Gordonia*—not after Garden's mentor, however, but after a well-known London nurseryman named James Gordon.

Garden kept after Linnaeus to honor Ellis, sending a "most superb lofty plant" and proposing that it be called Ellisia. Linnaeus fumbled that one, and to make up for it, he proposed to Ellis that an *Ipomoea*, a morning-glory, be renamed Ellisia—he could find one, Linnaeus told Ellis, in Collinson's garden. Ellis was somewhat miffed after he went to see Collinson's *Ipomoea*. "It was a mean-looking plant," he said, which reflected "no honor on the person to whose name it is given." In the end, Linnaeus gave Ellis's name to *Ellisia nyctelea*, one of the American waterleaf family, described in modern botanical manuals as "a small family of plants of no marked properties."

Garden remained irate, railing against European botanists who "assume a dictatorial power over us and our performances." There was apparently little the Americans could do about it. But, he added, "you can't take from us the power of grumbling and complaining which we certainly possess to a high degree."

While Garden had been campaigning for Ellis, Ellis had been lobbying for

Garden. He tried to persuade the uncooperative Linnaeus to name the fragrant *Calycanthus*, also called sweet shrub or Carolina allspice, after his Charleston friend, slyly suggesting that "Dr. Garden will take it as a compliment from you and may be most useful in sending you many many new undescribed plants." Linnaeus failed to rise to that bait. Some time later, Ellis informed Linnaeus of a new sensation in London, a plant from South Africa called a bay-leaved jasmine.

A Captain Hutcheson, putting in at the Cape of Good Hope on the way home from India, had ridden out into the country and was "most wonderfully surprised by a fine smell and, looking round, spied a large double white flower." He dug it up and took it home to London where only James Gordon, for whom Garden's *Gordonia* was named, seemed able to propagate it. As a result, he made a small fortune from it—five hundred pounds in three years. Ellis, in reporting to Linnaeus, proposed that its special beauty be acknowledged by calling it August. Linnaeus replied that he was tired of such hyperbolic names as "Superba, Augusta, Incomparabilis."

At this point, Ellis had had enough of the Swede's stubbornness. With a scathing politeness, he wrote, "I desire you would please to call" the bay-leaved jasmine "Gardenia, which will satisfy me and I believe will not be disagreeable to you." And to make refusal difficult, he added that he was telling Garden "that I have desired you to give the name of Gardenia to the Jasmine." Linnaeus did find the idea disagreeable, though he sounded altogether reasonable in his objection. He preferred that the name gardenia should be "applied to some genus first discovered by Dr. Garden. I wish to guard against the ill-natured objections often made against me that I name plants after my friends." But Ellis had boxed himself in by writing Garden. Linnaeus surrendered, agreeing to call the jasmine gardenia, even though he was sacrificing science for friendship.

Garden had been too often disappointed to take anything for granted. Not until Ellis assured him that the name gardenia had been approved by Linnaeus and presented to the Royal Society did he properly thank Ellis, who smugly informed him, "It has given great jealousy to our botanists that I have preferred you to them. I laugh at them."

He sent two gardenia plants to Garden in Charleston. One died on the voyage and the other, though given the most loving care, died after a year in the doctor's garden. The "sudden death I take to be no good omen for the continuance and duration of my botanical name and character," Garden wrote with rueful grace. "But if I do not outlive it, I shall be pleased and if I do, I shall certainly make myself happy in some other acquisition if it should only be, like the former, imaginary."

CHAPTER FIVE

PUC PUGGY IN XANADU

🌱 🌱 🌱 🌱 🌱 JOHN BARTRAM'S GOOD FRIENDS WERE ALL DRAWN INTO A problem that the practical Quaker could not seem to solve: what to do with his gifted, lovable and unanchored son William. "I don't want him to be what is commonly called a gentleman," John wrote Peter Collinson in 1755 when Billy was sixteen. "I want to put him to some business by which he may, with care and industry, get a temperate reasonable living. Hard labor don't agree with him. I have designed several years to put him to a doctor to learn physic and surgery."

Alexander Garden generously offered to take young Bartram as his apprentice and even, perhaps, as successor to his profitable practice. Bartram appreciated this "kindness for my son," he told Garden. "He longs to be with thee but it is more for the sake of botany than physic or surgery." Benjamin Franklin, when consulted, proposed that Billy become a printer, but John reminded Ben that, "as he well knew, he was the only printer that did ever make a livelihood by it in this place." Franklin then "sat and paused a while" and remarked that engraving was "a profitable business." Collinson approved of this as a career for Billy. It "may suit his genius," he decided.

As discussions of his future worried their way back and forth across the ocean and up and down the colonies, William Bartram was just finishing his schooling. His untutored father made sure William got a sound education at the Academy in Philadelphia where he studied under Charles Thomson, a teacher with a passion for the classics, a deep sympathy for Indians and an outspoken devotion to liberty—"the Sam Adams of Philadelphia," John Adams called him. (Thomson went on to serve as secretary of the Continental Congress and the first United States Congress, then spent seventeen years making a grand translation of the Bible from the Greek. It remained a standard throughout the nineteenth century.)

Billy must have been one of Thomson's most satisfying students. His later writing is studded with references to Vergil and Ovid and, unlike his "bang them stoutly" father, he always had a warm feeling toward the Indians. But it was nature that absorbed him. When he was fourteen, he sent some bird drawings to Collinson, who promptly sent back compliments, along with some fine paper and good ink. "Billy is much obliged to thee," John wrote Collinson. "He has drawn many rare birds to send thee and dried the birds to send to his friend Edwards."

This friend was George Edwards, the finest British bird artist of his time, whose landmark books *A Natural History of Uncommon Birds* and *Gleanings of Natural History* were best sellers in their time. Edwards used Billy's birds and drawings to guide his own work, on which Linnaeus relied heavily in classifying American birds. So Billy became a junior member of the international circle.

Learning from his father, William developed a profound respect for careful, firsthand observation that seemed to be at odds with his quirky poetic instincts. Eventually the contradiction helped make him a rare artist-scientist. He worked in the gardens, met the famous men who came to visit, went out on trips with his father and learned the perils a naturalist faced. In the Catskills, he wrote:

> I saw a singular and beautiful appearance which I remember to have instantly apprehended to be a large kind of fungus which we call Jews ears and was just drawing back to kick it over when my father cried out, "a rattlesnake, my son," and jerked me back which probably saved my life. I had never before seen one—this was very beautiful, speckled and clouded. My father pleaded for his life but our guide was inexorable, saying he never spared the life of a rattlesnake, and killed him.

After a visit to Coldengham, Billy asked Jane Colden's help in his drawing, but soon she wrote, "I can teach you no more. You have already surpassed me in skill and imagination." What with work and school, William had only Sundays for his drawing, and the household rule against working on the Sabbath was relaxed for him. In the spring he dissected birds of passage, and, finding immature eggs in the females, concluded that they had begun breeding during their migration. Taking into account Billy's love for the outdoors and for drawing, John for a while thought of making him a surveyor, but concluded that there were already five surveyors for every job available. Having asked everybody's advice, John discarded all of it. In late 1756, he apprenticed Billy to a merchant of Philadelphia. For four years, while he conscientiously tried to make himself a merchant, Billy kept at his drawings. His sketch of a "horn tailed turtle" was published, through Collinson, in the distinguished *Gentleman's Magazine* of London. William continued to supply Edwards with material, along with the observation that "many animals which abounded formerly in settled parts are no more to be found."

In 1761, when he was twenty-one, William left to set himself up as a merchant at Ashwood on Cape Fear, North Carolina, where his father's half brother William had a trading post. He was at Cape Fear through the years when his father took his second trip through the Carolinas and his brief journey with Bouquet down the Ohio. John's eyes had troubled him sorely, and Franklin fitted him with one of his new inventions, bifocal eyeglasses. "My eyesight is so well returned that I wrote this by candlelight and without spectacles," John wrote William in 1765. Some exciting news followed in a few days. John wrote that he had been appointed King's Botanist and proposed that William come along.

Years later, in a brief biography of his father, William described the journey and John:

> At the advanced age of near seventy years, he proceeded by land through part of Carolina and Georgia to St. Augustine in East Florida to search for the sources of the great river San Juan. He ascended that great and beautiful river (near 400 miles) to its sources, attending carefully to its various branches and the lakes connected with it. Having ascended on one side of the river, he descended by the other side. In the course of this voyage, he made an accurate draft and survey of the various widths, depths, courses and distance, both of the main stream and of the lakes and branches. He also noted the situation and quality of the soil, the vegetables and animal productions.

Nowhere does William mention that he went along.

The trip ended in March, 1766. Billy stayed in Florida. His father, after stopping over in Charleston for a last visit with Alexander Garden, was back in Philadelphia by May with a catalog of plants and complaints. "I have brought home with me a fine collection of strange Florida plants," he told Collinson, "the collecting of which has cost thy friend many score wounds, pains and sickness; in Florida, the fever and jaundice; a looseness through north and south Carolina and Georgia. Yet I lost not an hour's time of traveling."

After sending plants off to the King, Bartram busied himself with a journal of the trip. His *Description of East Florida*, published in 1767, sold so well that a second edition was printed in 1769 and a third in 1774.

Meanwhile, he could hardly wait to hear how George III liked his plants. Collinson's report was dampening. They "were carefully delivered and no doubt but were acceptable," he wrote, but the King would not pay the freight. "The honor of giving is sufficient," he said primly. "Consider thy salary is regularly paid."

Bartram had other things to worry him besides the King's indifference. "I have left Billy in Florida," he told Collinson. "Nothing will do with him now but he will be a planter upon St. John's River. This frolic of his and our maintenance drove me to great straits." Bartram put several hundred pounds into his son's frolic, and though he could well afford it by now, it was a bad investment. Henry Laurens, whom Bartram had met in Charleston (he was later a signer of the Declaration of Independence and president of the Continental Congress), went out of his way, during a trip to Florida, to see how William was doing. He sent a troubled report to John:

> His situation on the river is the least agreeable of all the places that I have seen—on a low sheet of sandy pine barren, in a bight or cove of the river, the water almost stagnated, exceedingly foul. The swamp and adjoining marsh will, without doubt, produce good rice, when properly cleared and cultivated; but both will require more strength than Mr. Bartram is at present possessed of. That sort of work goes on very heavily, for want of strong hands. He assured me that but two, among the six negroes that you gave him, that could handle an axe tolerably. The house, or rather hovel, that he lives in, is extremely confined, and not proof against the weather. His provision of grain, flesh, and spirits is scanty, even to penury. He had the fever, when I was first with him, and looked very poorly the second visit. No coloring can do justice to the forlorn state of poor Billy Bartram. A gentle, mild young man, no wife, no friend, no companion, no neighbor, totally void of all the comforts of life, except an inimitable degree of patience, for which he deserves a thousand times better fate.

William stuck it out for almost a year, farming, collecting plants, sending some drawings to Collinson. In the fall of 1767, he came home—and the worried mail about him once again started across the ocean. "Nothing but marrying will settle him," Collinson concluded. Get him a farm girl for a wife, he advised. To Billy he sent not sententious comment but an affectionate reminder that "I can truly say I have never had thee long far from my mind." He mixed praise for William's "elegant masterly drawings" with a scolding for using "such vile paper" for them. And later on sent him a guinea for his expenses.

William took a job as day laborer in Philadelphia, and went into business for himself. Collinson, distressed at Billy's "servile drudgery," was ecstatic over a drawing of a *Colocasia* he had sent over. "So great was the deception, it being candlelight, that we disputed for some time whether it was an engraving or a drawing." Triumphantly he wrote John in 1768 that the Duchess of Portland, "a great virtuoso in shells and all marine production" (and owner of the famous Portland vase), had come to dinner and, shown William's work, offered twenty guineas for "drawings of all land, river and sea shells." The letter had not yet reached America when Collinson was writing excitedly about another meal and another patron: Dr. John Fothergill had come to breakfast and stayed to admire Billy's "elegant performances." The doctor wanted drawings of shells and turtles.

Having now found patrons for a second Bartram generation, Collinson went on to instruct Billy as carefully as he had, three decades before, set down rules for his father: "Don't crowd the shells; a few in a sheet shows better. Send all to me rolled on a roller and put in a little box for fear of getting wet."

IT WAS ON THIS FAMILIAR NOTE THAT THE LONG AND LOVING correspondence between Peter Collinson and the steadfast friends he had never seen came to an end. In August, 1768, at the age of seventy-five, the mercer of London died. His last days had been sad. His business had fallen off; he was in debt and a modest request for a government pension, customary in those days, had been rejected—cruel reward for a man who had given so much of his time and resources for science and his country. To the very end, he found solace and pleasure in his friends and his plants—they were one and the same to him, as he told Cadwallader Colden in a charming letter:

> I am this instant come in from seeing your skunkweed (*arum Betafol*); its early appearance and its singularly spotted flowers attract the notice of everyone. As often as I survey my garden and plantations it reminds me of my absent friends by their living donations. See there my honorable friend, Governor Colden. Sir, I see nobody but two fine trees, a spruce and a larch, that's true, but they are his representatives. Look yonder at the late benevolent Duke of Richmond, his everlasting cedars of Lebanon, see with what vigor they tower. Those balm of Gilead firs renew a concern for my dear Lord Petre, they came young from his nursery. Ye variety of trees and shrubs, mountain magnolia, sarsifax, rhododendrons, Calmias and azaleas are all the bounty of my curious botanic friend J. Bartram of Philadelphia and those pretty fringe trees, halesias and Stuartia, great beauties, I must thank Mr. Clayton.

John Bartram did not learn directly of his old friend's death, though he heard some rumor of it. He was almost seventy now and his once clear Quaker mind was a bit clouded. When Dr. Fothergill wrote chiding him for not taking any notice of Collinson's passing, John replied that he did not know whom or where to write. Now he addressed himself to Michael Collinson, who proved a true son of Peter. He paid Bartram more than two hundred pounds still owed him and for years kept up an affectionate correspondence with him.

The Florida trip had taken much from Bartram physically. Collinson's death and William's troubles further eroded his spirit. Bartram's Gardens, a solidly profitable business, were run by John, Jr., four years younger than William and far more responsible. Other local seedsmen, cashing in on the reputation Bartram had given Philadelphia's botanists, were competing briskly for business, but as Collinson had scornfully remarked, "Their seeds do well enough for the Scots." John, Sr., still solicited customers and had a standard answer to inquiries. "I would undertake to supply your demands if your generosity is equal to them."

His eyes grew worse, though with Franklin's bifocals he could bring a book to meals and read as he ate. He missed Ben, who was in London representing the colonies, using his enormous prestige as a scientist to abet his political lobbying. He wrote Bartram faithfully—letters, Bartram said, that "have a magical power of dispelling melancholy fumes and cheering up my spirits."

The King's pension continued but there was no other sign of royal interest, even when Bartram sent a box of bullfrogs. "The frogs came safe and lively," reported Dr. Fothergill, but nothing more was heard. "I imagine they are quite forgot and will never be called for."

With Collinson gone, Fothergill was attentive to Bartram, but it was William he was really interested in. Is your son "sober and diligent?" he asked John, admitting that "this may be an uncommon question to ask a father of his son and yet I know thy integrity will not suffer thee to mislead me. I would lend him some little assistance if he is worthy." The man who now stepped in to become for William Bartram what Peter Collinson had been for John and what Ellis had been for Alexander Garden was one of the finest men in England. "A worthier man never lived," said his friend and patient Ben Franklin.

Like Collinson, Fothergill had the Quaker interest in botany bred into him and, like Mitchell and Garden, had studied at Edinburgh under Dr. Alston. A brilliant and prosperous physician, he helped restore the health of John Wesley by persuading the founder of Methodism to resume the drinking of tea, which he had stopped for religious reasons. He tended Lord Grenville, the chancellor of the exchequer, taking advantage of his calls to argue against Grenville's harsh policy toward the colonies. He would have been Royal Physician, too, but for the fact that, as a Quaker, he would not conform to the laws of England by swearing loyalty to the crown, or to any ruler but God.

Fothergill gave much of his life to good works. He served the poor of London without fee, took part in early antislavery movements and was a mainstay of the Society for the Recovery of the Apparently Drowned, a strangely popular cause that for half a century enlisted the support of the most eminent men in England and the Americas in spreading the techniques of resuscitation. Fothergill tried to help Franklin in his efforts to reconcile crown and colonies. Finally and reluctantly turning against the King, he wrote to Franklin that "through the infatuation of the times we shall be rendered a severe scourge to each other, the labor of ages ruined; what little lay within my reach to do, I have endeavored to do it honestly; but it is all in vain."

Through all this, he also served science. He corresponded with James Logan about his corn-tassel experiment and had Logan's work published in England. With Colden, he exchanged ideas about diphtheria, which he was the first to describe and diagnose correctly. With Collinson, he introduced Franklin's papers on electricity to English scientists. Put in touch with John Bartram by Collinson, he solicited seeds and fossils from him and then tried to persuade Bartram to put together a natural history of the colonies.

His garden, at Upton in Essex, became one of the finest in Europe, stocked with plants from America, China, Hindustan, Siberia, the West Indies. Bartram sent a special prize—a water lily that was, he wrote, "so coy a lady as to not bear a touch from any other species without faulting." Fothergill usually had time to visit his garden only after dark. With a lantern, he would make his way to a favorite spot where, in the shelter of a garden wall, he grew laurel and azalea from the Carolinas.

William Bartram proved an elusive protégé to Fothergill. In 1770, he left Philadelphia suddenly and secretively, leaving large debts behind. He stayed in North Carolina for two years, sending drawings to Fothergill but no longer trying to make himself into a businessman. In his mind was the plan for an extensive exploration over the routes he and his father had taken through Georgia and Florida. Fothergill's mind was set in an opposite direction. He wanted Billy to go to "the back parts of Canada" for plants that would be better suited to his garden. But Billy, perhaps, had had too much of doing what others wanted him to do. He insisted on Florida, and Fothergill gave in.

The doctor asked Dr. Lionel Chalmers of Charleston to act as his agent with Billy, who "is not quite a systematic botanist. He knows plants and draws prettily. I wish to encourage him, not to injure him by proposing a provision that may make him idle." He commissioned Chalmers to pay Billy fifty pounds a year, which was what John got as King's Botanist.

Chalmers, impressed by Billy, gave his father a long-overdue scolding for not having encouraged "this genius of his as a naturalist" sooner: "You endeavored to curb it by putting him to a merchant. John Bartram has a son who I hope will perpetuate both his father's and his own name."

John had shown no sympathy with William's new project—a "wild notion" he called it. But he must have been moved into consenting by Chalmers's remarks and Fothergill's faith. "It is a pity that such genius should sink under distress," Fothergill had told John. William came back to Philadelphia in 1772 to prepare for the great journey, which was to save his genius from sinking and more than fulfill Dr. Chalmers's hopeful prophecy.

The journey, which William Bartram recounted in his *Travels through North and South Carolina, Georgia, East and West Florida*, lasted almost four years—from March 20, 1773, when he sailed south from Philadelphia, until shortly after New Year's Day, 1777, when he returned to a home he was hardly ever to leave again. Though a sharp and accurate observer of nature, William was a careless recorder of dates and distances. His travel reports are full of errors in both. By patient detective work, Dr. Francis Harper, in his authoritative edition of the *Travels*, has established the chronology and route of the journey.

According to Bartram's account, he left from Philadelphia in April, 1773. Actually, it was March 20th. Arriving in Charleston, he sailed to Savannah and rode down to Darien. *Travels* then tells of a trip up the Altamaha River, south to the St. Mary's River and its source in the Okefenokee Swamp. This, however, took place sometime later. After several excursions in the back country, and a few short coastal trips, he left in March, 1774, for Florida, where he traveled up and down the St. John's River, east to the coast near New Smyrna, then west across the great Alachua Savannah to the Suwannee River. He returned to Charleston in March, 1775, set out overland through the country of the Creek Indians to the Tennessee border, then south and southwest through Georgia and Alabama to Mobile. Sailing along the Gulf of Mexico, he went up the Mississippi to the present site of Baton Rouge. Retracing his route, he came back to Savannah, went up to Charleston, where he used Dr. Garden's Linnaeus to check some of his observations, and as winter came near, rode north for home.

Bartram's *Travels* runs upward of 175,000 words of narrative, description, botanical and zoological observation, social comment, ethnological reporting, anecdotes, evocations, philosophizing and high-flown phraseology.* In the style

---

*In the excerpts that follow, Bartram's words are unchanged but the many internal elisions are not indicated.

he would maintain throughout, poetical description laced with homely fact, he begins dutifully:

> At the request of Dr. Fothergill, of London, to search the Floridas, and the western parts of Carolina and Georgia, for the discovery of rare and useful productions of nature, chiefly in the vegetable kingdom; in April, 1773, I embarked for Charleston, South Carolina, on board the brigantine *Charleston* packet. For the first twenty-four hours we had a prosperous gale, and were cheerful and happy in the prospect of a quick and pleasant voyage; but, alas! how vain and uncertain are human expectations! how quickly is the flattering scene changed! The powerful winds, now rushing forth from their secret abodes, suddenly spread terror and devastation; and the wide ocean, which, a few moments past, was gentle and placid, is now thrown into disorder, and heaped into mountains, whose white curling crests seem to sweep the skies!
>
> This furious gale continued near two days and nights. The storm having abated, we descried a sail. We hailed each other, being joyful to meet, after so many dangers. As he ran by us, [the captain] threw on board ten or a dozen bass, a large and delicious fish.

He had come with useful letters of introduction. The governor of the province "showed me every mark of esteem and regard" while the superintendent of Indian Affairs offered to "introduce my business to the chiefs of the Cherokees, Creeks, and other nations, and recommend me to their friendship and protection."

He goes on:

> Obedient to the admonitions of my attendant spirit, curiosity, as well as to gratify the expectations of my worthy patron, I again set off on my southern excursion. The road is straight, spacious, and kept in excellent repair by the industrious inhabitants; and is generally bordered on each side with a light grove, consisting of the following trees and shrubs: Myrica cerifera, Calycanthus, Halesia tetraptera, Itea, stewartia, Andromeda nitida, Cyrilla racemiflora, entwined with bands and garlands of Bignonia sempervirens, B. crucigera, Lonicera sempervirens and Glycine frutescens; these were overshadowed by tall and spreading trees, as the Magnolia grandiflora, Liquidambar, Liriodendron, Catalpa, Quercus sempervirens, Quercus dentata, Q. Phillos; and on the verges of the canals, where the road was causewayed, stood the Cupressus disticha, floriferous Gordonia lasianthus, and Magnolia glauca, all planted by nature, and left standing by the virtuous inhabitants, to shade the road, and perfume the sultry air.

Wherever he went, people welcomed him and pressed him to stay. "The Hon. B. Andrews Esq. [later a member of the Continental Congress] entertained me with hearty welcome, plain but plentiful food, free conversation." At the home of a "venerable gray headed Caledonian I was treated with some excellent venison." A Mr. Bailey "received me very civilly, inviting me to stay with him." At the home of Lachlan McIntosh, "the friendly man, smiling, and with a grace and dignity peculiar to himself, took me by the hand, and accosted me thus: 'Friend Bartram, come under my roof, and I desire you to make my house your home, as long as convenient to yourself.' "

Going past the farthest white settlements, Bartram had an experience that recalls his father's meeting with the Indian who chewed his hat. William orchestrated the encounter as if he were composing a pastoral piece:

> The gaily attired plants which enameled the green had begun to imbibe the pearly dew of evening; nothing appeared to ruffle the happy moments of evening contemplation: when, on a sudden, an Indian appeared crossing the path. I endeavored to elude his sight, but he espied me, and came up on full gallop. I never before this was afraid at the sight of an Indian, but at this time, I must own that my spirits were very much agitated: I resigned myself entirely to the will of the Almighty, trusting to his mercies for my preservation: my mind then became tranquil, and I resolved to meet the dreaded foe with resolution and cheerful confidence. The intrepid Seminole stopped suddenly, his countenance angry and fierce. I advanced towards him, and offered him my hand, hailing him, brother; at this he hastily jerked back his arm, with a look of malice, rage, and disdain, when again looking at me more attentively, he instantly spurred up to me, and with dignity in his look and action, gave me his hand. Possibly the silent language of his soul, during the moment of suspense (for I believe his design was to kill me when he first came up), was after this manner: "White man, thou art my enemy, and thou and thy brethren may have killed mine; yet it may not be so, and even were that the case, thou art now alone, and in my power. Live; the Great Spirit forbids me to touch thy life; go to thy brethren, tell them thou sawest an Indian in the forests, who knew how to be humane and compassionate." In fine, we shook hands, and parted in a friendly manner, in the midst of a dreary wilderness.

At the next trading post, Bartram learned that the Indian, an outlaw from his own tribe, had been beaten up by the traders and had gone off declaring that he would kill the first white man he met.

Bartram went on toward "a vast lake or marsh called Ouaquaphenogaw," the Okefenokee Swamp. He mused about its legendary inhabitants—not Pogo and his friends but Indians of a hazy past.

> This vast accumulation of waters, in the wet season, appears as a lake, and contains some large islands or knolls, of rich high land, one of which the present generation of the Creeks represent to be a most blissful spot of the earth: they say it is inhabited by a peculiar race of Indians, whose women are incomparably beautiful; they also tell you that this terrestrial paradise has been seen by some of their enterprising hunters, who being lost in inextricable swamps and bogs, and on the point of perishing, were unexpectedly relieved by a company of beautiful women, whom they call daughters of the sun, who kindly gave them such provisions as they had with them, and then enjoined them to fly for safety to their own country; for that their husbands were fierce men, and cruel to strangers: they further say that these hunters had a view of their settlements, but that in their endeavors to approach it, they were involved in perpetual labyrinths, and, like enchanted land, still as they imagined they had just gained it, it seemed to fly before them. Their young warriors were enflamed with an irresistible desire to make a conquest of so charming a country; but all their attempts hitherto have proved abortive, never having been able again to find that enchanting spot, nor even any road or pathway to it.

Where his father, having told the story of the Indian goddess and her gift of squashes, dismissed it irritably as "a silly story," William gently gave a plausible explanation of the Okefenokee maidens: they were probably fugitives of the Yamassee tribes finding refuge from the Creeks, who had all but exterminated them.

Natural history, of course, was his main business. He tended to it diligently, listing the plants and their habitats, noting a new andromeda "which far exceeds in beauty every one of this family," measuring black oaks and finding some of them an almost unbelievable eleven feet in diameter, giving the earliest known descriptions of the physical geography and vegetation of the area and telling how an accident on a steep hillside led him to discover a new species of pink: "On reaching to a shrub, my foot slipped, and, in recovering myself, I tore up some of the plants, whose roots filled the air with animating scents of cloves and spicy perfumes."

When he felt he had gathered enough specimens, he sent a shipment off to Dr. Fothergill—high time he did. Dr. Chalmers, hearing from him at last, replied that he had "feared the Creeks must have catched you," and Dr. Fothergill was annoyed at the delay and disappointed in the shipment, which contained "very few drawings and neither a seed nor a plant."

Indian troubles, which so often frustrated John, now kept William from traveling freely in the Carolinas. Recollecting his journey with his father and having "reasons to think that very many curious subjects had escaped our researches," he set out for Florida.

He started up the St. Johns River in company with a young man who was interested in sharing his adventures, but

> my fellow traveller, though stouter and heartier than myself, having repented of his promise to accompany me to the Indian trading houses, chose rather to stay behind, amongst the settlements, where he might be enabled to procure, without much toil and danger, the necessaries and conveniences of life. Whilst I, continually impelled by a restless spirit of curiosity, in pursuit of new productions of nature, my chief happiness consisted in tracing and admiring the infinite power, majesty, and perfection of the great Almighty Creator, and in the contemplation, that through divine aid and permission, I might be instrumental in discovering, and introducing into my native country, some original productions of nature, which might become useful to society. Each of our pursuits was perhaps equally laudable.

Up the river, he paddled through a host of mating mayflies. This inspired a fine set piece, which ended, as his so often did, with a sermon.

> I observed this day, during my progress up the river, incredible numbers of small flying insects, of the genus termed by naturalists Ephemera, continually emerging from the shallow water near shore. This resurrection from the deep, if I may so express it, commences early in the morning, and ceases after the sun is up. At evening they are seen in clouds of innumerable millions, swarming and wantoning in the still air. This fly seems to be delicious food for birds, frogs, and fish. They spring into the air after this delicious prey.
>
> Solemnly and slowly move onward, to the river's shore, the rustling clouds of the Ephemera. How awful the procession! innumerable millions of winged beings, voluntarily verging on to destruction, to the brink of the grave, where they behold bands of their enemies with wide-open jaws, ready to receive them. But as if insensible of their danger, gay and tranquil each meets his beloved mate in the still air, inimitably bedecked in their new nuptial robes. What eye can trace them, in their varied wanton amorous chases, bounding and fluttering on the odoriferous air? With what peace, love, and joy, do they end the last moments of their existence!
>
> The importance of the existence of these beautiful and delicately formed little creatures in the creation whose frame and organization are equally wonderful, more delicate, and perhaps as complicated as those

of the most perfect human being, is well worth a few moments' contemplation. And if we consider the very short period of that stage of existence, which we may reasonably suppose to be the only space of their life that admits of pleasure and enjoyment, what a lesson doth it not afford us of the vanity of our own pursuits!

Such reveries gave way to matter-of-fact notes:

> I was awakened in the morning early, by the cheering converse of the wild turkeycocks (Meleagris occidentalis) saluting each other, from the sun-brightened tops of the lofty Cupressus disticha and Magnolia grandiflora. The high forests ring with the noise, like the crowing of the domestic cock, of these social sentinels, the watch-word being caught and repeated, from one to another, for hundreds of miles around; insomuch that the whole country is for an hour or more in a universal shout.

He came to Rollestown, an offbeat Utopia founded by Denys Rolle, an English M.P. who sought to redeem the prostitutes, pickpockets and beggars of London by transporting them to America and a new life. "But," said Bartram, "it seems, from an ill-concerted plan in its infant establishment, negligence, or extreme parsimony together with a bad choice of citizens, the settlement by degrees grew weaker, and at length totally fell to the ground." The first batch of settlers coming in 1767 grew tired of prying up palmetto stumps to clear the land, and most of what a chronicler called the "miserable females" lit out for St. Augustine. Rolle brought new shiploads of settlers, but one group jumped ship at Charleston and those who arrived succumbed to fever or discontent. Finally, giving up his ideals, Rolle stocked his colony with slaves and made a modest profit from it.

Sailing up the St. John's in a small boat, Bartram passed Mount Hope, "so named," he remarks, "by my father John Bartram when he ascended this river about fifteen years ago." But where John's journal of the river trip had been full of businesslike detail, William's account was full of dangerous encounters and suspenseful scenes. He was a master of dramatic narrative, and no part of the *Travels* shows this off better than his accounts of the alligators.

He set the scene. The prudent traveler picked a place to spend the night:

> The evening was temperately cool and calm. The crocodiles began to roar and appear in uncommon numbers along the shores and in the river. I fixed my camp in an open plain, near the utmost projection of the promontory. From this open, high situation, I had a free prospect of the river, which was a matter of no trivial consideration to me, having good reason to dread the subtle attacks of the alligators, who were crowding about my harbor.

Nearby was a lagoon where he thought he might catch his dinner:

> The verges and islets were elegantly embellished with flowering plants
> and shrubs; the laughing coots with wings half spread were tripping over
> the little coves and hiding themselves in the tufts of grass; young broods
> of the painted summer teal, skimming the still surface of the waters, and
> following the watchful parent unconscious of danger.

Now came the beast—

> the subtle, greedy alligator. Behold him rushing forth from the flags and
> reeds. His enormous body swells. His plaited tail, brandished high, floats
> upon the lake. The waters like a cataract descend from his opening jaws.
> Clouds of smoke issue from his dilated nostrils. The earth trembles with
> his thunder. When, immediately from the opposite coast of the lagoon,
> emerges from the deep his rival champion. They suddenly dart upon
> each other. The boiling surface of the lake marks their rapid course, and
> a terrific conflict commences. They now sink to the bottom folded to-
> gether in horrid wreaths. The water becomes thick and discolored. Again

Captioning his drawings of alligators, Bartram noted that when they "bellow in the spring
season, they force the water out of their throats which falls from their mouth like a cataract

they rise, their jaws clap together, re-echoing through the deep surrounding forests. Again they sink, when the contest ends at the muddy bottom of the lake, and the vanquished makes a hazardous escape. The proud victor exulting returns to the place of action. The shores and forests resound his dreadful roar, together with the triumphing shouts of the plaited tribes around, witnesses of the horrid combat.

The hero was shaken. My "apprehensions were highly alarmed after being a spectator of so dreadful a battle." But he was hungry and set out to catch some fish. "I furnished myself with a club for my defense and paddled with all my might towards the lagoon." The alligators were waiting.

Ere I had halfway reached the place, I was attacked on all sides, several endeavoring to overset the canoe. Two very large ones attacked me closely, at the same instant, rushing up with their heads and part of their bodies above the water, roaring terribly and belching floods of water over me. They struck their jaws together so close to my ears as almost to stun me,

and a steam or vapor rises from the nostrils like smoke" and when they devour "fish they rise up out of the water." "A very large alligator is lord or chief" of the alligator hole.

and I expected every moment to be dragged out of the boat and instantly devoured, but I applied my weapons so effectually about me, though at random, that I was so successful as to beat them off a little. I made good my entrance into the lagoon, though not without opposition from the alligators, who formed a line across the entrance, but did not pursue me into it.

He quickly caught more trout than he needed, and on returning to his camp was chased by an old alligator,

who kept close after me, and when I stepped on shore rushed up near my feet and lay there for some time, looking me in the face; I resolved he should pay for his temerity, and having a heavy load in my fusee, I ran to my camp, and returning with my piece, found him with his foot on the gunwale of the boat, in search of fish. On my coming up he withdrew sullenly and slowly. I soon dispatched him by lodging the contents of my gun in his head, and then proceeded to cleanse and prepare my fish for supper, when, raising my head, I saw before me, through the clear water, the head and shoulders of a very large alligator, moving slowly towards me; I instantly stepped back, when, with a sweep of his tail, he brushed off several of my fish. It was certainly most providential that I looked up at that instant, as the monster would probably, in less than a minute, have seized and dragged me into the river.

It was by this time dusk, and I was again alarmed by a tumultuous noise. I saw a scene which threw my senses into such a tumult that it was some time before I could comprehend what was the matter. The river from shore to shore appeared to be one solid bank of fish, of various kinds, pushing through this narrow pass of St. Juan's; and the alligators were in such incredible numbers, and so close together from shore to shore, that it would have been easy to have walked across on their heads, had the animals been harmless. What expressions can sufficiently declare the shocking scene that for some minutes continued, whilst this mighty army of fish were forcing the pass? During this attempt, thousands, I may say hundreds of thousands of them were caught and swallowed by the devouring alligators. I have seen an alligator take up out of the water several great fish at a time, and just squeeze them betwixt his jaws, while the tails of the great trout flapped about his eyes and lips, ere he had swallowed them. The horrid noise of their closing jaws, their plunging amidst the broken banks of fish, and rising with their prey some feet upright above the water, the floods of water and blood rushing out of their mouths, and the clouds of vapor issuing from their wide nostrils, were truly frightful.

With his enemies too busy with the fish to threaten him, he returned to the camp and to an almost comic-relief ending to his drama:

I had left my fish broiling, and my kettle of rice stewing, and having with me, oil, pepper and salt, and excellent oranges hanging in abundance over my head (a valuable substitute for vinegar) I sat down and regaled myself cheerfully; whilst I was revising the notes of my past day's journey, I was suddenly roused with a noise behind me. I seized my gun and went cautiously from my camp. I soon perceived two very large bears advancing towards me. I snapped my piece, but it flashed, on which they both turned about and galloped off, plunging through the water and swamp. They did not presume to return again, nor was I molested by any other creature, except being occasionally awakened by the whooping of owls, screaming of bitterns, or the wood-rats running amongst the leaves.

The next day, he started out fearfully but encountered little more than a sedate domestic sequel to his terrifying experiences—an alligator

coming up again, with the usual roar and menaces, passed close by the side of my boat when I could distinctly see a young brood of alligators, to the number of one hundred or more, following after her in a long train. They kept close together in a column, without straggling off to the one side or the other. [I] had frequent opportunities of seeing the female alligator leading about the shores her train of young ones, just like a hen does her brood of chickens, and when she is basking upon the warm banks, with her brood around her, you may hear the young ones continually whining and barking like young puppies.

The voyage grew more peaceful. He was reminded of distant places and times by the anhinga,

a very curious and handsome bird, the people call them Snake Birds; I think I have seen paintings of them on the Chinese screens and other India pictures: they seem to be a species of cormorant or loon (Colymbus cauda elongata), but far more beautiful and delicately formed than any other species that I have ever seen. The head and neck of this bird are extremely small and slender, the latter very long indeed, almost out of all proportion, the bill long, straight, and slender; all the upper side, the abdomen, and thighs are as black and glossy as a raven's. The breast and upper part of the belly are covered with feathers of a cream color; the tail is very long, of a deep black, and tipped with a silvery white, and when spread, represents an unfurled fan. They delight to sit in little peaceable communities, on the dry limbs of trees. When we approach them, they drop off the limbs into the water as if dead, and for a minute or two are not to be seen; when on a sudden, at a vast distance, their long slender head and neck only appear, and have very much the appearance of a snake. I doubt not but if this bird had been an inhabitant of Tiber in Ovid's days, it would have been furnished him with a subject for some beautiful and entertaining metamorphoses.

This Wattoolla or great Savannah crane (it would now be called a sandhill crane) was shot in Florida. Bartram drew details of it before eating it for dinner.

At night, he was surprised from sleep by "the terrifying screams of owls in the deep swamps around me; and what increased my extreme misery was the difficulty of getting quite awake, and yet hearing at the same time such screaming and shouting, which increased and spread every way for miles around, in dreadful peals vibrating through the dark extensive forests, meadows, and lakes."

By day, he delighted in the "musical clangor" of the

> sonorous, savanna cranes (Grus pratensis). They spread their light elastic sail: at first they move from the earth heavy and slow; they labor and beat the dense air; they form the line with wide extended wings, tip to tip; they all rise and fall together as one bird; now they mount aloft, gradually wheeling about; each squadron performs its evolution, encircling the expansive plains, observing each one their own orbit; then lowering sail, descend on the verge of some glittering lake; whilst other squadrons, ascending aloft in spiral circles, bound on interesting discoveries, wheel round and double the promontory, in the silvery regions of the clouded skies, descend to the earth near the flowery border of the lake; with dignified, yet slow, respectful steps, approach the kindred band, they confer, and treat for habitation; the bounds and precincts being settled, they confederate and take possession.

Bartram's imagery is lavished on a fish,

> gliding to and fro, and figuring in the still clear waters, with his orient attendants and associates: the yellow bream or sunfish. It is nearly of the shape of the trout, of a pale gold (or burnished brass) color, darker on the back and upper sides; scales everywhere variably powdered with red, russet, silver, blue, and green specks, so laid on the scales as to appear like real dust or opaque bodies, each apparent particle being so projected by light and shade, and the various attitudes of the fish, as to deceive the sight; for in reality nothing can be of a more plain and polished surface than the scales and whole body of the fish; the fins are of an orange color; and, like all the species of the bream, the ultimate angle of the branchiostege terminates by a little spatula, the extreme end of which represents a crescent of the finest ultramarine blue, encircled with silver and velvet black, like the eye in the feathers of a peacock's train; he is a fish of prodigious strength and activity in the water; a warrior in a gilded coat of mail.

He ends his paean to the sunfish on a brisk practical note: "They are delicious food and in great abundance." He goes on to a blissful garden where "the balmy Lantana, ambrosial Citra, perfumed Crinum, perspiring their mingled odors, wafted through Zanthoxilon groves," dines on trout heads stewed in orange juice and talks about a tree that was involved in one of Dr. Garden's tangles over nomenclature:

> The tall aspiring Gordonia lasianthus, which now stood in my view in all its splendor, is every way deserving of our admiration. Its thick foliage, of a dark green color, is flowered over with large milk-white fragrant blossoms, on long slender elastic peduncles, at the extremities of its numerous branches, from the bosom of the leaves, and renewed every morning; and that in such incredible profusion, that the tree appears silvered over with them, and the ground beneath covered with the fallen flowers. It at the same time continually pushes forth new twigs, with young buds on them, and in the winter and spring, the third year's leaves, now partly concealed by the new and perfect ones, are gradually changing color, from green to golden yellow, from that to a scarlet, from scarlet to crimson; and lastly to a brownish purple, and then fall to the ground. So that the Gordonia lasianthus may be said to change and renew its garments every morning throughout the year; and every day appears with unfading lustre.

None of Bartram's brilliant passages show off his art as a painterly poet better than his description of one of those Florida fountains that beguiled him and had so surprised his father.

> I seated myself upon a swelling green knoll, at the head of the crystal basin. Near me, on the left, was a point or projection of an entire grove of the aromatic Illicium floridanum; on my right, and all around me, was a fruitful Orange grove, with Palms and Magnolias interspersed; in front, just under my feet, was the enchanting and amazing crystal fountain, which incessantly threw up, from dark, rocky caverns below, tons of water every minute, forming a basin, capacious enough for large shallops to ride in, and a creek of four or five feet depth of water and near twenty yards over, which meanders six miles through green meadows. Directly opposite to the mouth or outlet of the creek is a continual and amazing ebullition, where the waters are thrown up in such abundance and amazing force as to jet and swell up two or three feet above the common surface: white sand and small particles of shells are thrown up with the waters, near to the top, when they diverge from the center, subside with the expanding flood, and gently sink again.
>
> At the same instant innumerable bands of fish are seen, some clothed

in the most brilliant colors; the voracious crocodile stretched along at full length, as the great trunk of a tree in size; the devouring garfish, inimical trout, and all the varieties of gilded painted bream, the barbed catfish, dreaded stingray, skate, and flounder, spotted bass, sheepshead and ominous drum; all in their separate bands and communities, with free and unsuspicious intercourse performing their evolutions: there are no signs of enmity, no attempt to devour each other; the different bands seem peaceably and complaisantly to move a little aside, as it were to make room for others to pass by.

But behold yet something far more admirable, see whole armies descending into an abyss, into the mouth of the bubbling fountain, they disappear! are they gone forever? I raise my eyes with terror and astonishment; I look down again to the fountain with anxiety, when behold them as it were emerging from the blue ether of another world, apparently at a vast distance, at their first appearance, no bigger than flies or minnows, now gradually enlarging, their brilliant colors begin to paint the fluid.

Now they come forward rapidly, and instantly emerge, with the elastic expanding column of crystalline waters, into the circular basin or funnel; see now how gently they rise, some upright, others obliquely, or seem to lay as it were on their sides, suffering themselves to be gently lifted or borne up by the expanding fluid towards the surface, sailing or floating like butterflies in the cerulean ether.

Traveling west across Florida, usually in the company of traders, William Bartram went through the country of the Seminoles and the Creeks. He described the inhabitants and their customs as carefully as he did the flowers and fish:

At Cuscowilla, the chief, who is called the Cowkeeper, attended by several ancient men, came to us, and in a very free and sociable manner, shook our hands (or rather arms). He was then informed what the nature of my errand was, and he received me with complaisance, giving me unlimited permission to travel over the country for the purpose of collecting flowers, medicinal plants, etc., saluting me by the name of Puc Puggy, or the Flower Hunter.

Continuing on, he was saluted at the next Indian town

by a party of young Indian warriors, under the conduct of a young prince or chief of Talahasochte. They were all dressed and painted with singular elegance, and richly ornamented with silver plates, chains, etc., after the Seminole mode, with waving plumes of feathers on their crests. The young prince informed our chief that he was in pursuit of a young fellow who had fled from the town, carrying off with him one of his favorite young wives or concubines; he said merrily he would have the ears of both of them before he returned. Having a band of music with them, consisting of a drum, flutes, and a rattle gourd, they entertained us during the night with their music, vocal and instrumental. There is a languishing softness and melancholy air in the Indian convivial songs, especially of the amorous class, irresistibly moving, attractive, and exquisitely pleasing, especially in these solitary recesses, when all nature is silent.

In the white trading post, where a party of Creeks had bought twenty kegs of liquor, he witnessed

one of the most ludicrous bacchanalian scenes that is possible to be conceived. White and red men and women, without distinction, passed the day merrily with these jovial, amorous topers, and the nights in convivial songs,

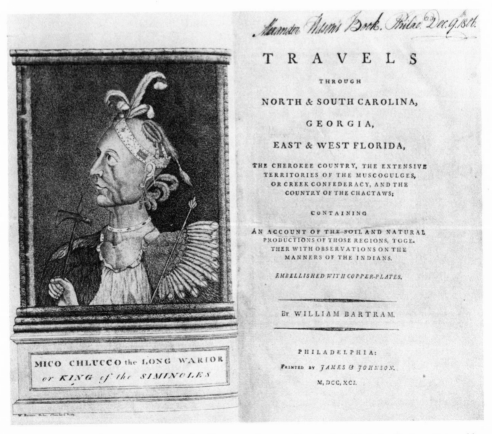

For the frontispiece of his Travels, *Bartram drew a Seminole chief he had met on his journey. This copy of the book belonged to his protégé, the ornithologist Alexander Wilson.*

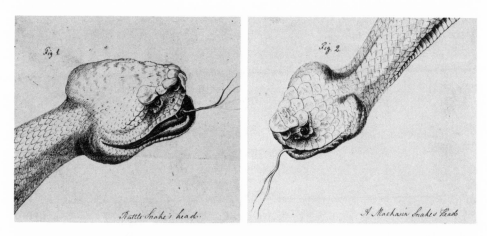

The diamondback rattlesnake Bartram drew may be the one he killed in camp, thereby becoming a hero to the Indians. He considered the water moccasin (right) to be "a horrid serpent."

dances, and sacrifices to Venus. At last their liquor running low, they became more sober; and now the dejected lifeless sots would pawn everything for a mouthful of spirits. This was the time for the wenches to make their market by a very singular stratagem; for, at these riots, every fellow has his own quart bottle of rum in his hand, he roves about continually, singing, roaring, and reeling to and fro, presenting his bottle to everyone, and is sure to meet his beloved female whom he complaisantly begs to drink with him. But the modest fair, veiling her face in a mantle, refuses, but he presses. She being furnished with an empty bottle concealed in her mantle, at last consents, and taking a good long draught, blushes, drops her pretty face on her bosom, and artfully discharges the rum into her bottle, and by repeating this artifice soon fills it: this she privately conveys to her secret store, and then returns to the jovial game, and so on during the festival; and when the comic farce is over, the wench retails this precious cordial to them at her own price.

One morning he was

drawing some curious flowers; when, on a sudden, my attention was taken off by a tumult without, at the Indian camp. I stepped to the door where I met my friend the old interpreter, who informed me that there was a very large rattlesnake in the Indian camp, which had taken possession of it, having driven the men, women, and children out, and he heard them saying that they would send for Puc Puggy to kill him or take him out of their camp. I at length consented, and attended on them to their encampment, where I beheld the Indians greatly disturbed indeed, collected together at a distance in affright and trepidation, whilst the dreaded and revered serpent leisurely traversed their camp, picking up fragments of their provisions, and licking their platters. Being armed with a lightwood knot, I approached the reptile, who instantly collected himself in a vast coil (their attitude of defense). I cast my missile weapon at him, which luckily taking his head, dispatched him instantly. I took out my knife, severed his head from his body, then turning about, the Indians complimented me with every demonstration of satisfaction and approbation for my heroism, and friendship for them. I carried off the head of the serpent bleeding in my hand as a trophy of victory.

Along the way, Bartram made notes on snakes and frogs, the earliest detailed descriptions of many of these creatures. He came upon the coachwhip snake while riding along a road.

At a good distance before me, I observed a large hawk on the ground; he seemed to be in distress endeavoring to rise; when, coming up near him, I found him closely bound up by a very long coachwhip snake, that had wreathed himself several times round the hawk's body, who had but one of his wings at liberty: beholding their struggles a while, I alighted off my horse with an intention of parting them; when, on coming up, they mutually agreed to separate themselves, each one seeking his own safety, probably considering me as their common enemy.

The coachwhip snake is a beautiful creature. When full grown they are six and seven feet in length, and the largest part of their body not so thick as a cane or common walking stick; their head not larger than the end of a man's finger; their neck is very slender, and from the abdomen tapers away in the manner of a small switch or coachwhip. They are extremely swift, seeming almost to fly over the surface of the ground; and that which is very singular, they can run swiftly on only their tail part, carrying their head and body upright. One very fine one accompanied me along the roadside, at a little distance, raising himself erect, now and then looking me in the face, although I proceeded on a good round trot on purpose to observe how fast they could proceed in that position. His object seemed mere curiosity or observation; with respect to venom they are as innocent as a worm.

In cataloging some of the local frogs, he showed that his ear was as acute as his eye. The voice of a large Florida frog "is loud and hideous, greatly resembling the grunting of a swine." The bell frogs, "so called because their voice is fancied to be exactly like the sound of a loud cow bell," utter "their voices in companies or by large districts, when one begins another answers, thus the sound is caught and repeated from one to another, to a great distance round about, causing a surprising noise for a few minutes, rising and sinking according as the wind sits."

The noise of a beautiful green frog "exactly resembles the barking of little dogs, or the yelping of puppies," while the notes of "a less green frog" are "remarkably like that of young chickens." A little gray speckled frog utters its

> language or noise in chorus; each particular note resembles the noise made by striking two pebbles together under the surface of the water, which when thousands near you utter their notes at the same time, does not ill resemble the rushing noise made by a vast quantity of gravel and pebbles together at once precipitated from a great height. The shad frog are very noisy; and at some distance one would be almost persuaded that there were assemblies of men in serious debate.

Bartram had now been traveling for two years. Having gone up and down the St. John's and back and forth across Florida, he went to touch base in Charleston. After sending shipments and letters to Dr. Fothergill, he consulted with Dr. Chalmers on where to go next. Though he starts Part Two of his *Travels* with "April 22d, 1776, I set off from Charleston for the Cherokee nation," he actually left Charleston a year earlier, in the spring of 1775. The wild shrubbery that covered the hills was in its most opulent bloom—

> fragrant Calycanthus, blushing Rhododendron ferrugineum, delicate Philadelphus inodorus, which displays the white wavy mantle, with the sky-robed Delphinium, perfumed Convalaria and fiery Azalea, flaming on the ascending hills or wavy surface of the gliding brooks. The epithet fiery I annex to this most celebrated species of Azalea, as being expressive of the appearance of it in flower, which are in general of the color of the finest red lead, orange and bright gold, as well as yellow and cream color; these various splendid colors are not only in separate plants, but frequently all the varieties and shades are seen in separate branches on the same plant; and the clusters of the blossoms cover the shrubs in such incredible profusion of the hillsides, that suddenly opening to view from dark shades, we are alarmed with the apprehension of the hills being set on fire.

For almost the first time in the *Travels*, a somber note intrudes, a sense of uneasiness. Perhaps it was that he was so long away from his family. Perhaps the news of the Revolution disturbed him, though he never mentions the war at all. He wrote that he felt

> dejected and unharmonized: all alone in a wild Indian country, a thousand miles from my native land, and a vast distance from any settlements of

white people; the savage vindictive inhabitants lately ill-treated by the
frontier Virginians; the Cherokees extremely jealous of white people
travelling about their mountains, especially if they should be seen peeping
in amongst the rocks, or digging up their earth.

His spirits were clearly better a few days later when he went walking up
into the hills with a trader he met. Throwing off his chaste demeanor, he re-
veals himself to be a warm-blooded male:

We began to ascend the hills of a ridge; and having gained its summit,
enjoyed a most enchanting view, green meadows and strawberry fields,
flocks of turkeys strolling about them and companies of young, innocent
Cherokee virgins, some gathering the rich fragrant fruit, others having
already busily filled their baskets, lay reclined under the shade of floriferous
and fragrant native bowers of Magnolia, Azalea, Philadelphus, perfumed
Calycanthus, sweet Yellow Jessamine and cerulean Glycine frutescens, bath-
ing their limbs in the cool fleeting streams; whilst other parties, more gay
and libertine, were yet collecting strawberries, or wantonly chasing their
companions, tantalizing them, staining their lips and cheeks with the rich
fruit.

The sylvan scene of primitive innocence was perhaps too enticing for
hearty young men long to continue idle spectators. In fine, nature pre-
vailing over reason, we wished at least to have a more active part in their
delicious sports. We cautiously made our approaches, yet undiscovered, almost to the joyous scene of action. Now, although we meant no other than
an innocent frolic with this gay assembly of hamadryades, we shall leave
it to the person of feeling and sensibility to form an idea to what lengths
our passions might have hurried us, thus warmed and excited, had it not
been for the vigilance and care of some envious matrons who lay in ambush,
and espying us, gave the alarm, time enough for the nymphs to rally and
assemble together. We however pursued and gained ground on a group
of them, who had incautiously strolled to a greater distance from their
guardians, and finding their retreat now like to be cut off, took shelter
under cover of a little grove; but on perceiving themselves to be discovered
by us, kept their station, peeping through the bushes; when observing our
approaches, they confidently discovered themselves, and decently advanced
to meet us, half unveiling their blooming faces, incarnated with the modest
maiden blush, and with native innocence and cheerfulness, presented their
baskets, merrily telling us their fruit was ripe and sound. We accepted
a basket, sat down and regaled ourselves on the delicious fruit, encircled
by the whole assembly of the innocent jocose sylvan nymphs.

Yet his mind and heart must have been heavy, for soon the somber note of alienation recurs.

> After waiting two days at Cowe expecting a guide and protector to the Overhill towns, and at last being disappointed, I resolved to pursue the journey alone, though against the advice of the traders; the Overhill Indians being in an ill humor with the whites. I was left again wandering alone in the dreary mountains, not indeed totally pathless, nor in my present situation entirely agreeable, although such scenes of primitive unmodified nature always pleased me. I could not help comparing my present situation in some degree to Nebuchadnezzar's, when expelled from the society of men, and constrained to roam in the mountains and wilderness, there to herd and feed with the wild beasts of the forests.

He traveled—almost without aim, it seems—through the back country, studying the plants, soils and rocks, making a list of all the inhabited towns and villages of the Cherokee nation. He had a tact that Indians found attractive. Coming upon a company of Indians, headed by a famous chief,

> I turned off from the path to make way in token of respect. His Highness with a gracious and cheerful smile came up to me and clapping his hand on his breast offered it to me saying I am Ata-cul-culla and asked me if I knew it; I answered that the Good Spirit who goes before me spoke to me and said that is the great Ata-cul-culla and added that I was of the tribe of white men of Pennsylvania who esteem themselves brothers and friends to the red men but particularly to the Cherokees.

Ata-cul-culla, also known as Little Carpenter, was a very sophisticated chief, having been to England some years earlier to treat with the British. He told Bartram he was "welcome in their country as a friend and brother" and, after shaking hands heartily, went on his way.

In the summer of 1775, Bartram set out with a "company of adventurers" on a long trek over an old Indian trading route to Mobile and the Mississippi and upriver to the site of present-day Baton Rouge. It was new territory for a botanist, and he observed dozens of undescribed plants. For several days on his journey, he had the company of William Dunbar, a young Scot with his own deep interest in science.

An eye ailment cut Bartram's trip short, and in 1776 he was back in Georgia. There, for a time, he took part in the Revolution. His friend Lachlan McIntosh, with whom he had stayed earlier in his travels, was raising a company of volunteers to fight off an expected British incursion. Bartram joined the detachment and may have served as a scout—his known occupation as a botanist would provide an excellent cover while his knowledge of the territory and his friendship with the Indians would help him. But the British never showed up, and Bartram, though offered an officer's commission, went on his way. After a few short excursions in Georgia, he went to look for

> a flowering tree, of the first order for beauty and fragrance of blossoms: fifteen or twenty feet high, the flowers are very large, expand themselves perfectly, are of a snow-white color, and ornamented with a crown or tassel of gold-colored refulgent stamina in their center. This very curious tree was first taken notice of about ten or twelve years ago, at this place, when I attended my father (John Bartram) on a botanical excursion; but, it being then late in the autumn, we could form no opinion to what class or tribe it belonged. We never saw it grow in any other place, nor have I ever since seen it growing wild, in all my travels, which must be allowed a very singular and unaccountable circumstance; at this place there are two or three acres of ground where it grows plentifully.

He named it, he added, after "the illustrious Dr. Benjamin Franklin." This was the Franklinia, the most famous "lost" tree of America. Though generations of naturalists have searched for it, it has not been seen in its wild state since 1803. Changing conditions of soil and water are apparently responsible for its extinction. It survives as a cultivated tree largely through plants and seeds the Bartrams took back to their gardens.

Finally, in the autumn of 1776, Bartram started back home, stopping in Charleston to consult Dr. Garden on the material he was sending to Dr. Fothergill. On the way north, he paused to observe the "ludicrous Dionaea muscipula," the tipitiwichet, or Venus's flytrap, which, he remarked, "seems to be distinguished in the creation, by the Author of nature, with faculties eminently superior to every other vegetable production; specimens of it were first communicated to the curious of the old world by John Bartram, the American Botanist and traveller, who contributed as much, if not more, than any other man towards enriching the North American botanical nomenclature, as well as its natural history."

Winter overtook him on the road and when he reached the Susquehanna, the river was freezing over and the ferries could not run. Joining a "number of traders with their pack horses loaded with leather and furs, we all agreed to venture over together; and keeping at a moderate distance from each other, examining well our icy bridge, and being careful of our steps, we landed safe on the opposite shore, and arrived at my father's house January 1778."

For years, William Bartram's biographers accepted this return date and ended their accounts of his travels on a wistful note: John Bartram had died in September, 1777, and Billy had thus missed by three months seeing his father alive for a last time. But William had, characteristically, ended his account as he had begun it, by making an error in the date. This time, instead of a few weeks, he was a full year off. In straightening out the chronology, Dr. Harper has established that William came home in January, 1777, not 1778—more than half a year before John died and time enough to tell him of his adventures and discoveries in the places where the two of them had traveled together a dozen years before.

DURING THE YEARS OF WILLIAM'S ABSENCE, JOHN BARTRAM continued to work at his business. His garden, capably managed by John, Jr., was filled with plants grown from the seeds and shoots he brought back in three decades of botanizing. Though Collinson was gone, Bartram still had dozens of steady clients in Europe and his botanical friendships continued. Dr. Fothergill was pleased to receive frogs and a turtle from Bartram, then apologetically asked for another pair of bullfrogs. "Mine are strayed away," he apologized, "notwithstanding my best endeavors." The salary as King's Botanist continued until the Revolution, and his credit balance in London, when war cut off all further business, was a considerable three hundred pounds. Franklin, now the American envoy in Paris, stepped in loyally to provide another market. "Dear old friend," he wrote Bartram in May, 1777, a time when he had the whole weight of the French alliance to worry about, "If you incline, you may send the same number of boxes here that you used to send to England. Enclosed is a list of the sorts wished for here. I will take care of the sale and returns."

Events closer to home disturbed the aging naturalist. When the British, after the battle of Brandywine, ravaged the countryside, he was sure that they would destroy the gardens, knowing the Bartrams's patriotic sentiments. They gave no trouble at all.

John had "never coveted old age," William wrote,

> and often observed to his children and friends that he sincerely desired that he might not live longer than he could afford assistance to himself; and that when death came to perform his office, there might not be much delay. His wishes were gratified in a remarkable manner, for although he lived to about eighty years of age, yet he was cheerful and active to almost the last hours. His illness was very short. About half an hour before he expired, he seemed, though but for a few moments, to be in considerable agony and pronounced these words, "I want to die."

This was September 22, 1777, and John Bartram's generation of pioneers had passed. Mitchell died in 1768 at the age of seventy. Clayton died in 1773; he was seventy-nine. Cadwallader Colden died in 1776. He was eighty-nine and a political power to the end, stepping up from his post as lieutenant governor to act as governor when the constant turnover of officials left that office vacant. Governor through the Stamp Act troubles, he was burned in effigy in the streets of New York and the garden at Coldengham was ransacked. He took over as governor in 1769 for more than a year, and again in 1774 when the province was boiling over. At the age of eighty-seven, he was still indomitably trying to hold New York for the King when, with the news of Lexington, the patriots took over the city. For the last time, Cadwallader Colden left his busy world for his country home. His appointed successor as governor did not have the courage even to land in the rebellious city. On September 24, 1776, from a warship in the harbor, he published a curt official obituary: "On the 21st instant, Lt. Gov. Colden departed his life at Flushing. This makes a vacancy on the Council."

Colden's son David went on to make a small name for himself as a physicist. Colden's grandson became mayor of New York. His talented daughter Jane lived very happily with her husband—but all too briefly. She died in childbirth after only seven years of marriage.

Carl Linnaeus survived John Bartram by five months, but he did not have Bartram's good fortune in confronting death. When he was 67, he gave up his post as rector of the University of Uppsala. "This cold season," he told his students, "this cold cathedral, my cold years and your patience, gentlemen, which is beginning to cool, command me to desist." The years grew even colder for him. His bright optimism turned to the bleakly pessimistic view that life was governed by a cruel, divine nemesis. His gay poetizing about sex was replaced by cynical suspicion of women expressed in perverse tales of unchaste wives and cuckolded men. A series of strokes muddled his marvelous memory. A pupil recalled seeing him "be led down into the garden," and remarked of the man who handled and defined more kinds of plants than any man of his time that he "delights in the plants but no longer knows them."

The youngest of that generation survived. At Goose Creek, a dozen miles from the city, Alexander Garden bought a plantation of seventeen hundred acres and filled an elaborate garden with the native plants he had come to know better than anyone else in the world—and the world had come to know largely through him. He called his estate Otranto, and a Charleston poet, George Ogilvie, gave it a rapturous, flower-filled description:

> Here early blossoms deck the unfledg'd Thorn,
> and yellow Jasmines leafless trees adorn.
> Th' Azalea climbs the Cypress loftier bough,
> and Pericyclemons low shaded blow,
> blending their lovely tubes of roseate hue,

William Bartram's portrait was painted by Charles Willson Peale, a close friend to whose museum Bartram made many welcome contributions of birds, plants and general knowledge about nature.

with the Glycine's variegated blue.
Whilst fragrant Calycanths appear to bring
The fruits of Autumn midst the flow'rs of Spring;
white Chionanths, with flaky fringe, display
December freezing in the lap of May.

Political troubles cut into Garden's enjoyment of Otranto. While sharply critical of British policy, he would not renounce his King. When Charleston was taken over by the patriots at the start of the Revolution, Garden, through his friendships and the respect in which he was held, was able to live and work freely without taking sides. When the British captured Charleston, Dr. Garden treated British and American soldiers alike. The war over, he was banished to England, most of his property confiscated and many of his patients' bills unpaid—including sixty-nine pounds still owed him by Eliza Lucas Pinckney. Garden's son Alexander, captured by the rebels at Otranto, joined their forces and had a distinguished military career in the American army. Years later, he wrote patriotic best sellers about Revolutionary heroes.

William Bartram had sent journals of his trip to Dr. Fothergill, expecting that they might be published as a scientific work. They vanished in Dr. Fothergill's files and were not seen again for almost a century. Expanding his journals into a full-length report, Bartram published it years later, in 1791, as *Travels Through North and South Carolina, Georgia, East and West Florida, the Cherokee Country, the Extensive Territories of the Muscogulges, or Creek Confederacy, and the Country of the Chactaws, Containing an Account of the Soil and Natural Productions of Those Regions, Together with Observations on the Manners of the Indians*. A thousand copies were printed and President Washington, Vice-President Adams and Secretary of State Jefferson all subscribed. Critics and readers in America gave the book a respectful but rather tepid reception. The response abroad, however, was astonishing.

In 1792, a pirated edition of *Travels* was printed in London. The next year, three other editions were published—one in Dublin, a translated version in Berlin, another in Vienna. The demand was so persistent that a second London edition was published in 1794. The same year, a Dutch translation was printed in Haarlem—and reprinted in 1797. A French translation was issued in Paris in 1799 and reissued in 1801. In a single decade, the modest American book went into nine foreign editions.

Even more surprising than the European popularity of *Travels* was its effect on two towering poets of the budding Romantic movement in England. Samuel Taylor Coleridge all but memorized the book. William Wordsworth carried a copy on a trip to Germany, where, having lost it, he wrote home asking that another be sent immediately. The images Bartram conjured up in the *Travels*, his stories and his philosophizing all flare up again and again in the finest works of the two poets.

Coleridge's voluminous notebooks, where he jotted passing thoughts, fragments of verse and verbatim passages from books he was reading, are filled with excerpts from *Travels*—and his poems are filled with echoes of it. The haunted fragment beginning "In Xanadu did Kubla Khan/A stately pleasure-dome decree" is rich with Bartram's inspirations. The "caverns measureless to man" come from Bartram's speculations on the underground waterways of Florida. The landscape of Xanadu, with its "sinuous rills" and "many an incense-bearing tree," are only a poet's step away from Bartram's "serpentine rivulet," his "balmy Lantana, ambrosial Citra, perfumed Crinium, perspiring their mingled odors."

What caught Coleridge's extraordinary imagination most of all were the fountains of Florida, which jolted John Bartram into exclaiming "What a surprising fountain!" and brought enchanted descriptions from his son. In "Kubla Khan," Coleridge writes of "ceaseless turmoil seething,/As if this earth in fast thick pants were breathing . . . /Huge fragments vaulted," of waters sinking into "caverns measureless to man." Bartram had written of a fountain "which incessantly threw up, from dark, rocky caverns below, tons of water every minute . . . a continued and amazing ebullition" and of "vast heaps of fragments of rocks."

Reminders of Bartram pervade a quite different poem, "The Rime of the Ancient Mariner." The iridescent many-colored fish that Bartram painted again and again swim, as watersnakes, around the old sailor's ghostly ship: "Blue, glossy green, and velvet black . . . every track . . . a flash of golden fire."

Just as impressive is Wordsworth's debt to Bartram. His poem "Ruth" is unabashedly borrowed from *Travels*. Its hero, a Cherokee chief, is a replica of the plumed prince Bartram met at Talahasochte. Wordsworth wrote:

> He told of girls—a happy rout!
> Who quit their fold with dance and shout,
> Their pleasant Indian town,
> To gather strawberries all day long . . .
> He spake of plants that hourly change
> Their blossoms, through a boundless range
> Of intermingling hues;
> With budding, fading, faded flowers . . .
> From morn to evening dews.
> . . . —Of flowers that with one scarlet gleam
> Cover a hundred leagues, and seem
> To set the hills on fire.

They are all from Bartram—the Indian girls he accosted, the ever-changing *Gordonia lasianthus*, the fiery azaleas. But the impact of Bartram on Wordsworth goes deeper than language. The germ of the poet's summation that there is "a motion and a spirit that impels all thinking things, all objects of all thought, and rolls through all things" can be found in William Bartram's musings on the Venus's-flytrap: "We see in this plant motion and volition"; and in his belief that the "essential principle" which empowers animals "to act must be divine and immortal." Ernest Earnest, in his discerning study of the Bartrams, traces Wordsworth's debt back to old John Bartram, who, insisting that plants behaved as if guided by some higher will, declared that there is "a portion of universal intellect diffused in all life."

🌱 🌱 🌱 🌱 🌱 ALL THE WHILE THAT THE POETS WERE MAKING OFF WITH HIS Florida fountains and fiery hills and transporting Puc Puggy from Cherokee country to Xanadu, William Bartram stayed put on the Kingsessing. He never married, but lived with his brother John and his family. The world now came to him, to see his gardens and to talk to this man who, once aimless and un-directed, had now become a sage of natural science. Every naturalist of standing or ambition in America felt he must visit the Bartram Gardens. And the direct heir of the Colden-Bartram-Garden triumvirate became mentor to a newer generation of naturalists—a Scottish poet named Alexander Wilson, a grand-nephew named Thomas Say, a Yorkshire printer named Thomas Nuttall.

During the Constitutional Convention in Philadelphia in 1787, the delegates made visits to the Gardens as a part of the local sightseeing. George Washington, in his diary, notes: "June 10, Rid to see the Botanical gardens of Mr. Bartram which tho' stored with the many curious plants, trees and shrubs and trees, many of which are exotic, was not laid out with much taste." Nevertheless he gave the Gardens a rather large order for trees. One day a party of delegates including Alexander Hamilton, James Madison, John Rutledge and George Mason rode out to the Gardens and found William Bartram "barefooted, hoe in hand, chopping at the weeds." Shy at first, he loosened up to explain the names of the plants "so far as he knew them." Jefferson, who became a good friend of Bartram's, was a frequent visitor to the Gardens, especially in 1793 when he moved out to Gray's Ferry to escape an epidemic in Philadelphia.

Bartram still did some local botanizing, but his interest shifted to the study of birds. Carefully observing them, dissecting them, studying their eating and breeding habits, chronicling their passages, he completed a catalog of two hundred American birds, the most complete systematic list compiled up to that time, and a base for future compilations. In the meticulous, objective way he studied bird habits and in the case-history style he adopted to present his information, he anticipated a distinctly American school of ornithology.

For all his poeticizing, William Bartram was a true scientist who believed the basis of science was observed fact. Naturalists have found him a remarkably reliable source. His stirring accounts of the alligators, once dismissed as tall tales, have stood up as accurate fact. Botanists, geologists, zoologists, ornithologists and geographers in later generations have testified to the honesty and pertinence of his reports. His discussions of Indian ways are cited repeatedly by ethnologists and his brief passages on Seminole music are virtually the only first-hand reports of their kind that musicologists can draw on.

The years and the community of naturalists treated William Bartram kindly. He lived surrounded by a little menagerie of pets—a possum, some snakes and frogs, a salamander and a crow named Tom—"a bird of happy temper and good disposition," wrote Bartram—who teased the family dog, stole his master's spectacles and came out to help him weed the garden. Visitors to the Gardens would come upon Bartram, as the writer William Dunlop once did, out in a tulip bed "breaking clods of earth. His hat was old, his waistcoat and breeches were both of leather. He ceased his work and entered into conversation with the ease and politeness of nature's noblemen, his countenance was expressive of benignity and happiness."

CHAPTER SIX

PRESIDENT OF
THE WEST

❦ ❦ ❦ ❦ ❦ NOT EVEN THE PRESIDENT OF THE UNITED STATES, WHO offered him a whole new western world to botanize in, could budge William Bartram from his home on the Kingsessing once he had returned from his travels. In 1803, he was asked to join an expedition that would head up the Red River into the Rockies. "Come on," the invitation vainly urged. "You are not too old. Remember that your venerable father continued to make botanical tours after he had reached your age."

If anyone could have moved the reluctant traveler out of his garden, it was the man who was behind the expedition: Bartram's good friend and fellow naturalist, Thomas Jefferson. For twenty years Jefferson had been trying without success to get Americans to go out and see what lay in the huge, unknown tracts of land that lay west of the Mississippi. As a politician, Jefferson was concerned for the national interest. Though the land belonged to a foreign power, he realized that it was an inevitable part of America's future. But Jefferson was also, like John Bartram, a curious man. The pursuit of knowledge always absorbed him as much as the pursuit of politics and he simply wanted to know what was out there.

Back in 1783, he had asked George Rogers Clark, hero of the Revolutionary frontier wars, to scout the region. Clark begged off—he didn't have the time or money. A few years later, when he was ambassador in Paris, Jefferson tried to use a Yankee named John Ledyard for his purpose.

Ledyard and his partner, John Paul Jones, the naval hero, were interested in going into the fur trade in the American West—Ledyard had once sailed along the West Coast on Captain Cook's last voyage. When Ledyard and Jones failed to raise the necessary capital, Jefferson worked on a way to get Ledyard into the American West by the back way—across Russia to the Pacific, over to Alaska and down the coast. From there he would walk eastward across the continent, contracting for furs and making notes on everything as he went. Ledyard actually got within a few hundred Russian versts of bringing off this implausible scheme. Careening across Siberia in a three-horse cart, he reached Yakutsk. There, on instructions from Queen Catherine, a pair of suspicious officials (one of whom had been a botany student of Linnaeus) turned him back.

In 1792, now Secretary of State, Jefferson received a proposal from a man whose grand ambition meshed with his own. "For the sum of 3,600 pounds," André Michaux offered to "travel to the sources of the Missouri River," and "the rivers which emptied into the Pacific Ocean," and report what he found to the United States government. This brief suggestion masked a formidable project: a journey over unmeasured distances through a strange and hostile land to a far-off ocean. But, as Jefferson was aware, André Michaux was a formidable figure: the farthest-traveled and best-trained scientist yet to enter the American community of naturalists.

In a few years, André Michaux had earned a respected place in this community. William Bartram, for example, knew him as one of the very few collectors who could go over the ground that he and his father had covered and come back with plants neither of them had found. Along with his scientific skills, Michaux had a special grace of character. In Paris, his official patrons trusted him so completely that they gave him an unlimited letter of credit and never questioned how he used it. In the American backwoods, settlers gladly gave him food and lodging, held letters for him and even, in an ultimate act of frontier friendship, lent their horses to the man they came to call "the French wanderer."

In his native France, Michaux had studied under Bernard de Jussieu, whose natural system of classification challenged the Linnaean method. He had herbalized with Jean Baptiste Lamarck, known then as author of a popular botany manual and remembered today for his brilliant though discarded theory of evolution based on acquired characteristics. Sent to Persia by the French government to collect botanical specimens, Michaux crisscrossed the wild regions between the Caspian Sea and the Indian Ocean, poked around for plants amid the ruins of the Semiramis's palace and was captured by bandits who stripped him of everything he had and left him naked and half dead on the scorching desert. He survived to bring home thousands of seeds, a magnificent herbarium, a French-Persian dictionary he had compiled and a lovely bellflower now named *Campanula michauxia*.

Pleased with this Persian haul, French officials sent Michaux to America to establish a headquarters and find plants, especially trees, that would be useful to France. Michaux was thirty-nine when he came to the United States in 1786. His first move was to set up a nursery in New Jersey, fill it with local plants and start sending prodigious shipments to Paris—in the first year alone, five thousand tree shoots, a dozen cases of seeds and some live grouse, which took happily to the royal estate at Versailles. Heading south, he called on William Bartram, and went to Virginia to give George Washington a present from the Marquis de Lafayette—seeds of a pyramidal cypress, a tree which for years grew at the garden gate in Mount Vernon.

The same rich regions of the South which had repeatedly drawn the Bartrams now drew Michaux. In 1787, he began exploring the Carolina back country, a region with a wonderfully mixed-up flora—northern plants toward the mountain summits, semitropical plants in sheltered valleys.

A wide-eyed French biographer depicted the way the wanderer's life went: "The forests are impenetrable. There are no paths except for the trails made by bears. You can live only on the uncertain killing of game or acid fruits you find by chance." Only hints of the loneliness and uncertainties he faced came through in the journals Michaux scrupulously kept—small, crammed, weather-beaten, rain-stained little books—whose entries were written with fingers stiffened by cold, in a kind of French shorthand at the end of exhausting days by the un-reliable light of campfires. When he refers to something as *"peur affreux,"* the reader knows it must have been really hair-raising.

He was accompanied by his fifteen-year-old son François André. Their pro-

In his journal for January 1790, Michaux recorded the seeds he sowed in his Charleston garden. The July 15, 1793, entry described his moonlight departure on his mission for Genêt.

visions and equipment were piled into a little horse-drawn two-wheeled cart. But, as was to happen regularly with Michaux, his horse ran off. They had to pull the cart themselves "across swampy areas that we had to cross in water up to our knees, torrents that we had to cross over fallen trees with the risk of being attacked by alligators, which abound."

They went on through fog that made it seem as if they "were enveloped in a profound night," and under the "continual fear of stepping on snakes." One snake proved both harmless and interesting. "Black-colored snake of the veepcoach species," Michaux called it, meaning a coachwhip snake. He collected an attractive sweet pepper bush, *Clethra Accuminata* Michaux and a heath that was a favorite food of bears—*Vaccinium erythrocarpum* Michaux, one of the many plants called mountain cranberry or bearberry.

Later on in this area he found "a new *arbuste* with toothed leaves." Now called *Shortia galacifolia*, it grows nowhere except in the Carolina mountains. Like Bartram's Franklinia, it became one of America's famous "lost plants." After Michaux, it was not found again in the wilds for nearly a century and its rediscovery, as told in a later chapter, involved another famous botanist, Asa Gray.

Having followed the Bartrams in Carolina, Michaux now went down to another of their hunting grounds, Florida—"a very disagreeable place where alligators and snakes abound," he grumped. He traveled along the St. John's, counted the number of teeth an alligator has (seventy-two) and from what had started out as a "fruitless trip" he came back with scores of uncommon and unknown plants.

Michaux had set up a second nursery, in Charleston, putting it in charge of Louis Bosc d'Antic, a compatriot after whom a fine pear is named. During his stays in the Carolinas, Michaux was welcomed into the homes of cultivated residents, where he found the company agreeable though sometimes long-winded. One young and pretty hostess launched into an explanation of the fine distinctions of belief among Methodists, Anabaptists and Quakers. After three and a half hours of nonstop theological dissection, Michaux noted with immense forbearance, "I began to get bored in spite of the pleasantness of the lady, and retired." Some less learned ladies made for other complications. Out camping with an Indian chief, his wife, his mother and two daughters, he dined well on boiled deer, corn bread and sweet potatoes but felt uncomfortable because "the ladies were naked down to the waist and wore nothing else but a skirt." Between prattling bluestockings and topless Cherokees, Michaux had his social problems.

He never forgot his prime mission: to send useful trees back to France. In search of the hardiest varieties on the continent, he headed into Canada, stopping off, as was his custom, to report to Bartram. With three Indians and an interpreter, he made his way northwest toward Hudson Bay. It was still August, but his journal gives a wintry catalog of fog, rain, ice, snow and "great windstorms with thunder and lightning and the terrible cold. We came to nine rapids therefore made nine portages." When they reached the 100-mile-long Lake Mistassini, "the rain was like melted snows." The Indians, though brave and willing, "trembled, drenched with water." Showers of hail hit them as they went up the lake. Finally, the Indians could not bring themselves to go any farther. Snow, they said, would make it impossible to return and the wind on the lakes would swamp the canoes. But they also knew that the great Manitou lived in a marble grotto at the head of the lake, and they feared he would rouse the waves against the trespassers.

Michaux, who never seemed satisfied with what he accomplished, must still have taken some pride in his northwest journey. No botanist before him had ventured so far into the inhospitable land. And he found, along with the hardiest evergreens and oaks, a sturdy primrose, *Primula mistassinica*. Now he had an even larger project in mind. Back in Philadelphia, he enlisted Bartram and other members of the American Philosophical Society in his plan to go to the Pacific.

As a leading member of the Philosophical Society, Jefferson was asked to draft a reply. He filled it with detailed instructions. In agreeing to sponsor and finance the trip, the Society would expect Michaux to "find the shortest and most convenient route of communication between the U.S. and the Pacific Ocean." He continued:

> You will cross the Mississippi to the nearest part of the Missouri above the Spanish settlements that you may avoid the risk of being stopped, then pursue the largest streams of that river as shall lead by the shortest way and lowest latitudes to the Pacific Ocean, take notice of the country you pass through, its general face, soil, rivers, mountains, its productions— animal, vegetable and mineral—the names, members and dwelling of the inhabitants, languages, society, arts, commerce, animal history, that of the mammoth particularly, whether the llama or paca of Peru is found in those parts. The method of preserving your observations is left to yourself noting them on skin might be the best for such as are most important and further details committed to the bark of the paper birch which may not excite suspicions among the Indians.

When he reached the Pacific, Jefferson went on, speaking as if Michaux were to come out on a fully civilized shore, he was to go to any settlement of Europeans "within convenient distance" and prove that he had really been there by obtaining "certificates from the Europeans."

After laying out this arduous course through uncharted lands, the instructions wound up with a caution: "It is strongly recommended to expose yourself in no case to unnecessary dangers." It would be interesting to know what the French wanderer, who had confronted perils from the marauder-infested deserts of Arabia to the marble abode of Manitou, would consider "unnecessary dangers."

Jefferson, of course, had a special reason for backing Michaux. Spain owned the regions—the Louisiana Territory—that Michaux would cover, and was suspicious of intruders. But its officials would hardly notice a single scientist, with only a couple of men in his party, going through, and in any case could not dispute his credentials. The Philosophical Society set out to raise money for Michaux, soliciting the leading men of the country. George Washington's audit book notes: "Paid Dr. Collins one fourth part of the President's subscription toward enabling M. Michaux to explore the western countries to the South Seas. 25 dols."

The Society got more money than Michaux asked for, and, with his usual scruples, he refused to take it all. Everything was set when, in the spring of 1793, André Michaux was caught up in the machinations of a headstrong Frenchman named Edmond Charles Édouard Genêt, better known as Citizen Genêt.

Genêt had been sent over to carry out a complicated intrigue designed to involve the United States in France's running war with England and Spain. Using American settlers to attack Spain's American possessions, he would raise a frontier army, recruiting Kentucky riflemen by promises of land and enlisting Indian chiefs by making them generals. The scheme's uncertain prospects were immensely improved when André Michaux offered, as a patriotic Frenchman, to give up his own plan and go west for Genêt instead of for the Philosophical Society. He knew the country well, was highly regarded by influential Americans and, under the guise of picking plants, could safely play politics.

Though this meant still another setback to his hopes, Jefferson approved the idea. He was not, it must be said, very straightforward about the whole business. He would let Michaux go as a private citizen but would not recognize him as a French consul. While clearly abetting Genêt's plans, he reminded him that any Americans taking up arms against a friendly country ran the risk of being hanged. "Leaving out that article," he added cavalierly, he "did not care what insurrections should be excited in Louisiana."

With this ambiguous backing, Michaux left Philadelphia in July, his journal beginning in cloak-and-dagger style. "I started at ten o'clock at night to travel by moonlight." He moved through the West, alternately politicking and botanizing. "The 28th," his journal notes, "visited Mr. H. Breckinridge." This was Hugh Breckinridge, an influential Pittsburgh lawyer and supporter of the Whiskey

Rebellion. The journal goes on, "29th, herborized recognized on the banks of the Monongahela *Dracocephalum virginican* [a dragonhead]." In Lexington, Michaux called on Alexander Orr and Henry Lee, founding fathers of the state of Kentucky, and then went to a tar pit to see "bones of these monster animals supposed to be elephants"—mammoths. He detoured to talk over Genêt's plan with General Benjamin Logan, the famous Indian fighter. "Recognized many plants not found elsewhere," he wrote at that point. As if regretting that his time was taken up with other matters, he remarked, "The neighborhood would be very interesting for a botanist to visit."

Finally he reached the man chosen to lead Genêt's army, General George Rogers Clark. Michaux brought Clark a commission as major general and the promise that he would be made a field marshal as soon as he had taken New Orleans. But Clark responded with the dismaying news that Genêt's project had been totally abandoned.

There was nothing for Michaux to do but go back and see what had happened. After borrowing a horse from Clark, he hurried over the Wilderness Trail through crowds of westbound settlers and also, he noted, through several acres of an interesting climbing fern. He observed some landmarks in the young history of American botany, the *Mitchella repens, Claytonia virginica* and *Kalmia latifolia*, and found a grass which would be named *Jeffersonia diphylla*.

In Philadelphia, Michaux found that Genêt had overplayed his hand, arousing the open anger of Washington and losing Jefferson's support. His great intrigue was collapsing.

Michaux was stranded. The trip to the Pacific was no longer possible for a politically compromised person. He contented himself with what would have been a major undertaking for anyone else but for him was an anticlimax: a 1,100-mile journey west, out over much of the ground he had brushed on his mission to Clark, across the Mississippi to the edge of the prairies which he was the first botanist to visit.

His work in America finished, he left for France. In his eleven years, he had outdone everyone before him in the numbers of plants he had discovered or identified. Just as important, he had set straight many wrong classifications and doubtful identifications. Present-day botanical guides are studded with the attribution "Michx." crediting him with having found, placed or named the plant described.

❦ ❦ ❦ ❦ ❦ WHILE JEFFERSON WAS PROJECTING THE MICHAUX TRIP, HE was approached by Meriwether Lewis, a young Virginian he knew. Lewis lived so close to Monticello that when Jefferson wanted to see him, he would signal by reflecting the sun's rays with a mirror. Now an army officer serving in the West, Lewis had heard of the Michaux plans and volunteered to go along. Jefferson put him off, worried that the presence of an American soldier on a scientific expedition might alarm the Indians.

Ten years later, President Jefferson found himself addressing a letter to Captain Meriwether Lewis, commander of the Corps of Discovery. With Captain William Clark as his second in command, Lewis was preparing to set out on the expedition Michaux had proposed and abandoned. Now, writing to Lewis, Jefferson sounded as if he had gone back to his files and copied the letter he had written Michaux before Citizen Genêt came on the scene—even down to the suggestion that a copy of the report be written on "the paper of the birch." "The object of your mission," he wrote, "is to explore the Missouri River and such principal streams of it as, by its course and communication with the waters of the Pacific Ocean, may offer the most direct and practicable water communication across this continent, to acquire what knowledge you can of . . . the soil and face of the country, its growth and vegetable productions, the animals especially those not known in the U.S., the remains of any which may be extinct, the mineral productions." He even wanted to know "the dates at which particular plants put forth or lose their flower or leaf, times of appearance of particular birds, reptiles or insects."

Such items betrayed Jefferson's special concerns with natural history. He was a true virtuoso in that science, as learned and enthusiastic as any of the expert amateurs of Europe—and, as President, in far better position to further his interest. This was, of course, just one of his many scientific concerns, but it ran deep. Once, writing to William Bartram about some experiments on the Hessian fly he was conducting for the American Philosophical Society, Jefferson said: "I long to be free for pursuits of this kind instead of the detestable ones in which I am now laboring." Politics, he declared, was his duty, but natural history was his passion.

He indulged his passion always and everywhere. At home in Virginia, he kept a garden book where, in his careful handwriting, he noted all that happened in his woods and fields. The account for 1766 opens with the coming of Virginia's spring: "March 30: Purple hyacinth begins to bloom. April 6: Narcissus and puckoon open. April 13: Puckoon flowers fallen. April 16: A bluish-colored funnel-formed flower in lower grounds in bloom." Interspersed with these botanical observations were a husbandman's record of when carrots and peas were planted, how many peas were in a pint (2,500), statistics on cucumber production ("50 hills will yield 400 cucumbers a week"). One terse entry states: "May 6: Aurora Borealis at 9 P.M. A quart of currant juice makes 2 blue teacups of jelly." In Paris, when he ordered plants from Bartram's Gardens, Jefferson identified each by its Linnaean name. In Washington, a friend recalled, he would ride out into the countryside and botanize on horseback. Not a plant "from the lowliest weed to the loftiest tree escaped his notice." He would dismount to "climb rocks or wade through swamps to obtain any plant he discovered or desired and seldom returned from these excursions without a variety of specimens." At the White House, a pet mockingbird perched on his shoulder as he worked at his desk, and sang to him when he lay down for a Presidential nap.

Wherever he was, Jefferson was always proclaiming the glories of nature in America. "What a field we have at our doors to signalize ourselves," he wrote the president of Harvard. "The botany of America is far from being exhausted, its mineralogy untouched, its natural history or zoology totally mistaken or misrepresented." It was this misrepresentation and his irritation at it that involved Jefferson in his most important work on natural history—and in one of the most passionate and preposterous disputes that science ever stumbled into.

The work was *Notes on the State of Virginia*, an admirably researched and constructed monograph on the natural history, climate, resources and geography of his native state, along with dissertations on its education and politics. It was written originally to answer a questionnaire circulated by François de Barbé-Marbois, secretary to the French legation in Philadelphia in 1780, when the French were concerned with getting hard facts about their struggling ally. It was hardly the time for Jefferson, then governor of Virginia, to deal with such a matter. The traitorous Benedict Arnold was leading British troops into Virginia. Jefferson's wife and young daughter were mortally ill. Such "present occupations," Jefferson wrote Barbé-Marbois, made it difficult for him to set down answers. When his term as governor ended, however, he was able to deal with the questions. His reply was so impressive that, at the urging of friends, Jefferson published it, after many revisions.

For the most part, the *Notes* is an objective study, but it wanders every now and then into personal observation. "Our mountains," Jefferson writes, as if praising the convenient aspects of American topography, "are not solitary and scattered confusedly over the face of the country. They commence at about one hundred and fifty miles from the sea coast, are disposed in ridges one behind the other running nearly parallel with the seacoast."

Nature, as it does in even the most practical of men, brought out the adventurer and poet in Jefferson. The Natural Bridge, which was on property he owned, is so high, he wrote, "that few men have the resolution to look into the abyss." But, like every naturalist, he had to see for himself: "You involuntarily fall on your hands and feet, creep to the parapet and peep over it. Looking down from this height about a minute gave me a violent headache. If the view from the top be painful and intolerable, that from below is delightful in an equal extreme, so beautiful an arch, so elevated, so light and so springing as if it were up to heaven! The rapture of the spectator is really indescribable." Then, back to earth, he told of lead and iron ore and listed 130 native plants, giving their Linnaean names and referring to "The Flora Virginica of our great botanist, Dr. Clayton."

After a while, he gets to his main and patriotic purpose: to refute the misguided European scientists who were libeling his native land. In doing so, he took on one of the era's monumental figures, Georges Louis Leclerc, Comte de Buffon. The most omniscient of all living natural scientists and one of the big four of French literature (with Montesquieu, Voltaire, and Rousseau), Buffon had awed Europe with his magnum opus, *Histoire Naturelle, Générale et Particulière*, which set down thousands upon thousands of facts and theories— botanical, zoological, geographical, geological, and so on. The *Histoire* ran to forty-four volumes and became a colossal best seller: 52 editions in French, 20 or more in other languages, plus 325 blessedly abridged versions. It rivaled Diderot's *Encyclopédie* in prestige and circulation, and ranks with that Enlightenment classic as an apotheosis of an age which sought to set down and explain everything.

Buffon had begun it as a simple catalog of the Jardin du Roi, the royal botanical gardens of which he was superintendent. But everything he touched became a large project. To justify an optical theorem, he once re-created Archimedes' famous feat of burning the Roman fleet at Syracuse by focusing the sun's rays on it with an array of mirrors. To build a château and garden worthy of the author of the *Histoire*, he cut off the entire top of a small mountain. A man of imperious ways and unassailable self-confidence, he was flattered by both Catherine the Great and Frederick the Great, was slapped by Mme. Pompadour's fan for his defense of physical love and was summed up by Mme. Necker, wife of the French finance minister, in her remark, "M. de Buffon has never spoken to me of the marvels of the earth without inspiring in me the thought that he himself was one of them." Buffon himself felt his own famous aphorism fitted him best: "Style is the man."

It was this world-straddling scientist that the provincial virtuoso Thomas Jefferson challenged in defense of his country. With all his knowledge and wisdom, Buffon was abysmally ignorant of the New World and utterly foolish in his concept of it. To him, nature in the New World was inferior in all ways to that of the old. Animals, plants, natives, climate were all underdeveloped or degenerate forms of Old World life. "In thinly inhabited regions [like America]," he stated, "nature is always rude and sometimes deformed. The air and the earth overloaded with humid and noxious vapors are unable either to purify themselves or to profit by the influence of the sun, who darts in vain his most enlivening rays upon this frigid mass." All that America can produce, Buffon said, "are reptiles and insects. The place can afford nourishment only for cold men and feeble animals."

"The animals of America are tractable and timid," he went on, "very few ferocious and none formidable. There is no North American animal comparable to the elephant: no giraffes, lions or hippopotami. All animals are smaller in North America than Europe. Everything shrinks under a 'niggardly sky and unprolific land.'" As for the natives of America, "Nature treated them like a stepmother. The organs of generation are small and feeble. They have no beard or body hair and no ardor for the female."

This incredible nonsense, as has been pointed out earlier, was derived in part from descriptions of a few disgruntled early travelers who had expected all the New World to be lush tropics. It was bolstered by snippets of quasi-fact dropped by more admiring visitors: for example, Kalm's casual observations that American cows were smaller than Europe's (which were generally better kept) and that many American women could not bear children after the age of thirty (many were too worn out by their hard life). The man who translated Kalm's travels into French dwelt lovingly on these observations, distorting Kalm's intentions. Such stuff was support for Buffon's grand theory that the New World had been actually created later than the old. By that time the "basic molecules of life" had lost most of their initial energy and had little left to give life in the New World.

Buffon was the most respectable of the New World's detractors but others had more impact on Europe. Notable among them was a Dutchman named Corneille de Pauw, one of whose kinsmen, Michael, briefly owned Staten Island, while another, who came over with Lafayette to fight in the Revolution, had a descendant who became benefactor of DePauw University. Corneille, though he never saw the New World, was repelled by it. In a book called *Recherches Philosophiques sur les Américains*, which was published first in 1768, he presented a distorted description of America which was accepted as absolute truth by many of Europe's scientists and teachers. De Pauw himself was a learned and diligent scholar, independent of mind, intolerant of criticism and marvelously duped by his own mistakes. He would brook no amendments to his analysis of the New World. The land there, he declared, was either desert or swamp, forest or mountain. The water was putrid, the fog poisonous, the climate so cold that even in relatively benign regions seeds planted too deep froze to death and trees sent their roots out horizontally to avoid the icy subsoil. Serpents, lizards and reptiles overran the place and the only animals larger than those of the Old World were the "monstrous insects which grew to prodigious size and multiplied beyond imagining." Even the crocodiles were too weak to be vicious, dogs lost their barks and camels could not reproduce. Animals had syphilis and men were so lacking in virility that they had milk in their breasts. All this was contradicted, of course, by the specimens and evidence that the American naturalists had been sending over, but many intellectuals of Europe, notably the *philosophes* of France, endorsed de Pauw. So did many rulers who, alarmed by the emigration of their subjects, tried to discourage it by disparaging America. Frederick the Great, who employed de Pauw as a counselor, was particularly pleased with what he was saying.

Americans were so flabbergasted by this error that, in their exasperation, they hardly knew how to begin to contradict it. John Adams attacked Buffon and Tom Paine castigated a leading French propounder of the distortions, the Abbé Raynal, an esteemed *philosophe*. Ben Franklin tried to make a dent in the Abbé's ideas in his own fashion. He invited the Abbé to a dinner party where, as Jefferson used to tell the story, half the guests were French, the other half American. During the dinner, Jefferson related,

> the Abbé got on his favorite theory of the degeneracy of animals and even man in America and urged it with his usual eloquence. The Doctor at length noticing the accidental stature and position of his guests at table, "Come," says he, "M. l'Abbé, let us try this question by the fact before us. We are here one-half American and one-half French and it happens that the Americans have placed themselves on one side of the table and our French friends on the other. Let both parties rise and we will see on which side nature has degenerated." It happened that his American guests were of the finest stature and form while those of the other side were remarkably diminutive and the Abbé himself, particularly was a mere shrimp.

Jefferson's methods of refutation were more laborious than the deft Dr. Franklin's. In *Notes on the State of Virginia*, he went directly at Buffon with logic and provable data. First he set up his target: "The opinion advanced by the Count de Buffon is that (1) that the animals common both to the old and new world are smaller in the latter, (2) that those peculiar to the new are on a smaller scale, (3) that those which have been domesticated in both have degenerated in America, and (4) that on the whole it exhibits fewer species."

After attacking Buffon's ideas in general, Jefferson gets down to particulars with an elaborate list of animal weights and measures. He cites the reliable John Bartram, who reported one American bear that weighed 410 pounds. The largest reported European bear weighed 153.7 pounds. The average American beaver outweighs his European counterpart 45 pounds to 18.5; the American otter 12 pounds to 8.9; the marten 6 pounds to 1.9. He does, however, give the European red deer a small edge over the American, 288.8 pounds to 273.

Domestic animals, he proves, are at least as large in the New World as in the old, provided they are given equal care. As for quantity and diversity, he states that there are eighteen quadrupeds that are found in the Old World but not in the new, while there are seventy-four in the New World that are not found in the old.

He comes to the defense of American virility. "The Indian," he states, "is neither more defective in ardor nor more impotent with his female than the white man reduced to the same diet and exercise." As for Buffon's scornful observation that the lack of hair on an Indian's face and body betokened impotence, Jefferson pointed out that Indians had a fastidious aversion to bodily hair. They say it "likens them to hogs. They therefore pluck the hair as fast as it appears." Providing delicate proof of this, he observed that traders who marry Indian women "and prevail upon them to discontinue this practice say that Nature is the same with them as with the whites."

A written rejoinder was not enough for Jefferson. When he was assigned to replace Franklin as ambassador in Paris, he bought the largest American panther skin he could find and delivered it to Buffon, who listened with skeptical good humor to his guest's boast that a European reindeer "could walk under the belly of our moose." Whereupon Jefferson set about backing up his boast with a unique display of chauvinistic diplomacy.

At his request, General John Sullivan, the Revolutionary hero who was now president of the state of New Hampshire, set out to get him a good-sized moose. It took a troop of twenty soldiers two weeks to bag a proper specimen and cart it out of the winter woods. "Every Indian near," Sullivan informed Jefferson, "had been set to working to remove the flesh, clean the bones and treat the skin." Packed into a huge crate, the moose was shipped across the ocean. First the box missed the boat. Then the bill went to the embassy in London, where a puzzled John Adams paid it. Finally the boxed beast arrived in Paris. Jefferson, though distressed at the delay and expense, was delighted with the moose's dimensions and with the fact that the skin was so sewn that it could be drawn off and on the skeleton. Though the horns were rather small, General Sullivan had thoughtfully sent along some sizable elk and deer antlers, which, he said, "could be fixed on."

Jefferson presented the animal to the doubting Buffon, along with an apology for the size of the horns. Buffon promised Jefferson to set things right, but never did. As Jefferson told Daniel Webster some years later, the great Frenchman "died directly afterwards."

The efforts of Jefferson and other Americans helped bring most Europeans to their senses, but the silly slanders persisted well into the next century, promulgated by, among others, an eminent Scottish historian named Robertson, who was ranked at the time with Gibbon, and by the German philosopher Hegel,

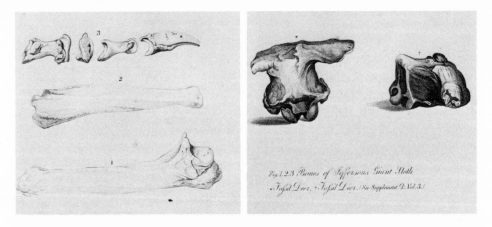

The bones of the Megalonyx make plain that it was a huge animal, but it was an oversized sloth, not the ferocious lion-like creature Jefferson imagined.

who picked up his facts from de Pauw. Even gentle Oliver Goldsmith contributed to the outrage. In a four-volume compendium of natural history, *A History of Earth and Animated Matter*, which borrowed big chunks from Buffon, Goldsmith belittled American animals, people and plants, admitting only that America "exceeds us in the size of its reptiles." This work went into more than twenty editions, the last one printed in 1876. Even more widely read, of course, was Goldsmith's attack on America in "The Deserted Village," where, bemoaning the fate of those who left their pleasant English homes, he described the "torrid tracts . . . Where Wild Altama [the Bartrams's Altamaha, of course] murmurs to their woe . . . Those matted woods where birds forget to sing . . . Those poisonous fields . . . The rattling terrors of the vengeful snake." It was no wonder that for generations in the United States orators at Fourth of July celebrations regularly and resoundingly denounced that perfidious French count and all his deluded followers.

Patriotism, which stood Jefferson in good stead in this instance, almost proved his scientific undoing in his study of fossils. Like other intellectuals of his day, he was captive to a belief in what was called "the Great Chain of Being," a theory that God had created all things at once in a perfect, closely dovetailed succession from the lowest creatures to the highest. There was never any—and could never be any—change in the chain: nothing could be added, altered or dropped out. This ruled out the possibility that any creature could become extinct or evolve into something different.

This theory plagued Jefferson when he made an ambitious venture into paleontology. In 1795, two friends in Virginia sent him an exciting find: bones of a large animal "of the clawed kind," found in a cave by saltpeter diggers.

They were prehistoric, but Jefferson believed that if the animal existed once, it must still exist somewhere. Besides, his friends told him, they had found drawings of a lionlike figure on nearby rocks and local hunters had heard a roaring loud as thunder resounding through the woods. Examining the bones and swallowing the stories, Jefferson concluded he had the remains of a big cat of "the family of lion, tiger, panther, etc., but as preeminent over the lion in size as the mammoth is over the elephant." He called it Megalonyx, or "great claw," and declared that the existence, past and present, of such a huge beast would once and for all destroy the Buffon–de Pauw myths. It was "victorious evidence against the pretended degeneracy of animal nature" in the New World.

Jefferson had just been elected president of the American Philosophical Society, and he announced from the chair that he would shortly present a paper on his American superbeast. Just before he did, while browsing through an English magazine, he came across an account of a fossil skeleton dug up in Paraguay. It was written by a young Frenchman whose name, Georges Cuvier, was unfamiliar to Jefferson, as it was then to most scientists. The description of the Paraguay fossil was so close to that of the Megalonyx that Jefferson knew it must be the same animal. On the basis of evidence Jefferson did not have, Cuvier deduced that the creature was herbivorous and could not be any kind of cat. It was, in fact, a giant sloth, which Cuvier named Megatherium. It was big, certainly, but it was not to be compared in fierceness to a lion or tiger.

Disappointed at the comedown of his Megalonyx but probably relieved at having stumbled on the facts, Jefferson made some hedges in his paper. Cuvier had lost Jefferson an argument against the Buffonites but saved him from an embarrassing paleontological goof. Years later, when he was recognized as the preeminent paleontologist of his time and the true founder of that science, Georges Cuvier graciously praised Jefferson for having helped to introduce the fossil animal to science through his "enlightened love and extensive knowledge of the sciences."

This "enlightened love and extensive knowledge," all through the Jeffersonian era, served to awaken Americans to an interest and a delight in the natural sciences and swelled their pride in the republic. With this love and knowledge, Jefferson could give to the Lewis and Clark expedition—which finally carried out his long-held dream of exploring the West—its historic inspiration and impetus.

🌱 🌱 🌱 🌱 🌱 JEFFERSON'S CHOICE OF MERIWETHER LEWIS TO LEAD THE party shows an admirable insight. In André Michaux he had had a man superbly qualified by learning and experience to serve science. In Meriwether Lewis he had an untrained man of little formal learning who was nonetheless an instinctive naturalist. Jefferson himself, in a biographical sketch of Lewis, wrote that

> when only 8 years of age he habitually went out in the dead of night alone with his dogs into the forest to hunt the raccoon and opossum, plunging through winter snows and frozen streams in pursuit of his object. His talent for observation which had led him to an accurate knowledge of plants and animals would have distinguished him as a farmer: but at the age of 20, yielding to the ardor of youth and a passion for more dazzling pursuits, he engaged as a volunteer in the body of militia which were called out by General Washington on occasion of the discontents produced by the excise taxes.

This discontent was the Whiskey Rebellion of 1794. The large force sent out against the rebels never had to fire a shot—the protesters faded away from battle—but Lewis was completely taken with the soldier's life. "We have mountains of beef and oceans of whiskey," he wrote his mother, who, incidentally, was an herb doctor and had taught her son a practical kind of botany. Staying in the army, Lewis served briefly in a company commanded by his future partner William Clark and undertook several difficult and delicate missions for the army. In 1800, ready to take office as President, Jefferson engaged Lewis as his private secretary. He thought it would be "advantageous," he explained, to have someone on hand who knew the "western country."

By 1802, Jefferson and Lewis were making hard plans for a western expedition, and Congress was asked in a secret message—secret because Louisiana was then still foreign territory—for permission to send a party of about a dozen men to the Pacific and back. Its purpose, Jefferson told Congress, would be to establish trading with the Indians and set up posts.

To his friends in the American Philosophical Society, Jefferson confided his deeper scientific purpose and asked for their help. The ideal leader, he wrote the botanist Benjamin Smith Barton, was "a character who, to a complete science in botany, natural history, mineralogy and astronomy, joined the firmness of constitution and character, prudence, habits adapted to the woods and a familiarity with the Indian manners and character. All the latter qualifications Captain Lewis has." He was, however, lacking in formal science. The President asked Barton to help set up a quick course in botany and zoology for Lewis, while other Philadelphia intellectuals were recruited to give Lewis cram courses in other sciences: Dr. Caspar Wistar, natural historian and mineralogist; Dr. Benjamin Rush, the famous physician; Andrew Ellicott, the naturalist-surveyor who had laid out the new capital at Washington. Lewis consulted William Bartram, who introduced him to a younger generation of natural historians.

When Lewis finally set out, he carried—along with such predictable necessities as 7 tons of food, 1 blacksmith's forge, 30 yards of common flannel, 6 copper kettles, 10 pounds of Epsom salts, 5 pounds of wampum and several dozen strings of blue beads—a copy of Dr. Barton's *Elements of Botany* and two Linnaean volumes.

Meanwhile, Lewis had chosen a partner who became, in effect, co-commander of the Corps of Discovery: Lieutenant William Clark, younger brother of General George Rogers Clark, the man who had been Jefferson's choice as leader of his first Louisiana expedition and Genêt's choice to lead his invasion. William Clark turned out to be, above all else, an instinctive geographer, able to take in the legend-laden Indian descriptions of vague lands, the contradictory tales of trappers, the feel of the terrain, the look and flow of rivers and, with these fragments of information, chart with repeated accuracy the routes the party should take. Though not so literate as Lewis, he shared his partner's diligence and care in observation.

All through the trip, Lewis insisted that his men keep their eyes open for strange plants and animals and bring him descriptions and specimens. Lewis's own descriptions were so specific in details of size, color and habits that botanists, zoologists and ornithologists, generations later, could identify what he found by the way he wrote of them.

Lewis and Clark and their forty-two men spent the winter of 1803–1804 near St. Louis, training for the trip and getting to know each other. During that time, Lewis undertook a special errand for Jefferson, going down to Big Bone Lick in Kentucky to report on a cache of fossil bones uncovered by a doctor named Goforth. When some of the bones arrived in Washington, Jefferson hardly knew what to do with them. He finally stored them in the East Room of the White House, thus giving another use to that all-purpose room where Abigail Adams used to hang up the weekly wash. On another side trip, Lewis sent back the plant now called the Osage orange. The Indians prized its wood for their bows, he reported, and gave "an extravagant account of the exquisite odor" of the fruit. The Osage orange was afterward offered for sale by Bartram's Gardens as a plant with "beautiful foliage and curious fruit."

Meanwhile, a great event had taken place. In 1802, Spain had ceded the Louisiana Territory to France, but Napoleon, ready to start a new Continental war and disgusted by his army's setback in rebellious Haiti—"Damn sugar, damn cotton, damn colonies" he is supposed to have said—wanted to rid himself of a territory he could not have defended anyway against England. So he sold it to the United States, and now Lewis and Clark were exploring not a piece of foreign property but the new American destiny.

"Monday, May 14th," Clark's journal of the expedition began. "Rained the forepart of the day" as the Corps of Discovery in a keelboat and two pirogues pulled into the Missouri. A few days out, Clark, who kept the official records for the first year of its trip, noted that "Capt. Lewis went out to the woods and found many curious plants and shrubs."

As they made their way upriver, they found new varieties of beaver and bull snakes, gathered some clammyweed and cleome that botanists had not known, and came to a mystifying phenomenon: a three-mile raft of white feathers floating in the river. Pushing through, they came upon a host of white pelicans, five or six thousand jammed on a sandbar. Lewis bagged one and poured water in its beak to measure the capacity. Five gallons, Sergeant Gass put down in his notes.

When they reached the High Plains, Lewis and Clark, out walking on a "very cold morning, discovered a village of small animals that burrow in the ground." Lewis added a description:

> The little animal which I have called the *barking squirrel* weighs from 3 to 3½ pounds, its form is that of the squirrel, its color is a uniform light brick red grey, the red rather predominating. They generally associate in large societies placing their burrows near each other and frequently occupy in this manner several hundred acres of land. When at rest above ground, their position is generally erect on their hinder feet and rump, thus they will generally set and bark at you as you approach them. Their note being much that of the little toy dogs, their yelps are in quick succession and at each they give a motion to their tails upwards.

The gregarious little creature is, as Lewis correctly said, a squirrel, but it goes by the name of "prairie dog." Lewis, incidentally, found a practical use for the animal. "As we had not killed or eat anything today," he wrote, "we each killed a burrowing squirrel to make sure of our suppers. I found the flesh well-flavored and tender; some of them were very fat."

A few miles farther up the Missouri, Clark "killed a buck goat about the height of a grown deer, its body shorter, the horns not very hard and forked 2/3 up, one prong short, the other round and sharp arched. He is more like the antelope or gazelle of Africa than any other species of goat." It was the fleet and abundant pronghorn. Lewis was to add to the description:

> I had this day an opportunity of witnessing the agility and the superior fleetness of this animal. I had pursued and twice surprised a small herd. I got within about 200 paces of them when they smelt me and fled; I gained the top of the eminence on which they stood as soon as possible, from whence I had an extensive view of the country. The antelopes which

The mountain goat was an elusive beast. Lewis never saw it. Clark saw one only at a distance. The pronghorn was comparatively common, found on both sides of the Rockies.

had disappeared in a steep ravine now appeared at a distance of about three miles. So soon had these antelopes gained the distance I doubted at first that they were the same that I had just surprised, but my doubts soon vanished when I beheld the rapidity of their flight along the ridge before me. It appeared rather the rapid flight of birds than the motion of quadrupeds. I think I can safely venture the assertion that the speed of this animal is equal if not superior to that of the finest blooded courser.

That same day, John Shields came into camp with "a hare like the mountain hare of Europe, its ears large, his tail long, thick and white"—the white-tailed jackrabbit. Lewis measured the leaps and found them "commonly from 18 to 22 feet." Near the mouth of the White River, Clark killed "a prairie wolf, about the size of a gray fox, bushy tail, head and ears like a wolf, burrows in the ground and barks like a small dog. What has been taken heretofore for a fox was those wolves." This was the most widespread denizen of the West: the coyote. Nearby they killed a curious kind of deer whose "ear and tail so well comported with those of the mule," said Lewis, "that we have adapted the appellation of the mule deer." That same day, Clark noted, Lewis killed "a remarkable bird (Magpy) of the Corvus species. Abt. the size of a large pigion, a butifull thing." The magpie was as pesky as it was beautiful. It flew into their tents, snatched food from their plates, stood by as they skinned game and darted in to steal pieces of meat.

These familiar animals, embedded now in the tales and traditions of the West but virtually unknown to Americans when the Corps of Discovery found them, would be found again by later naturalists, who would mark them as their own discoveries and give them names and classifications. But it was Lewis and Clark and their men who first came upon them.

By October, the party had encountered cold weather and the troublesome Teton Indians, who tried to stop the Corps from going farther. They literally held Clark's boat back. "We were not squaws but warriors," Clark wrote that he told them, and when a chief turned "very insolent, his gestures were of such a personal nature that I felt myself compelled to draw my sword." The Indians withdrew. "We anchored off a willow island," Clark's account winds up. "I call this island Bad Hummered Island as were in bad humer."

The Tetons did teach the Americans something of Indian botany, introducing them to the useful pomme blanche or prairie apple with which, Lewis wrote, the Indians "thicken their soup, boil with their meat, prepare an agreeable dish of the consistency of a hasty pudding." At the powwows, they were introduced to Teton tobacco, the dried inside bark of red willow, which, mixed with leaves of a local tobacco plant, "answered for smoking, but not for chewing." Lewis found it "does not affect the nerves in the same manner that the tobacco cultivated in the U.S. does."

The Corps wintered at Fort Mandan. There Lewis helped a young squaw get through a difficult labor by providing her with two rings of a rattlesnake's rattle. She produced a boy whom the men named Pompey. The squaw, named Sakawajawa, had been kidnapped from the Shoshone Indians, far to the west, and sold to a trapper named Charbonneau, who settled in with the Corps at Mandan.

The winter over, Lewis sent off a shipment of plants, animals and artifacts to Jefferson, along with five Indian chiefs, who were to visit the Great White Father. Then on April 7 the Corps of Discovery once again set out upriver.

> Our vessels consisted of six small canoes and two large pirogues [wrote Lewis]. This little fleet altho' not quite so respectable as those of Columbus or Capt. Cook were still viewed by us with as much pleasure as those deservedly famed adventurers ever beheld theirs and I dare say with quite as much anxiety for their safety and preservation. We were now about to penetrate a country at least two thousand miles in width, on which the foot of civilized man had never trodden. I could but esteem this moment of my departure as among the most happy of my life.

Charbonneau, Sakawajawa and her papoose Pompey went along as members of the party. Sakawajawa quickly made herself useful. "When we halted for dinner," Lewis wrote, "the squaw busied herself in searching for the wild artichokes which the mice collect and deposit in large hoards. The flavor resembles that of the Jerusalem artichoke."

Signs of spring multiplied. Along with "great numbers of geese, flowers in the prairies," Clark noted, "I saw a musquetor today." They were soon into idyllic land where "the buffalo, Elk and antelope are so gentle that we pass near them without appearing to excite any alarm among them."

Well up the Missouri, the party divided. Lewis took a shortcut across the land on foot while Clark took the boats up the winding river. At the mouth of the Yellowstone, Lewis camped, sending Joseph Field up the tributary to see what lay there. When Clark and the flotilla caught up, Lewis, "much pleased at having arrived at this long wished for spot and in order to add in some measure to the general pleasure, ordered a dram to be issued to each person. This soon produced the fiddle and they spent the evening with much hilarity singing and dancing and seemed as perfectly to forget their past toils as they appeared regardless of those to come."

Into this gay scene in the middle of terra incognita walked a weary Joseph Field with a report on "several big horned animals" and a large horn he had picked up. No white American had ever seen the bighorn sheep before. Lewis wrote:

> The places they generally select to lodge is the crannies or crevices of the rocks in the faces of inaccessible precipices. These animals bound from rock to rock and stand apparently in the most careless manner on the sides of precipices of many hundred feet. They are very shy and are quick of both scent and sight. The horns occupy the crown of the head almost entirely. They are compressed, bent backwards and lunated; the surface swelling into wavey rings which encircling the horn continue to succeed each other from the base to the extremity and becoming less elevated and more distant as they recede from the head. This horn is used by the natives in constructing their bows; I have no doubt but it would make elegant and useful hair combs.

The bighorn was to be a staple of their diet all through the mountains— "the flesh much resembles mutton though not so strong," wrote Lewis approvingly.

They were into grizzly country and, though confused at first by the varying color of the big bears, the party soon learned to recognize and fear them. Lewis wrote the first specific description of the grizzly:

> The legs of this bear are somewhat longer than those of the black, as are its talons and tusks incomparably larger and longer; its color is yellowish brown, the eyes small, black and piercing; the front of the forelegs near the feet is usually black; the fur is finer, thicker and deeper than that of the black bear; it is a much more ferocious and formidable

An American having struck a Bear but not killed him, escapes into a Tree

A grizzly bear, far less fierce than those Lewis encountered, was shown treeing a well-dressed explorer in Sergeant Patrick Gass's published account of the expedition.

animal, and will frequently pursue the hunter when wounded. It is astonishing to see the wounds they will bear before they can be put to death.

One grizzly, shot through the lungs, ran for half a mile after a hunter before giving up the pursuit. Another, with eight bullets in him, chased six men and came so close that two of them threw away their guns and jumped into a river to get away.

Lewis himself, having shot a buffalo, was standing in the open with an unloaded gun.

> While I was gazing attentively at the poor animal discharging blood in streams from his mouth and nostrils a large bear crept up on me within 20 steps. It was an open level plain. I thought of retreating in a brisk walk until I could reach a tree about 300 yards below me, but I had no sooner turned myself about but he pitched at me, open-mouthed and full speed. I ran hastily into the water about waist deep and faced about, the moment I put myself in this attitude of defense he suddenly wheeled about as if frightened and retreated with quite as great precipitation as he had just before pursued me. I saw him run through the level open plain about three miles.

Further troubles waited for Lewis after the bear had fled:

> In returning, my direction led me directly to an animal that I at first
> supposed was a wolf; but on nearer approach or about sixty paces distant
> I discovered that it was not. Its color was a brownish yellow; it couched
> itself down like a cat looking immediately at me as if it designed to spring
> on me. I took aim at it and fired. It instantly disappeared in its burrow.
> I loaded my gun and examined the place, which was dusty, and saw the
> track from which I am still further convinced that it was of the tiger kind.
> It now seemed to me that all the beasts of the neighborhood had made a
> league to destroy me, or that some fortune was disposed to amuse herself
> at my expense, for I had not proceded more than three hundred yards
> from the burrow of this tiger cat, before three bull buffalo, which were
> feeding with a large herd about half a mile from me, separated from the
> herd and ran full speed towards me. I altered my direction to meet them;
> when they arrived within a hundred yards they made a halt, took a good
> view of me and retreated with precipitation. I then continued my route
> homewards passed the buffalo which I had killed, but did not think it
> prudent to remain all night at this place which really from the succession
> of curious adventures wore the impression on my mind of enchantment; at
> sometimes for a moment I thought it might be a dream, but the prickly
> pears which pierced my feet convinced me that I was really awake.

Almost every member of the party had his own narrow escape from the
grizzly. On June 2nd, a "bear was very near catching Drewyer; it also pursued Charbonneau who fired his gun in the air as he ran." On June 4th, a
grizzly chasing Joseph Field got "so near that it struck his foot." As for his
own feelings about the grizzly, Lewis remarked: "I must confess that I do not
like the gentleman and had rather fight 2 Indians than one bear."

Past the Yellowstone, the Corps came to the mouth of the Marias River
and into a land that delighted Lewis:

> One of the most beautiful picturesque countries that I ever beheld,
> through the wide expanse of which innumerable herds of living animals are
> seen, its borders garnished with one continued garden of roses while its
> lofty and open forests are the habitation of myriads of the feathered tribes
> who salute the ear of the passing traveler with their wild and simple yet
> sweet and cheerful melody.

Near the Great Falls of the Missouri, they came upon two animals new
to them: the bushy-tailed wood rat or pack rat, one of the most annoying
thieves of the animal kingdom, and the pretty little kit fox, which lives in

underground villages. They met the sage grouse, largest of the grouse family, which they dubbed "cock of the plains" and found to be indifferent eating; the white-rumped shrike; and the western meadowlark, which was noted by Lewis but not described by anyone else until Audubon rediscovered it forty years later. In the water around the Falls, they found the cutthroat trout.

They were in new land, but they made the same complaints that naturalists had sounded, with variations in spelling, since the first days in the colonies: "July 14th Sunday 1805: Musquetors and Knats verry troublesom." They did meet a plague that their predecessors had missed. "The prickly pear is now in full blume," wrote Lewis, "and forms one of the beauties as well as the greatest pests of the plains." Clark had no feeling for its beauty: "My feet constantly stuck full of prickly pear thorns. I pulled out 17 by the light of the fire tonight." Even double soles of buffalo hide did not keep out the thorns. "Our trio of pests, musquetos, eye knats and prickly pears," sighed Lewis, "equal to any three curses that ever poor Egypt labored under, except the Mohametant yoke."

Nature did offer some pleasures. The ripening currants were sweet and juicy and brought on, incidentally, one of the few recorded disagreements between the two partners. Clark preferred the yellow varieties, while Lewis was so taken by the black kind—"a charming fruit"—that he gathered seeds for President Jefferson. Pushing into the mountains, Lewis got his first glimpse of a woodpecker: "black as a crow, the belly and breast is a curious mixture of white and blood red which has much the appearance of having been artificially painted or stained of that color." It is now called Lewis's woodpecker.

They came to Shoshone country—homeland for Sakawajawa, where she found roots the men could eat and had a dramatic reunion with her chieftain brother. Going across the Great Divide, the party found a matching namesake for Lewis's woodpecker, Clark's nutcracker, a large black-and-white bird with "a loud squawking note something like the mewing of a cat."

Having made their difficult way to the Pacific, the Corps spent a miserable winter at Fort Clatsop, at the mouth of the Columbia. Here they found and described the superb western salmon, but the fish that caught their interest most was the small eulachon or candlefish.

> They are filled with roes of a pure white color and have scarcely any perceptable alimentary duct [wrote Lewis]. I find them best when cooked in Indian style, which is by roasting a number of them together on a wooden spit without any previous preparation whatever. They are so fat they require no additional sauce, and I think them superior to any fish I ever tasted, even more delicate and luscious than the white fish of

Charles Willson Peale drew a mountain quail and a Louisiana tanager for Meriwether Lewis. Then he proudly put them on display in his museum.

the lakes which have heretofore formed my standard of excellence among the fishes. The bones are so soft and fine that they form no obstruction in eating this fish.

New water birds were seen; the fluttering western grebe, the white-fronted goose, the ring-necked duck, the lesser Canada goose, and a large swan whose call, wrote Lewis, "begins with a kind of whistling sound and terminates in a round full note; from the peculiar note I have called it the Whistling Swan."

When the Corps started back east in late March, the spring flowers were up, and whereas Lewis, on his way west in autumn, had listed mostly animals and birds, now he filled his journal with long lists of plants: the big-leaf maple, the Oregon grape, a dogwood Audubon was later to name Nuttall's dogwood, showy phlox, the salmonberry, a pink cleome, a yellow bell, a purple trillium, the beautiful mariposa lily and a pink evening primrose or ragged robin which is botanically known as *Clarkia pulchella*. Best known of all was the bitterroot or *Lewis rediviva*, whose rosy blossom is Montana's state flower.

Interspersed on the lists are notes on birds. The one on the mountain quail is a classic of detailed ornithological description:

> The upper part of the head, sides and back of the neck, including the crop and about ⅓ of the under part of the body is of a bright dove colored blue; underneath the under beak, as high as the lower edge of the eyes, and back as far as the hinder part of the eyes and thence coming down to a point in front of the neck about two-thirds of its length down-

wards, is a fine dark brick red. Between this brick red and the dove color there runs a narrow stripe of pure white. The ears are covered with some coarse stiff dark brown feathers. Just at the base of the under chap there is a narrow transverse stripe of pure white. From the crown of the head two long round feathers extend backwards nearly in the direction of the beak and are of a black color. The longest of these feathers is two inches and a half; it overlays and conceals the other which is somewhat shorter and seems to be wrapped in the plumage of that in front which folding backwards collapses behind and has a round appearance. The tail is composed of twelve dark brown feathers of nearly equal length. The large feathers of the wings are of a dark brown and are rather short in proportion to the body of the bird in that respect very similar to our common partridge. The covert of the wings and back are of a dove color with a slight admixture of reddish brown. A wide stripe which extends from side to side of the body and occupies the lower region of the breast is beautifully variegated with brick red white and black which predominate in the order they are mentioned and the colors mark the feathers transversely. The legs are covered with feathers as low as the knee; these feathers are of a dark brown tipped with dark brick red as are also those between and about the joining of the legs with the body. They have four toes on each foot of which three are in front and that in the center the longest, those on each side nearly of equal length; that behind is also of good length and are all armed with long and strong nails. The legs and feet are white and imbricated with proportionably large broad scales. The upper beak is short, wide at its base, black, convex, curved downwards and rather obtusely pointed. It exceeds the under chap considerably which is of a white color, also convex underneath and obtusely pointed. The nostrils are remarkably small, placed far back and low down on the sides of the beak. They are covered by a thin protuberant elastic, black leather-like substance. The eyes are of a uniform piercing black color. This is a most beautiful bird. I preserved the skin of this bird retaining the wings, feet and head which I hope will give a just idea of the bird. Its loud note is single and consists of a loud squall, entirely different from the whistling of our quails or partridge. It has a churping note when alarmed something like ours.

The explorers were hurrying, impatient when snow held them up in the mountains—splitting into two parties, with Lewis going north and Clark taking a new short way south. The river currents were with them and they moved rapidly down the Missouri as summer was ending. They met a surprised army artillery captain, who "informed us that we had been long since given out by the people of the U. States generally and almost forgotten. The President of the United States had yet hopes for us." At last, in St. Louis, Lewis wrote Jefferson, summing up his great expedition:

It is with pleasure that I announce to you the safe arrival of myself and a party at 12 o'clock today at this place with our papers and baggage. On obedience to your orders we have penetrated the continent of North America to the Pacific Ocean. I have brought with me several skins of the Sea Otter, two skins of the native sheep of America, five skins and skeletons complete of the Bighorn or mountain ram, and a skin of the Mule deer beside the skins of several other quadrupeds and birds natives of the countries through which we have passed. I have also preserved a pretty extensive collection of plants.

The men went on to Washington, with their animal skins, dried plants and tales of the dangers and wonders they had encountered. Then they separated, Lewis to a troubled career and a mysterious death, Clark to a long and useful life as an administrator in the West. Sakawajawa ran out her life as a white man's squaw on the upper Missouri. Pompey, the son whom Lewis's rattlesnake rattler had helped bring into the world, was educated by Clark. Taken up by a German prince who was sightseeing in the West, he spent several years in Europe and returned to a nondescript life on the frontier as a guide, translator and historic curiosity.

Naturalists have been arguing almost since the expedition ended over whether Jefferson made a mistake in not sending a trained scientist instead of relying on Meriwether Lewis's lay knowledge and instincts. Considering everything—the demands of such a journey, the need to keep the party small and efficient, Lewis's remarkable record of bringing everyone back alive and in good shape—Jefferson was undoubtedly right in his decision, especially in view of what Lewis accomplished as a naturalist. A thorough and diligent observer, he overlooked very little along the way. Later naturalists making their "discoveries" were more often than not simply rediscovering things Lewis had found in the first place. He was careful in his descriptions, repeating himself for clarity or to emphasize exceptions or differences. He used Latin names and correct botanical terms, although, oddly, he avoided the Linnaean binomials.

Of the several hundred plant and animal specimens the expedition collected, some two hundred survived. Its scientific data, however, were overlooked because the original publication of the expedition's journals omitted most of it. It was not until late in the century that naturalists, going back over the original journals, finally realized the scope and depth of the Corps findings. Recent works by Raymond Darwin Burroughs and Paul Russell Cutright have affirmed the

significance of the expedition. In his *Lewis and Clark, Pioneering Naturalists,*
Cutright lists the species and subspecies that the explorers first described.
Though it makes dense reading, the list is an impressive suggestion of what the
leaders of the Corps of Discovery accomplished as naturalists.

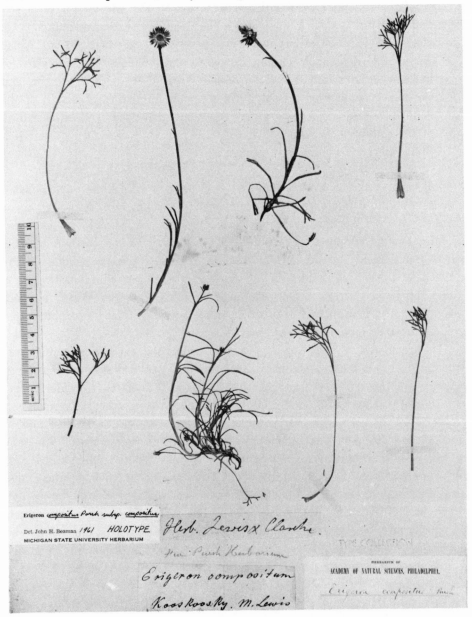

Lewis's handwriting on a specimen of cut-leaved daisy notes that he found it near the Koos-
koosky River. It was named Erigeron compositus *by the botanist Frederick Pursh.*

Subalpine fir, vine maple, Rocky Mountain maple, bigleaf maple, western red baneberry, Oregon sunshine, Geyer's onion, Tolmie's onion, white alder, red alder, wavy-leaved or Sitka alder, Saskatoon serviceberry, cutleaved sideranthus, Lyall's angelica, small-flowered Collinsia, northwest crimson columbine, madrone, hoary sagebrush, linear-leaved wormwood, long-leaved mugwort, dark-leaved mugwort, sagebrush, long-tailed wild ginger, aromatic aster, Oregon white-topped aster, Missouri milk vetch, bushy atriplex, Nuttall's atriplex, Oregon grape, dull Oregon grape, spring birch, western paper birch, rabbit brush, fetid rayless goldenrod, wild hyacinth, large mountain brome grass, balsam root, mariposa lily, camas, scarlet gilia, buckbrush, sticky laurel, netleaf hackberry, leafy or dwarf thistle, edible thistle, ragged robin, western spring beauty, linear-leaved montia, sugar bowls, pink cleome, narrow-leaved collomia, Nuttall's or mountain dogwood, California hazelnut, black hawthorn, red false mallow, mountain lady's slipper, Menzies's larkspur, slender toothwort, narrow-leaved purple coneflower, silverberry, giant rye-gass, cut-leaved daisy, western wallflower, yellow fawn lily, white-margined spurge, blue bunch wheatgrass, Oregon ash, mission bells, yellow bell, great-flowered gaillardia, salal, shrubby pentstemon, tassels, broad-leaved gum plant, linear-leaved phacelia, western blue-flag, western larch, yellow-flowering pea, bitterroot, Lewis's wild flax, cous, orange honeysuckle, involucred fly-honeysuckle, silvery lupine, seashore lupine, silky lupine, Osage orange, uropappus, Lewis's monkey flower, large monkey flower, Indian tobacco, scapose primrose, northern sun-cup, brittle opuntia, many-spined opuntia, owl's clover, Oregon wood-sorrel, silver oxytrope, Oregon boxwood, lousewort, cascade pentstemon, Gairdner's yampah, biscuit root, common lomatium, virgate phacelia, Lewis's syringa, showy phlox, Engelmann's spruce, Sitka spruce, whitebark pine, lodgepole pine, western white pine, ponderosa pine, slender popcorn flower, large-flowered clammyweed, American Jacob's ladder, white milkwort, western snakeweed, narrow-leaf cottonwood, plains cottonwood, black cottonwood, silver-leaf psoralea, pomme blanche, lance-leaved psoralea, few-flowered psoralea, western bracken, antelope brush, Oregon crab apple, Sitka mountain ash, Oregon white oak, cascara sagrada, California rhododendron, squaw bush, golden currant, white squaw currant, Umatilla gooseberry, straggly gooseberry, canyon gooseberry, red flowering currant, sticky currant, Nootka rose, cluster rose, Woods's rose, thimbleberry, salmonberry, Pacific blackberry, peach-leaved willow, slender willow, blue elderberry, rayless camomile, greasewood, narrow-leaved skullcap, narrow-petaled stonecrop, silvery buffalo-berry, pestle parsnip, common matchweed, inland cord-grass, ocean spray, needle-and-thread grass, clustered swertia, common snowberry, Lewis and Clark's synthyris, tansy, Pacific yew, western red cedar, large-headed clover, small-headed clover, western wake-robin, petioled wake-robin, mountain hemlock, Lyall's nettle, blue huckleberry, western huckleberry, evergreen huckleberry, California false hellebore, bear grass, glaucous zygadene

white sturgeon, goldeye, blue catfish, channel catfish, Columbia River chub, mountain sucker, starry flounder, northern squawfish, cutthroat trout, steelhead trout, sauger, eulachon, soft-shelled turtle, Columbian toad, northern Pacific rattler, prairie rattler, western hog-nose snake, Pacific tree frog, pigmy horned toad, plains horned toad, bull snake, water terrapin, western frog, western fence lizard, western garter snake, northwestern garter snake, California newt

western grebe, white-fronted goose, Lewis's woodpecker, ring-necked duck, Oregon ruffed grouse, Hutchins's goose, lesser Canada goose, Montana horned owl, dusky horned owl, Franklin's grouse, western willet, sage grouse, Pacific nighthawk, northern flicker, western common crow, northwestern crow, American raven, black-headed jay, Richardson's blue grouse, Harris's woodpecker, Cabanis's woodpecker, western pileated woodpecker, prairie horned lark, Brewer's blackbird, Pacific fulmar, Pacific loon, piñon jay, white-rumped shrike, glaucous-winged gull, western gull, Bonaparte's gull, Clark's nutcracker, long-billed curlew, whistling swan, mountain quail, Columbian sharp-tailed grouse, prairie sharp-tailed grouse, Oregon jay, double-crested cormorant, Nuttall's poor-will, black-billed magpie, western tanager, red-necked grebe, McCown's longspur, broad-tailed hummingbird, pale goldfinch, Forster's tern, least tern, western meadowlark, western winter wren, western mourning dove

Shiras's moose, pronghorn, Oregon pronghorn, mountain beaver, short-tailed shrew, coyote, plains gray wolf, Missouri beaver, Roosevelt's elk, black-tailed prairie dog, mule deer, Columbian black-tailed deer, white-tailed deer, sea otter, yellow-haired porcupine, Townsend's chipmunk, mountain lion, white-tailed jackrabbit, Oregon bobcat, northern bobcat, yellow-bellied marmot, striped skunk, long-tailed weasel, ermine, bushy-tailed wood rat, eastern wood rat, mountain goat, Audubon's mountain sheep, harbor seal, raccoon, Townsend's mole, western gray squirrel, Columbian ground squirrel, thirteen-lined ground squirrel, desert cottontail, Douglas's squirrel, Richardson's red squirrel, westen badger, pocket gopher, grizzly bear, great-tailed fox, swift fox.

CHAPTER SEVEN

THE NATURAL SHOWMAN

☙ ☙ ☙ ☙ ☙ As the Corps of Discovery was pushing from Fort Man-dan up the Missouri into the Rockies, the first samples of what it had found were making their roundabout way toward Washington. "Cage 6 containing four liveing Magpies," said the invoice, "7 containing a liveing burrowing squirrel of the praries. 9 containing one liveing hen of the Prarie." When it arrived at New Orleans after a 2,500-mile trip by keelboat and riverboat, the cargo was given special treatment by the governor, William Claiborne, an amateur naturalist himself, who wrote Jefferson that the prairie squirrel "seems to be sick and I fear will not live" but the magpies "have excellent appetites." The prairie hen had apparently succumbed on the way. A couple of days later, the solicitous governor sent off a dispatch to Jefferson saying the prairie squirrel—the prairie dog—had recovered and they would all soon be sent on to Washington. When the ship-ment arrived at the White House in August, the maître d'hôtel advised Jefferson, who was away at Monticello, that "the magpie and the kind of squirrel are very well; they are in the room where the Monsieur receives his callers."

On returning to Washington, the President set about disposing of the specimens. Some of the Indian objects he kept "for an Indian hall I am forming at Monticello," he explained. The plants and seeds he sent to the American Philosophical Society, which dispersed the seeds to nurserymen. As for the animals, living and preserved, there was never any question about where they would go: to Jefferson's good friend, the artist-patriot-naturalist-impresario Charles Willson Peale, for display at Peale's Museum of Philadelphia, the country's only working natural history museum where tens of thousands of Americans were given a serious introduction to natural science.

In terms of science and showmanship, there was nothing in the young republic that could compete with Peale's Museum, and there were few men in the nation who, for art and ingenuity, could compare with its proprietor and unresting promoter. No development in the early days of American natural science seemed to begin with a set purpose and proceed to it by a logical process —and both Peale and his institution fitted this pattern.

The museum started with some prehistoric bones that had been found at Big Bone Lick, which for half a century had been yielding fossils that fascinated and puzzled scientists on both sides of the Atlantic. Peter Collinson had obtained a four-pound tooth in 1762 and suggested to John Bartram that he go to the Lick for more bones.

Soon after, the site was visited by an Indian agent named George Croghan. One of the versatile adventurers of the frontier, Croghan had served as supply master for Braddock's troops in their disastrous attack on Fort Duquesne, speculated grandly in land and wound up heavily mortgaged to, among others, Cadwallader Colden. At the Lick, Croghan unearthed a number of bones, but lost them when he was captured by the Indians. After persuading the savages not to scalp him, he wangled his release and promptly went back to fetch more bones. He sent a parcel of them to Franklin in England. Collinson got his hands on some of them and sent a few on to Buffon.

A confused discussion arose in the international circle. The bones looked like those of elephants and hippopotamuses, but the region was too cold for those beasts. Franklin's astute suggestion that it might once have been warm enough for them was brushed off by the Europeans—nothing so benign was possible in the New World. Some scientists thought that the elephantlike animal still lived in the unexplored north. Indian legends, which always seemed to have some basis in fact, supported this. Any possibility that they were the remains of some extinct animal was ruled out. This would contradict the Great Chain of Being and indicate that God had made some mistakes in creating the world. For Him to permit anything to vanish because of original error or later carelessness was both scientific and theological heresy.

In any case, a man named George Morgan, who had gone with Croghan on his trip back to the Lick, picked up some bones and sent them to his brother Dr. John Morgan of Philadelphia. Dr. Morgan piled them in his home, where they drew many interested visitors. John Adams noted in his diary that he went to see "bones of an animal of enormous size found on the banks of the Ohio." Some years later, in 1783, Morgan was approached by a physician named Christian Friedrich Michaelis, who had come to America as doctor to the Hessian troops and stayed on after the war. Michaelis was a studious naturalist. He observed the habits of rattlesnakes so closely that he was bitten by one of his subjects, happily surviving his research. Michaelis wanted to buy the bones but Dr. Morgan refused to sell, agreeing, however, to let Michaelis have some drawings made of them.

This is where Peale entered. The best-known artist in Philadelphia, he was commissioned by Michaelis to do the drawings and took the bones off to his studio on Lombard Street. The studio was already a kind of public place. People came there to see the portraits Peale had done of Washington and other American leaders and to listen to his little lectures about his work. Having set up the bones so he could draw them, Peale discovered that they attracted more attention than his portraits. His businessman brother-in-law, Nathaniel Ramsay, told Peale he would go twenty miles out of his way to see the bones and there were many who would "prefer seeing such articles of curiosity to any paintings." For a brilliant opportunist like Peale, the next move was inevitable, and so in this roundabout way his natural history museum came into being.

Peale's personal progress to this point was just as roundabout as the museum's. His father, a bright and extravagant Englishman, had been caught flagrantly forging notes in his job at the post office, and had, in effect, been given optional sentences: either he be hanged or leave England forever. He removed himself to Virginia where, in 1741, Charles Wilson Peale was born. (Later, for no stated reason, he put an extra "l" in his middle name.) Apprenticed to a saddler, young Charles branched out into metalworking and watch repairing and tried his hand at portrait painting. By the gift of a saddle to a professional painter named John Hesselius, who today enjoys a considerable reputation as a primitive artist, he was permitted to watch Hesselius while he worked. With the tips he picked up, Peale began to do portraits of well-off neighbors. In 1765, after falling into debt, he escaped jail only by fleeing to Boston.

At that point, everybody turned to help Peale develop his art. In Boston the noted painter John Singleton Copley gave him advice. Back home, when he was able to arrange his debts, his friends raised money to send him to London to study. In London, Benjamin Franklin offered him introductions even after Peale walked in on Ben unannounced and found him with a young lady in his lap. Benjamin West, the colonial who had become court portraitist, took Peale on as student and assistant. When he came back to America in 1769, Peale was a sure-handed professional: a good draftsman, a fine colorist, a sharp reader of personality and a persuasive salesman.

His business and reputation as a portraitist flourished. In 1772, he called at Mount Vernon where he found a reluctant client with a stubborn wife. When she was still Mrs. Daniel Parke Custis, Martha Washington had had her portrait done as part of the conventional husband-and-wife pair. Now she wanted one of her new husband to keep her portrait company. After talking with Peale, she coaxed her husband to get into his old uniform as colonel of the militia and pose. Washington gave in without much grace. "Inclination having yielded to importunity," he wrote a friend, "I am now contrary to all expectations under the hands of Mr. Peale; but in so grave—so sullen a mood— and now and then under the influence of Morpheus that I fancy the skill of this gentleman's pencil will be put to it in describing to the world what manner of man I am." The man Peale portrayed was not the Jovian figure of later portraits but a stoutish 40-year-old squire, his uniform rather tight, awkwardly reenacting his role as a young officer of the king.

In 1776, Peale moved himself and his family to Philadelphia, the center of colonial culture, and plunged promptly into the war. As an officer in the militia, he fought under Washington at Princeton and proved himself a highly practical commander. When his men went barefoot, he used his old skills as a saddle-maker and made shoes for them. When some of the soldiers broke ranks to steal fruit from an orchard, he kept discipline simply by ordering the whole company to fall out so all could join in the foraging. His paints and palettes went with him into battle, and the scenes he sketched provided backgrounds for two portraits of General Washington. During the winter at Valley Forge, he became a friend of the young Marquis de Lafayette.

The war had just ended when the old bones from Big Bone Lick intruded on Peale's life and diverted him into natural history. He virtually had to invent his new profession as a museum-keeper, since there was little to serve as a model. Some cultured gentlemen of the time did possess "cabinets"—collections of minerals, stuffed animals, plants, curiosities. Such cabinets were indiscriminately filled with mummies, shark teeth, unicorn horns, bones of creatures said to have been giants and, most prized of all, prehistoric stone axes believed to have been, quite literally, thunderbolts hurled down from the sky. A few of the establishments in Europe had already changed from confused collections into organized semipublic museums.

In America, Charleston had founded a natural history museum, but it had an on-and-off life. In Philadelphia, Peale had become familiar with something called the American Museum, a haphazard batch of bones and artifacts owned by an elderly Frenchman named Pierre Eugène du Simitière, who opened it to the public for a few hours a week and charged the rather high admission fee of fifty cents. When du Simitière died in 1784, Peale had Dr. Morgan's mastodon bones in his gallery and the idea for a museum in his head. This was put aside, however, when he heard about a new theatrical device called the Eidophusikon, which was a sensational attraction at the Drury Lane Theatre in London. By moving transparent painted panels in quick succession against varying backlight, a remarkable illusion of motion could be obtained. Adapting the idea, Peale depicted the coming of dawn, the breaking of a thunderstorm, the turning of a mill wheel on the Schuylkill River and a melodramatic sequence of Lucifer

In his painting The Artist in His Museum, *Peale summed up his life's work: the specimen-filled Long Hall, the mastodon and its bones, his palette, himself at the age of 81.*

rising in flames from the underworld. Turning his gallery into a theatre, he gave public performances to crowded houses, business being especially brisk in 1787, when Philadelphia was filled with the delegates to the Constitutional Convention. Peale eventually discarded the cumbersome name Eidophusikon and called his device simply "moving pictures."

Despite the distraction, Peale kept at his museum project, and in the summer of 1786 announced that he was making "a part of his house a repository for natural curiosities, the wonderful works of nature," which would be open to the public. Within a year, he had a respectable collection displayed in ways novel for the times and clearly the precursor of those used in natural history museums today. Manassah Cutler of Massachusetts, himself a naturalist of some note, visited Peale's Museum and found the

> natural curiosities arranged in a most romantic and amusing manner. There was a mound of earth, considerably raised and covered with green turf, from which a number of trees ascended and branched out in different directions. On the declivity of this mound was a small thicket, and just below it an artificial pond; on the other side a number of large and small rocks of different kinds, collected from different parts of the world and represented in the rude state in which they are generally found. At the foot of the mound were holes dug and earth thrown up, to show the different kinds of clay, ochre, coal, marl, etc., which he had collected from different parts; also, various ores and minerals. Around the pond was a beach, on which was exhibited an assortment of shells of different kinds, turtles, frogs, toads, lizards, water snakes, etc. In the pond was a collection of fish with their skins stuffed, waterfowls, such as the different species of geese, ducks, cranes, herons, etc.; all having the appearance of life, for their skins were admirably preserved. On the mound were those birds which commonly walk the ground, as the partridge, quail, heath hen, etc.; also, different kinds of wild animals—bear, deer, leopard, tiger, wildcat, fox, raccoon, rabbit, squirrel, etc. In the thicket and among the rocks, land snakes, rattlesnakes of an enormous size, black, glass, striped and a number of other snakes. The boughs of the trees were loaded with birds, some of almost every species in America and many exotics. What heightened the view of this singular collection was that they were all real, either their substance or their skins finely preserved. Mr. Peale's animals reminded me of Noah's Ark but I can hardly conceive that even Noah could have boasted a better collection.

Most of the specimens were preserved and mounted by Peale himself, who, with his usual skill and enthusiasm, had taught himself the art of taxidermy. One of his first subjects was Benjamin Franklin's deceased Angora cat, but

Peale botched the job and Ben's pet never appeared in the museum. George Washington's pheasants did. Learning that some exotic foreign game birds had been sent to Mount Vernon, Peale asked the general to let him have any that might be so unfortunate as to die. Washington replied with the quiet wit he so often showed in his private letters: "I cannot say that I shall be happy to have it in my power to comply with your request by sending you the bodies of my pheasants; but I am afraid it will not be long before they will compose a part of your museum as they all appear to be drooping." A few weeks later, there was another letter from Mount Vernon: "Sir, you will receive by the stage the body of my gold pheasant packed in wool. He made his exit yesterday, which enables me to comply with your request sooner than I wished to do. I am afraid the others will follow him but too soon."

Year by year, Peale added specimens, soliciting them at home and abroad, going out and gathering specimens for himself. Though the institution, which he called the American Museum but everybody else called Peale's Museum, was a steady attraction at twenty-five cents admission, he still relied on painting for income. When he went south to do some portraits, he came back with a batch of baby vipers given him by the French consul at Baltimore, on whom he had called to discuss the latest volumes in Buffon's *Histoire Naturelle*.

He soon made another trip south, this time for a different purpose. Rachel, his faithful spouse of almost thirty years, had died, leaving him at the age of forty-nine with four sons and three daughters, all named for famous artists: Raphaelle, Rembrandt, Titian, Rubens, Angelica, Sophanisba and Rosalba. Peale went to Maryland to find another wife, and though he came back without a bride, he did bring a prize for his museum—a five-legged cow with six feet and two tails.

One day at the museum, he was introduced to a young visitor, Elizabeth De Peyster. He gave her a piece of coral and a good deal of attention. A few weeks later, she agreed to marry him and preside over his brood of children, his turbulent home and his impromptu zoo, which by now included a caged rattlesnake, a bear chained in the front yard and the five-legged cow, which, notwithstanding her aberration, provided milk for the family. Three years later, Peale showed how much his interests had changed from art to science by the name he gave his newborn son: Charles Linnaeus Peale.

Peale had become a devoted Linnaean, scrupulously using the Linnaean system in arranging the sequence and juxtaposition of his exhibits. His untutored public may have found this edifying, but they were more impressed by the way he presented his stuffed animals, putting them in dramatic but not dishonest attitudes against backgrounds full of recognizable details. Accompanying them were clear and vivid explanations enlivened by homely facts and anecdotes. The whole effect was to entertain and teach at the same time.

As he educated the rest of America, Peale educated himself. Moving into the international circle of naturalists, all changed from the days of Colden and Collinson, he corresponded with Buffon and with Sir Joseph Banks, sponsor of Captain Cook's famous expeditions. A London dealer named Hall, on the lookout for showpieces for the ambitious American museum-keeper, sent a mixed-up Australian mammal he called the duck-billed platypus. At home, Peale enlisted the cooperation and the reputations of David Rittenhouse, the famous astronomer, who had been his comrade on Revolutionary battlefields; Miers Fisher, a wealthy lawyer who was to be useful to the two great ornithologists, Alexander Wilson and John James Audubon; Dr. Caspar Wistar, who helped straighten Jefferson out on his Megalonyx. William Bartram was an ever-helpful friend and source of specimens. When Peale proposed that his museum become a national institution, Thomas Jefferson and Alexander Hamilton took turns presiding over meetings to consider ways of getting public funds. Nothing came of this scheme.

Through his own energies and the enthusiasm of contributors, Peale found himself so crowded in his studio quarters that he had to move. The American Philosophical Society was honored to let him use its new quarters as both his home and his museum. Never one to miss a showman's chance, Peale mustered the neighborhood boys to move the museum's possessions. As he described it (using the third person), they formed a procession: "at the head was carried the American buffalo, then followed the panthers, tyger catts and a long string of animals of smaller size. The parade brought all the inhabitants to their doors and windows to see the cavalcade. It was fine fun for the boys and Peale saved some of the expense. He lost only one article, a young alligator."

The museum and its proprietor prospered in the new home, which was heated by a stove of Peale's own invention. Peale profited immensely by the assistance of a learned Frenchman, Baron Ambrose Marie François Palisot de Beauvois, who was possibly the world's unluckiest naturalist. As a young man, the baron went to Africa to do field work in tropical botany. On the voyage down, two hundred and fifty of the three hundred people aboard died, and after he had laboriously made a collection of plants in Guinea, the British sacked the colony and burned all his specimens. Sent off on a slave ship to Haiti, he started all over again, making another large botanical collection. It was destroyed in a slave rebellion and de Beauvois barely managed to get aboard a ship going to the United States. On the way, the vessel was stopped by the British, who stripped the hapless refugee of his few remaining possessions. When he reached Philadelphia in 1793, he learned that the revolutionary regime in France had condemned him as an aristocrat and would not let him come home.

A man of enormous patience and fortitude, who kept saying "never mind," de Beauvois settled in Philadelphia and made a living by teaching French and playing the bassoon in local bands—there were plenty of patriotic parades in the new capital and bands were kept busy. They lost their bassoonist, however, when Peale hired him for his museum. There the Frenchman worked at classifying the exhibits, while doggedly starting on still another botanical collection. Traveling down to the Carolinas, he met his countryman André Michaux. By the time he got permission to go back to France, he had made a third major collection, and sailed off with it. Fate still had a baleful eye on him. A fierce storm sank his ship and, with it, his American collection. He himself made it to shore and to Paris, where he settled at last into an uneventful life.

With de Beauvois's help, Peale issued a "scientific and descriptive catalogue" of the museum. After a little discourse on the Linnaean method, it took up the animal displays. The mandrill had been "fond of being caressed" when he was alive and had "died of cold though kept in a cellar with plenty of hay." The coaita monkey caught fish with its tail, which was so strong that it could break oyster shells with a blow. The sloth moved slowly, "crying in the night," and dogs that ate its entrails died.

The exhibits went on—stuffed and living sea lions, barbet dogs, red and gray foxes, Mexican cats, a cougar, a margay, civet cats, a mongoose, coatimundi, ermine, black bears and a Madagascar jackal whose cries disturbed the whole neighborhood at night. There was a raccoon which was very playful but hated children and a hyena that tolerated women but snarled at men. An English traveler named Henry Wansey, who had been impressed by a two-headed snake at Yale, was overwhelmed by the three-headed snake at Peale's.

In 1801, Peale learned that a farmer not far from Cadwallader Colden's old estate at Coldengham had plowed up a cache of ancient bones. Rushing to see for himself, Peale identified them as mammoth bones, and knew he had to have them for his museum. The farmer knew it, too. For giving Peale the right to dig for more of the beast, he demanded three hundred dollars in cash, plus city-made gowns for his daughters and a gun for his son. Peale turned for help to the American Philosophical Society, which advanced five hundred dollars, and to President Jefferson, who ordered the War Department to lend Peale some pumps and tents. Thus equipped, Peale set out on the country's first organized paleontological dig.

At the site he dug a huge pit, and when water seeped in faster than pumps could pull it out, he built an endless bucket-chain strung to a 20-foot-high wooden wheel inside which three men walked, like squirrels running in a cage, to turn the wheel and keep the buckets filling and emptying. Sightseers caused traffic jams on the country lanes, and when a bone came up, said a Peale

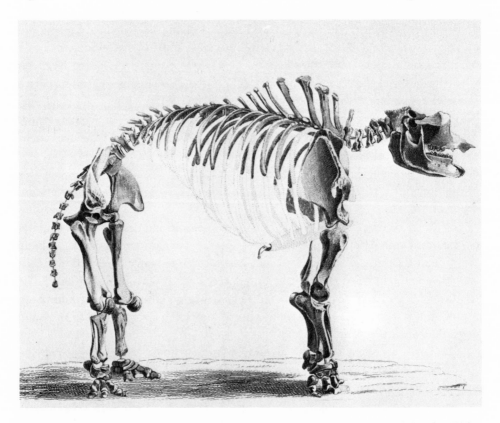

The components of this mastodon's skeleton were carefully drawn and labeled by Titian Peale. It was 15 feet long (not counting the 11-foot tusks or tail), 11 feet tall and almost 6 feet across the chest.

report, "the unconscious woods echoed with repeated huzzahs which would not have been more animated if every tree had participated in the joy. Gracious God, what a jaw! How many animals have been crushed between it?" And how disappointed they would have been to know that the huge herbivore had never crushed anything more than grass or tree branches between its outsize teeth. Some privileged sightseers were permitted to get inside the wheel and keep it moving. This flattered them while sparing Peale's men, who, finding the work tedious, the water cold and the mud unbearable, were kept going only by high pay and frequent cups of rum. Five months of work in the area unearthed three nearly complete skeletons. It cost a thousand dollars, far more than the budget, but such an unprecedented haul was worth it.

Now came the complex job of fitting the bones into a complete mammoth. (It was, to be precise, a mastodon, which differs slightly from a mammoth.) Nobody had ever put one together before, and Peale and his helpers found that, as in a jigsaw puzzle, what fitted together most easily almost always proved wrong. The ablest reconstructor turned out to be Peale's Negro man of all work, Moses Williams, who, with no preconceived paleontological ideas, fitted the most improbable joints and found they belonged. Finally the rebuilt mammoth, eleven feet high and thirty feet long from the tip of its 11-foot tusks to the end of its bony tail, was installed in the Mammoth Room, where on Christmas Eve in 1801, the public pushed in, paying fifty cents admission to see "The Ninth Wonder of the World."

A second skeleton, assembled from leftover pieces, was introduced with a gala dinner held virtually inside the skeleton. A table for thirteen was set up beneath the rib cage, with a grand piano alongside. At the meal, the fossil was given a patriotic toast: "The American people, may they be as preeminent among the nations of the earth as the canopy we sit beneath surpasses the fabric of the mouse." At which the pianist broke into "Yankee Doodle."

The patriotism was not misplaced. Peale's mammoth was as much a triumph for the American people as it was for science. No other country had ever produced such a stupendous native. No other people had the wit and ingenuity to re-create it. Not even the Megatherium-Megalonyx could match Peale's mammoth. How could the followers of Buffon and de Pauw dismiss this overwhelming fact of nature? It was even more convincing than Jefferson's moose. And when Peale sent his second skeleton on a tour of Europe, Georges Cuvier noted with envy that America owned the only two mammoths in the world.

For Peale, as for so many other Americans, natural science was a patriotic endeavor, offering testimony to the greatness of his country and its inherent superiority over all others. The new republic was beginning to enjoy a cultural euphoria and naturalists were leading the way. What was American was, just because of that, wonderful: to be studied, admired and proclaimed. Peale's hope, he told Jefferson, was to make the museum "an honor to my country." "Such a museum," he declared, "easy of access, must tend to make all classes of people in some degree learned in the science of nature without even the trouble of study. Whether a diffused knowledge of this kind may tend to mend their morals is a question of some import. Furnishing the idle and dissipated with a great and new source of amusement ought to divert them from frivolous and pernicious entertainments." Here Peale was not only anticipating the American impulse for easy-to-come-by education but also the missionary belief, which sprouted later in the lyceums and the Chautauqua meetings, that popular educational projects would improve people both spiritually and materially. As Peale's indispensable biographer (and descendant) Charles Coleman Sellers explains, Peale lived in an age of vast changes and "expected to see mankind's emergence into an era utterly new." The key to it was "Nature, opening new ranges of beauty and understanding, length of days and joy in life."

A true disciple of the Enlightenment, Peale made himself the first significant American popularizer, capitalizing on the Americans' innate curiosity about how things worked, as well as their close feeling for nature. His museum grabbed the sightseer's attention. The skins of its animals were stretched realistically over wooden limbs carved to imitate the swell and stretch of muscles. A llama, one visitor reported, was shown "in the act of spitting through the fissure of his upper lip." Snakes were caught gulping toads "with the hindquarters projecting from the mouth" or "charming a stuffed bird with its beady eyes." A wolf "with bloody fangs" was dismembering a lamb "whose innards looked as though they had that instant been torn out of the body, and the blood besmeared upon the whole body seemed yet warm." Comic relief lightened the gruesome realism. Monkeys dressed up as people were "a subject of much amusement to the country people, particularly those human-looking animals who dressed in clothes sitting on stools engaged at shoemaking."

By 1802, Peale had amassed 1,800 different kinds of birds, 250 quadrupeds, 150 reptiles, hundreds of fishes and thousands of insects. Needing more room, he moved once again. So great was the museum's prestige that the Pennsylvania legislature invited him to occupy the State House, giving him, rent-free, not only the upper floors and the Tower Room but also the hallowed chamber in which the Declaration of Independence had been signed.

In its new quarters the museum became an even greater attraction. Outside, two bear cubs sent from the West by Colonel Pike romped engagingly—and when they grew old and too fierce, they were stuffed and set up inside. In the Quadruped Room, specimens of antelope and bighorn brought back by Lewis and Clark shared the stage with the faithful old five-legged cow which, having succumbed to old age, still served in death by offering her stuffed udders to a two-legged calf. In the Long Room, above glass cases of natural objects ranged in good Linnaean order, hung portraits of famous Americans almost all painted by the proprietor.

Visitors to the museum wrote many accounts of the experience, none more charming than the one set down by a Moravian sister named Catherine Fritsch, who journeyed to Philadelphia from Lititz, Lancaster County:

> When Renata and I, dressed for traveling, came out of the Sisters' House, at 4 o'clock in the morning of May 29th, 1810, the robins in the square were singing gaily—happy, as we were, too. Christel's stage drove up with the rest of our party inside. In high spirits we rode away. We

sang a few verses with an accompaniment of trombones—Polly B. and her father having a cunning knack of imitating those instruments by putting a leaf between their lips. We came to a succession of high and steep hills, and so, Polly B. and Magdelene G., also "Mother" Muecke, alighted to ease the load by walking. I was heartily sorry that because of a swollen foot I could not walk with them.

Continuing our journey, a never-to-be-forgotten view burst upon us; for there, not far away—O, happy surprise—lay the splendid city of Philadelphia! After we had rested awhile, "Mama" B. proposed a walk to the river, my only worry about it being how was I to get on my shoe? "Ach," said "Mama" B, "just stick your toes into it and *schlap* along as best you can!" We went down Chestnut Street to visit what of all city sights I most wished to see: namely Peale's Museum. Having come to the State House where the museum is located, we passed through it and into a fine square. Two great bears amused us exceedingly by their clumsy play, or as they drew from the recesses of their den vegetables—mostly asparagus—and ate them. On the top of the bears' house two parrots, apparently quite contented, chatted together; in the next cage an eagle sat right majestically on his perch—above his head a placard with this petition on it: "Feed me daily for 100 years"; and next to it there was a monkey, who kindly showed us his whole assortment of funny capers and wonderful springs.

Over the lower door leading to the museum we observed this good advice: *Whoso would learn Wisdom, let him enter here!* At the foot of the stairway each of us paid 1/4 dollar, and on the second floor we were shown into a large hall which was filled entirely with animals, finely mounted and in natural positions. In this room was located the Oracle— a lion's head; had I talked into it I should have fancied myself a priestess of a heathen temple; but we knew not where the sound outlet was, and it was only after we had gone through the three rooms that I discovered it. Then Mr. Steinman at the lion's head and Christel at the other end of the tube, quite a distance apart, talked together; but the novelty of it caused them, and us, to laugh so immoderately that they could hardly ask or reply to any questions.

I went about the rooms with my spectacles on under my bonnet, so that I could read the finely written labels. Here we could observe abundant instance of the wisdom of God in His creation, as we viewed, with astonishment, the many different animals, birds and fish, and the infinite variety of exquisite butterflies and insects.

All this time I was looking forward to seeing the mammoth. A gentleman told us that he had seen it and had to pay 1/2 dollar for the privilege. All the party, but myself, declared that the price was entirely too high —a quarter they would give willingly, but not a cent more! I was keenly disappointed yet did not wish to go in alone and be there among strangers. Just to content me, Christel went to the doorkeeper and asked him whether, as we were a large company, there might be a reduction in the charge for us—but he would not grant it; only he led us to some old bones that we had already seen! I had not the happiness to meet Mr. Peale. Don't laugh! there's no danger—I shall not set my cap for him, even if he is a widower.

Catherine was making a standard joke about Peale's repeated searches for a wife. When his second wife died, in 1804, he spent a year looking for a third and in 1805, in his middle sixties, married a Quaker lady named Hannah Moore. He now had ten children from his two marriages. From their earliest years, the children had been involved in their father's enterprises and acquired considerable versatility in switching from carpentering showcases to stuffing snakes to building backgrounds to keeping the museum's account books. The Peale home sounded with the banging of hammers, the squawks of caged birds, the sound of Rembrandt's flute.

Raphaelle, the eldest son, became an accomplished painter on his own, doing perhaps the best still-lifes in America in his time and showing a devilish skill at trompe-l'oeil scenes. On the wall of the museum, he painted a likeness of the catalog so realistic that visitors would reach to take it down and read it. Warm, engaging, full of jokes, Raphaelle was an adept ventriloquist. Walking innocently about the museum, he would make the stuffed animals talk to spectators, and at Thanksgiving dinner the turkeys he carved would beg for their lives and cry as the knife cut in.

When, in 1794, the elder Peale declared that he was giving up painting for natural science, he passed his portrait business on to Raphaelle and Rembrandt. Rembrandt was more diligent, and gradually took over as the family's working portraitist. In 1795, when he was seventeen, his father got him a commission to portray President Washington. While the President sat for Rembrandt, Charles Willson stayed to keep an eye on things, and did a little portrait himself to occupy the time. As a matter of fact, four Peales in all took advantage of Rembrandt's sitting. Charles's brother James worked on a portrait sketch to be carved in ivory and Raphaelle did a profile. Gilbert Stuart, in town doing one of his many likenesses of Washingon, heard of the ensemble and warned Mrs. Washington to be careful lest her husband be "pealed all around."

Rembrandt went on to do very well as a painter, especially with a huge allegory called "The Court of Death," which in a year's tour of Europe and America netted the artist nine thousand dollars.

For many years, his younger brother Rubens managed the museum for his father, building up the museum's collection of minerals and installing elaborate electrical demonstrations.

The child who inherited Peale's bent for mechanics was the youngest son, born in 1795 and at first named Aldrovandi, after an Italian naturalist and museum-keeper. A few months later, Peale showed up at a meeting of the American Philosophical Society and introduced an item that was not on the agenda. "Mr. Peale," read the minutes of the meeting of February 19, 1796, "presented to the Society a young son of four months and four days old, being the first child born in the Philosophical Hall, and requested that the Society would give him a name. On which the Society unanimously agreed that, after the name of the chief founder and late president of the Society, he should be called Franklin." When he grew up, Franklin Peale devised a cotton mill which produced superb yarn but could not compete with cheap foreign cottons. He later helped Matthias Baldwin, a friend, build Old Ironsides, one of the earliest American locomotives, and wound up as chief coiner of the United States Mint.

The naturalist among the sons was Titian Ramsay Peale, who became a prominent member of Philadelphia's natural history community. There was a new generation of naturalists now, and its members had in Peale's museum an advantage their predecessors did not have: a reliable and well-kept source of specimens and data. Peale kept up the museum's integrity, maintaining detailed records of its contents, exchanging data with museums in Europe, constantly adding new specimens. As the prestige of the museum rose, so did its popularity. By 1810, it was grossing more than eight thousand dollars a year. Wearying of the work it involved, Peale handed the museum over to Rubens in return for a guaranteed income of four thousand dollars a year.

In the summer of 1811, Peale received a letter from an old friend, now retired to Monticello. "It is long, my dear sir, since we have exchanged a letter," Thomas Jefferson wrote.

> I shall be anxious to know that you are well and happy. I have heard that you have retired from the city to a farm. Does not the museum suffer? And is the farm as interesting? I have often thought that if heaven had given me a choice of my position and calling it should have been on a rich spot of earth well-watered and near a good market for the productions of the garden. But though an old man, I am but a young gardener. Think of me sometimes when you have your pen in hand.

Peale's pen came promptly to hand and he sent a rambling reply describing his new life. He had bought a large farm near Germantown, which he called Farm Persevere. (He later changed the name to the less bleak Belfield.) Here he labored happily, contour-plowing the land by a method prescribed by Jefferson, mechanizing his chores by use of his own millstream contraptions, careening about the farm at twelve miles an hour on his "fast walking machine," a primitive bicycle without pedals, throwing all his energies and enthusiasms into agriculture. Jefferson, reading Peale's account, worried to his 70-year-old friend that "zeal and age" would bring him down.

Four years on the farm were enough for Peale. In 1815, he resumed work at the museum and in 1822 took it over for the next few years. As imitators sprang up in several cities, Peale's establishment became less and less a unique wonder. Though Peale still kept to his scientific purpose, he was forced to offer popular entertainment—on one occasion hiring an Italian musician named Signor Hellene, who played simultaneously the viola, drums, cymbals, pipes and Chinese bells.

Charles Willson Peale was now eighty, so much a permanent part of Philadelphia that he was looked on patronizingly as "old Mr. Peale," a relic like those in his glassed cabinets. Turning back to portraiture, he went to Washington and was welcomed with warmth and deference by the men who now ran the republic. President James Monroe, John Quincy Adams, Andrew Jackson, John Calhoun all gladly sat for the man who had known and painted the founding fathers. But his hometown ignored Peale, snubbing him cruelly on the great occasion in 1824 when Lafayette made his triumphal return to America. Riding through jubilant throngs, the marquis came to Independence Hall and went inside to pay homage to that landmark of liberty. There standing on the stairs, shut out of the festivities, stood Peale.

It was more like a sentimental story than a piece of history. Rushing over, Lafayette embraced and kissed his comrade of Valley Forge and the Revolution. Unwilling to let him go, he pulled Peale along to stand beside him during the welcoming speeches and the endless lines of handshakers. With all that over, the two went off to Peale's gallery to look at the portraits of the legends who had been their friends and exclaim over a drawing Peale had made of Lafayette when the marquis was nineteen. Later, inviting Lafayette to come to see his museum, Peale set down a sparse but complete history of his project. "A few mammoth bones gave me the idea of forming a musuem, begun in 1784," he wrote. "This object has had my unceasing labors for many years and," he added in an understatement that could not hide his pride, "is now in high estimation with the lovers of natural history."

$\mathcal{A}$ PEDDLER OF BIRDS

❦ ❦ ❦ ❦ ❦ ONE MAY MORNING IN 1802, WHEN THE BIRD MIGRANTS WERE flying over Pennsylvania, Charles Willson Peale and his son Rubens were out hunting specimens for their museum in the woods near Bartram's Gardens, using, Rubens noted in a journal, "the finest mustard-seed shot" so as to do the birds as little injury as possible. The father went off while his son remained beside a spring "taking a breakfast of smoked herring and bread." He stopped eating when he spied a flower new to him, a double anemone. After marking it carefully with some twigs, he went back to his smoked herring. He was interrupted again, this time by a lanky, glowering man who stared at the birds the Peales had shot and, in bitter tones, declared that one of the victims was a cardinal he knew well: it would come and sing at his window every morning. Peale, more surprised than sorry, explained what he was doing and the conversation grew more amiable.

"His name," Peale wrote, "was Alexander Wilson. He taught school in a small log cabin near Darby Road." Wilson had taken the job only that February, it turned out, but already knew the woodlands and its birds. Rubens finally had to move off. He was to meet his father at the Bartram house and induced Wilson to come along. There they found William Bartram at breakfast with the elder Peale. As they sat, William's younger brother John came in with delight in his eyes and a flower in his hand. Walking through the woods, he had noticed a small pile of twigs and right next to them a rare double anemone. Rubens listened as the botanical brothers exclaimed over the find but tactfully did not claim it. John grew the flower in the garden and later gave Rubens one of the offspring.

In the room that morning, past and future generations of American naturalists were firmly joined—that of Colden, John Bartram and Garden, whom William knew, to that of the nineteenth-century ornithologists whom the schoolteacher Wilson was to lead. In Bartram and Peale, Wilson found two men who were to help him crucially in his short and astonishing career as the first complete student and painter of American birds, a role for which he had no training as a scientist and no practice as a painter.

It seems necessary in these accounts of America's first naturalists to stop abruptly and try to explain how a politician, an unlettered farmer, a soldier all turned into significant naturalists. How did a schoolteacher, who had been a peddler and wrote poetry, become a major ornithologist? Possibly because, like the fairy-tale sleeping princess smitten by the first creature she saw on awakening, Alexander Wilson fell in love with the first thing of beauty he saw in America—a woodpecker. As he walked away from the ship that had brought him into Delaware Bay, he came into a land that was—as it had been to so many before him—"a new world to us, filled with strange birds. I did not observe one such as those in Scotland, but all much richer in color." The first one he really noticed, and the most beautiful he had ever beheld, was a red-headed woodpecker. He shot it and was promptly distressed that he had. Years later he made amends by writing a fond description of the bird: "His tri-colored plumage, so striking—so excellent a connoisseur in fruit that wherever an apple or pear is found broached by him, it is sure to be among the ripest and best flavored. A gay and frolicsome disposition, diving and vociferating around the high dead limbs of some large tree, amusing the passenger with their gambols."

The birds of his homeland had never aroused such enthusiasm in Wilson, although they had all been familiar to him. He worked as a weaver in the town of Paisley, and his occupation had sent him on long walking tours over the moors and hills, peddling the cloth he wove. The peddler's life, as he pictured it, was a melancholy one. He wrote in one of his poems:

> His lonely way a meagre peddlar took,
> Deep were his frequent sighs, careless his pace
> And oft the tear stole down his cheerless face,
> Beneath a load of silk and sorrows bent.

All through his life Wilson had deep fits of feeling sorry for himself and being a peddler could not have been that doleful. Along with his wares, he carried a gun to shoot game for his dinner, a flute to solace him while he rested and books of poetry to read as he walked between farms. Although his schooling had stopped when he was apprenticed at the age of ten, he read avidly as he worked his loom and made his way through Milton and Pope. This was nothing exceptional. At the next loom a young friend of his read Vergil and did Latin conjugations so that he could become a schoolmaster. As

Wilson went across the moors selling his Paisley cloth to farmers' wives, he took side trips to browse around old castles, and once, watching some noble Scotsmen at the "game of golph," he concluded that it was "good exercise but dull sport." He took notice of all the happenings in nature and began to set down his feelings in stilted verse. After a while, along with his cloth, he was peddling a small book of poems he had written and published on his own.

It was the time of Robert Burns, and excitement over poetry had spread through Scotland. Wilson's book brought recognition from his fellow poets and went into a second printing. Wider popularity came when he wrote *Watty and Meg*, a comic dialect poem about a roistering husband who tamed his shrewish wife by threatening to enlist in the army. Printed and reprinted for half a century, *Watty and Meg* was compared to Burns's *Tam O'Shanter* and sometimes even attributed to Rab himself.

The reprints were all pirated and brought Wilson no money. Another poem, moreover, brought him serious trouble. In a short verse called "The Shark," Wilson angrily attacked a local millowner for cheating his workmen. Accused of libel and blackmail, he was thrown into jail, and settled his case only by publicly burning a copy of "The Shark" on the courthouse steps. In May, 1794, feeling oppressed and unwanted in his native land, Wilson, at the age of twenty-eight, set out for America on a ship so crowded that he and his nephew, whom he was taking with him, could find sleeping place only on deck.

Landing at New Castle, they walked to Philadelphia and settled finally in a Scottish colony on Pennypack Creek where they found jobs as weavers. A literate man among a largely unlettered people, Wilson was soon hired to teach school, first at Bustleton, and then at Milestown, closer to Philadelphia. To understand his pupils and their Pennsylvania Dutch parents, the new schoolmaster learned German. He studied mathematics and, to augment his pay, did surveys for the farmers. To satisfy his love for the birds of his new homeland, he was out whenever he could find time to watch them as, in flocks undreamed of in Scotland, they swarmed along the Atlantic flyways and filled the Pennsylvania woodlands. He shot them so he could study them, trapped and caged them so he could have them close at hand and, within a few months, came to know them far better than men who had been surrounded by them all their lives. "When we came to America," he later wrote, "we found ourselves with respect to the feathered tribes in a strange country where the manners, languages and faces were utterly unknown to us. Now we find ourselves among interesting and well-known neighbors and acquaintances, and in the notes of every songster, recognize the voice of an old friend and companion."

❦ ❦ ❦ ❦ ❦ THE SURROUNDING PRESENCE OF THE BIRDS ENTHRALLED HIM—
their sounds, habits, excited comings and goings. He would watch and listen to
the goldfinches "on their first arrival in February assembling in great numbers
on the same tree to bask and dress themselves in the morning sun, singing
in concert for half an hour together; the confused mingling of their notes forming a kind of harmony not at all unpleasant." He played games with a yellow-
breasted chat that began scolding every time he came near "in a great variety
of odd and uncouth monosyllables, which may be readily imitated so as to deceive
the bird itself and draw him after you for half a quarter of a mile, as I have sometimes amused myself in doing." He became, "as it were, acquainted" with one
thrush "whose notes I could instantly recognize on entering the woods. The
top of a large white oak was usually the favorite pinnacle from whence he
poured the sweetest melody; to which I had frequently listened till night began to
gather in the woods and the fireflies to sparkle among the branches."

In 1801, suddenly and inexplicably, Wilson left his teaching post and went to
New York, taking nothing with him but an overcoat and telling nobody what
he was about. A series of anguished letters to a friend hinted that he had had a
shameful love affair. A year later, he was back teaching again, this time at
Gray's Ferry where, on that May morning, he met Rubens Peale. "I gave
Mr. W an invitation to see the Museum," Rubens recalled, "and he came next
Saturday afternoon. I don't remember ever to have seen anyone as much delighted especially with the birds. We were ever after bosom friends to the
death." There were hundreds of specimens to study and the museum proprietor
to talk to. The elder Peale gave Wilson advice on how to draw birds and
may have given him a proper pen to use.

William Bartram, settled comfortably into the role of counselor to young
naturalists, befriended but did not press himself on the intense and solitary
Scotsman. He guided him through his library where Wilson was introduced to
the work of Catesby, Edwards, Buffon and Pennant. Studying Linnaeus, he
taught himself the methods of classifying. There were, Wilson soon discovered,
few reliable works on American birds. Even from his own brief observations, he
could find errors and omissions in the respected authorities. There was nothing
in America that could match the European tradition of ornithological scholarship,
which went back four centuries to Frederick II, the Hohenstaufen Holy Roman
Emperor, an imperial genius whose fondness for things Arabic led him to
acquire a harem (and be excommunicated by the Pope) and whose love of
music made him the patron of the minnesingers. Out of his own study of
falconry, Frederick produced a brilliant work on bird habits and anatomy that
became a model for later ornithologists. By the time New World birds began

coming to them, ornithology was a fairly substantial science in Europe and North American birds were quickly classified, though not always correctly. All sorts of misconceptions crept in. An American thrush, for example, was called a robin because its breast gave it a resemblance to Europe's robin redbreast, to which it is only distantly related.

Catesby's work provided Europeans with direct, accurate observations. A mixed bag of amateurs contributed further bits of information. Thomas Anburey, a British soldier who had fought under Burgoyne, made many interesting notes on American birds—but also burdened ornithology with a nagging myth: that if a young mockingbird were captured and caged, its parents would come and feed it poisoned berries, death being preferable to captivity. The adventurer Gilbert Imlay, whose liaison with Mary Wollstonecraft broke the heart of that pioneer feminist, wrote a *Topographical Description of the Western Territory of North America* in which he sensibly cataloged 111 American birds. The Frenchman Louis Jean Pierre Viellot, the finest of all eighteenth-century ornithologists working in America, studied the birds in Peale's Museum in the 1790s, and in his *Natural History of the Birds of America* published the most useful work available up to then. The best firsthand study of American birds had been done by William Bartram, and Wilson was lucky to have access to his notes and his knowledge.

Wilson was, as he described himself in his poem "The Solitary Tutor," a "strange recluse and solitary wight," who would go out into the woods near Bartram's Gardens to "a woody vale" where under a "mossy cliff beside a little grot" a pair of phoebes, year after year, built their nests. There, with the birds as company, he would read Milton, Goldsmith, Gibbon and "thro' Georgia's groves with gentle Bartram" stray, listening to the "wild choir of songsters" until evening when "homeward thro' the moonlight trees, the owl salutes him with her trem'lous sound."

There was nothing in what he did or the way he lived that betrayed his ambition. As he taught the stolid schoolchildren and instructed himself in nature, a grand scheme formed in his mind. He confided it to William Bartram in 1803: "I have had many pursuits, Mathematics, the German language, music, drawing, etc., and now I am about to make a collection of all our finest birds." The modest word "collection" barely suggested his real purpose: to make the first comprehensive study of all the birds of America and illustrate them with his own painting. He did not mention that he lacked every obvious qualification for the job. He could not draw or paint from nature; he had never studied bird anatomy or physiology; he had observed few living American birds save those that came flying past his home. The wonder is not only that he did what he set out to do but that, in the end, he did it so superbly.

Alexander Wilson sat for a revealing portrait by Rembrandt Peale. All the Peales were good friends of Wilson, and the senior Peale was his invaluable guide and counselor.

When he started drawing birds, Wilson kept a stuffed owl on his desk and doggedly practiced making likenesses of it. This was one of his better tries.

He brushed aside anyone who mentioned his shortcomings. "Now I don't want you to throw cold water, as Shakespeare says, on this notion, Quixotic as it may appear," he wrote a friend. "I have been so long accustomed to the building of airy castles and brain windmills that it has become one of my earthly comforts, a sort of rough bone that amuses me when sated with the dull drudgery of life."

The man to whom Wilson wrote this was another Scottish expatriate, Alexander Lawson. He had left Scotland to join the revolution in France, but since he could not sail directly to that enemy land, he chose to go by way of America, where he decided to stay. Hard-working and firm-minded, Lawson became the finest engraver in Philadelphia. Wilson fought off his first friendly advances but, after a while, became a frequent visitor at Lawson's home, where the city's younger intellectuals gathered. Lawson was dubious about the ornithology project but this did not deter Wilson. He soon was sending drawings to Bartram, "hoping that your good nature will excuse their deficiences while you point them out to me. They were chiefly colored by candle-light."

How did Wilson learn to draw birds, knowing nothing to begin with? Simply by trying and discarding, trying again and complaining about himself, asking and taking the advice of others, among them Bartram's niece Ann, who had a deft hand with pen and paints. He kept a stuffed owl on his desk as a model and drew it over and over again. The first likeness was ludicrous—"The face of an owl and the back of a lark have put me to a nonplus," he groaned. Though he would not surrender his ambition, he sometimes wondered at it.

> While others are hoarding up their bags of money, without the power of enjoying it [he wrote Bartram], I am collecting, without injuring my conscience, or wounding my peace of mind, those beautiful specimens of Nature's works that are forever pleasing. I have had live crows, hawks, and owls—opossums, squirrels, snakes, lizards, etc., so that my room has sometimes reminded me of Noah's ark; but Noah had a wife in one corner of it, and in this particular our parallel does not altogether tally.

One of his pupils brought him a mouse, and while he was drawing it, he said, the

> pantings of its little heart showed it to be in the most extreme agonies of fear. I had intended to kill it, in order to fix it in the claws of a stuffed owl, but happening to spill a few drops of water near where it was tied, it lapped it up with such eagerness and looked in my face with such an eye of supplicating terror, as perfectly overcame me. I immediately untied it, and restored it to life and liberty. The agonies of the prisoner at the stake, while the fire and instruments of torment are preparing, could not be more severe than the sufferings of that poor mouse; and, insignificant as the object was, I felt at that moment the sweet sensations that mercy leaves on the mind when she triumphs over cruelty. My dear friend, you see I take the liberty of an old acquaintance with you, in thus trifling with your time. You have already raised me out of the slough of despond.

Again and again he thanked Bartram for lifting him from his fits of despondency, and a deepening attachment to his friend comes through in a poem "The Rural Walk."

> In Bartram's green emblossomed bowers . . .
> The genius of this charming scene
> From early dawn till close of day
> Still busy here and there is seen

> To plant, remove or prune . . .
> But well to him they are all known,
> Their names, their characters and race.
> Their virtues when each bloom is gone
> Their favorite home, their native place.

The poem was published in the most eminent literary magazine of the day, the *Port Folio*. In the midst of all his other occupations, Wilson had returned to his original art, poetry, and found a ready audience. The burgeoning culture of the day encouraged newcomers, and if he had cared to, Wilson could have become one of the country's most active literary figures. But he held off, keeping mostly to his ornithology.

In the fall of 1804—he had been in the country for barely a decade—he went on the first of his long American journeys. It took him over the same general territory that John Bartram had covered with Weiser and Shickellamy sixty years before—from Philadelphia, up to the Great Lakes and Niagara Falls. Wilson had two purposes. The first was to spend some time with his nephew, whom he had installed on a farm in upstate New York. The second, and of deeper importance, was to test his ability to travel through wild country. He started out when, as he described it in verse,

> The sultry heats of summer's sun were o'er,
> The corn stood topped . . .
> And driving clouds of blackbirds wheeled around.

After traveling for twelve hundred miles, mostly on foot, "through almost un-inhabited forests, over stupendous mountains and down dangerous rivers," he walked home over winter-hardened roads. The trip produced Wilson's laborious attempt at an epic poem, *The Foresters*, whose two thousand lines plod on in a succession of heroic couplets and dogged rhymes relieved by brief flashes of eloquence ("mountains headlong over mountains thrown"); by some wrathful descriptions of the dreadful lodgings on the roads (at "Pat Dougherty's Hotel and drygoods store . . . man and beast with equal honors meet"): by some startling celebrations of the life of professional hunters feasting on their kill ("while piles of bones like polished ivory rise") and an almost gloating description of the scores of birds taken ("ducks, plover, teal, the dying and the dead . . . cranes, storks, snipes . . . splendid summer ducks and divers wild").

The trip proved to Wilson that he could successfully make the difficult kind of journey necessary for his ornithology. "With no family to enchain my affections," he wrote Bartram, "no ties but those of friendship, and the most ardent love of my adopted country; with a constitution which hardens amidst fatigues, and a disposition sociable and open, which can find itself at home by an Indian fire in the depth of the woods, as well as in the best apartment of the civilized world, I have at present a real design of becoming a traveller."

He had come home with a strange bird, a kind of jay unknown in Pennsylvania—his first new species, he thought. He had it stuffed for Peale's Museum, and sent a drawing of it, along with some others he had made, as a kind of inauguration present to President Jefferson, who was just starting his second term. Wilson enormously admired Jefferson and his democratic principles. In fact, a patriotic speech he had been asked to make, as schoolmaster, for a local celebration of Jefferson's first inaugural had been widely reprinted in pro-Jefferson newspapers. The President thanked Wilson for "the elegant drawings," and asked him to solve the mystery of a bird whose identity had long puzzled him. It was, Jefferson said,

> to be found or rather heard in every part of America and yet scarcely ever to be seen. It is in all the forests from spring to fall and never but on the tops of the tallest trees from which it perpetually serenades us with some of the sweetest notes and as clear as those of the nightingale. I have followed it for miles without ever but once getting a good view of it. It is of the size and make of the mockingbird, lightly thrush-colored on the back and a greyish white on the breast and belly.

Back from a trip north, Wilson wrote President Jefferson that he had discovered a rare new species of jay. He was disappointed when it turned out to be the common Canada jay.

Flattered by Jefferson's commission, Wilson set out to identify the bird. But in both his own discovery and Jefferson's he was disappointed. His new jay turned out to be the Canada jay, seldom seen as far south as Philadelphia but common to the North. Ornithological data was so sparse and scattered that even as informed a naturalist as William Bartram did not know it. As for Jefferson's unseen singer, Wilson concluded that it was the wood thrush. "It seems strange," Wilson wrote Bartram, "that the President should represent it as so hard to be seen." Tactfully, he did not say this to Jefferson, though years later he reprinted the President's letter in his *American Ornithology*.

Settled at home, Wilson patiently drew and practiced, drew and discarded, drew and corrected. He went out watching birds, shooting and trapping them, bringing skins home to draw, keeping tame birds in his room as his models. His drawings took on life and natural form and his ambition grew firmer: to publish his birds in a 10-volume set, for which he would charge $120. But how many Americans would pay that much to see birds they already knew, painted by a schoolteacher they never heard of?

Wilson ignored this question. By the summer of 1805, he had twenty-eight drawings he thought good enough to show as finished work to Bartram—"they may yet tell posterity that I was honored with your friendship and that to your inspiration they owe their existence." To keep costs down, he tried his own hand at engraving plates. The indulgent Lawson lent him tools, and two days later the novice rushed into the shop with his first attempt, demanding a proof at once. It could be better, he admitted, looking at the result, but he persisted.

At the beginning of 1806, less than three years after he had made his first dismaying drawings of the owl that looked like a lark, Wilson described his progress to his eminent correspondent Jefferson: "Upwards of one hundred drawings are completed; and two plates in folio already engraved." But he had a further purpose in writing the President. He needed specimens of western birds and "faithful representations of them can only be taken from living nature or from birds newly killed." The President, he had learned, was sending an expedition to the Red and Arkansas rivers. Could Wilson go along as a naturalist? He never received an answer (it is not clear why Jefferson never replied) and he put off any western travel plans.

Leaving his teaching job, he became editor of a new American edition of Rees's *Cyclopaedia*, published by Samuel Bradford, whose great-grandfather had hired Benjamin Franklin when that roll-munching young man first came to Philadelphia. Wilson was paid a generous nine hundred dollars a year, and given time to work on his own. Bradford, soon to become the biggest book publisher in the country, also undertook to publish the *Ornithology*.

Living in Philadelphia, Wilson edited by day, drew by night, went off into the country on Sundays to find birds he lacked. In the spring of 1807, a prospectus of his proposed work was sent out to twenty-five hundred potential subscribers, a large list for those days. They were offered ten volumes or folios, each of twelve color plates, with several different birds depicted on each plate. The complete set would be issued over a period of years and only subscriptions to the whole set would be accepted. Nothing so ambitious or expensive had ever been tried in America. Bradford and Wilson agreed that Volume I would be printed when two hundred subscriptions came in.

Encouragement came unexpectedly from the country's newest hero. Meriwether Lewis, who had met Wilson when he was in Philadelphia studying up on natural science for his expedition, had returned with skins of new western birds. He gave them to Wilson. At "the request and particular wish of Captain Lewis made to me in person," wrote Wilson proudly, he drew several of the birds, naming the woodpecker after Lewis and the nutcracker after Clark. It was a coup for Wilson to report on these discoveries. Lewis's endorsement gave Wilson invaluable recognition and prestige. And it confirmed his own faith in himself and his project.

While he waited anxiously for subscribers to respond, Wilson faced production problems. The engravings, done mostly by Lawson, had to be colored by hand. The color had to be clear and true but not so strong as to obscure the lines of the engraving. Wilson hired professional artists to help him, including the well-known Alexander Rider, but got uneven results. Talented young ladies were enlisted but had to be carefully supervised. Wilson found no one who could do it as well as he himself could until, by a stroke of luck, he met Charles Robert Leslie, an apprentice clerk in Bradford's bookstore who haunted the exhibits at Peale's Museum and loved to paint. He proved an even better colorist than Wilson, able to look at the bird skins and match the color subtly and exactly. He was impressed by Wilson. "I remember the extreme accuracy of his drawings," Leslie later recalled, "and how carefully he counted the number of scales on the tiny legs and feet of his subject." The youth was too talented to keep. After three years, Wilson and some friends bought up his apprenticeship and sent Leslie to England where, after working under Benjamin West, he became a leading artist of the early-Victorian era, painter to the Queen and author of a widely used instruction book on painting.

The response to the prospectus was good in Philadelphia. Elsewhere, subscriptions came in slowly. Wilson made a quick trip to solicit them in New York and Albany. Albany produced no subscribers but in New York, Robert Fulton, busy with the trials of the *Clermont*, signed up. Disconsolate, Wilson returned to Philadelphia and was cheered by a subscription and a note that the subscriber "salutes Mr. Wilson with great respect, [signed] Thomas Jefferson."

The *American Ornithology* was to be not a simple picture book, but a scientific study. Wilson set himself to write a suitable text. Just as his drawings, in their accuracy and vividness, were to be like nothing Americans had ever seen before, so his life histories were, in their lively style and homely detail, like nothing they had ever read before. The admiring twentieth-century critic Van Wyck Brooks once said that "there was no living American novelist who could make people as real as Alexander Wilson made his birds."

The first bird in Volume I was the blue jay. Wilson's essay is precise and engaging.

> This elegant bird, which, as far as I can learn, is peculiar to North America, is distinguished as a kind of beau among the feathered tenants of our woods, by the brilliancy of his dress; and, like most other coxcombs, makes himself still more conspicuous by his loquacity, and the oddness of his tones and gestures. The jay measures eleven inches in length; the head is ornamented with a crest of light blue or purple feathers, which he can elevate or depress at pleasure; a narrow line of black runs along the frontlet, rising on each side higher than the eye.
>
> The blue jay is an almost universal inhabitant of the woods, frequenting the thickest settlements as well as the deepest recesses of the forest. He appears to be among his fellow musicians what the trumpeter is in a band, some of his notes having no distant resemblance to the tones of that instrument. These he has the faculty of changing through a great variety of modulations, according to the particular humor he happens to be in. When disposed for ridicule, there is scarce a bird whose peculiarities of song he cannot tune his notes to. When engaged in the blandishments of love, they resemble the soft chatterings of a duck.
>
> He sneaks through the woods plundering every nest he can find of its eggs. He will sometimes assault small birds. There are, however, individual exceptions to this general character for plunder and outrage.

And he told of a jay he caught and put in a cage with a female orchard oriole, which

> put on airs of alarm, as if she considered herself endangered and insulted by the intrusion; the jay, meanwhile, sat mute and motionless on the bottom of the cage. After displaying various threatening gestures (like some of those Indians we read of in their first interviews with the whites), she began to make her approaches, but with great circumspection, and readiness for retreat. Seeing, however, the jay begin to pick up some crumbs of broken chestnuts, in a humble and peaceable way, she also descended, and began to do the same; but, at the slightest motion of her new guest, wheeled

round, and put herself on the defensive. All this ceremonious jealousy vanished before evening; and they now roost together, feed, and play together. When the jay goes to drink, his messmate very impudently jumps into the water to wash herself, throwing the water in showers over her companion, who bears it all patiently. He seems to take pleasure in his little fellow prisoner, allowing her to pick (which she does very gently) about his whiskers, and to clean his claws from the minute fragments of chestnuts which happen to adhere to them.

[Jays] are common in the eastern states, and are mentioned by Dr. Belknap in his enumeration of the birds of New Hampshire. They are also natives of Newfoundland. Blue jays and yellow birds were found by Mr. M'Kenzie, when on his journey across the continent, at the headwaters of the Unjigah, or Peace River, in N. lat. 54°, W. lon. 121°, on the west side of the great range of Stony Mountains. Mr. William Bartram informs me that they are numerous in the peninsula of Florida. Captain Lewis, and Clark, and their intrepid companions continued to see blue jays for six hundred miles up the Missouri.

When Volume I was completed in 1808, Wilson was ready for another of his prodigious efforts: a series of journeys that would eventually take him more than ten thousand miles up and down and across the country, peddling his *Ornithology*. With a sample copy of Volume I in his bag, he headed in September for New England. From the days when he carried his cloth from door to door in Scotland, walking had been his accustomed means of travel. Weather and distance scarcely bothered him; miserable lodgings were an old story and he was not shy about accosting strangers. Taking the stagecoach for his first leg to Princeton, he grew impatient at the long stops and walked on for several miles until the coach caught up. Going through Connecticut, he often walked between towns. As his money began to run low, he walked much of the way from Hartford to Boston. From Boston he walked to Portsmouth, and on to Portland, then all the way to Dartmouth College and on to Albany. The distances he covered could not be measured in straight lines between destinations, for he went back and forth to villages, out into the country to farms, up and down the streets of cities. He seemed at home with anyone he talked to—farmers, businessmen, backwoodsmen, scholars—telling them or asking them about the birds of their country.

What he showed the prospects in his sample Volume I was a large 10" x 13½" folio with pages of heavy paper. There were five plates, with colored engravings of forty birds, starting with the very familiar: blue jay, yellowbird or goldfinch, Baltimore bird (oriole), wood thrush, red-breasted thrush or robin. They were usually shown in profile and their attitudes were stiff. But the drawing was patiently detailed, the coloring true. The accompanying text contained references to such authorities as Linnaeus, Buffon, Latham, Bartram and, frequently, the catalog number of the specimen in Peale's Museum. Reading, the potential subscriber would come across touches he could appreciate: the Baltimore oriole was "so solicitous to procure proper materials for his nest that the women in the country are under the necessity of narrowly watching their thread that may chance to be out bleaching." With the text on the bluebird was a little poem by Wilson: "Oh, then comes the bluebird, the herald of spring,/ And hails with his warblings the charms of the season." In with the dissertation on the orchard oriole is an attack on the ignorance of the Comte de Buffon, who gave the orchard oriole the title "spurious" because he couldn't tell it from a female Baltimore oriole.

The price was high—what a man might pay for a team of good carriage horses. But it was a very pretty book. Its author came with fine references and its publisher was the best known in the country. And there was nothing else like it to be had. It was the first American ornithology, and the fact that it was all American—its author (now a citizen), publisher, paper, type, engravings and, of course, the birds—made a nice selling point. But right from the start Wilson found that people were more ready to admire the book than to buy it. In Newark, he wrote, his "book attracted as many starers as a bear or mammoth would have done" but no subscribers. In New York, the governor, a plain-spoken man named Daniel Tompkins, said he "would not give a hundred dollars for all the birds you intend to describe even had I them alive." Wilson signed half a dozen subscribers in the city, including the famous Federalist, Rufus King; Dr. David Hosack, about to start work on an ambitious botanical garden; and an old hero of his, Tom Paine, whom he found "wrapt in a night-gown, the table before him covered with newspapers, with pen and ink beside him. Paine's face would have excellently suited the character of Bardolph; but the penetration and intelligence of his eye bespeak the man of genius and of the world. He examined my book, leaf by leaf, with great attention; desired me to put down his name as a subscriber." Paine, sadly, died before his subscription started.

"Few Americans have seen more of their country as I have done," Wilson once said, "and none love her better." He tempered his affection, however, with blunt reporting. Henry Adams, drawing repeatedly on Wilson for his *History of the United States*, called him "a confirmed grumbler but a shrewd judge and the most thorough of American travelers who knew every nook and corner of the United States." As he traveled, Wilson noted almost everything he encountered in journals and in letters to his friends. He then embedded his observations in his *Ornithology*, which became a book not just about the birds of America but about the people, customs, economics, geography and social conditions.

At Middletown, Connecticut, Wilson found the streets

> filled with troops, it being muster-day. I observed a row of twenty or
> thirty country girls drawn up, with their backs to a fence, and two young
> fellows supplying them with rolls of bread from a neighboring stall, which
> they ate with a hearty appetite, keeping nearly as good time with their
> grinders as the militia did with their muskets. In another place, the crowd
> had formed a ring, within which they danced to the catgut scrapings of an
> old negro. The spectators looked on with as much gravity as if they were
> listening to a sermon, and the dancers labored with such seriousness, that
> it seemed more like a penance imposed on the poor devils for past sins,
> than mere amusement.
>
> My journey through New England has rather lowered the Yankees in
> my esteem [he went on]. Except a few neat academies, I found their school-
> houses equally ruinous and deserted with ours; fields covered with stones;
> wretched orchards; the taverns along the road, dirty, and filled with
> loungers, brawling about lawsuits and politics.

In Boston, looking for Bunker's Hill, "that eminence, so justly celebrated in
the history of the revolution of the United States," he was hurt

> at the indifference with which the inhabitants directed me to the place. I
> inquired if there were any person still living here who had been in the
> battle, and I was directed to a Mr. Miller, who was a lieutenant in this
> memorable affair. I introduced myself and said that I was proud of the
> honor of meeting with one of the heroes of Bunker's Hill—the first un-
> conquerable champions of their country. Tears instantly glistened in his
> eyes, which as instantly called up corresponding ones in my own. In our
> way to the place, he called on a Mr. Carter, who, he said, was also in the
> action. As they pointed out to me the rout of the British—the American
> entrenchments—the place where the greatest slaughter was made—the spot
> where Warren fell, and where he was thrown amid heaps of the dead—I
> felt as though I could have encountered a whole battalion myself in the
> same glorious cause. We drank a glass of wine to the memory of the
> illustrious dead, and parted almost with regret.

He sold disappointingly few subscriptions in Boston. After going north to
Portland, he turned west and walked 157 miles to Dartmouth where "Dr.
Wheelock, the president, made me eat at his table and the professors vied with
each other to oblige me." The president subscribed, as had all the other college
presidents he called on in New England. By now, snow was several inches deep,
but "though sick with a severe cold and great fatigue," he walked to
Albany. There he paused and summed up his journey: "I have labored with

the zeal of a knight-errant, in exhibiting this book of mine, wherever I went, traveling with it, like a beggar with his bantling. I have been loaded with praises, with compliments, and kindnesses. I have wandered among strangers, hearing the same Oh's and Ah's, and telling the same story, a thousand times over, and for what? Ah, that's it!" People balked at paying $120, he told Lawson. "Sorry I am to say, that the whole number of subscribers which I have obtained amounts only to forty-one."

That left him still well short of the two hundred required before Bradford could start publication. Shortly Wilson set out to peddle his project again, this time on horseback, headed south. Making his first call in Baltimore on Peale's brother-in-law Nathaniel Ramsay, he got only the same "compliments, and kindnesses" he received in New England. Then, miraculously, everything changed. Complete strangers whom he solicited subscribed without hesitation. He sold seventeen subscriptions in Baltimore, a third as many as in all New York and New England. In Washington, though Jefferson had already subscribed, Wilson sought further endorsement from him. Calling at the White House, he sent in a formal note: "Alexander Wilson, author of *American Ornithology*, would be happy to submit the first volume of this work to the inspection of Mr. Jefferson if he knew when it would be convenient for the President." That very moment, it turned out, was convenient. Jefferson "ordered me immediately to be admitted," Wilson said, and he and his work were received "very kindly."

After this, everything seemed easy. Secretary of State James Madison, and Albert Gallatin, Secretary of the Treasury, subscribed, as did the Postmaster General and Benjamin Latrobe, architect of the Capitol. Washington produced another seventeen subscribers. Richmond, to Wilson's astonishment, produced twice that: thirty-four, including the governor.

It hardly mattered now, as he continued south, that the roads between cities were longer and subscribers fewer. The trip was already a success and, besides, the countryside was filled with birds in their winter quarters. It was fascinating travel, but arduous and lonely in a way that modern Americans cannot imagine. Henry Adams noted that "the grumbling Wilson who found New England so dreary painted this part of North Carolina in colors compared to which his sketch of New England was gay." He rode

> through solitary pine woods, perpetually interrupted by swamps, that covered the road with water two and three feet deep, frequently half a mile at a time, looking like a long river or pond. They were covered every morning with a sheet of ice, from half an inch to an inch thick, that cut my horse's legs and breast. The taverns are the most desolate and beggarly imaginable. At supper, you sit down to a meal, the very sight of which is

sufficient to deaden the most eager appetite, and you are surrounded by half a dozen dirty, half-naked blacks, male and female, whom any man of common scent might smell a quarter of a mile off.

He was better received and lodged at the plantations where he called—"the hospitality was such that I could scarcely get away again." One planter took a fancy to Wilson's horse, which Wilson was willing to swap for another, but they could not agree on a deal until the planter

followed me to the sea beach under pretext of pointing out to me the road; and there on the sands, amidst the roar of the Atlantic, we finally bargained; and I found myself in possession of a large, well-formed, and elegant sorrel horse, that ran off with me, at a canter, for fifteen miles and travelled, the same day, forty-two miles, with nothing but a few mouthfuls of rice straw. The least round of the whip made him spring half a rod at a leap. Two or three times he had nearly broke my neck.

In Wilmington, North Carolina, he had acquired a problem, an ivory-billed woodpecker (the model for his later painting of that bird) which he had shot:

This bird was only wounded slightly in the wing, and, on being caught, uttered a loudly reiterated, and most piteous note, exactly resembling the violent crying of a young child. I carried it with me, under cover. In passing through the streets, its affecting cries surprised every one within hearing, particularly the females, who hurried to the doors and windows with looks of alarm and anxiety. At the hotel the landlord came forward, and a number of other persons, all equally alarmed at what they heard; this was greatly increased by my asking whether he could furnish me with accommodations for myself and my baby. After diverting myself for a minute or two at their expense, I drew my woodpecker from under the cover, and a general laugh took place. I took him upstairs and locked him up in my room. In less than an hour I returned, and, on opening the door, he set up the same distressing shout, which now appeared to proceed from grief that he had been discovered in his attempts at escape. He had mounted along the side of the window, nearly as high as the ceiling, a little below which he had begun to break through. The bed was covered with large pieces of plaster; the lath was exposed for at least fifteen inches square, and a hole, large enough to admit the fist, opened to the weather-boards. I now tied a string round his leg, and fastening it to the table, again left him in search of suitable food for him. As I reascended the stairs, I heard him again hard at work. He had almost entirely ruined the mahogany table to which he was fastened. While engaged in taking the drawing, he cut me severely in several places. He lived with me nearly three days, but refused all sustenance, and I witnessed his death with regret.

In Charleston, one after another, residents subscribed: the descendant of a man who had taken Catesby into his home a century before; families who had known Alexander Garden; Eliza Lucas's descendants the Pinckneys; a glamorous soldier, General James Wilkinson, commander of the U.S. armies, who had been involved in Aaron Burr's conspiracy to set up an empire in the American West. The general was a man of wide interests, and birds were among them. Wilson later cited data on birds from Wilkinson, identifying him as "a gentleman in whose judgment he could rely." The general not only subscribed to the *Ornithology* but insisted on buying Wilson's sample copy of Volume I. The twelve dollars he paid for the volume was the first actual cash Wilson received for his work.

In Beaufort, Wilson visited Stephen Elliot, a plantation owner whose *Botany of South Carolina and Georgia* is a minor classic of American natural history. Elliot pressed Wilson to use his home on the Ogeechee River, introduced him to birds he had never seen and, of course, subscribed. Near Elliot lived an almost unknown naturalist named John Abbot, on whose knowledge Wilson drew heavily. Savannah yielded thirty-five subscribers, including the mayor. Triumphantly, Wilson wrote Bartram that by now he had "visited all towns within one hundred miles of the Atlantic from Maine to Georgia and done as much on this bantling book of mine as ever another did for any progeny of his brain." Too tired to ride back home, he took a boat, and in Philadelphia the discussions with the publisher now were not whether to publish but how many copies to print. With two hundred and fifty subscribers signed up and only the seaboard solicited, it was decided to print five hundred copies.

As he started work on Volume II, he renewed an old effort to get William Bartram to go west with him. They would travel to St. Louis where their friend Meriwether Lewis was territorial governor and could give invaluable help. At this point, news came that Lewis had died on his way to Washington—by his own hand, it was said. Then Bartram begged off from taking such a rigorous journey. Wilson set out by himself from Pittsburgh, where, "beyond expectations," he signed nineteen subscribers, Wilson tried a new mode of transportation. "I have resolved to navigate myself in a small skiff which I have bought, and named the *Ornithologist*, down to Cincinnati, a distance of five hundred and twenty-eight miles," he wrote Lawson. "As soon as the ice clears out of the Allegheny, I shall shove off." He did so at the end of February.

My stock of provisions consisted of some biscuit and cheese, and a bottle of cordial; my gun, trunk, and greatcoat occupied one end of the boat; I had a small tin, occasionally to bail her, and to take my beverage from the Ohio with. The current went about two and a half miles an hour, and I added about three and a half miles more to the boat's way with my oars. I could only discover when I was passing a clearing by the crowing of cocks, and, now and then, in more solitary places, the big horned owl made a most hideous hollowing, that echoed among the mountains. In this lonesome manner, exposed to hardships all day, and hard berths all night, to storms of rain, hail, and snow—for it froze severely almost every night—I persevered.

A violent storm of hail and snow roiled the river and filled his boat with water. Making shore, he spent the evening in "learning the art and mystery of bear-treeing, wolf-trapping, and wildcat-hunting from an old professor. This man was one of those people called *squatters*, who neither pay rent nor own land, but keep roving on the frontiers, advancing as the tide of civilized population approaches. They are the immediate successors of the savages, and far below them in good sense and good manners, as well as comfortable accommodations."

He shot into a flock of parakeets and, he said, "anxious to try the effects of education on one of those which was but slightly wounded in the wing, I fixed up a place in the stern of the boat and presented it with some cockleburs which it freely fed on in less than an hour after being on board. The intermediate time between eating and sleeping was occupied in gnawing the sticks that formed its place of confinement in order to make a practicable breach."

He stopped in Cincinnati, where a leading citizen named Dr. Daniel Drake showed him a "collection of curiosities" from a large Indian mound. Reaching Big Bone Creek, Wilson "set out for the Big Bone Lick, that great antediluvian rendezvous of the American elephants. I found numerous fragments of large bones lying scattered about. In pursuing a wounded duck across this quagmire, I had nearly deposited my carcass among the grand congregation of mammoths below, having sunk up to the middle, and had hard struggling to get out."

His river voyage ended at Shippingport where he sold his skiff for half what it cost him. "The man who bought it wondered why I gave it such a droll Indian name (the *Ornithologist*). 'Some old chief or warrior, I suppose?' said he."

It was at this rude river town, just above Louisville, that the most celebrated—and argued-about—meeting in American ornithology took place. Fretting at the absence of prospects and congenial companions, Wilson went to call on a local storekeeper who advertised himself as an artist and portrait painter. He entered the establishment of Rozier and Audubon and inquired for Mr. Audubon.

Years later, John James Audubon recalled "Wilson's sudden entrance. His long rather hooked nose, the keenness of his eyes and prominent cheekbones stamped his countenance with a peculiar character. His dress too was of a kind not usually seen in Kentucky: a short coat, trousers and gray cloth waistcoat." Wilson showed his folio and Audubon was about to subscribe when his partner, speaking in French, told him not to. "Your drawings are certainly far better," said Rozier, and Audubon put down his pen. Wilson, who understood Rozier's French, suggested that Audubon show him some of his own drawings. As Audubon recorded it, Wilson was surprised that anyone else was making a series of bird drawings. And even more surprised when Audubon said he had no intention of publishing them, Wilson asked to borrow a few.

Wilson himself seems to have noted the meeting only briefly in his journal: "March 19. Rambling around town with my gun. Examined Mr.——'s drawings in crayons—very good. Saw two new birds he had . . . both *Motacillae*."

On the basis of these few fragments of information, the partisans of Wilson and of Audubon later spread contradictory interpretations of the meeting: the one version picturing Audubon as a liar and credit-grabber who exaggerated Wilson's interest and admiration; the other insisting that Wilson was an ingrate who borrowed Audubon's drawings in order to make use of them. The whole incident was confused by the questionable way in which a future editor dealt with Wilson's papers.

Wilson lodged at the inn where Audubon stayed. "His retired habits exhibited a strong discontent or a decided melancholy," Audubon recalled. "The Scotch airs he played sweetly on his flute made me melancholy too." Feeling sorry for his visitor, he said, he took him out hunting several times. Wilson's existing journal barely acknowledges this. "March 20. Set out this afternoon with gun. No naturalist to keep me company. March 21. Went out this afternoon with Mr. A——. Saw a number of sand-hill cranes; pigeons numerous." Then Wilson shrugged Shippingport off in a passage that years later outraged Audubon. "I neither received one act of civility, one subscriber, or one new bird," Wilson wrote of that town. "Science or literature has not one friend in this place."

His boat sold, Wilson reverted to his old mode of travel. With his half-tamed parakeet wrapped in a silk handkerchief and stuffed into a pocket, he walked on toward Lexington. Near Shelbyville, he went out of his way to visit a passenger-pigeon roost and added his own description to those of so many other bird watchers:

> [Pigeons] were flying in such immense numbers as I never before had witnessed. From right to left, far as the eye could reach, the breadth of

this vast procession extended, seeming everywhere equally crowded. Curious to determine how long this appearance would continue, I took out my watch to note the time, and sat down to observe them. It was then half past one. I sat for more than an hour, but instead of a diminution of this prodigious procession, it seemed rather to increase both in numbers and rapidity. About four o'clock in the afternoon I crossed the Kentucky River, at which time the living torrent above my head seemed as numerous and as extensive as ever. Long after this I observed them in large bodies, that continued to pass for six or eight minutes, and these again were followed by other detached bodies, all moving in the same south-east direction, till after six in the evening.

There were, he estimated, some two billion birds in that torrent.

Much taken by Kentucky's horses, Wilson bought himself a stallion and rode on through new and delightful country: "Every day was producing wonders on the woods, while the voices of the feathered tribes, many of which were to me new and unknown, were continually engaging me in the pursuit." He overtook a family caravan moving westward.

In the front went a wagon drawn by four horses, and filled with implements of agriculture; another heavy-loaded wagon, with six horses, followed, after which came a numerous and mingled group of horses, steers, cows, sheep, hogs, and calves, with their bells; next followed eight boys, mounted double; also a negro wench, with a child before her; then the mother, with one child behind her, and another at the breast; ten or twelve colts brought up the rear. The singular appearance of this moving group, the mingled music of the bells, and the shouting of the drivers, mixed with the echoes of the mountains, joined to the picturesque solitude of the place, and various reflections that hurried through my mind, interested me greatly; and I kept company with them for some time, to lend my assistance, if necessary.

His account reads like a picaresque tale as he talks of the people he met and the risks he took along a frontier still full of resentful savages and murderous backwoodsmen. "In the woods I met a soldier on foot who had been robbed and plundered by the Choctaws. 'Thirteen or fourteen Indians' said he, 'surrounded me before I was aware, cut away my canteen, tore off my hat, took the handkerchief from my neck, and the shoes from my feet, and all the money I had from me, which was about forty-five dollars.'"

Next came a comic encounter with a man mending his stirrup leathers, who walked round my horse several times and observed that I seemed to be armed. I told him I was well-armed with gun and pistols, but I hoped he was not afraid to travel with me on that account, as I should be better able to assist in defending him as well as myself, if attacked. This man furnished me with as much amusement as Strap did to Roderick Random. He was a most zealous Methodist, and sung hymns the first day almost perpetually. Finding that I should be obliged to bear with this, I got him to try some of them to good old song tunes.

When the preacher endeavored, sometimes with great vehemence, to convert his companion, Wilson would get away by riding

hard down hill, which, the preacher being unable to do, generally broke the thread of his discourse. He was, however, very useful to me in taking charge of my horse while I went into the woods after strange birds. I stopped five days in the Barrens of Kentucky in the house of a good Presbyterian, who charged me nothing, and would have kept me a month for some lessons in drawing which I gave his two daughters. Here my psalm-singing Methodist left me.

During his stay with the good Presbyterian, Wilson explored the Barrens and the huge caves that underlay them. "Frightful stories are told of tavern keepers who are suspected of destroying travelers and secreting the bodies in these caves," he wrote, and he ventured into one that belonged to "a man of notoriously bad character, and strongly suspected of having committed a foul murder. He was a dark mulatto, and walked lame. His countenance bespoke a soul capable of deeds of darkness." He and another man led Wilson into his cave, Wilson "with my hand on my pistol, reconnoitering on every side. After examining this horrible vault for forty or fifty yards," he realized he was alone with the notorious owner.

I fixed my eye steadily on his, and observed to him that he could not be ignorant of the reports circulated about the country relative to this cave. "I suppose," said I, "you know what I mean?" "Yes, I understand you," returned he, without appearing the least embarrassed—"that I killed somebody, and threw them into this cave. I can tell you the whole beginning of that damned lie." I asked him why he did not get the cave examined by three or four reputable neighbors, whose report might rescue his character from the suspicion of having committed so horrid a crime. He acknowledged it would be well enough to do so but did not seem to think it worth the trouble; and we returned.

Wilson must have been a welcome companion and guest everywhere along the way, with his painting, his stories, his flute and his pet parakeet. At one inn, the landlord, whose name was Isaac Walton, refused "to take anything for my fare or that of my horse saying 'You seem to be traveling for the good of the world and I cannot and will not charge you anything. Whenever you come this way, call and stay with me, you shall be welcome.' "

Dark sides of life in the West aroused his sarcastic anger:

> This is a charming country for ladies. From the time they are first able to handle a cowskin, there is no amusement they are so fond of as flogging their negroes and negro wenches. The landlady of the tavern where I lodge is a great connoisseur at this sort of play; and while others apply their cowskin only to the back, she has discovered that the shins, elbows, and knuckles are far more sensitive, and produce more agonizing screams and greater convulsions in the "black devils," as she calls them, than any other place. My heart sickens at such barbarous scenes.

And his journal notes furiously: "Horses selling by auction. Negro woman sold the same way . . . 'three hundred and twenty-five dollars for this woman and boy! Going! Going' . . . Damned, damned slavery."

He had not sold very many subscriptions along this stretch but he was content. He had seen innumerable new birds and a great deal of the country. Though pressed for time, he went out of his way to redeem the reputation of a friend.

Meriwether Lewis, appointed governor of the territory he had explored, had found himself unsuited for the job of administering his formless domain and even less suited for the political infighting it required. When his financial accounts and his loyalty were questioned, he set out from St. Louis in great distress to defend himself in Washington. Traveling over the Natchez Trace, the ancient Indian way that follows the wavering line of ridgetops through Tennessee, he stopped at a place called Grinder's Stand and there died mysteriously of bullet wounds. Testimony of members of his party brought an official verdict of suicide, but many of Lewis's friends were convinced that he had been murdered. Wilson set out to learn what he could at the scene of the tragedy. He wrote:

> I prepared for a journey through the wilderness. I was advised by many not to attempt it alone, that the Indians were dangerous, the swamps and rivers almost impassable without assistance. I equipped myself for the attempt, a loaded pistol in each pocket, a loaded fowling piece belted across my shoulders. I rode to a man's home by the name

of Grinder, where our poor friend Lewis perished. In the same room where he expired, I took down from Mrs. Grinder the particulars of that melancholy event. Governor Lewis, she said, came thither about sunset, alone, and inquired if he could stay for the night. There were two servants behind who would soon be up. He called for some spirits, and drank a very little. When the servants arrived, he inquired for his powder, saying he was sure he had some powder in a canister. Lewis walked backwards and forwards before the door, talking to himself. Supper being ready, he sat down, but had eaten only a few mouthfuls, when he started up, speaking to himself in a violent manner. He lighted his pipe, and, drawing a chair to the door, sat down, saying to Mrs. Grinder, in a kind tone of voice, "Madam, this is a very pleasant evening." He said he would sleep on the floor, and desired the servants to bring the bear skins and buffalo robe. The woman could not sleep, but listened to him walking backwards and forwards, she thinks, for several hours, and talking aloud, as she said, "like a lawyer." She then heard the report of a pistol, and something fall heavily on the floor, and the words, "O Lord!" Immediately afterwards she heard another pistol; and, in a few minutes she heard him at her door, calling out, "O Madam! give me some water, and heal my wounds." She saw him stagger back, and fall. He crawled for some distance, raised himself by the side of a tree, where he sat about a minute. She then heard him scraping the bucket with a gourd for water, but it appeared that this cooling element was denied the dying man! As soon as day broke, and not before, the terror of the woman having permitted him to remain for two hours in this most deplorable situation, she sent two of her children to the barn to bring the servants; and, on going in, they found him lying on the bed. He uncovered his side, and showed them where the bullet had entered; a piece of the forehead was blown off, and had exposed the brains, without having bled much. He begged that they would take his rifle and blow out his brains, and he would give them all the money he had in his trunk. He often said, "I am no coward; but I am so strong —so hard to die!" He expired in about two hours, or just as the sun rose above the trees. He lies buried close by the common path, with a few loose rails thrown over his grave. I gave Grinder money to put a post fence round it, to shelter it from the hogs and from the wolves.

The woman's melodramatic story, Wilson concluded, was hysterical and its details unconvincing. Lewis, he decided, had been murdered—a verdict that he undoubtedly favored even before his investigation. His published account, the only one ever taken firsthand at the scene, has led many historians, in the

years since, to believe that Lewis did not kill himself. Still, though suspicion
of murder persists, the official verdict remains suicide.

Wilson left the place "in a very melancholy mood." In the middle of the
forest he dismounted to write a brief, mournful memorial for Lewis:

> The anguish that his soul assailed,
> The dark despair that round him blew,
> No eye, save that of heaven beheld,
> None but unfeeling strangers knew . . .
> Pale pity consecrate the spot
> Where poor, lost Lewis now lies low.

His mood soon changed. The profusion of flowers delighted him: "Sweet
William of all tints, a superb thistle, a passion flower, a stately sunflower,
the button of the deepest orange and the radiating petals bright carmines; a
large white flower like a deer's tail, great quantities of the sensitive plant that
shrunk instantly on being touched." As if taunting the immovable Bartram,
he wrote him, "This must be a heavenly place for the botanist."

He stopped to deliver a lecture to an Indian who had shot a mockingbird.
"I told him this was bad, very bad, that this poor bird had come from a far
distant country to sing to him. I told him that the Great Spirit was offended
at such cruelty and that he would lose many a deer."

He still had his pet parakeet with him.

> When I stopped for refreshment I unbound my prisoner, and gave
> it its allowance, which it generally despatched with great dexterity, un-
> husking the seeds from the bur in a twinkling. In recommitting it to
> "durance vile," we generally had a quarrel; during which it frequently
> paid me in kind for the wound I had inflicted, and for depriving it of
> liberty, by cutting and almost disabling several of my fingers with its
> sharp and powerful bill. The path through the wilderness is in some
> places bad beyond description, where I had to fight my way through;
> the paroquet frequently escaped from my pocket, obliging me to dis-
> mount and pursue it through the worst of the morass before I could re-
> gain it. On these occasions, I was several times tempted to abandon it;
> but I persisted in bringing it along. When at night I encamped in the
> woods I placed it on the baggage beside me, where it usually sat with
> great composure, dozing, and gazing at the fire till morning. In this
> manner I carried it upwards of a thousand miles in my pocket. In passing
> through the Chickasaw and Choctaw nations, the Indians wherever I
> stopped to feed, collected around me, men, women, and children, laughing,
> and seeming wonderfully amused with the novelty of my companion. The

A Carolina parakeet, caught by Wilson, was his companion during his entire trip through the West. He kept it with him until, sailing home, it flew overboard and drowned.

Chickasaws called it in their language "Kelinky"; but when they heard me call it Poll, they soon repeated the name; and, wherever I chanced to stop among these people, we soon became familiar with each other through the medium of "Poll."

An attack of dysentery so weakened him that he could scarcely ride, but he cured himself by eating raw eggs for a week. At Natchez, that copy of the first volume of the *Ornithology* he had sold General Wilkinson in Charleston produced an unexpected dividend. Wilson was handed a note from William Dunbar: "The perusal of your first volume of *Ornithology* lent me by General

Wilkinson has produced in me a very great desire of making your acquaintance." He invited Wilson to stay at his plantation, The Forest. "My house stands literally in the forest and your beautiful orioles [the ones painted by Wilson in Volume I] with other elegant birds are our courtyard companions." Along with the message, Dunbar sent an extra horse for Wilson.

The son of a Scottish laird, Dunbar had been a prodigy in mathematics at home but he left the virtuoso's life and emigrated to America. He was a partner of John Ross, the merchant-patriot who had helped finance the Continental Army during the Revolution's worst days. Going south, Dunbar set up a plantation where he pioneered in growing cotton and devised a useful way of packing his crop in square bales. No man, a friend of Dunbar's wrote, was held in higher regard in the territory for "science, probity and general information." Dunbar remembered William Bartram as a traveling companion twenty years before and sent his best wishes through Wilson.

Wilson found his host incurably ill, able to see him for only a short time each day, but his large family—there were seven children—kept their visitor busy. They knew their guest not just for his birds, but for his poetry. The *Port Folio*, where *The Foresters* had just appeared, was in their library. As Dunbar had promised, the land was filled with birds, many of which Wilson had never seen before.

His parakeet was also happy at The Forest. On arriving, Wilson procured a cage and placed it under the piazza. Poll

soon attracted the passing flocks; such is the attachment they have for each other. Numerous parties frequently alighted on the trees immediately above, keeping up a constant conversation with the prisoner. One of these I wounded slightly in the wing, and the pleasure Poll expressed on meeting with this new companion was really amusing. She crept close up to it as it hung on the side of the cage; chattered to it in a low tone of voice, as if sympathizing in its misfortune; scratched about its head and neck with her bill; and both at night nestled as close as possible to each other, sometimes Poll's head being thrust among the plumage of the other. On the death of this companion, she appeared restless and inconsolable for several days. I placed a looking glass beside the place where she usually sat, and the instant she perceived her image, all her former fondness seemed to return, so that she could scarcely absent herself from it a moment. It was evident that she was completely deceived. Always when evening drew on, and often during the day, she laid her head close to that of the image in the glass and began to doze with great composure and satisfaction.

With Dunbar to introduce him, Wilson was welcomed in all the great houses of the region. Planters, government officials, merchants had him as a guest and, as a matter of course, subscribed to the *Ornithology*. In New Orleans alone, by walking up one street and down another, he signed sixty-three subscribers. As he traveled from plantation to plantation, exploring the bayous, Wilson collected birds he had never known.

The sea voyage home proved fatal to his parrot. "Poor Poll, having one morning about daybreak wrought her way through the cage while I was asleep, instantly flew overboard and perished in the Gulf of Mexico." Settled again in Philadelphia in August, he calculated the distance he had covered in those six exhausting months: "Philadelphia to Pittsburgh 320 miles. Down the Ohio in small boat alone 720. By land to Lexington 75. Ditto to Nashville 200. Through the wilderness to Natchez 470. To New Orleans along the Mississippi 252. Total to New Orleans 2,037." To which he could add another thousand miles by sea back to Philadelphia. It was more than worth it. He had signed over a hundred subscribers and there were now more than four hundred sets spoken for. Some fifty thousand dollars would eventually be paid for the *Ornithology* —and Wilson had done it all himself. The first two volumes, already in circulation, were widely admired.

A vast amount of work remained on the *Ornithology*. There were drawings to be done, mainly of the birds he had first seen or studied more closely on his trip. He had to supervise the engravings, oversee the coloring of each plate and, after Leslie left, do much of the coloring himself. For the first time, there was nothing to distract him from his work. All through the years since he started it, he had had other jobs—teacher, editor, traveling salesman. Now he gave himself full time to the *Ornithology*. An enormously efficient man, he seems to have wasted nothing, gathering just the material he needed and using virtually all of it. Fiercely dedicated to his work, he had little time for diversion and none for argument. "He was of *genus irritabile*," wrote his disciple George Ord, "and was obstinate in opinion. It ever gave him pleasure to acknowledge error when the correction resulted from his judgment alone but he could not endure to be told of his mistakes." His obstinacy was justified. Though he made his mistakes, his observations as a whole have withstood a century and a half of checking. His birds are drawn with almost all their important markings correct, the more surprising since only toward the end of his bird-watching did he use field glasses. All in all, he described some 260 of the 350 species of birds known in his day, adding 48 new species on his own.

No work of that scope could rely on the observations of a single man. Wilson had, by now, built a network of correspondents so extensive that, he boasted, "scarcely a wren or a tit could reach the Canadian border before I had

received intelligence of it." His correspondents were a wonderfully miscellane-
ous and helpful aggregation of Americans, dedicated to nature and eager to
share what they learned. Their notes, printed in Wilson's life histories, show
how common an interest natural history was in America and how deep a part
of the American spirit was touched by the transplanted Scotsman's work. What
he described were familiar parts of American lives, city or country. What he
set out to satisfy was an American ambition. His work reflected the open patriotism of the day, which found a reason to admire America in everything the
land offered, a patriotism often grandiloquently expressed, but utterly sincere.

Sometimes Wilson refers to his correspondents by name, sometimes by in-
direct descriptions. A "curious and correct observer" informed him that when
a bluebird "first begins his amours, it is pleasing to behold his courtship, his
solicitude to secure the favor of his beloved female. He sings to her his most
endearing warblings. If he espies an insect delicious to her taste, he takes
it, spreads his wings over her and puts it in her mouth." Few correspondents
were so poetically inclined as this curious observer, who, it turns out, was William Bartram.

Bartram was the most immediate source of information and advice, and
the *Ornithology* is studded with his facts and phrases—"the coots, loquacious
and noisy, talking to one another night and day." Wilson fondly tells stories
about his friend. Once, he gave a young tanager to Bartram who hung
it in a cage in a pine tree where its cries attracted the parents. For several
days, they brought food to the cage and tried vainly to get in. The bird's
distress, wrote Wilson, "was too much for the feelings of my venerable friend;
he procured a ladder, opened the cage, took out the prisoner and restored him
to liberty and to his parents who with notes of great exultation accompanied
his flight to the woods." Another time, observing an exhausted sandpiper trying
to defend its nest from a squirrel, Bartram, "like one of those celestial agents
who in Homer's time so often decided the palm of victory, stepped forward from
his retreat and rescued the innocent from destruction."

Peale, whose museum was a basic source of information, told Wilson of
the two hummingbirds he had raised from the nest that used to fly about the
museum chasing motes of dust in the streaks of sunlight that shone into the
chamber. A "Mr. Coffer of Fairfax County, Virginia, a gentleman who has
paid great attention to the manners and peculiarities of our native birds," gave
facts about the hummingbird's diet. Wilson added his own experience with a captured hummingbird, which, all but dead, revived when "a lady in the house
undertook to be its nurse, placed it in her bosom, dissolved a little sugar in her
mouth" which "it sucked with great avidity."

Trying to ascertain whether the goldfinch, called the wild canary, would mate with the familiar cage bird, Wilson was told by "an ingenious French gentleman who resides in Pottsgrove, Pennsylvania," that he had tried repeatedly to breed them and they would not. However, "Mr. Hassey of New York" did get the two kinds to mate, though their eggs never hatched.

"A lady who resides near Tarrytown" enabled Wilson to refute authorities who declared that a caged robin never sings: "She raised and kept one of these birds for seventeen years which sung as well at that age as ever, but was at last unfortunately destroyed by a cat." A "young lady in Middletown, Connecticut," helped fill out sparse data on the bay-breasted warbler by sending him "a very neat drawing of this bird." His "respected friend, Mordecai Churchman, cashier of the bank" at Easton, Pennsylvania, kept track of the behavior of the local chimney swallows which nested by the scores at the courthouse until the young could fly, when they "entirely foresook the courthouse chimney and rendezvoused in the southernmost chimney of John Ross's mansion." John Joseph Henry, Esq., "Judge of the Supreme Court of Pennsylvania, a man of most amiable manners," compiled a learned account of the purple martin, citing observations from as far away as Quebec and Tierra del Fuego. A "very worthy gentleman living in the Genesee County" told about a pet crow, which, having left home, met his old master on the river's shore and came to sit on his shoulder to "gabble away with great volubility as one long-absent friend naturally enough does on meeting with another." An "obliging correspondent in New York" told of the wounded goose which, tended by a farmer until it was well enough to fly off, came back next year with three offspring "to share with them the sweets of civilized life." Local data on the eagle came from "Mr. John L. Gardiner who resides on an island about three miles from the eastern shore of Long Island." He sent Wilson a well-preserved skin of the bald eagle with the information that he had once come upon an eagle making off with a lamb which the eagle dropped when Gardiner "went running, hallooing" after it.

Many of the correspondents were naturalists of standing. Stephen Elliot of South Carolina, whom Wilson had visited, sent him considerable information and "a very fine specimen" of the wood ibis. "Mr. Ainsley, a German naturalist, collector in this country for the Emperor of Austria," sent a crossbill. François André Michaux, "son to the celebrated botanist," wrote about the migrations of cardinals. "A gentleman of observation who resided for many years not far from Hudson in the State of New York" informed him about the Canada jay, the bird which had been the cause of some disappointment to Wilson.

Of all his correspondents, the one who, next to Bartram, was most valuable to Wilson was John Abbot of Georgia. There have been few American naturalists so prolific as Abbot and few so long forgotten. When Wilson called on Jefferson at the White House at the start of his trip south, Jefferson told him to look up a man named Abbot in Georgia. For some reason, Wilson seemed irritated by the President's suggestion. "I am to receive a world of facts and observation from him," he wrote a friend sarcastically. That, in fact, is exactly what Wilson did receive, after he had called on Abbot in his home near the Altamaha River.

Wilson found him a weather-beaten man of almost sixty. According to a brief autobiography Abbot wrote, which did not come to light until 1948, he was born "in the year 1751, the first of June Old Stile, at the west end of the Town London. My peculiar liking for insects was long before I was acquainted with any method of catching or keeping them." An introduction to the president of the Linnaean Society gave "a new turn to my future life. I had immediately a mahogany cabinet made of 26 draws and begun to collect with an unceasing industry. Lady Honeywood made me a present of Catesby's Nat. Hist. of Carolina." That determined him to come to America and, settling in Georgia, he joined the Revolutionary forces. His services as a soldier were rewarded after the war with a large farm.

Farming must have been a secondary occupation, for Abbot was one of the most industrious naturalists who ever lived—collecting, drawing, shipping insects by the thousands to Europe. One of his clients was James E. Smith, an Englishman who brought off a great scientific coup for his country. Hearing that Linnaeus's heirs were putting his papers up for sale, he rushed over to Sweden and, despite last-minute intercession by the King, bought the priceless collection for a thousand pounds and took it to England. Smith commissioned Abbot to paint American moths and butterflies and published them in 1797 as *The Natural History of the Rarer Lepidopterous Insects of Georgia*. He made it seem as if he were mainly responsible for the book, merely acknowledging that it was "Collected from Observations by John Abbot." The paintings, along with those he did of birds, affirm Abbot as one of the finest naturalist-artists who ever worked in America.

Making a business out of natural history, Abbot hired assistants to help fill his orders and colorists to flesh out his drawings. To his main patron in England, John Francillon, a famous silversmith, he sent drawings of 1,664 American insects, each with a life history. "He has been drawing plants since boyhood," wrote a naturalist who met Abbot when he was eighty-three, "and never knew anything of Linnaeus's classification till I demonstrated it to him and created his astonishment."

"Mr. Abbot, who has been engaged these thirty years in collecting and drawing subjects of natural history," told Wilson about the eccentric migratory habits of the hummingbird, pointed out a puzzling change in the color of the iris in the towhee's eye and explained how the pine creeping warbler makes its hanging nest of "grape-vine bark, rotten wood and caterpillars' webs, with sometimes pieces of hornets' nests." Wilson contracted with Abbot for bird specimens, paying forty-five dollars per shipment, much more than Abbot's English clients had been paying. It was only through repeated mentions in the *Ornithology* that Abbot finally became known at all.

The most eminent of Wilson's correspondents, though possibly the least useful (except for sending him to see Abbot), was Thomas Jefferson. An extract from his letter on the elusive nightingalelike bird he asked Wilson to find is included in the text on the wood thrush as having come from "a distinguished American gentleman whose name, were I at liberty to give it, would do honor to my humble performance." Jefferson must have been pleased to see how Wilson had used the thrush to attack Buffon and the other European detractors of America. Buffon had stated, Wilson wrote, that the wood thrush was the descendant of the European thrush, which "had, at some time after the creation, rambled round by the northern ocean and made its way to America; that it had there become degenerated by change of food and climate so that its cry is now harsh and unpleasant." Very precisely he traces the sources of Buffon's errors and points out that the bird Buffon describes looks nothing at all like the wood thrush.

Again and again through the *Ornithology*, Wilson takes out after Buffon who, he says, "with equal eloquence and absurdity," committed error after foolish error. Buffon had described the golden-winged woodpecker (the flicker) as leading "a mean and gloomy life without intermission of labor, the narrow circumference of a tree circumscribes his dull round of life." Nonsense, said Wilson. It is a "sprightly bird who spends the sweetest hours of the morning calling on his companions or gamboling with them."

Buffon, who seems to have had a special contempt for American woodpeckers, further complained that the downy woodpecker was doomed to "incessant toil and slavery, painful posture, dull and insipid existence." Not at all, Wilson insisted. The posture is one to which its "frame is particularly adapted" and its labor "is as pleasant and as amusing as the sucking of flowers to a hummingbird," while "the cheerfulness of his cry and the liveliness of his motion while dislodging vermin" indicate a full and happy life. It seems, Wilson winds up, that "the whole family of woodpeckers must look sad, sour and be miserable to satisfy the caprice of a whimsical philosopher."

Unable to hold back his anger at the scorn foreigners visited on his beloved American birds, Wilson finally burst out: "This eternal reference of every animal of the new world to that of the old with all the transmutations it is supposed to have produced would leave us in doubt whether even the ka-te-dids of America were not originally nightingales of the Old World degener-ated by the inferiority of the food and climate of this upstart continent." If Ben Franklin's dinner-table strategy and Jefferson's moose did not lay the European libels low, Wilson's wrathful sarcasm certainly should have.

Patriotic Americans, applauding Wilson's defense of their birds, must have glowed at his appreciation of them. Sharp in observing, Wilson was specific and poetic in his writing. In certain lights, the plumage of the indigo bunting "appears of a rich sky blue and in others of a vivid verdigris green; so that the same bird, in passing from one place to another before your eyes, seems to undergo a total change of color." He set down the smallest details: the way the native oriole had adapted European silk thread for its nest "with the sagacity of a good architect"; how a great heron always swallows a fish "head foremost, such being their uniform position in the stomach." His images jump out of the pages: flocks of woodpeckers, nuthatches, chickadees and tit-mice "proceeding through the woods like a corps of pioneers"; the clapper rail "rising and disappearing again with the silence and celerity of thought."

His ear was superb and so was his way of describing what he heard. The kingfisher has a "voice not unlike the twirling of a watchman's rattle." The mourning dove expresses "the hopeless woe of settled sorrow." Some idea of the bobolink's song "may be formed by striking the high keys of a pianoforte at random, singly and quickly, making as many sudden contrasts of high and low notes as possible." The thrush "pipes his clear and musical notes in a kind of ecstasy, the prelude to which strongly resembles the double tonguing of a Ger-man flute." His descriptions can be bleak (the nuthatch's call in winter—"quank quank heard in the leafless woods among the howling branches") or cheerful (the oriole "with the pleasing tranquility of a careless ploughboy whistling merely for his own amusement") or visceral (the heron's "hoarse and hollow qua has been compared to that produced by the retching of a person attempting to vomit") or grotesque (this same heron's noise at breeding time "almost induces one to suppose that two or three hundred Indians were throttling each other").

A fine description of a frustrated singer comes in his anecdote about the baby cowbird he had put in a cage with a cardinal, which "seemed to adopt it as his own, feeding it with all the assiduity and tenderness of the most affection-ate nurse." The cowbird tried to repay "the affectionate services of his foster parent with a frequent display of all the musical talents with which nature has gifted him. He spreads his wings, swells his body and with great seeming dif-ficulty, utters a few low spluttering notes. To see the red bird, who is himself so excellent a performer, silently listening to all this guttural splutter, reminds me of the great Handel contemplating a wretched catgut scraper."

And Wilson touched with special eloquence on his belief that God manifested himself most truly in nature when he described the barred owl's wing with its "web of wing quills of a delicate softness covered with an almost imperceptible hair and edged with a loose silky down so that the owner passes through the air without interrupting the most profound silence. Who cannot perceive the hand of God in all these things!"

After his trip south, Wilson never ventured far from Philadelphia except for one trip to New England to collect money from delinquent subscribers and agents. He spent his summers at Bartram's Gardens, with his still alert and venerable friend, and at Cape May, where he was preoccupied with water birds. His companion there was George Ord, a wealthy Philadelphian who later became Wilson's posthumous collaborator and acrimonious apostle.

Looking back, Wilson saw himself "a solitary exploring pilgrim." Others overflowed with admiration for his single-handed accomplishment. He was gifted, Henry Adams said, "with a dogged enthusiasm which in spite of obstacles gave to America an ornithology more creditable than anything yet accomplished in art or literature." Naturalist Elliot Coues remarked that he had accomplished this "though he had genius and not much of anything else—very little learning, scarcely any money, not many friends and a paltry share of the world's regard while he lived." Mostly true except for his last years, when he had a host of friends and his world held him in very high regard indeed. "The extent of Wilson's achievement in so brief a period was explicable only as a sustained creative inspiration," writes his perceptive biographer Robert Cantwell. "Wilson's aim was to discover the design of the world of birds as a link to an unspoiled past of nature. His creation in the *American Ornithology* was so rare, strange and hauntingly beautiful that it transformed a work of science into a work of art, the vindication of his faith that the wonder of nature was sufficiently evident to warrant our finding in it proof of the wisdom and goodness of its creator."

Wilson worked on, giving himself totally to finishing the *Ornithology*. "I am myself far from being in good health," he wrote William Bartram in the summer of 1813, when he was forty-seven years old. "My eighth volume is now in the press and will be published in November. One more volume will complete the whole."

To a friend in Scotland he summed up his accomplishments. "I was a wanderer when I was in Scotland and I have been much more so since my arrival here. Fortune has not yet paid me all her promises after all the wild goose chases she had led me; but she begins to look a little more gracious than usual and I am not without hope."

L

CHAPTER NINE

ℐ CHAOS
OF KNOWLEDGE

❦ ❦ ❦ ❦ ❦ "DEAR SIR: IT GIVES ME GREAT PLEASURE TO REPLY TO YOUR letter of the 12th instant asking of me information concerning the grouse of Long Island," began a letter Alexander Wilson received in 1810 from Samuel Latham Mitchill of New York. "The more popular name for them is heath hens. By this name they are designated in the act of our legislature for the preservation of them and of other game. I well remember the passing of this law. The bill was introduced by Cornelius J. Bogert Esq., a member of the Assembly from the city of New York. It was in the month of February, 1791, the year when as representative from my native county of Queens I sat for the first time in a legislature."

Wilson read on, turning page after page of information about eastern Long Island, the heath hen's habitat: the kinds of soil found there, including a sand used by glassmakers; the kinds of trees in the region; the benefits of growing trees for firewood and a prediction that the area could provide New York City with firewood for ages; finally an apology for not having provided much data on the subject in hand.

Whereupon the letter launched into an exposition on the size of the heath hen (3 pounds); the market price (recently risen from one dollar to five dollars a brace); their "amours" (the male's "tooting may be heard on a still morning for three miles"); their food (partridgeberry, hurtleberries, insects, acorns and, perhaps, wintergreen); their migratory habits (they don't migrate, but stay put); their "manners" (the males, in a strutting ceremony, "frequently cast looks of insult and utter notes of defiance" at each other). The letter pauses to remind Wilson that Mitchill's "short memoir in the eighth volume of the *Medical Repository* ventured an opinion as to the genus and species." And, with an air of polite abruptness, it ends with: "It remains to repeat my joy to contribute somewhat to your elegant work."

As he kept reading, Wilson must have realized that he was being told far
more than he had to know about the heath hen. But he knew that he would print
the letter in full in his *American Ornithology* for, next to Thomas Jefferson,
Dr. Samuel Latham Mitchill was the most eminent of all his correspondents.
Like Jefferson, he was both a politician and a scientist. Unlike the President,
he put science ahead of politics—and Americans, in his time, put Mitchill
ahead of all other living scientists. He was an anthropologist, botanist, chemist,

As printed in his Ornithology, Wilson's *drawing of the heath hen was accompanied by a
lengthy letter from Samuel Latham Mitchill, an early protector of that vanishing bird.*

entomologist, geologist, herpetologist, ichthyologist, mineralogist, ornithologist, paleontologist and zoologist. He was, as well, a former member of the New York State Assembly, of the House of Representatives and of the Senate. He carried in his head—and imparted it on any and all occasions—so much information on everything that his contemporaries outdid themselves in trying to explain him.

A historian of New York wrote of Mitchill that

> an essay on composts, a tractate on the deaf and dumb, verses to the Indian tribes might be eliminated from his mental alembic within the compass of a few hours. He was now engaged with the anatomy of the egg, and now deciphering a Babylonian brick; now involved in the nature of meteoric stones; now in the different species of brassica; now in the evaporization of fresh water, now in that of salt; now scrutinizing the geology of Niagara; now anatomizing the tortoise; now offering suggestions on the angle of the windmill; and now concurring with Michaux on the beauty of the black walnut for parlor furniture; now in the investigation of bivalves; and now with the learned Jewish Rabbi Gershom Seixas in exegetical disquisitions on Kennicott's Hebrew Bible.
>
> One day, in workmanlike dress, he might have been engaged on the natural history of the American elk, or perplexed as to the alimentary nature of tadpoles; another, attired in the costume of a native of the Feejee Islands, he was better accoutred for illustration, and for the reception, at his house, of a meeting of his philosophical acquaintances.

To his colleagues in Congress, Mitchill was known as "the walking library." Jefferson called him "the Congressional Dictionary." To his partner in public works and natural history, Governor DeWitt Clinton of New York, the doctor was "the Delphic oracle." The president of Columbia University considered him "a living encyclopedia," and a New York bishop, desperately trying to encompass Mitchill, summed him up as "a chaos of knowledge."

Mitchill lived during the last period in American science when a single man could involve himself in many disciplines and achieve a reasonable mastery of them all. His countrymen, often limited in learning but avid for knowledge of all kinds, submitted willingly to the barrages of fact and philosophy that Mitchill kept firing at them. In spanning so much knowledge and, at the same time, becoming a bulwark of American politics, he recalled an earlier New Yorker, Cadwallader Colden. The skeins of his career, curiously enough, wind back to that redoubtable scientist-politician.

At about the time that he was indoctrinating his daughter Jane into the Linnaean system, Colden invited a 14-year-old boy named Samuel Bard to stay at his home. Samuel's father, Dr. John Bard, had been recommended to Colden by Benjamin Franklin and the two men became close friends. When young Samuel fell sickly, Colden suggested he come out to mend in the fresh frontier air at Coldengham. There the young man quickly attached himself to Jane and her botanical projects, helping her collect and draw specimens. At Colden's suggestion, Samuel went off to the University of Edinburgh, still a center of medical-botanical study. Graduated and back in America, Samuel became a leading physician of New York, twice helping to save President Washington's life. Once, with his father, he cut out a carbuncle which had given Washington a frighteningly high fever. Another time, he brought Washington through a bout of pneumonia which had left Jefferson "in total despair" at the chances of the President's survival.

Bard's interest in botany, begun at Coldengham and reinforced at Edinburgh, drew him to one of his medical apprentices, a Quaker farm boy named Mitchill, who showed considerable skill at collecting and classifying plants. In his turn, Dr. Bard encouraged his protégé to go to Edinburgh, and it was inevitable, when Mitchill came back to be professor of chemistry at Columbia College, that he include botany and other natural history subjects in his courses.

Building up a successful medical practice and marrying the widow of a wealthy shipbuilder, Mitchill could afford to spend more and more time as a naturalist. Soon he all but gave up medicine for natural science. Since he was interested in opening new fields rather than adding to old ones, he concentrated on ichthyology, the study of fishes. What meadows and forests were to the Bartrams and flyways were to Wilson, the inexhaustible waters around New York were to Mitchill. He came to know them intimately but also learned that he could explore their life by proxy, going down to the fish markets and browsing through the stalls for unfamiliar specimens. In his house overlooking the East River, he would classify a fish by reference to his large library and dissect it in his operating room. A thoroughgoing man, he would then call Jenny, his housekeeper, and tell her to cook the fish so he could judge its table use. The long-suffering Jenny grew adept at making a meal out of strange sea creatures that seemed all head or all tail or more bones than flesh, though she did complain once at having to prepare a dish of spotted snakes. Called to dinner, the doctor would beg a few moments more to examine some new specimen and, when he showed up hours later, would find his wife and Jenny gone to bed and his latest subject cooked and cold on the kitchen table. His wife tried valiantly to keep to his schedule and tidy up his study, but finally gave up when the doctor came in one day with a moth-ridden anteater skin she recognized as something she had just thrown out in the rubbish. Waving it triumphantly, he announced that he had obtained it from some street boys, to whom he had given fifty cents along with a lecture on the animal's dietary habits.

Before long, the local fishermen knew all about the doctor's ichthyological obsession, and would show up at his home with the latest odd creature they had brought up in their nets. Standing wet-booted in his library, they would listen amazed as the doctor told them more about their catch than they thought it possible for a man to discover. "Give me a fin, and I will tell you the fish," he used to say to them, and would always make good on the boast.

The result of his research was the first American work on ichthyology, *The Fishes of New York*, published in 1815. It described 166 different species, classifying some two dozen new ones and bringing some order to a disorganized branch of American natural history. His approach was scientific but touched by his concern for the practical. For example, fishermen waiting for the blackfish to run in spring were advised to consult the dogwood trees. When their blossoms opened, the fish would come in. If there were no dogwoods in the vicinity, chestnut trees would do.

For the most part, Dr. Mitchill curbed his tendency to wander off into byways of fact, but when he came to the sheepshead, he could not contain himself. After going through dutiful descriptions of the fish's large lips, double nostrils, brown eyes, smooth gills, concave tail, horny scales and convoluted intestines (filled, he found, with pieces of crab), and noting that the fish gets

One of Dr. Mitchill's favorite fish, the sheepshead (top right) appeared in his Fishes of New York, *the first authoritative work of its kind to be published in America.*

its name because "the form of the mouth and a certain smuttiness of the face have a distinct resemblance to the physiognomy of a sheep," his admiration for this "noble fish" welled forth. "The outfit of a sheepsheading party is always an occasion of considerable parade and high expectation," he declared. "Whenever a sheepshead is brought on board more joy is manifested than by a possession of any other kind of fish. The feats of hooking and pulling him in furnish abundant material for the most pleasing and hyperbolical stories. Nothing in the opinion of a New Yorker can exceed boiled sheepshead served up at a sumptuous dinner." He also had good things to say for the striped bass, called *Perca mitchilli*—"large, distinguished," he wrote, "beyond the generality of fishes," as, of course, anything bearing the name of Mitchill should be. For the most part, he himself collected and examined the fish he discussed, but he did go afield to describe a shark caught by Joshua Terry of Sag Harbor and a 100-pound numbfish, or ray, that had been pulled in by Captains Rose and Dodge of the town of New Shoreham.

Fish conservation concerned him. While in the New York legislature, he opposed construction of a dam on the upper Hudson that might obstruct migrating fish. "I considered myself the advocate of the fish," he explained, "the counsel for their silent tribes, like Saint Antonio." The dam project, he was glad to report, "was negatived by a very large majority." But his advocacy still did not do enough for the silent tribes. "The life of the herring," he added rather sadly, "has never been thought important enough to be put under the protection of the law in New York."

Local fishermen were a handy but very small segment of the doctor's circle of contributors. Naturalists always seemed to need someone to serve as a center of knowledge, and here Mitchill fulfilled that role. In a single week, he was sent an assortment that might have taxed even his wide-ranging talents. As an ichthyologist, he got a fish from Monte Bolca in Italy; as a herpetologist, a serpent from the Linnaean Society in Boston; as a botanist, a *Spiraea tomentosa* (steeplebush) from Connecticut; as a mineralogist, Istrian quicksilver from Trieste and volcanic rock from Tenerife; as a conchologist, shells from St. Jago; as an anthropologist, some antiquities from Aquileia.

When Meriwether Lewis wanted to identify some things he had brought back with him, he turned to the doctor for answers. When Henry Schoolcraft, who explored the sources of the Mississippi, wanted to verify a new species of squirrel that European naturalists were skeptical about, Mitchill confirmed it—and patriotically named it the "Federation squirrel." Having made some pioneering studies on amphibians and snakes, the doctor was deluged with specimens and stories of sea serpents. He declared one to be a badly mutilated land snake and another to be a huge mackerel, and he took special delight in demonstrating that the long serpent sighted slithering across Lake Ontario was a mother duck leading her ducklings over the waves.

The doctor was not belligerent about his knowledge, but he did not run from controversy. In fact, he was an outspoken partisan in two of the fiercest scientific battles of his time. In geology, he took sides in the earthshaking arguments between the Neptunists and the Vulcanists. The Neptunists held that all the earth's land masses had been built up from the primeval deposits of the sea. The Vulcanists believed that heat, water and volcanic action were responsible for its geologic structure. The doctor was a Neptunist, and its adherents were glad to have him on their side. His *Sketch of the Mineralogical History of New York*, published in 1798, was the earliest American effort to study a single region—New York, from the eastern tip of Long Island to Niagara Falls—at first hand and to organize the data into a coherent description of the area. The first significant paper on American geology, it was to be a model for geologists who followed Mitchill. Of course, in the Neptunist-Vulcanist controversy, Mitchill would have been wrong no matter which theory he had chosen. Not until the mid-nineteenth century did geologists accept the modern concept that it was not a single force that shaped the earth but all those forces acting on it— volcanic upheavals, rise of sea floors, glacial movement, erosion.

In chemistry, a field in which he had few American peers, Mitchill boldly took issue with a long-unchallenged dogma: that combustion was caused by a substance called phlogiston, supposedly present in all inflammable material, which escaped during combustion in the form of flame and heat. No one had ever seen or detected phlogiston itself, but its existence was accepted without question all through the eighteenth century. Its most prominent adherent came to be Joseph Priestley, the discoverer of oxygen, who had settled in Pennsylvania after British mobs, outraged by his radical religious and political beliefs, had sacked his home. Though an admiring friend of Priestley's, Mitchill could not accept his theory. He was drawn to the discoveries of Lavoisier, the French chemist whose work in quantitative chemistry denied and destroyed phlogiston, once and for all. By introducing Lavoisier's theories, which are the basis for modern chemistry, Mitchill helped set the course of American chemistry.

Mitchill got caught up, unhappily, in his own chemical crotchet, an element that he called septon. This, he declared, was the instrument of decay and the cause of most diseases. Like Cadwallader Colden with his explication of Newton's principles, Mitchill could neither prove his point nor let go of it. He lectured on septon, wrote papers on it and even composed a long poem called "The Doctrine of Septon," in which the doctor's doggerel elucidated the "principle of dissolution" and blamed septon for cancer, leprosy, scurvy and ringworm. Mitchill's intuition, it must be said, was sounder than his conclusions.

His nonexistent septon bore some resemblance to nitrogen, which is a product of decay. Had he been a little more modest in his claims for septon, Mitchill might have added a valuable bit of scientific husbandry with his studies of decay. But, like so many men of his time, he was out after a grand principle that would explain a universal truth, and he stretched his insights further than fact could carry them.

All this other work drew Mitchill away from his first love in natural science. In botany, he was more inclined to receive information than search for it and more interested in passing it on to others than in developing it himself. Still, he provided much botanical data for the first *United States Pharmacopœia*, published in 1820. And somewhere he found time to write the first proper history and bibliography of New World botany. He began his discourse, as might be expected, with an account of the first recorded botanical garden, the Garden of Eden. Running quickly through other Biblical references, he paused in classical times to note that Daphne had been transformed into a shrub and Narcissus into a flower, and finally came with the explorers to his subject: the New World. He detailed the work of Catesby, Colden, Bartram, Kalm and Garden, setting down facts and recollections still fresh in the men's memories. And he praised "the industry and learning" of a new force in botany, his colleague David Hosack.

A large and convivial Scotsman, Dr. Hosack studied at Edinburgh and came to New York to become the medical partner of Jane Colden's pupil Samuel Bard and to take over Mitchill's chair at Columbia. When Bard retired, he left Hosack with the richest practice in America. An adventurous scientist, Hosack was the first American doctor to use the stethoscope and one of the most forthright in advocating vaccinations. As the leading physician in New York, he was summoned in 1804 to the heights of Weehawken, across the Hudson, to attend the duel between Alexander Hamilton and Aaron Burr. He could not save Hamilton after that mortal bullet wound, and though he considered Burr a murderer, he helped him flee to the South to escape prosecution.

A man of "profuse expenditure" able to earn huge fees but unable to hold on to them—"Had he the wealth of Astor," a later friend remarked, "he would have died poor"—Hosack poured his money into the most ambitious botanical project ever attempted in America, the Elgin Gardens. For some five thousand dollars, plus an annual payment of "16 bushels of good merchandisable wheat," he bought from the city twenty acres of rocky swamp on Middle Road at the northern limits of the city—today the area from Forty-seventh to Fifty-first streets west of Fifth Avenue. There, in 1809, he set up his Elgin Gardens, a wonder of the time. Within two years, he had two thousand species of American plants growing in outdoor plots and three greenhouses. These were augmented by plants gathered on the Lewis and Clark expedition and brought to the garden

The Elgin Gardens, the finest botanical garden of its day, was built by Mitchill's friend David Hosack on the site where Rockefeller Center stands today.

by Frederick Pursh, a German botanist working in Philadelphia. Hired by Lewis to describe and classify the plants, Pursh came to look on them as his own property, taking some of them with him to New York and later to London. Though he was denounced by fellow botanists for this, Pursh performed a major service to science—and to the Lewis and Clark expedition—in the way he presented the plants in his *Flora Americae Septentrionalis*.

During Pursh's three years in New York, he and Hosack made the Elgin Gardens the finest in America and were in part responsible for a major shift in American natural history. Up to now, Philadelphia had been the unchallenged center of the natural sciences—the two Bartrams, Peale, Wilson and the American Philosophical Society had seen to that. Now anyone who wanted to see the best display of American flora, more complete and orderly and scholarly than Bartram's Gardens, would have to come to New York and take the long drive up Middle Road to the Elgin Gardens. Anything so well done was, of course, very costly, and even the free-spending Dr. Hosack could not afford his gardens. After some confusing transactions, by which he lost thousands of dollars, Hosack sold the land to the College of Physicians and Surgeons. When the college became part of Columbia University, it brought the Elgin Gardens along as a kind of dowry—an immensely rich one, since the land on which the doctor grew his plants is today the property (still owned by Columbia) on which Rockefeller Center is built.

In a more important way than Hosack's gardens, Dr. Mitchill raised New York as a center of natural history. Like Charles Willson Peale, he was a superb popularizer and promoter of science. In 1817, he founded the Lyceum of Natural History in New York. Though it had large collections and exhibits, the Lyceum was intended for serious study rather than popular sightseeing. Dr. Mitchill, of course, became its first president and its busiest contributor, not just of his knowledge and wisdom but also of his varied collections of fish, fowl and minerals. At the Lyceum, as at home, he carried science to the table. The minutes of a dinner meeting noted that through him, "the members were gratified with a taste of the boiled tongue of the sea elephant, *Phocaelephantinia*."

All in all, Mitchill wrote about two hundred papers for the Lyceum and delivered innumerable addresses. In one he declared his belief that the horse had been native to America, a concept affirmed by paleontologists decades later. He brought leading scientists of past and future generations to lecture, among them old Mr. Peale, whom the doctor introduced glowingly as "the father of natural history in America," though he privately confessed that he had once found Peale's lectures "desultory." The Lyceum, which was housed in a building near City Hall, had another attraction for Peale, an institute for the deaf and dumb. Here he came to woo an elderly teacher. Widowed for a third time at the age of eighty-five, he offered to teach the lady his newest accomplishment: making porcelain false teeth. In return, he hoped she would teach him the deaf-and-dumb language and consider becoming his wife. The offer and the suit were both kindly received and gently refused.

As influential as the Lyceum was another of Mitchill's creations, the *Medical Repository*, founded in 1797 as the first independent scientific journal in the country. In its 20-year life, the *Repository* was the most stimulating, authoritative and wide-ranging scientific publication in the Western Hemisphere. Mitchill presided over it with an open mind for new talent and the theories of scientists he did not agree with. Of course, he gave full space to his own work—but getting a hearing for himself was never any problem for the doctor. His lectures at the Lyceum were automatically abstracted in the *American Journal of Science and Arts*. The Literary and Philosophical Society, of which the doctor was a founder, published his *Fishes of New York*. The New York Historical Society, which he helped found, gratefully sponsored his natural history lectures. On the podium, the doctor was a past master of the show-and-tell technique. As he started to empty his pockets, his audiences always wondered what would come next. At various times he produced "the snout, tail and fins of an 11-foot swordfish harpooned near Sandy Hook," "arms and domestic utensils from the Sandwich Islands," a steel file found in the belly shell of a tortoise and "several teeth of the mammoth lately discovered by Judge Haring of Rockland County."

The Historical Society also served as forum for one of Mitchill's favorite nonscientific causes: to change the name of the United States of America to Fredonia, a cause he promoted in debates, in speeches to legislatures and in a poem praising Fredonia's achievements, expectations, heroes and women:

> Whenever Fredonia's fair appear,
> Begins resplendent beauty's reign,
> Grace, virtue, modesty are near.
> And taste and delicacy are in their train.

Mitchill's political programs were not generally so far-fetched as this. He was, in fact, an industrious and effective public official, serving for two decades as a state and national legislator. His public career began only three years after he returned from schooling in Scotland. In 1790, when he was twenty-six, he was elected to the New York Assembly. His first assignment was suited to his formidable talents. He was instructed to go through the expiring laws of New York, decide which ones should be kept and which discarded, then make a list of new laws the state would require. His record was impressive enough to send him, in 1801, to Congress. There, as an ardent supporter of Jefferson, he led the administration forces in supporting the Louisiana Purchase. That epic bargain had been a shambles of noncommunication and unconstitutional procedure. Because Napoleon proved to be in such a hurry to sell, the American commissioners in Paris could not keep their government abreast of the negotiations, and they had bought the whole tract before anyone back home really knew what they were up to. Having approved the deal, Jefferson then looked for something in the Constitution that would permit the purchase—and found nothing. Mitchill became a leader of a pragmatic group in Congress which held that though the Constitution did not authorize the purchase, neither did it forbid it. What would happen, he rose to ask, should some oceanic upheaval create a new island off Cape Hatteras? Would the Constitution forbid the erection of a lighthouse on land not part of the United States? Of course not. Or, what would happen when the United States, its population expanding, grew too crowded? If the Constitution forbade the acquisition of new territory, he declared, there would be only one alternative, "the Chinese custom of infanticide to get rid of the tender little beings for whom food could not be procured." Between unconstitutional lighthouses and slaughtered babies—and the plain fact that the country couldn't possibly turn down such an opportunity—Congress voted almost four to one to buy the land.

During his second term in the House, Mitchill was appointed to a vacant seat in the Senate where he soon became noted for his endless erudition and the unyielding exhaustiveness of his speeches. In a major defense of Jefferson's Embargo Act, which sought to restrict the use of foreign ships in United States commerce, Mitchill started with "a survey of the mercantile conditions of the U.S.," touching on the East India Company, Nantucket whalers, early-American diplomatic missions and so on for quite a while until he announced, "This brings me to the year 1798. I shall now make a hasty retrospect of the American people," which, after a while, took him into a glowing catalog of American industry, "the manufactures in iron, forgings and refining, the casting of hollow ware, the preparation of nails, the fabrication of cannon, works in pelts and skins, paper mills, gazettes, pamphlets, books, Greek and Latin classics. . . . Fourthly," he began . . . "but I check myself," and went into a patriotic peroration. "When Mr. Mitchill concluded," wrote the Congressional recorder with an almost audible sigh of relief, "the Senate adjourned."

Though he kept straying into arcane byways, Mitchill was a valued legislator. Out of his expansive knowledge of physics, geology and botany, he could provide data and sound reasoning in debates on roads, canals and agriculture. Because of his Indian studies—he had translated Indian war songs and been made an honorary Mohawk—he could give prudent advice on frontier affairs. As a physician, he helped improve naval sanitation and public health procedures. If he told his colleagues too much about the matter in hand, he still set them straight on it, and if members of Congress often felt like schoolchildren listening to teacher, they were grateful that they had at hand a ready and reliable fountain of fact. They had daily evidence of the aptness of the contemporary quip: "Tap the doctor and he will flow."

The dinner tables of Washington welcomed the doctor's flow. John Quincy Adams, though he disagreed with Mitchill's Jeffersonian views, wrote that the doctor's conversations at White House dinners were very various "of oils, grasses, beasts, birds, petrifactions and incrustations, Pike and Humboldt, Lewis and Barlow and a long train of etcetera, for the doctor knows a little of everything and is communicative of what he knows, which makes me delight in his company."

Mitchill's fund of information included the latest capital gossip. He wrote to his wife that James Madison, Washington's most eligible bachelor, was torn between two attractive widows but he was sure Dolley Todd, whose smile and blue eyes made her a "queen of hearts," would catch him. And after one dinner at the White House, he described a novel dessert: "Ice cream in the form of balls of the frozen material enclosed in covers of warm pastry exhibiting a curious contrast as if the ice had just been taken from the oven." Jefferson or his chef must apparently be credited with having invented the baked Alaska.

In 1813, the doctor retired from politics and gave his time to science and public works, successfully promoting two projects derided at the time as hare-brained: the steamboat and the Erie Canal. When he was in the New York legislature, he had pushed through a bill enabling Robert Fulton to pursue what was called "an idle and whimsical project." An early biographer of Fulton —David Colden, Cadwallader's grandson, who became mayor of New York City —gave the doctor most of the credit for Fulton's success. The biographer incidentally noted the fact that Fulton, having triumphantly sailed the *Clermont* up to Albany, had trouble finding passengers for the return trip. "Only two Frenchmen had the courage to embark with him," the account states. One of them was François André Michaux, the botanist's son, who was in America preparing a work on American trees.

In both the steamboat project and the Erie Canal scheme, Mitchill was allied with another politician-naturalist, DeWitt Clinton, who served as mayor of New York City and as governor of the state. A well-grounded Linnaean, Clinton studied and collected in several fields of natural science. Sent out to explore routes for a canal connecting the Great Lakes and the Hudson River, he turned parts of his report into a natural history of the region. He noted in passing that all the squirrels he encountered were black, and that the population of red-winged blackbirds was increasing. He reported an abundance of ginseng and mandrake and remarked on the way fireweed sprang up in burned-over woods where the plant had not appeared for decades (a phenomenon also noted after World War II in bombed-out London). Analyzing the rocks of the area, he found them to be of oceanic origin, and discovering an interesting periwinkle shell, he sent it to Peale's Museum. Later, as "Hibernicus," Clinton became one of the most widely read naturalists of the time, writing a newspaper column called *Letters on Natural History and Internal Resources of New York*, which was reprinted all over the East. Aimed primarily at promoting the canal project, the column made observations on the life cycle of the *Libellula* (a dragonfly) and criticized the whippoorwill's call, which, "although the call of love, tends to inspire melancholy." Clinton had his own answer to the old question that Peter Kalm had asked Cadwallader Colden: Was the cockroach a native American or a foreigner? The roach, declared Clinton, was all-American.

The Mitchill-Clinton alliance was to do a very good turn for American botany. An upstate New Yorker named Amos Eaton, influenced by Mitchill and Hosack to turn away from law to natural history, was charged with forgery and convicted on what seem to have been trumped-up charges. After four years in prison, he was released by Governor Tompkins (the one who wouldn't buy Wilson's birds), with an astonishingly archaic condition: that he never set foot in New York State again. Eaton spent several years in Connecticut until

Mitchill, among others, took his case to Governor Clinton, who not only ended the exile with an unconditional pardon, but also invited Eaton to deliver a series of lectures to the state legislature. The community of naturalists certainly had a way of helping its members out, even when it didn't involve swapping plants or finding birds. Eaton went on to write and sponsor botanical guides that made him the most important popularizer of natural history after Peale.

The most impressive accomplishment of the Clinton-Mitchill alliance was the Erie Canal. No one was wiser in advising or stauncher in supporting Clinton, through all the skepticism and over all the obstacles, than Dr. Mitchill. When the canal was completed in 1825, the doctor stood beside the governor on the deck of a vessel in New York Bay. First Governor Clinton poured a keg of Lake Erie water into the bay, bringing together the West and the Atlantic. Then Dr. Mitchill stepped forward to give the event its proper scale. Though he came near losing his balance on the pitching deck, he never lost the thread of his discourse. After evoking the ancients and talking of their river gods, he conjured up a wedding between the Ruler of the Deep and the Belle of the Inland Waters. He declaimed,

> On the wings of the wind the Atlantic supplied
> And the flood of the river as upward it goes . . .

At last, as recounted in the official report by David Colden, whose grandfather himself had projected such a canal, "Dr. Mitchill completed the ceremony by pouring into the briny deep, bottles of water from the Ganges and Indus, the Nile and the Gambia, the Thames, the Seine, the Rhine, the Danube, the Mississippi and Columbia, the Orinoco, La Plata and Amazon." The doctor then declared that "The virtue infused in these waters has spread from this spot by a combination of mechanical impulse, chemical attraction and diffusive propagation through the whole mass of waters with an electrical rapidity and magnetical subtlety that authorizes me to pronounce the circumfluent ocean republicanized. It is done. I pronounce this union blessed." And the applause of the admiring crowd acknowledged that no man alive was better equipped than the all-knowing doctor to authorize, republicanize and bless such a grand union of nature.

CHAPTER TEN

THE AMERICAN WOODSMAN

❦ ❦ ❦ ❦ ❦ Dr. Mitchill's family learned to put up with the things he did at home in the name of science. But the people who lived on a street some blocks away were less forbearing when the smell of formaldehyde floated from a rented room where the doctor busied himself evenings with some noisome project. A constable coming to investigate found the doctor in the company of several dead birds and a young man with a French accent. He was trying out some interesting ideas in taxidermy, the doctor explained, and his friend was helping. The constable heard him out, as one always did with the doctor, and then told him and his helper to stop annoying the neighbors with their experiments.

Perhaps if the meddling policeman hadn't tried to interfere with destiny, John James Audubon, the doctor's assistant, might have entered more directly on his career. But it might also have been a less glorious career. For Audubon, the hardest way round was the surest way home. Setting out to make his fortune as a businessman on the exuberant American frontier, he wound up making it as an artist in the dour industrial cities of England. And bad fortune again and again proved to be his best friend, moving him away from what he was doing into what he should have been doing.

But paradox was part of Audubon's character. He was an artist of the Romantic era, which is to say, a contradictory genius—wild-eyed in his vision and down-to-earth in his work, reckless in his ambitions and prodigiously patient in achieving them, disdainful of the world's opinion and cunning in his way of cultivating it. Audubon was a true romantic: a charming, impetuous man and a dogged, immovable artist.

He was French by birth and became an American for the most practical reason: to avoid being drafted into Napoleon's army. The illegitimate son of a sea captain, he had been born on his father's plantation in Santo Domingo in 1785. His mother, a French country girl Captain Audubon had met aboard ship,

died a few months after bearing her son, Jean Jacques. The captain took Jean
to France where his childless wife adopted and indulged the boy, letting him go
out and draw birds when he should have been doing his lessons. His sterner
father, though he encouraged Jean's interest in birds, tried to make a sailor
out of his son (who all his life suffered from seasickness). The boy flunked
out of the navy. To keep him from being taken by army recruiters, and to look
over some property he owned in Pennsylvania, the captain sent Jean to America,
instructing him to change his name from Jean Jacques to John James. Jean-
turned-John was eighteen when he arrived in 1803. Falling desperately ill, he
was nursed back to health by Captain Audubon's agent, Miers Fisher, an
intellectual Philadelphia merchant whose disposition toward natural history
made him one of Alexander Wilson's best patrons—his family bought five
subscriptions to the *American Ornithology*.

When he recovered, young Audubon settled on his father's farm at Mill
Grove, making the acquaintance of the unreasonable American language, the
exciting American outdoors, the astonishing American birds and Lucy Bakewell,
who lived nearby. A well-mannered, well-educated English girl, Lucy had
gained an appreciation of nature back home from the family physician, Erasmus
Darwin, an imaginative botanist (and grandfather of the evolutionist) who set
the Linnaean system to verse in a popular poem, "The Loves of Plants."

Audubon courted his two American loves—the birds and Lucy—at the same
time. In a cave near Perkiomen Creek, he found some phoebes building their
nests. Only a couple of dozen miles away, at about the same time, Alexander
Wilson was watching the phoebes in a grotto near Bartram's Gardens. Where
Wilson went to watch with a book of poems in his hand, Audubon went with
a pretty girl on his arm—and alarmed Lucy's father, who misinterpreted the
trips to the cave. But Audubon was truly absorbed in his birds. At first as he
watched the phoebes, they were hostile. "The male flew violently, snapped his
bill sharply with a tremulous rolling note," Audubon wrote years later. After a
while, they accepted the watcher and "would often come in close by me as if I
had been a post." He lifted out the first egg "so white and so transparent, the
sight was more pleasant than if I had met with a diamond the same size." Soon
he could reach in and pick the mother off the eggs and handle the fledglings when
they were hatched. Then he undertook one of the earliest experiments in bird-
banding. "I attached light threads to the legs of the young but these they or their
parents invariably removed. When they were about to leave I fixed a light silver
thread to the leg of each, so fastened that the bird could not remove it." The
threads were still on some of the birds when they returned next spring. Two
springs later he approached a pair of phoebes. One of them was shy; the other
permitted him to come close. This was one of the early pair, Audubon decided,
who remembered the creature that had kept them company in the cave.

Audubon's early drawings had a whimsical grace. These grebes were done in 1805 when the 20-year-old Audubon returned home to France for a visit.

Audubon's room at the farm became a small-scale nature museum. Lucy's younger brother William Bakewell, taken to see it, was "astonished and delighted." The walls, he wrote, "were festooned with all kinds of birds' eggs, carefully blown out and strung on a thread. The chimney piece was covered with stuffed squirrels, raccoons and opossums; the shelves were crowded with fishes, frogs, snakes, lizards. Paintings were arrayed on the walls, chiefly of birds. He had great skill in stuffing and preserving animals." And besides, added Bakewell, running on breathlessly, "he had a trick in training dogs. He was an admirable marksman, an expert swimmer, a clever rider possessed of prodigious strength, notable for the elegance of his figure, musical, a good fencer, danced well, had some acquaintance with legerdemain tricks, worked in hair and could plait willow baskets."

The bird paintings on the wall showed the bare beginnings of Audubon's art. "Stiff unmeaning profiles," he called them, and suffered the same frustrations Alexander Wilson had met when he began to draw birds. Now, "watching a pair of peewees at Mill Grove, a thought struck my mind like a flash of light: that nothing could ever answer my enthusiastic desires to represent nature except to copy her alive and moving." He drew "hundreds of outlines of the peewees, either alighted or on the wing, but could finish none of my sketches." Trying to fashion a lifelike model,

> I cogitated a mannequin, labored with wood, cord and wires and formed a grotesque figure, a tolerable-looking Dodo. I gave it a kick and thought again. One morning I leaped out of bed, went off at a gallop towards Norristown. When I arrived there, not a door was open, for it was not yet daylight. I went to the river, took a bath and returning to the town inquired for wire of different sizes, bought some and was soon again at Mill Grove. I shot the first kingfisher I met, pierced the body with a wire, fixed it to the board, another wire held the head, smaller ones fixed the feet. The last wire proved a delightful elevator to the bird's tail and at last—there stood before me the real kingfisher. I outlined the bird, colored it. This was my first drawing actually from nature.

Birds did not distract him from his social life: "Not a ball, a skating match, a house or riding party took place without me." But the world of natural science in and around Philadelphia did not attract him. Miers Fisher, though a kind of guardian to Audubon and a patron to Alexander Wilson, never brought the two together. Audubon never mentions visiting Bartram's Gardens or Peale's Museum. His purpose in America was not to study nature but to make money for his father by exploiting a vein of lead ore on his father's property.

He was not very good at this, and in 1805 he impulsively returned to France to discuss business ventures and to get consent to marry Lucy. Captain Audubon promised to consider the marriage and gave him money to set up a partnership with a young family friend named Ferdinand Rozier. With money to invest but not much sense about how to use it—he once sent eight thousand dollars in cash to a bank in an open envelope—Audubon went to New York in 1806 to be apprentice clerk to Lucy's merchant uncle, Benjamin Bakewell. But birds still held him. He bought waterfowl in the early-morning markets, drew them whenever he could and then, after Mr. Bakewell introduced him to his friend Dr. Mitchill, stuffed them by night. Meanwhile he invested unwisely in indigo, one of the most volatile New World commodities.

His intended partner, Ferdinand Rozier, was not doing much better—he had lost in a scheme to export American hams to the West Indies. Old ways and places, the two concluded, were not for them, and they set out for the West. By coach, which was so slow and uncomfortable that they walked as much as rode, and by river, in an open flatboat so poorly navigated that they were always jumping off to shove it off snags and sandbars, they traveled to the river port of Louisville.

There they opened a store, Rozier stocking it while Audubon went out to find customers and make friends. George Rogers Clark told Audubon about untamed forests and Revolutionary battles. The general's brother William, back from the expedition with Meriwether Lewis, described the birds and animals in the still wilder western lands. A good friend of Dr. Mitchell's, Dr. William Galt, a frontier virtuoso, talked knowledgeably about local botany and ornithology. William Croghan, a friend of Audubon's father and kin to the freebooter who dug up the fossil bones that aroused those arguments half a century before, took Audubon out to see a local phenomenon, a hollow sycamore tree where chimney swifts roosted.

> The sun was going down [Audubon wrote], thousands of swallows were flying closely above me and three or four at a time were pitching into the hole like bees hurrying into their hive. I remained, my head leaning on the tree listening to the roaring noise made within by the birds as they settled. Next morning I arose early and placed my head against the tree. All was silent within when suddenly I thought the great tree was giving way. The swallows were now pouring out in a black continued stream. I listened with amazement to the noise within which I could compare to nothing else than the sound of a large wheel revolving under a powerful stream.

He had a hole cut in the tree so he could get inside at night and count the birds: "There would be 375 square feet of surface. Each square foot would contain 32 birds. The number of swallows therefore that roosted in this single tree was 9,000." It is an interesting calculation but most interesting is the fact that Audubon took the trouble to make it.

When the winter ended, Audubon went back east, married Lucy and brought her out to live at the Indian Queen, the best inn in town. He took easily to both of his frontier worlds. In the pathless forests, he was becoming, as he came to call himself, an American woodsman—a superb marksman, a patient fisherman, an alert observer of everything that went on around him. He was as much at ease among the cultivated French settlers at nearby Shippingport, who enjoyed his fiddling, his dancing and his animated mind.

He had been in Louisville for two years when Alexander Wilson called. Their meeting, which soured Wilson, stirred Audubon's ambition and self-esteem. He felt he could draw birds as well as his visitor or even better. From then on, Wilson was Audubon's mark. His writings are studded with references to Wilson, his own works compared—favorably—with Wilson's.

Audubon's diligence as a merchant slackened. Off hunting for birds when he should have been selling his merchandise, and drawing them when he should have been tending to customers, he came to know the birds intimately. He watched the snowy owl lying "flat and lengthwise with its head down near the water. One might have supposed the bird sound asleep. The instant a fish rose to the surface, the owl thrust out the claw that was next to the water, seized it and drew it out like lightning." He saw how the wood-duck drake "chases his rivals away from some coquetting female, raises his head, curves his neck, bows before her and, his silken crest high, lets a guttural note emerge from his swollen throat. To the female it is as the song of the wood thrush." Riding through a forest, he came on an avocet's nest: "Softly I crawled within three feet of the sitting avocet. Her head was almost mournfully sunk among her plumage, her eyes were half closed as if she were dreaming."

Business went poorly. The partners moved down river to Henderson and then, at Rozier's insistence, to the village of Ste. Genevieve, on the Mississippi. Audubon immensely enjoyed the trek through the woods, filled with wintering flocks of ducks, swans and parakeets. They camped near some Osage Indians and Audubon proved himself to be a fine wilderness entertainer. The Indians "were delighted to see me draw and when I made a tolerable portrait of one in red chalk, the others laughed to excess." Nat, their clerk, "played the fiddle and I had a flute. The squaws laughed heartily."

Ste. Genevieve would be too rough for Lucy, Audubon decided, and dissolved his partnership with Rozier, who went on to make a very good thing of his new business. Back in Henderson, Audubon set up a new partnership with Lucy's brother Thomas and twice went east to raise money. In Philadelphia he called on Wilson. "He was drawing a white-headed eagle," Audubon recalled. "He received me with civility and took me to the Exhibition Rooms of Rembrandt Peale to see 'Napoleon Crossing the Alps.' Mr. Wilson spoke not a word of birds or drawings. Feeling, as I was forced to, that my company was not agreeable, I parted from him."

On the way home from one trip, riding a spirited horse named Barro, he had a more congenial meeting with

> a gentleman from New Orleans whose name was Vincent Nolte. He was mounted on a superb horse. As I approached and praised his horse he observed very courteously that he wished I had as good a one. I asked

A thorough ornithologist, Audubon collected birds' nests and eggs for study and made detailed drawings of them. Some were collected in Louisiana, at Elizabeth Pirrie's plantation.

when he would reach Bedford. "Just soon enough to have some trout ready for our supper if you will join me when you get there." I almost imagined that Barro understood our conversation. He pricked his ears and lengthened his pace. At this, Mr. Nolte caracoled his horse and put him into a quick trot—but all in vain; for I reached the hotel a quarter of an hour before him.

This Vincent Nolte was a merchant and adventurer who, according to his autobiography, *Fifty Years in Both Hemispheres*, did banking chores for the Pope, advised Lafayette on finances and traveled in the most interesting political and intellectual circles of Europe and America. He achieved posthumous fame in the 1930s when Hervey Allen introduced him in his best-selling novel *Anthony Adverse*, calling him by his real name and making him his fictional hero's best friend. In his autobiography, Nolte recalled coming upon Audubon sitting at an inn, "with a madras handkerchief wound around his head. 'You are a Frenchman, sire?' 'No sare,' he answered, 'hi emm an Henglishman.' 'How do you make that out? You look like a Frenchman and you speak like one.' 'Hi emm an Henglishman becas hi got a Heenglish wife.'"

Audubon stuck to his store in Henderson for seven years with some success. He owned a log store, a log house, some real estate, three or four slaves. Often as not, a partner or the clerks tended the store while he was off in the woods hunting birds or out in back of the store stuffing and drawing them. Always a sociable man, he made a good friend of Daniel Boone. The old backwoodsman, who was reluctant because of his seventy-odd years to go out hunting with Audubon, demonstrated the way to "bark" squirrels.

Pointing to a squirrel crouched on a branch about fifty paces distance [Audubon wrote], he raised his rifle. A whip-like report reverberated through the woods. Judge of my surprise when I perceived that the ball had hit the piece of bark just beneath the squirrel and shivered it into splinters. The concussion killed the animal and sent it whirling through the air as if blown up by a powder magazine explosion.

Audubon also made a most unlikely enemy—John Keats. The poet, scraping together some money, had sent his younger brother George off to build it into a fortune in America. George and his 16-year-old bride Georgiana settled in Henderson. Audubon showed the tenderfoot Englishman how to chop logs and Lucy befriended Georgiana. George invested in a steamship Audubon partly owned and, having lost his money, told his brother it was all Audubon's fault. The poet was outraged. "I cannot help thinking Mr. Audubon a dishonest man," he wrote Georgiana. "Tell Audubon he's a fool."

The steamship was one of several miserable ventures that eventually ruined Audubon. Another was a lumber mill, which, badly conceived and poorly built, siphoned off the profits of his store. In 1819, after having been jailed by his creditors, Audubon declared himself bankrupt. With only his gun and his drawings left to him, he trudged away from Henderson, "the saddest of all my journeys—the only time in my life when the wild turkeys that so often crossed my path and the thousands of lesser birds that enlivened the woods and the prairies all looked like my enemies and I turned my eyes from them as if I could have wished that they had never existed."

They were, fortunately, as much to blame for Audubon's business failure as anything. He had come to love and understand them better than almost anyone then alive in America. He still lacked Wilson's deep and hard-learned lore but even now, in his hundreds of drawings, he was surpassing Wilson as an artist.

Trouble, which always seemed to turn Audubon in his fated direction— from France to America, from the East to the frontier—now turned him from business to art. Here he was, at the age of thirty-four, discredited as a businessman, all but destitute, living with Lucy's relatives in Shippingport. "That I was a good draughtsman was a blessing," he wrote. "I began to take black chalk portraits. In a few weeks I had as much work as I could possibly wish." It was a macabre way to make a living: "I was sent for from four miles away to take likenesses of country people on their death beds. A clergyman had his dead child disinterred that I, the best delineator of heads in that vicinity, might make a facsimile of his face, which I gave as faithfully as if he were still alive."

After a few months, he found a job that would use his skills as a natural-

Audubon's quick hand at portraiture helped in hard times. These are crayon and chalk drawings of James Berthoud and his wife, good friends of Audubon in Louisville.

ist—in Cincinnati, working for an old friend of Dr. Mitchill's, Dr. Daniel Drake. Drake was, in his own way, as remarkable a character as the New York know-it-all. The child of impractical pioneers, Drake was brought up on the emigrant trail. Crudely educated, he was apprenticed in 1800 at the age of fifteen to Dr. William Goforth of Cincinnati, which was then a small military outpost. Dr. Goforth was a dandy and a dreamer who called on his log-cabin patients with powdered head, gloves and a gold-topped cane and who kept looking for ways to make a fortune—out of a yellow ore, which turned out to be fool's gold, and out of fossil bones from Big Bone Lick, which Peale would not buy.

Young Daniel Drake was Goforth's first student. Barely able to make out the words in the medical books, he memorized the herbals, used his wilderness knowledge to find medicinal herbs and let his master experiment on him with vaccines. After four years, Goforth grandiloquently gave Daniel a diploma and sent him to Philadelphia for further study. Drake returned to take over Goforth's practice and became the civic leader of Cincinnati, now grown into a busy port. Medicine, learning, natural history and most of all Cincinnati were dear to Drake's heart and mind. He exulted in Cincinnati's present and future, goaded its citizens into improving it, bombarded outlanders with its praises and became the prototype of all the generations of boosters who saw in their crossroads settlement a New World Athens or Rome. Hoping to improve the city's intellectual life, Drake wrote learnedly about local botany, zoology and geology, while establishing a medical school, a library and a museum.

When Audubon arrived in 1820, Dr. Drake's Western Museum was a small but thriving institution. Hired at $125 a month, Audubon used the skills he had learned in that smelly room in New York to stuff and preserve the museum's specimens. It was a good job, even though the pay was slow in coming, and it gave him plenty of time to hunt and draw birds. Dr. Drake was impressed by the drawings, and in a speech at the museum—ever the booster —declared that the great Mississippi flyway boasted migrating birds that the East never saw and that "might have escaped the notice of their greatest ornithologist [Wilson] in the single excursion he made to the Ohio. As proof of this supposition, Mr. Audubon, one of the artists attached to the museum, who has drawn from nature in colored crayons several hundred species of American birds, has in his portfolio a large number that are not figured in Mr. Wilson's work which do not seem to have been recognized by any naturalist."

Drake was the first person of any authority to couple Wilson and Audubon. When eastern naturalists came through town and stopped at the museum, he showed them Audubon's drawings and they seemed impressed. Among them were Charles Peale's artist son Titian, and John Bartram's great-grandson Thomas Say, an entomologist. Audubon had been dreaming of doing his own ornithology of American birds. The approval of established naturalists turned the vague idea into a concrete proposal. He put it down in a letter to Henry Clay, his Kentucky congressman. He had spent fifteen years drawing American birds "with a view of publishing them," he wrote Clay, and had already drawn many birds peculiar to the West. But before he presented them "to my country in perfect order, I intend to explore the territories southwest of the Mississippi." Would Mr. Clay give him "such introductory aid necessary to a naturalist?" No one would guess from the letter that Audubon was a failed storekeeper with no formal training in art or science. Fifteen years before, he had scarcely known how to draw a bird.

Clay sent the requested introduction: "I have the satisfaction of personal acquaintance with Mr. John J. Audubon and have learned from others that his character and conduct have been uniformly good." In a separate letter, he cautioned Audubon to find out how well Wilson's *Ornithology* had done before he committed himself too far. But Audubon was not holding back for anything. On October 12, 1820, at the age of thirty-four, he began his new—his real—life.

Leaving Lucy and their two sons in Cincinnati, he embarked on a flatboat for New Orleans with his drawing materials, his gun, his flute, a volume of Linnaeus and a young companion named Joseph Mason, a 13-year-old boy who had been one of Audubon's students in Cincinnati and showed so much promise that Audubon proposed to have him do botanical backgrounds for his birds.

Audubon earned his passage by supplying the ship's food, shooting or fishing for the meals. Mason was the cook, plucking a fowl or scaling a fish and throwing it into the embers of the fire on the open deck. Audubon's journals tell what he saw: "hosts of paroquets, cranes, turkeys, ducks, geese, grouse, the frost heavy and when the sun shun on it, it looked beautifully beyond expression, two eagles catitating, the female was on a very high limb and squatted at the approach of the male who came like a torrent, alighting on her and quackled shrill until he sailed off, the female following him and zigzagging herself through the air." Asserting himself as an ornithologist, he found fault with Wilson for misidentifying a warbler and even with Linnaeus for calling snow geese stupid. He made a whopping error himself, mistaking an immature bald eagle for a new species, which he later named the "Bird of Washington." He often drew the birds he shot before turning them over to Mason for dinner.

The voyage grew tedious. Depressed and fearful, Audubon looked back to happier days and wrote a fanciful autobiography, dotted with invented facts. Audubon was always making up myths about himself. It took the brilliant scholarship of two twentieth-century biographers, Francis Hobart Herrick and Alice Ford, to clear up the confused trail he left with his statements and suggestions that his father had fought at Valley Forge (where there was no fighting), that his mother was a wealthy Spanish lady, that he himself was a native American, born in Louisiana, or, alternately, a Frenchman of royal blood.

At Natchez, Audubon quickly earned five dollars doing a portrait and borrowed a copy of Wilson's *Ornithology* from a merchant who had subscribed when Wilson was staying with Dunbar at The Forest. In New Orleans, he picked up a few portrait commissions and had a titillating adventure, which he described in a little story called *A Remarkable Femelle*:

"On February 21 on Levee Street I was accosted by a female of fine form, her face heavily veiled. She addressed me in animated French: 'Pray monsieur, are you the one sent by the French academy to draw the birds of America?' I answered that I drew them for my pleasure. 'It's you who draws likenesses so remarkably strong in black chalk.' I granted that I took likenesses in that medium."

The lady told Audubon to call on her in thirty minutes, and when she received him, "she threw back her veil to show me one of the most beautiful faces I ever saw. 'Are you married?' she asked. 'Is your wife in the city?' A numbness stole through me. 'Have you ever drawn a full figure naked?' Had I been shot with a forty-eight pounder through the heart, my power of speech could not have been more suddenly cut off. To her impatient 'Why don't you answer?' I said yes. 'I want you to draw the whole of my form. Return in an hour.'"

He returned, and the remarkable femelle, having locked the door, went behind a curtain. After a moment, she instructed him to pull the curtain aside; Audubon saw her lying nude on a couch.

> "Will I do, so?" she asked. I eyed her but only dropped my black lead pencil. She smiled and I began. Fifty-five minutes later she asked that I close the curtain. In an instant she was dressed and looking at what I had done. Very rightly she discerned an error and made me correct it. Then she called for a servant to bring cakes and wine. For ten days I had the pleasure of this beautiful woman's company, undraped. On our last morning she had a beautiful frame ready to show me. She put her name at the lower edge of the drawing as if the work were her own. Mine she wrote in a dark, shaded bit of drapery. Taking me by the hand she gave me a delightful kiss. "Keep my name forever secret," she said. We parted. She did not ask me to call again. I tried several times, in vain. Always the servant said: "Madame is absent."

The story, even its chaste ending, is bizarre but believable. Because of his intense face, his flowing hair, his wiry body, his graceful attitudes and his on-tap charm, Audubon found female admirers everywhere. His letters and journals show him all through his life to have been a flirt and even a philanderer. Setting himself up in New Orleans as a teacher of drawing, he took as a pupil a young woman, Mrs. Heerman, who responded unduly to Audubon's undue attentions. At least it seemed that way to Mr. Heerman, who not only fired Audubon but refused to give him his pay. In the meantime, the mother of another pupil, 15-year-old Elizabeth Pirrie, had asked Audubon to come out to Oakley, her plantation, and be Elizabeth's resident tutor. Audubon wanted a hundred dollars a month, but when the Heerman scandal broke, he hastily accepted Mrs. Pirrie's terms of sixty dollars a month and went up the bayous to Oakley.

There could not have been a more compelling place to urge on his project. "The aspect of the country, entirely new to us, amazed me," Audubon wrote.

> The thousands of warblers and thrushes, the richly blossoming magnolias, the long-wished-for Mississippi kite and swallowtailed kites hovered over us. I found seventeen nests with eggs or young of the orchard oriole in two days. An Indian of the Choctaw nations brought me a female chuck-

will's-widow in full handsome plumage. In its craw were many pinch bugs including a curious one with two pairs of pincers. Several red-cockaded woodpeckers watched my every move from their hiding place.

Here was a chance to show himself better than Wilson. "Sorry am I to say that Wilson's drawing of this species could not have been made from a fresh killed bird. He puts its small streak of red feathers immediately over the eye instead of a white line. The red should be placed far back of the ear."

He had his job to think of. When he drew a "very fine rattlesnake, ten rattles," his "amiable pupil" also drew it. Daily he gave Miss Pirrie lessons "in drawing, music, dancing, arithmetic and such trifling acquirements like working hair for jewelry." Elizabeth was, in fact, not as good a student as Audubon made her appear to be—nor was Audubon really an honest teacher. "I had to do two-thirds of all her work," he wrote, "so that her rapid progress was truly astonishing to some observers." It was his own progress that could truly be called astonishing. "I continued my close application to my ornithology," he wrote, "writing all day, correcting my notes, rearranging them and painting land birds."

Both the man and his art had suddenly matured. He had arrived in New Orleans with twenty finished bird drawings, which he sent on to Lucy. Several of them—the great-footed hawk, the white-headed eagle, the hen turkey —went almost unchanged into his final *Birds of America*. At Oakley, he drew the pine creeping warbler, mockingbird, Mississippi kite, yellow-throated vireo, red-cockaded woodpecker, American redstart, summer redbird, prairie warbler, Tennessee warbler. He was both inspired and methodical. Having shot a bird, he wired it into a lifelike pose, bending it into attitudes that would fit it into a 30" x 40" drawing space. He then set it against a background drawn with squares, like graph paper, so that he would know the scale. He measured the bird with calipers and set down the figures. Drawing with either his right hand or his left, sometimes even with both at once, he roughly sketched the subject. After working over it, he traced it onto a second sheet, where further refining was done and backgrounds drawn in, usually by young Joseph Mason.

His working paradise at Oakley, presided over by a determined mother and a drunken father, was too good to last. Audubon seemed to be taking more than a teacher's interest in Elizabeth. "A girl well formed but not handsome," said Audubon, she had several suitors, "no particular admirers of her beauty but anxious for her fortune." One of them, a doctor, grew jealous of Audubon, and when Elizabeth fell ill he forbade any lessons and in effect quarantined her from her teacher. The household turned cool and then hostile,

Mrs. Pirrie fired him and would have sent him off without pay had not her alcoholic but sympathetic husband roused himself to promise Audubon his money. Audubon made his goodbyes "as simple as ever an honest Quaker might" and left "without a single sigh of regret."

Back in New Orleans, Audubon totted up what he had done: "Since I left Cincinnati I have finished 62 drawings of birds and plants, 3 quadrupeds, 2 snakes, fifty portraits." He sent some money to Lucy, keeping forty-two dollars for himself. Irritated because the city people derided his backwoods appearance, he threw away his old clothes, cut off his hair and felt "much as a handsome bird robbed of all its feathers." Angry and depressed, he was abruptly cheered when Lucy and his two sons arrived.

They struggled to make a living, Lucy as governess and companion, Audubon as portraitist and teacher. Adversity seemed about to break the family apart when Lucy was hired by a widow named Mrs. Percy to set up a small school at her plantation, Beech Woods, not far from the Pirries' Oakley. Audubon, on a visit, charmed Mrs. Percy into taking him on as instructor in drawing and music. Drawn by the nearness of Oakley, he paid a visit to Elizabeth Pirrie and found her in mourning for her husband—not the jealous doctor but a cousin with whom she had eloped. Carrying her across a creek on their flight, the cousin had contracted a fatal pneumonia. Poor Elizabeth married twice again and was twice widowed.

Mrs. Percy, though attached to Lucy, quarreled with Audubon and ordered him to leave. He did, but sneaked back one night to see Lucy. Caught in her bed, and thoroughly humiliated, he left a second time. Misfortune once again forced him into a crucial move. A few months before, he had met a traveling Englishman who, impressed by Audubon's paintings, urged him to work over them and get them published. With Audubon jobless, he and the steadfast, far-seeing Lucy agreed that this was the time to try for publication. In the autumn of 1823, Audubon set out for the East. After spending the winter in Louisville, where he supported himself by painting everything from portraits to store signs, he arrived in Philadelphia in April, 1824.

❦ ❦ ❦ ❦ ❦ THE CITY WAS STILL THE COUNTRY'S FIRST—THOUGH FADING— center of natural history. Of its great figures, only old Mr. Peale survived and he was no longer active. William Bartram had died the year before. He had shared his father's wish not to live on too long in lingering uselessness, and the wish was also granted him. "A few minutes before his death," wrote George Ord, in a memoir, "he wrote an article on the natural history of a plant and in rising from his desk to take a morning survey of the botanic grounds, he had proceeded only a few steps from his door when he burst a blood vessel which suddenly closed his useful life, July 22, 1823, in the 85th year of his age."

Alexander Wilson, the man Audubon was challenging, had finished eight volumes of *Ornithology* and begun the ninth when he took ill—according to uncertain evidence, after he had swum a river to retrieve a bird. He contracted a severe dysentery, and died on August 23, 1813. Now that it was too late to do him any good, Philadelphia had grown proud of Wilson, and rather possessive of him. George Ord, who had worked his way into Wilson's life, became his alter ego. Jealous of anyone who might try to share his hero, he took on the job of editing and finishing the *Ornithology*.

Ord was a contradictory man, in some ways overbearing and in others modest. Although he did essential work on systematizing American zoology, classifying specimens brought back by Lewis and Clark, he kept his own name off his most important papers. Audubon, arriving in Philadelphia, instantly antagonized Ord, who disliked both him and his paintings. He particularly disapproved of the way Audubon introduced what he considered extraneous details into his scenes—flowers, trees and butterflies, the elements that added so much to Audubon's art.

Another disciple of Wilson's was more friendly to Audubon: Charles Lucien Bonaparte. Son of Napoleon's younger brother Lucien, Charles Bonaparte became interested in natural history as a boy in France, gaining quick entry into scientific circles through his name but staying there through his own talents. In 1822, he came to America to visit his uncle Joseph Bonaparte, once King of Naples and of Spain, who had settled outside Philadelphia. Charles Bonaparte became a leader among Philadelphia's ornithologists. A specialist in bird names and relationships, he compiled the first systematized checklist of American birds.

When Audubon arrived, Bonaparte was preparing a supplement to Wilson's *Ornithology*, using Titian Peale as his illustrator. Seeing ways in which Audubon might be useful to him, Bonaparte introduced him at the Academy of Sciences and helped him show his drawings there. They were pleasantly received by many viewers but not by Wilson's old engraver Alexander Lawson. Bonaparte, whose books were being engraved by Lawson, wanted to have Audubon do some of the drawings. This was sacrilege to Lawson. "You may buy them," he coldly told Bonaparte, "but I will not engrave them, because ornithology requires truth in the forms and correctness in the lines. Here are neither."

When Audubon brought him a drawing of the boat-tailed grackle, Lawson was patronizing. Audubon's work, he remarked, was "extraordinary for one self-taught. But we in Philadelphia are used to seeing very correct drawing."

Stung, Audubon retorted that he had studied drawing under the famous French painter David. Whereupon Lawson replied, "Then you have made damned bad use of your time." The engraver did relent, however, and engraved a grackle Audubon drew for Bonaparte.

The comparisons with Wilson were inevitable and, in Philadelphia, usually unfavorable to the newcomer. Where Wilson in his work was scrupulous about accurate representation, Audubon seemed too much concerned with dramatic effect. Where Wilson was trustworthy and consistent, Audubon seemed given to contradictions and unsupported claims. Actually, the differences between the two artist-ornithologists have always been overemphasized. Wilson, the cautious Scot, was as adventurous in his ambition as Audubon. Audubon, the flashy Gaul, was as single-minded in his purpose as Wilson. Both men were self-taught in the disciplines of the art and science they mastered. Both showed stubborn courage in adversity and native skill in salesmanship, and both gave up everything else for the wild dream of painting all the birds of their adopted country.

The first Audubon bird painting to be published was the female grackle in the rear of this plate. Ironically it appeared in a supplement to the Ornithology *of his great rival, Alexander Wilson.*

By 1824, Audubon as an artist had already gone far beyond any other painter of birds anywhere, beyond Catesby, Bartram and Wilson. With these earlier artists, the effect is archaic—which, of course, lends a special charm today. Their birds are mainly in profile, done more in repose than in action, set against backgrounds which, except for some of Catesby's, seem like afterthoughts. But each had made significant steps in advancing his art—Catesby in his attention to plants and landscape, Bartram in his attention to identifying details, Wilson with his scientific care and the stiff poetic grace of his subjects. Audubon was an artist first of all and an ornithologist after that—an artist with a painstaking passion for nature as expressed in its birds. He mastered the techniques of exaggeration, of dramatizing attitudes and action so that his subjects seemed more lifelike than life itself, as if art were dictating to nature. The images of birds held in the mind's eye of future American generations were to be Audubon's visions as much as nature's models.

Giving up on Philadelphia, Audubon went to New York where Dr. Mitchill welcomed his bird stuffer and dashed off a letter of introduction to an influential friend: "Mr. A. is now sitting with me—I have been delighted and instructed by a display of his Port Folio containing Drawings Done from Life of North American Birds and illustrating the Connect, of ornithology with Botany." He put Audubon up for membership in the Lyceum, and Audubon thus entered the formal ranks of American naturalists.

No New York publisher would take on Audubon's project, and impulsively he went up to Albany to ask for DeWitt Clinton's help. Clinton was not in town, and almost out of money, Audubon headed back to Lucy. Perhaps because Wilson had gone there, he went by way of Niagara Falls and, when he signed the register at an inn, wrote after his name, "who, like Wilson, will ramble but never like that great man die under the lash of a bookseller." When he got to Pittsburgh, again emulating Wilson, he bought a skiff to take him down the Ohio.

He reached Lucy at Beech Woods, glum and penniless, "with rent and wasted clothes and uncut hair, altogether looking like the Wandering Jew." For Lucy's sake, Mrs. Percy made peace with him and let him stay at Beech Woods. Lucy, as determined as her husband that he publish his birds, rounded up students of music, French and drawing for him. He worked even harder and more productively at Beech Woods than at Oakley—out at dawn to see and shoot birds, busy during the day with his pupils, staying up into the night to draw. On Saturdays, he conducted a dancing class in the village:

> With my fiddle under my arm, I entered the ballroom. I placed the gentlemen in line. How I toiled before I could get one graceful step or

motion. I broke my bow and nearly my violin in my impatience. Next I had the ladies alone. Then I tried both together—pushed one here, another there—all the while singing to myself. At the close I was asked to dance to my own music. This I did until the whole room came down in thunderous applause.

The ladies found him compelling—"tall, slender, his blue eyes an eagle's in brightness, his hair beautiful chestnut brown very glossy and curly," recalled Martha Pope, a neighboring girl who had listened raptly as Audubon told needless lies about having been born in an orange grove on the Mississippi. When another fencing teacher spread old gossip about Audubon's flirtations, a few hints about Audubon's skill with gun and foils shut him up. For the most part, Audubon was discreet, prudent and even thrifty. In a year and a half, he and Lucy saved two thousand dollars, a considerable sum.

In April, 1826, at the age of forty-one, he left Beech Woods for England. He carried sixteen hundred dollars, some four hundred drawings and sketches of birds, voluminous notes on them and several letters of introduction: from the always helpful Henry Clay, DeWitt Clinton and Vincent Nolte, who recommended him to some business associates in Liverpool. At New Orleans, learning that his boat would not sail immediately, he dashed back to Beech Woods for another farewell, bursting in on Lucy at three in the morning. "The moments spent afterwards full repaid me," he wrote succinctly in his journal.

Audubon was an assiduous keeper of journals, intending them for his own reference and Lucy's reading. One of the few journals left in its original form is the one for 1826. Most of the others, edited by Lucy and his granddaughter Maria, were cut, rewritten, bowdlerized, erased or destroyed, in order to make Audubon seem an altogether decent genius. The 1826 journal, recovered and published raw and uncut by Alice Ford, shows Audubon as a writer of pointed whimsy, of crude humor, and of drunken expostulations, and yet a man possessing broad literary interests and intuition. He notes what he read on the voyage: Byron's *The Corsair* and Thomson's *The Seasons* and *The Castle of Indolence*. "I felt the all powerful extent of his genius operating on me as a cathartic," he wrote of Thomson. The light-hearted anecdotes he set down are a world away from the overblown prose which he, like so many other naturalists of the time, indulged in. Recounting the voyage on the ship, *Delos*, he told how the crew tried to get their favorite saints to bring a breeze. When invocations to St. Anthony failed,

St. Mark [was] appointed chief director of the breezes. The Delos moved at three miles per hour. I had heard that saints as well as men would accept light gifts. I conceived it my duty to try. My offering? It was not a bull

1. Red-headed Woodpecker. 2. Yellow-bellied W. 3. Hairy W. 4. Downy W.

The red-headed woodpecker (1) was Alexander Wilson's first love among American birds. The other woodpeckers in this plate from Ornithology are yellow-bellied (2), hairy (3), and downy (4).

1 American Siskin. 2 Rose-breasted Grosbeak.
3 Green black-throated Warbler. 4 Yellow-rump W. 5 Cærulean W. 6 Solitary Flycatcher.
17

Into a single plate, Wilson crowded half a dozen songbirds. The yellow-rump warbler (4) is also known as the myrtle warbler, and the solitary flycatcher (6) is not recognized as a species today.

Some of Wilson's water birds: goosander or merganser male (1) and female (2), pintail (3), blue-winged teal (4), snow goose (5). The pintail and teal, he noted, were fine eating and the snow goose's "singularly curious" beak gave it the name of "laughing goose."

Wilson's white-headed or bald eagle—"fierce, contemplative, daring and tyrannical," he called it—was painted against the background of Niagara Falls.

"A beautiful creature" but "most difficult" to paint, said Audubon of the common loon. He drew the female from a bird he shot on the Ohio. The male was shot in Labrador.

These common puffins seem comical here, but when Audubon pulled them from their Labrador nest they "bit most furiously, making a mournful noise all the time."

*Details from Audubon's paintings: a blue jay impaling a stolen egg
(above); a belted kingfisher gulping his catch (right).*

In his Winter Hawk *(in fact, an immature red-shouldered hawk), Audubon produced a cruelly
dramatic painting—the bird's claws drawing blood from its captive.*

These black-billed cuckoos were "in pursuit of flies, probably to amuse themselves," wrote Audubon. The lush magnolia was most likely painted by his young assistant, Joseph Mason.

The bush-tailed wood rat, which Audubon painted, was a plague to naturalists in the West, eating their books and blankets, stealing their razors and axes.

The jaguar, "its powerful limbs quivering with excitement," is by Audubon's son, John Wodehouse Audubon, who did most of the large animals in Quadrupeds.

The snowy owl appears in the only night scene Audubon did for Birds of America. *He used to watch them in winter on the Ohio River, "hidden in a pile of drift logs."*

resembling Jupiter in his pranks. Neither was it a heifer, snowy white. It was a ram's head. I assured the great unknown that it would be served up to his appetite either raw, boiled, toasted, roasted or pickled or fried or tarred and feathered. I have had no answer from this genie. Polite genies, I am told, never thank one no matter how much they get when in need.

Audubon did not have legs for the sea or a head for strong drink. He was seasick intermittently and drunk several times, as his silly remarks and his stumbling handwriting reveal.

Now where the devil are you running to Audubon? Why toward the shores of that England that gave birth to a Milton, to a Shakespeare, to a Dryden. Ah England! Is it possible that thou shouldst be untroubled by thy own sons? Thy hoary head ought not to suffer this. What strange itching will prevail and lead a poor devil to think on matters entirely unconnected with him? I will drink the residue of my glass. I recollect just now that when I first knew thee, dearest friend, I was asked if this passion of mine would be of long lasting duration. Help I am now entering on a sacred subject. "Husband shut thy book, pray."

Later, he lurched into scatology, as if trying to shock Lucy. Many Englishmen he wrote, read about England's troubles "without caring a f——. I know you blushed a little when the single letter F came into your sight. I will soon relieve you," he went on, belaboring his joke. "Do not dread any explosion from Mount Vesuvius. I intended to write Fig in full but my rascally pen was not supplied with material sufficient."

In Liverpool, that chance meeting and horse race on the Kentucky road took him, with Vincent Nolte's letter of introduction, to the homes of the Rathbone family. They received him with extraordinary warmth—partly because they would welcome any friend of Nolte, who had helped save them from severe financial losses in cotton; partly because of Audubon's charm; mostly because they were the Rathbones, a tolerant, affectionate, cultured Quaker family interested in natural science and acquainted with England's most respected naturalists. The matriarch of the family was Mrs. William Rathbone, whom Audubon dubbed "the Queen Bee." Her merchant sons Richard and William were men of substance, generous and independent. Richard's wife was learned and sweet but it was his dark-eyed sister, Hannah, who drew Audubon most strongly. And she was deeply drawn to Audubon. There is no evidence that their actions went beyond propriety, but their feelings seemed to have gone beyond friendship. She once gave him a knife to sharpen his quill pens, and when he lost it, she was coldly distressed, as if he had proved unfaithful by losing a love amulet.

The Rathbones, and very quickly their friends, were delighted with Audubon's quaint accent, his bursting temperament and his frontier appearance—a "long-haired Achaean," one observer described him, whose locks "flow over his ears and over the coat collar; you can smell the bear's grease across the street and if these amaranthine locks were to be raised you would see the shiny coating of bear's grease upon the velvet collar below."

He lugged his heavy portfolio to the Rathbones—ever since a porter in New Orleans lost his drawings, he had refused to let anyone else carry them. Out of the big white sheets he spread before them sprang a clamorous aviary—the wild turkey strutting large as life from an oversized page, parakeets chattering in clumps of cockleburr, a mockingbird attacking a marauding rattlesnake.

An admiring European writer expressed what the Rathbones must have experienced on first seeing Audubon's paintings:

> . . . a landscape wholly American, trees, flowers, grass, even the tints of the sky and waters quickened with a life that is real, peculiar, trans-

Audubon kept his drawings in this large portfolio. Unwilling to trust anyone else with it, he always carried it himself, balancing it on his head when his arms got tired.

In Kentucky, Audubon once found that rats had shredded 200 of his drawings. Somehow the story got to Japan, where an artist depicted Audubon's awful discovery.

In England, Audubon and his admirer Hannah Rathbone exchanged gifts. She gave him a knife for sharpening his pens. He gave her this exquisite drawing of a winter wren.

atlantic. On twigs, branches, bits of shore, copied by the brush with the strictest fidelity, sport the feathered races of the New World, in the size of life, each in its particular attitude, its individuality and peculiarities. Their plumages sparkle with nature's own tints; you see them in motion or at rest, in their plays and their combats, in their anger fits and their caresses, singing, running, asleep, just awakened, beating the air, skimming the waves or rending one another in their battles. It is a real and palpable vision of the New World.

In this unlikely smoky city, so different from the bayous of Beech Woods and the cave at Perkiomen Creek, the transplanted Frenchman caught up with his destiny. Within a week after he walked in on the Rathbones, he was ensconced not only in their household and their hearts but in the lively intellectual circles of the city. It was arranged for Audubon to visit Lord Stanley, a former Prime Minister and a virtuoso in the eighteenth-century tradition. Audubon was "troubled at the idea of meeting an English gentleman, called, moreover, a lord!" Then, astonished that a peer should do such a thing, he watched Stanley spread the drawings on the floor and get down on his knees to see them more closely, admiring them and also pointing out a mistake.

Only a few days after he arrived, Audubon was invited to show a selection of his birds at the Royal Institution. On opening day, the ladies of Liverpool, all agog over the romantic woodsman from America, crowded in. "I was in view of the world," Audubon wrote Lucy. " 'La, that's beautiful,' again and again." The crowds were so big that the Institution gave him a room in which he could hang more than two hundred of his drawings and, after much discussion, persuaded him to charge admission. Still the visitors crowded in—413, he noted, in two hours.

His new friends were as excited as he was and back at the house they made him supply a soundtrack for his drawings, gobbling like a wild turkey, hooting like a barred owl, cooing like a dove. "I am glad I was not desired to bray. They all appear very much surprised," he went on, "that I have no wonderful tale to relate, have not been devoured at least six times by tigers, bears, wolves, foxes. No, I was never troubled by any animals larger than ticks and mosquitoes."

To help pay expenses, Audubon began doing oil paintings, hackwork to keep him in cash. He painted a large oil of his wild turkey, finishing it in twenty-three hours of almost steady work while friends coming in to watch wondered that he could paint so fast and steadily with so much distraction. All blown up with the success of his exhibition, he went on to Manchester where the reception was lukewarm, both socially and professionally. He was being forced to play the amusing outlander. Having startled his friends in Liverpool by eating raw tomatoes, which were considered poisonous, he astonished a host in Manchester, who had thoughtfully served a native American dish, by eating corn on the cob "held by my two hands as if I intended gagging myself with the ear."

Lonely now and uncertain, Audubon was drinking regularly and it showed in his letters to Lucy, full of pathetic pleas that she pity his indiscretions and taunting references to the attractions that English ladies flaunted—"I could plainly hear the heaving breast of the fair maids through the rustling of their silky gowns." The prostitutes of Manchester swarmed so thickly around him, he complained, that he had to ask a watchman to escort him home. He drank too heavily at a formal dinner, waited on by three servants, "in livery trimmed with red on a white ground, like a killdeer."

Still he could find no one to publish his birds. Then he proceeded to Edinburgh, where he took his portfolio to William Lizars, the best engraver in Scotland. "I slowly unbuckled the straps and without uttering a word, turned up a drawing," Audubon wrote. "Mr. Lizars exclaimed, 'My God, I never saw anything like this before.' "

On the spot, Lizars proposed that he engrave the work and agreed with Audubon that the birds should be life-size—"the same size paper that is called double elephant," Audubon explained to Lucy. He and Lizars drew up a prospectus for *The Birds of America*. It would consist of four hundred drawings, one to a plate, five plates to a folio. Five folios would be issued every year, each to cost two guineas, about twelve American dollars. "If I can procure three hundred subscribers, we will be very rich indeed," he told Lucy.

The reception in Edinburgh, with Lizars to sponsor him, was as enthusiastic as it had been in Liverpool and far more significant. Edinburgh was still the center of natural science it had been when Colden, Garden, Mitchill and all the others had studied there. Sir William Jardine, editor of the British edition of Wilson's *Ornithology*, welcomed Audubon. Christopher North, the most eminent critic in the kingdom, praised him. The prestigious Wernerian Society watched Audubon show how he drew his birds, and when it was moved that he be made an honorary member, "everyone clapped hands and stamped the floor" in approbation.

The American woodsman, thrown into the cosmopolitan life of the Scottish capital, found that

> the great round of company does not agree with my early habits. I go dine at 6, 7 or 8 o'clock in the evening and it is 1 or 2 in the morning when the party breaks up. Then painting all day. My head is like a hornet's nest. My room was filled constantly by persons of the first rank in society. Think of poor Audubon, of Lords sending their carriage to Mr. A to go to spend days and nights at their hall. I was toasted by Lord Elgin.

He went to call on the Earl of Morton, whose huge castle "ornamented with great lions and all the signs of heraldry" intimidated him. He expected, he wrote, to meet "another Richard Coeur de Lion. Oh my imagination, where dost thou lead me? I saw a small slender man, tottering on his feet, weaker than a new hatched partridge, tears almost trickling from his eyes." The tottering earl was much pleased with Audubon and after Audubon gave her a drawing lesson, his wife subscribed to the *Birds*.

He ached to see Walter Scott, and finally a meeting was arranged. Audubon was all modesty with the great author, who was impressed—"no dash or glimmer or shine about him," he wrote, "great simplicity, countenance acute." Scott, whose taste inclined toward Landseer's overwrought animals, was reserved about Audubon's drawings, disliking their "extreme correctness." The Royal Institution gave him its exhibition rooms for his drawings, and on one Saturday Audubon took in fifteen pounds. "It is not the naturalist that I wish to please altogether, it is the wealthy part of the community," he told Lucy. "The first can only speak well or ill of me but the latter will fill my pockets."

All through the gray Edinburgh winter, Audubon worked hard and happily, more efficient now than ever. He wrote some papers for the scientific societies, one a slapdash account of a rattlesnake climbing trees to attack birds and

To amuse his English friends, who were fascinated by tales of the frontier, Audubon made this mocking portrait of himself as the American Woodsman.

squirrels that was to get him into a great deal of trouble. But he enjoyed his new standing as a scientist and signed a letter to Lucy with a flourish of capitals: "John J. Audubon, F.R.S.E., F.A.S., M.W.S.N.H., M.S.A., M.P.L.S., M.L.N.Y.," meaning that he was a Fellow of the Royal Society of Edinburgh, a Fellow of the Antiquarian Society, Member of the Wernerian Society of Natural History, Member of the Society of Arts of Scotland, Member of the Philosophical and Literary Society of Liverpool and Member of the Lyceum of New York.

About to try London, he took a step he had long put off. Playing the American woodsman, he had kept his long hair and his frontier dress, changing clothes only for very formal affairs. His friends, especially the Countess of Morton, worried that he would seem like a buffoon in the capital and nagged him to change. Reluctantly giving in, he wrote a mock mourning card to announce the sad occasion: "Edinburgh, March 19, 1827. This day my hair was sacrificed and the will of God was usurped by the wishes of man. As the barber clipped my locks rapidly it reminded me of the horrible times of the French revolution when the same operation was performed upon all the victims murdered at the guillotine. My heart sank low. John J. Audubon." Around the card he drew a wide black band.

Like Wilson, Audubon had to peddle his own work, from town to town and from house to house. On the way to London, he picked up five subscribers in Leeds and eighteen in Manchester, which had been so cool to him before. At Newcastle, he visited Thomas Bewick, the greatest of wood-carvers, whose *History of British Birds* and *General History of Quadrupeds* were already classics. Bewick directed Audubon to eight subscribers and Audubon later named a bird after him, Bewick's wren. At Liverpool, he was once again with the Rathbones and the beguiling Hannah, but stayed only briefly.

He arrived in London in the spring of 1827 with a pocketful of impressive introductions, including one to Thomas Lawrence, the painter, who, Audubon reported, "examined some of my drawings repeating frequently 'Very clever indeed.' From such a man these words mean much." Out soliciting subscribers, Audubon wrote, "I thought of poor Alexander Wilson. When, traveling as I am now to procure subscribers, he as well as myself was received with rude coldness and sometimes with that arrogance which belongs to parvenus."

Alarming news came from Lizars. His engravers were demanding more money. The work was going badly and he despaired of being able to get on with the job. Audubon was stunned but moved quickly to replace Lizars. In his walks around London, he had noticed an engraver's shop run by a man named Robert Havell. Audubon called on him, proposing that he take over from Lizars. The job was too big, Havell replied, and he was too old. Instead he took Audubon around to another engraver named Colnaghi, who thought for a moment, then showed them the proof of a lovely engraving. Havell studied it. "That's just the man," he said, upon which Colnaghi replied, "Then send for your son."

It was a storybook tale. Havell had wanted his son Robert to study for a profession. Young Robert wanted to be a painter. They had quarreled and the son became a landscape artist. Now, the elder Havell brought his son to Audubon, who, as a trial, asked him to engrave a warbler. When he saw the younger Havell's try, the story goes, Aubudon cried, "Ze jig is up, ze jig is up," dismaying and baffling the Havells until they realized that he meant the exact contrary, that the engraving was wonderful.

Once again Audubon profited by disaster. When Havell, Jr., took over the job, he proved a far better engraver than Lizars—and charged less. London craftsmen were more tractable than those of Edinburgh, and Audubon could be right at hand to supervise the coloring. For all of that, Audubon found London a trying town. People thought it unseemly for him to go through the streets carrying his own big portfolios, often balancing them on his head. By much maneuvering, he got George IV to look at his paintings and—to the surprise of his chamberlain, who usually had trouble getting His Highness away from his interminable games of whist—the King spent some time with them. Audubon, he said, could "publish the work under His Majesty's particular patronage." When the King later withdrew his patronage, Queen Adelaide, an amateur naturalist, agreed to substitute hers.

By 1828, Audubon had seventy subscribers and was ready to try another capital, Paris. In his few weeks there, he signed thirteen subscribers and garnered some priceless praise. The painter Gérard exclaimed: "You are the king of ornithological painters. Who would have expected such things from the woods of America?" And Cuvier, the paleontologist whose prestige was now almost as great as Buffon's or Linnaeus's once had been, declared in a ringing phrase that the paintings were "the greatest monument ever erected by art to nature."

Being back in France had a disturbing effect on Audubon. Long out of touch with his family, he learned for the first time that his adoring stepmother had died. Guilt and sadness added to his fears that somehow the fact of his illegitimate birth might come out. His diary, as published by his granddaughter, were full of mystifying references: "The cloud that hangs over my birth requires silence. I thought of my birth, of my curious life and of the strange incidents that have brought me to what I am *now* known to be. Now was the moment to dispel the cloud. I reflected on the consequences and concluded to carry my extraordinary secret to the grave."

Out of such cryptic statements, made even more baffling by the way Audubon's family edited the original documents, grew the myth that Audubon was really the lost Dauphin, the son of Louis XVI and Marie Antoinette, who, supposed to have died in prison, instead had been spirited off to Canada with an English colonizer, Lord Selkirk, and thence taken to America. Other random references in Audubon's letters have been picked up to support this implausible yarn.

In 1829, leaving enough drawings to keep the engravers busy for a year, Audubon set sail for America—to see his family, to get subscribers and to paint birds he still lacked. In New York, people praised his drawings but did not subscribe. Instead of going directly down to Louisiana, Audubon spent the summer in New Jersey, where the birds he had to draw were in residence and in proper plumage. An artist named George Lehman was hired to do backgrounds. "I wish I had eight pairs of hands and another body," Audubon wrote, but he "accumulated 42 drawings in 4 months, 11 large, 11 middle-size and 20 small plates, comprising 95 birds from eagles downwards with plants, nests, flowers and 60 different kinds of eggs." Shipping off a batch to Havell, he finally went home to gather up his family and take them back to England.

It was November before he reached Lucy. Put ashore at the river landing at midnight, he walked into a deserted village—yellow fever had been raging through the bayou country. At the inn "all was dark and silent. I called and knocked in vain, it was the abode of death alone. I went to another house, another and another but the living had fled." Losing his way in the dark, he finally came to the plantation in the morning. "I went to my wife's apartment. Her door was ajar. She was sitting by her piano on which a young lady was playing. I pronounced her name gently and the next moment I had her in my arms."

On New Year's Day, 1830, Audubon, with Lucy and their 18-year-old son John, set out for England, stopping in Washington where President Jackson received them "with great kindness" and Edward Everett persuaded the House of Representatives to subscribe to *Birds*. Back again in London, he found that fifty subscribers to *Birds* had canceled. Audubon still had about 130. They had advanced forty thousand dollars, which paid production costs.

Audubon was ready for the next step: writing a text that would supplement his paintings. Referring to his conscientious journals and notes, he began his *Ornithological Biography*. Though it was intended simply as text for the drawings, the *Biography* became—like Wilson's accounts—the story of Audubon's travels and adventures. Audubon's English prose was expressive but unreliable and he was lucky to find as an editor a Scottish naturalist named William MacGillivray, who later published a very respectable *History of British Birds*. MacGillivray had an empathy with Audubon that enabled him to set the artist's writing straight without making it stiff. Audubon wrote. MacGillivray read and revised. Lucy made a final copy. In this brisk fashion, the first volume of the *Biography* was finished in three months.

A persistent trouble flared up. The feud with George Ord that had begun in Philadelphia had followed him to England where Ord found an ally in a naturalist named Charles Waterton, author of *Wanderings in South America* and one of England's finer eccentrics. As a young man, Waterton climbed the cross on top of St. Peter's in Rome and left his glove on the lightning rod there. When the irate Pope ordered the glove taken down, no one was brave enough to obey, so Waterton climbed back up to retrieve it. He never slept in a bed, lying down on the floor at night with a wooden block for a pillow and a military cape for a cover. When he was twenty-five, Waterton attended the christening of a friend's daughter and vowed, half seriously, that he would marry the infant (whose grandmother was an Arawak princess) when she grew up. Seventeen years later, the day she left her convent school, he married her at four o'clock in the morning, and, as a honeymoon, took her on a tour of Europe's natural history museums. She died after bearing her first child and Waterton mourned her the rest of his life.

Waterton's *Wanderings in South America* was full of half-man, half-boy adventures—exotic descriptions of natives, detailed explanations of how to make a blowgun for shooting poison arrows or to capture a sloth or to eat wasp

grubs. It was studded with stiff-upper-lip comments: "Time and experience have
convinced me that there is not much danger in moving amongst snakes and wild
beasts provided only that you have self-command." Waterton was a writer
easy with learning and edifying to read though he annoyed other naturalists by
refusing to use Latin names in describing his specimens. His *Wanderings* was
reprinted again and again for almost a hundred years.

   Though he was a man of ascetic tastes and sometimes saintly behavior
(which his admirers traced to his ancestor Sir Thomas More), Waterton had a
rough tongue and unforgiving temper. Audubon had made some sarcastic
comments on Waterton's story of how he jumped on an alligator's back to
help capture it, and Waterton apparently never forgot it. He and Ord set out
to wreck Audubon's reputation. Audubon's drawings, Ord reported to his
English friend, were "wretched" and Audubon himself was a "clumsy liar." The
two spread reports that Audubon had plagiarized Wilson's drawings, attacked
Audubon's account of a rattlesnake climbing a tree to raid birds' nests and
found Audubon foolish in saying that vultures found their prey through sense
of smell rather than sight.

   The controversies make tedious reading today. Audubon did, in two or

three instances, copy Wilson's drawings—for his Mississippi kite, cerulean warbler and redwing. The plagiarism is inexcusable but in sum total insignificant, for Audubon was not really a copier of Wilson or anyone else. At that time, the evidence on the climbing rattler and the vulture's olfactory organs was contradictory. A blacksnake does climb to the tops of trees even if a rattler doesn't, and the vulture uses both sight and smell. But the quarrels were furious, enlisting scientists on both sides, distracting Audubon from his work and diminishing the participants, all of whom were men of high talent and interesting character.

By 1831, the engravers were catching up to Audubon. He had all but run out of subjects for them. Another birding trip to America was called for, and in August he sailed for the United States. The fine reviews in England had impressed Americans and in Philadelphia he finally knocked down the ramparts that Ord and his friends had held so long, signing up four subscribers, including two that mattered immensely: the American Philosophical Society and the Philadelphia Academy of Natural Sciences. Audubon's immediate problem was not to find subscribers but birds. He went south, accompanied by George Lehman, his background painter. While he was walking the streets of Charles-

In a few instances, Audubon copied Alexander Wilson's birds and presented them as his own. For example, at far left is Wilson's drawing of a female Mississippi kite. In the center is Audubon's original painting of a male Mississippi kite. At left is the final plate as it appeared in Birds of America. *Audubon had not painted a female kite, and needing one for the plate, his engraver appropriated Wilson's, reversing the image. Audubon may have been away from England when this happened. In any event, he let the "piracy" stand.*

ton with an acquaintance who was helping him find lodgings, a man rode up on horseback and introduced himself. He was the Reverend John Bachman. Listening to Audubon explain his reason for coming south, he immediately solved the lodging problem: Audubon must come and stay with him.

It was a fruitful meeting. In Dr. Bachman, himself a serious and well-known naturalist, Audubon was to find not only a host but a lifelong friend and a trusted collaborator. In Mrs. Bachman's sister-in-law Maria Martin he found a capable assistant who was to draw many details of his plates. And in Bachman's daughters he found wives for his two sons. Audubon was impressed to learn that Bachman had known Alexander Wilson. He had sent Wilson specimens, and Wilson had helped get Bachman the teaching job Wilson had given up. But Bachman was somewhat piqued with the earlier artist. In publishing material Bachman had sent him on the troublesome Canada blue jay, Wilson had referred to him anonymously as "a gentleman who resided not far from Hudson." Audubon was delighted to learn that Bachman was also acquainted with George Ord, and had no use for him.

"He is an excellent shot," Audubon wrote Lucy about his new friend. "Full of life and spirits. We laugh and talk as if we had known each other for twenty years." Bachman's study was filled with birds and animal specimens and his mind with wide and exact knowledge. Bachman called Audubon "old Jostle" and, after he had left, wrote Lucy: "Things seem quite a blank since he has gone." He was missed particularly by Maria Martin, who affectionately offered to be his amanuensis, painter, or anything else, not forgetting the darning of socks."

Audubon sailed to Florida on a navy schooner. Making his way through country he had read about in William Bartram's *Travels*, he wrote:

> I have been deceived most shamefully about the Floridas, scarcely a bird to be seen, these of the most common sort. The general wildness, the eternal labyrinths of waters and marshes; interlocked and apparently never ending; the whole surrounded by interminable swamps. Here I am in the Floridas which from my childhood I have consecrated in my imagination as the garden of the United States. A garden where all that is not mud, mud, mud is sand, sand, sand; where the fruit is so sour that it is not eatable and where in place of singing birds and golden fishes you have a species of ibis that you cannot get when you have shot it and alligators, snakes and scorpions. Mr. Bartram was the first to call this a garden but he is to be forgiven. He was an enthusiastic botanist, and rare plants in the eyes of such a man convert a wilderness at once into a garden.

Looking for a celebrated spring, one of those fountains that had so surprised the Bartrams, Audubon found "a circular basin having a diameter of about sixty feet from the center of which the water is thrown up with great force—transparent. The spring has been turned to good account by Colonel Rees, who has directed its current so as to run a mill which suffices to grind the whole of the sugar cane." So much for the fountains of Xanadu.

It was not the birds' fault that Audubon could not find them. He had come at a bad time of year—either earlier or later he would have caught them on their migrations. Finished with the South, he turned north to Labrador. It took a year to mount an expedition, but meanwhile he finished dozens of drawings and sent them off to Havell. Planning to make his enterprise a family business, he also sent his elder son Victor, now twenty-three, to London as his agent and began training John, nineteen, as an artist to assist him in his drawings. Originally, four hundred birds were planned for the folios. Now he proposed to add another sixty or seventy. Going on a selling trip for the first time to Boston, where Wilson had done so poorly, he wound up with fourteen subscribers, among them Daniel Webster, who shot a pair of diving ducks for him. They are immortalized in plates No. 332 and No. 333 of *Birds*.

The critics were all favorable. "The subscription price may be considered as large ($1,000)," wrote the *National Gazette* of Philadelphia, George Ord's stronghold, "but how rich, ornamental and instructive and entertaining is the work and how much preferable to the merely personal gewgaws of transitory gratifications upon which greater sums are as frequently expended." Philip Hone, the diarist-mayor of New York, expressed his praise in a way that must have pleased Audubon, remarking that "he illustrates his favorite science with the ardor of a lover to a mistress." Audubon made a platonic conquest of Fanny Kemble, who was touring the country. "He is enchanting, one of the great men of his country," wrote the actress. Fanny's younger sister in London later fell in love with Audubon's son Victor, and might have married him if Lucy hadn't considered it impractical.

Audubon sailed for Labrador in 1833. Though it was early summer, there was snow on the ground and there were no blossoms on the trees. But the land was filled with the songs of robins and whitethroats, and in the dawn silence he could hear the fox sparrow singing a quarter mile off. Where Florida had yielded Audubon little, barren Labrador showed him something new every day—unfamiliar ravens, gulls and mergansers "that had so glutted themselves with fish they were obliged to disgorge before they could fly off." Long files of gannets led Audubon to the nesting rock: "I thought it covered with snow to the depth of several feet. What we saw was not snow but a mass of birds of such a size as I never before cast my eyes on, all calmly seated on the eggs or newly hatched brood, their heads all turned to windward and towards us. The stench is unsufferable with the remains of putrid fish, rotten eggs and dead birds."

The land brightened. "Strawberry blossoms were under our feet at every step," and they sank to their knees in moss. When he put his hand into a puffin burrow "the bird bit most furiously and scratched shockingly with the inner claw, making a mournful noise all the time." The birds were in their loveliest summer plumage and he was kept busy shooting and drawing the new sparrows, the ruby-crowned kinglet, the white-billed crossbill, puffins, gannets, plovers. Rising at three to start work, he bemoaned the fact that "I am growing old too fast. This afternoon at half past five my fingers could no longer hold my pencil."

He marveled at how

> quickly the growth is attained of every living thing in this country. In six weeks I have seen the eggs laid, the birds hatched, their first moult half over, their association in flocks. That the Creator should have commanded millions of delicate diminutive tender creatures to cross immense spaces of country to all appearance a thousand times more congenial to them than this, to cause them to people this desolate land for a time, to enliven it by the songs of the sweet feathered musicians for two months and by the same command induce them to abandon it almost suddenly, is as wonderful as it is beautiful.

But he mourned the slaughter of birds and animals. Twenty-five hundred seals were killed by seventeen men in three days, clubbed as they lay on the ice. Four men gathered forty thousand eggs from the goose nests to sell in Halifax at twenty cents a dozen.

After Labrador there was another region Audubon wanted to explore, the western parts of the Gulf of Mexico. In Washington, frustrated in his attempts to get the use of a government cutter, he luckily ran into Washington Irving, whom he had met on a river boat some years before. Irving, an old State Department hand who knew his way around the capital, took Audubon in to see Roger Taney, the future Chief Justice, who was then Secretary of the Treasury. Taney offered Audubon use of a Treasury ship, but there would be a long wait for it.

Discouraged, Audubon took his family to London in 1834. There he solicited Baron Rothschild, "a corpulent man hitching up his trousers. 'I expect that you are the publisher of some book or other; you may send in your work and I will pay for a copy of it.' I sent the first volume and after eight or ten months my son made out his account. The Baron cried out: 'What, a hundred pounds for birds? I will give you five pounds and not a farthing more.' " Audubon took the volume back.

Then to America again, where people who had opposed him were now friendly and those who had been cool were helpful. Audubon could no longer expect to see every North American bird himself and he was anxious to buy or borrow skins. Thomas Nuttall, a friendly naturalist, generously sold him almost a hundred specimens that he and a companion had collected on a western expedition. In a winter of furious work, Audubon made more than seventy drawings, loyally helped by Maria Martin and by his son John, who was becoming an accomplished painter.

The old problem of getting to the Gulf was settled by President Jackson himself. He invited Audubon to dinner at the White House—the President ate milk and bread for dessert, Audubon noted. Though warning that a Seminole war might threaten the travels, Jackson said he would try to find him a boat. He did, and Audubon sailed from New Orleans to Galveston. Unhappily, there were few birds for him but he did meet a famous hero, Sam Houston, president of the new Republic of Texas, who "came dressed in a fancy velvet coat and trousers trimmed with broad gold lace. We were asked to drink grog with him which we did wishing success to his new republic."

The new birds from the West forced Audubon to change plans again. He added eighty-seven new species and, fearing that subscribers would complain if they had too many plates to pay for, he began using composite drawings, putting several species in one plate. There was another trip to England in 1837. On June 20, 1838, the last plate was engraved. By the following May, the fifth and final volume of *Ornithological Biography* had been finished, to be followed by a *Synopsis of the Birds of North America*, an index to both the *Birds* and the *Biography*. The financial panic in England, following that in the United States, confused the subscription lists but in the end some 175 sets of *The Birds of America*, each containing 435 plates and describing 489 species, were completed and sold. About a hundred sets were bought in England, the rest in America. From them, Audubon grossed some $175,000, most of which went for expenses. He profited more from the *Biography* and still more, a few years later, from a small octavo edition of *Birds*, which consisted of colored lithographs rather than engravings.

Leaving London for the last time, Audubon took with him a tribute from an admiring England. "The American Woodsman's hair—long since cut short—has grown white," wrote the London *Athenaeum*; "his magnificent undertaking is completed and he is now quitting England to settle himself whether by the side of a bayou in some forest clearing, report saith not. Few have quitted England carrying with them a larger portion of honest regard and sincere good wishes."

In America the triumphant completion of *The Birds of America* moved the *North American Review* to measure the man and the moment. "His trumpet of victory at the result must have given an uncertain sound," declared its perceptive writer, "partly exulting in his success and partly lamenting that his great work was finished."

THE GULLIBLE GENIUS

ONE DAY WHILE WALKING BY THE RIVER AUDUBON NOTICED a man landing with what seemed to be "a bundle of dried clover" on his back.

"What an odd-looking fellow," said I to myself. He ascended the banks with rapid step then asked if I could point out the house where Mr. Audubon lived. "Why I am the man," I replied. The traveler rubbed his hand with delight while I broke the seal of a letter of introduction that he handed me: "My dear Audubon, I send you an odd fish which you may prove to be undescribed. . . ." With all the simplicity of a woodsman I asked the bearer where the "odd fish" was. Again he rubbed his hands and with the utmost good humor said: "I am that odd fish, I presume!" I felt confounded and blushed but managed to stammer an apology to that renowned naturalist. Constantine Rafinesque himself.

Years later, in an episode of his *Ornithological Biography* entitled "The Eccentric Naturalist," Audubon was gleefully recalling how he had met one of the most sophisticated scientists of the day and made him the butt of his backwoods humor.

He pulled off his shoes [the account went on], drew his stocking so as to cover the holes about his heels telling us all the while in the gayest imaginable mood that he had walked a great distance. His agreeable conversation made us forget his singular appearance. A long loose coat of yellow nankeen cloth—stained all over with the juice of plants, nankeen waistcoat over a pair of tight pantaloons. His beard was long, his lank black hair hung loosely over his shoulders. His words afforded a sense of rigid truth. I listened with as much delight as Telemachus could have done to Mentor. I laid my portfolios open before him. He turned to the drawing of a plant quite new to him, inspected it closely, shook his head and told me no such plant existed in nature. I told my guest the plant was common in the immediate neighborhood. He importuned: "Let us go now." We reached the river bank and I pointed to the plant. I turned to Rafinesque and thought he had gone mad. He began plucking the plants one after the other, danced, hugged me, told me exultingly that he had not had now merely a new species, but a new genus.

That night Audubon heard a great uproar from the naturalist's room. "I opened his door and saw him running about naked in pursuit of bats. He had my favorite violin by the handle and proceeded to bash it against the wall in an attempt to kill the winged animals. He begged me to procure a bat for him—'a new species.' I took the bow of my battered Cremona violin, and soon got specimens enough."

At Rafinesque's request, Audubon took him out into

one of those thickets or brakes in which the cane grows from twelve to thirty feet in height. A fallen tree obstructed our passage. We were about to go round it when out of the center of the tangled mass of branches sprang a bear with such force and snuffing the air in so frightful a way that Rafinesque was terrified. In his haste to escape he fell and was pinioned between the stalks. Despite his thorough fright, I could not refrain from laughing at the ridiculous exhibition he made. The way became more and more tangled. The thunder began to rumble. Heavy rain drenched us. Briars had scratched us, nettles stung us. Rafinesque threw away all his plants, emptied his pockets of fungi, lichens and mosses. I led him first one way, then another until I myself, though well acquainted with the brake, was all but lost in it. I kept him stumbling and crawling until long after midday.

Leading his guest through the canebrakes was cruel enough but even crueler was a scientific hoax Audubon played on him, describing and drawing a dozen local fish which never existed except in his own tall tales. Taking Audubon at his word, Rafinesque included ten of Audubon's imagined creatures in his pioneering work on western fishes.

The Devil-Jack Diamond fish (Litholepsis admantinus) [Rafinesque wrote], the wonder of the Ohio. I have seen it but only at a distance and have been shown some of its singular scales. Wonderful stories are related concerning this fish but I have principally relied upon the description and figures given me by Mr. Audubon. Its length is 4 to 10 feet. The whole body is covered with large stone scales half an inch to one inch in diameter. They strike fire with steel! and are ballproof!

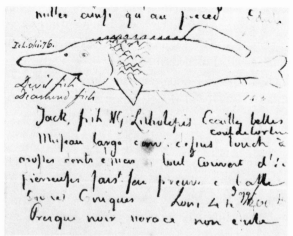

Audubon's mythical fish were solemnly entered by Rafinesque in his notebook. The nonexistent "devil fish" or "diamond fish" appeared on the same page with two real varieties.

It was perhaps inexcusable for Audubon to carry a joke so far. It was certainly inexcusable for a naturalist like Rafinesque to be gulled by such stuff. He was, after all, one of the most widely experienced scientists in America. "In knowledge," he wrote of himself, "I have been a botanist, naturalist, geologist, geographer, historian, poet, philosopher, economist, philanthropist. By profession, a traveler, merchant, manufacturer, collector, improver, professor, teacher, surveyor, draftsman, architect, engineer, author, editor. I hardly know what I may not become as yet." One of the most traveled men of his times, he covered "over 25,000 miles, half by sea, half by land. One-fourth pedestrian journeys . . . by mules, asses, litters, sedan chairs, chaises, men's backs, feluccas, tartans, boats, arks, scows, nearly all the possible manners except by camel and in balloons."

Every one of his journeys, whether into knowledge or new lands, was a journey of discovery for Rafinesque. He was so obsessed with finding new things, propounding new explanations, replacing old names with new ones that fellow scientists, however much they admired his talents, could hardly bear to deal with him. One loyal colleague complained: "He is the best naturalist I am acquainted with but he is too fond of novelty. He finds too many new things. All is new! new!" Another spluttered at that "foolish European foolery which leads him to treat Americans like half-taught school boys."

Yet if anyone had a right to be intellectually arrogant it was Constantine Samuel Rafinesque. Natural history, as he himself pointed out, did not contain him. As an anthropologist, for example, he astutely analyzed the similarities between American Indians and Asians and uncovered early clues to the meanings of pre-Columbian hieroglyphics. As a businessman, he founded one of the earliest and most successful savings banks in America and patented a coupon system that presaged the present forms of stocks and bonds. As a poet, he composed a verse epic about almost everything, and as a biologist, he had—by Charles Darwin's own acknowledgment—intimations of evolution long before *Origin of Species* was written.

Though his mind commanded respect, almost everything about Rafinesque invited mockery. His students at one school where he taught found him

> a corpulent man with a queer French accent, very large about the waist and wore wide Dutch pantaloons of a peculiar pattern and never wore suspenders. As he proceeded with a lecture and warmed up to his subject, he became excited, threw off his coat, his vest worked up to make room for the surging bulk of flesh and the white shirt which sought an escape, and heedless alike of his personal appearance and the amusement he furnished, was oblivious to everything but his subject.

Years later, the distinguished American scientist David Starr Jordan summed up Rafinesque's character as much as his achievements when he wrote, "No more remarkable figure has appeared in the annals of science."

He was only an embryo eccentric when, in 1802, he first came to America. He was twenty years old. Born in Turkey of a French father and a German mother, he was taken to France when, he wrote, he "was yet at the breast of [his] mother." A precocious student, he had read a thousand books by the time he was twelve years old and was a knowing naturalist when he first came ashore in Pennsylvania in 1802. The shock of discovery hit him, as it had Banister and Kalm and Wilson and all the others. "Everything was new to me," he recalled, including a plant he described as a new species and named *Draba americana*. "American botanists would not believe me," he grumbled, and they discarded his discovery only to have it verified decades later.

Settling in Philadelphia, and working as a clerk in a counting house, he wrote a paper classifying the birds in Peale's Museum, met William Bartram and explored the plant-rich regions of Pennsylvania. Rafinesque soon knew as much as anyone about the botany of the region. Characteristically he decided he would do the first comprehensive flora of the Middle Atlantic states and, proceeding south to do his research, found new plants in the mountains, new fish in the bays and strange trees in the Great Cypress Swamp. He called on Jefferson, who received him cordially but begged off when Rafinesque asked him to provide plants for the projected *Flora*. Regretting that "pursuits of an opposite nature to botany and natural history" kept the busy President from conferring this favor, Rafinesque had another request. Could he go as a botanist on one of the western expeditions Jefferson was planning? Jefferson said there was a place on an expedition William Dunbar, Wilson's friend, was taking up the Red River, "but

In Philadelphia, where he lived when he first came to America, young Rafinesque was portrayed in a charming miniature by the well-known artist of the city, Thomas Birch.

the government could pay only expenses and your time and labor have far other value."

Rafinesque probably would have gone anyway, but by the time Jefferson's answer came, he was back in Europe. Living for a decade in Sicily, he enlarged his naturalist's reputation by writing busily for European journals and Dr. Mitchill's *Medical Repository*. From his observations on two continents, he wrote a paper on European plants that had become naturalized in America. He was delighted to recognize an American acquaintance, the canvasback duck, swimming in Sicilian waters. Following his precept that anything anyone else could do Rafinesque could do better, he branched out into archaeology and volcanology and began reordering Linnaeus's classifications of fish. The local fishermen were agreeable to saving "the offal of their nets" for him and in these discards Rafinesque found dozens of new species. His careful way of describing the fish in their still-living colors confused other ichthyologists who, seeing only dead, faded specimens, concluded that Rafinesque was imagining the creatures he described.

A practical botanizer, Rafinesque set up a profitable export trade in medicinal plants. When anti-French feeling boiled up in post-Napoleonic Italy, he began to refer to himself as an American and, for "prudent considerations," tried to disguise his French name by taking on his mother's maiden name, calling himself Rafinesque-Schmaltz.

In 1815, with a cargo of botanical drugs, fifty boxes of books and collections including sixty thousand shells, he sailed again for the United States. It was a dismal voyage with a disastrous end. What with successive storms and endless calms, with stops for repairs and detours to elude hostile warships, the crossing took a hundred days. Off Block Island, the ship ran into a heavy fog and then into some rocks and capsized. Rafinesque reached the mainland in a longboat with no money, no cargo, none of his collections and no clothes except what he wore.

He made it to New York where Dr. Mitchill took him in, gave him clothes and soon had the whole natural history community of New York clucking over the half-drowned bird of passage. Dr. Hosack and DeWitt Clinton helped get Rafinesque a tutoring job, which kept him going until he collected some insurance money and set up a botanicals business in New York. He could hardly have paid much attention to it—he was too ready to take field trips with Dr. Mitchill. The two compendiums happily swapped information, and Mitchill illustrated one of his papers with some drawings Rafinesque had done on his voyage and happened to have in his pockets when his ship was wrecked. Made a member of the newly formed Lyceum of Natural History, Rafinesque was given the honor of presenting the first scientific paper. Naturally he refused to limit himself to a single subject, discussing fossil tubifore and aphids. As a member of the Committee on Lectures, he assigned himself papers on Helminthology, Polyology, Plyspes, Hydrogeology, Atmology and Taxonomy.

Though he seemed to be dispersing his talents, Rafinesque was more disciplined in New York than he had ever been—or ever would be again. Dr. Mitchill, however much he overflowed himself, seemed able to contain other scientists. While giving Rafinesque constant encouragement, he also kept him almost within bounds. Not that Rafinesque was completely accepted by the naturalist community. His interesting paper on fossil jellyfish—a concept other naturalists thought a contradiction in terms—was dismissed by one colleague as "the wild effusions of a literary madman." His campaign to replace the artificial sexual system of Linnaeus with the more broadly based natural system of classification proposed by the de Jussieus of Paris was attacked as heresy by America's loyal Linnaeans. But a young curator at the Lyceum, John Torrey, absorbed Rafinesque's arguments and went on to accomplish, by his cool and careful approach, what Rafinesque's fulminations could not.

Restless in New York, Rafinesque in 1818 started the American wanderings which were to take him back and forth across the Alleghenies five times, mostly on foot. "Horses do not suit botanists," he declared, no matter that they did suit John Bartram. He followed Bartram's course across Pennsylvania and followed Alexander Wilson's by riding down the river from Pittsburgh. At Hen-

derson, his autobiography notes, he "spent some days with Mr. Audubon, ornithologist, who showed me his fine collection of colored drawings." Rafinesque
seems never to have read Audubon's account of the visit, and may never have been
aware of the fishy hoax. The waters of the Ohio were unusually low and
revealed to his delighted eyes a host of univalves nobody had ever collected.
Before Rafinesque left on his trip, John Torrey had told a friend about it. "You
may imagine how many new discoveries he will make. He was almost crazy
with anticipation." When he had finished his trip, Rafinesque totted up his
claims: "Abt. 25 new species of Bats, Rats and other quadrupeds, abt. 20 N. Sp
of Birds. Abt. 15 N. Sp of snakes, turtles, lizards, and other reptiles, 64 N. Sp
of fishes of the Ohio: more than 80 N. Sp of shells, besides some new worms
and many fossils. And in Botany I have collected more than 600 Sp of Plants
of which one-tenth part at least are new."

The West attracted Rafinesque and he applied for a post at the University
of Transylvania in Lexington, Kentucky. Both the city and the university were
surprising citadels of culture to find on the rough frontier. Lexington, with a
population of 5,000, had several newspapers, two bookstores, an Athenaeum,
two philosophical societies (Union and Whig), private schools for girls and
boys and a piano manufacturer. Musical groups played the still radical music
of Beethoven, traveling theatre troupes brought the newest plays, and celebrities
from everywhere came to call on the leading citizen, Henry Clay. On his western
trip, Alexander Wilson sold several subscriptions to Lexingtonians. "A singularly
neat and pleasant town," wrote a visitor. "An air of leisure and opulence. Literature was most commonly the topic of conversation and the people are addicted to
giving parties."

Transylvania was central to the city's life. The first college set up west of the
Alleghenies, it became a Presbyterian university but lost its Fundamentalist
cast in 1817 when Horace Holley, a learned and cosmopolitan New England
Unitarian, was made president. Under his brilliant regime, in the 1820s,
Transylvania graduated more Bachelors of Arts than Columbia or Bow-
doin, and gave out more M.D.s than Yale, largely because Dr. Drake had come
down from Cincinnati to set up a medical faculty. The graduates of this decade
included seventeen future congressmen, six senators, three governors and the
president of the Confederacy. Shortly after taking over, Holley added natural
history to the curriculum and when Rafinesque applied, hired him to teach it.

The West had never had a professor of natural history before—nor seen anything like Rafinesque. "A man of very peculiar habits," a student recalled, "but
one of the most interesting men I have ever known. He lectured in a most entertaining manner. His lecture on the ants was peculiarly instructive, causing many
of the students to laugh heartily especially when he described them as having

lawyers, doctors, generals and privates and of their having great battles and of the care by physicians and nurses of the wounded."

Instead of relying solely on texts, as was the academic custom, Rafinesque brought specimens he had collected in the neighborhood into his classes and used them to illustrate his lectures—which, according to a modern scholar who has read the scripts, were "well prepared, well pondered." Though his class-rooms were, as a student described them, "the scene of most free and easy be-havior," he reached many of those who took his courses. One of his students, Jefferson Davis, was so affected that when he was imprisoned after the Civil War, he called for his old botany and conchology texts so that he might resume the interest that had been stirred by his ardent teacher at Transylvania.

The university was a turbulent place. Holley quarreled with his conserva-tive trustees, and the faculty members feuded freely and almost fatally with each other. (Professor Dudley of the medical department, having gravely wounded Professor Richardson in a duel, rushed over and, by applying his thumb to the proper pressure point, saved his mortal enemy from bleeding to death.) Rafinesque was always haggling about something—over not being properly paid, or not being adequately fed and lodged, or not given enough room for his col-lections or help in recruiting students, whose fees made up most of his pay. He grumbled when he wasn't given a graduate degree and was offended when he was finally given one that he thought did not recognize his full talents.

While at the university, he completed his *Ichthyologia Ohiensis*, or *Natural History of the Fishes Inhabiting the River Ohio and Its Tributary Streams*. A pioneer work in its field, it is an engaging book, explaining much about Rafinesque as well as about the Ohio's fishes. "The art of seeing well or of noticing and distinguishing with accuracy the objects which we perceive is a high faculty of the mind," he wrote. This faculty, he went on, aiming at his deprecators, is "unfolded in few individuals and despised by those who can neither acquire it nor appreciate its results."

In *Ichthyologia Ohiensis* he writes succinctly, with careful attention to detail —a reader can almost smell the air and earth, taste the waters, see the "very fine views and prospects." The fish are described mostly in English, not Latin, since the intention was to make it easy and attractive for laymen. The fishes' common names are given along with instructions on where and how to catch them (the golden-eye perch "bites at the hooks"), how to cook them, how they taste ("Most delicate are the salmon-perch, the Bubbler, the Buffalo fish, the sturgeons, the catfishes"). Like William Bartram, he was as ravished by the coloring of a fish as any ornithologist by the plumage of a bird. The Ohio gold-shade, he wrote, "is greenish gold above, silvery underneath, blue under the scales, sides, belly and throat with purple and violet shades. Top of head and neck clouded with brown, eyes black, iris silvery and gilt." Besides all this, it is "a fine fish, flesh esteemed, less bones than the shad." He had an eye—and ear— for the grotesque. He described the Grunting Bubbler crunching shellfish in its teeth and uttering a "strange grunting noise between the dumb grunt of a hog and the single croaking noise of the bullfrog. Every navigator of the Ohio is well acquainted with it."

In good temper when he compiled his Ohio fishes, Rafinesque gave credit to the work of others. His usual condescending manner is missing, though he does break in every once in a while with comments like "This genus was very badly defined by Linnaeus and Mitchill." In describing Audubon's creatures, Rafinesque suggests that his informant may have been a little confused in some cases—"the big-mouth Senber is a very doubtful species"—but he accepts "the description and figure given me by Mr. Audubon." Other ichthyologists found it irritating to have to reconcile some of the book's disparities, but they had to, for it proved to be a basic work on fishes of the region.

The years at Transylvania were in some ways Rafinesque's most productive. He wrote two hundred scientific papers, many for Dr. Mitchill and for Benjamin Silliman's new *American Journal of Science and Arts*. The Geographical Society of Paris awarded him the first gold medal they ever gave an American for his paper on the similarities between the primitive natives of Asia and America. A learned society in Bonn honored Rafinesque by conferring upon him the appellation *"Catesbaeus,"* that earlier painter of birds and fishes having now been established in the naturalists' pantheon.

Rafinesque, meanwhile, became a part of the Lexington social and cultural life. Hostesses welcomed him at their affairs, for although he was an unpredictable conversationalist—he had no small talk but could fascinate anybody willing to submit to his scientific discourses—he was a very graceful dancer and attentive to ladies. One of his minor productions at the time was a small book filled with drawings of the belles of Lexington. To eke out his salary and fees, he gave public lectures on botany. "I am patronized by the ladies," he complained, "and must endeavor to please them by telling them pretty things, yet have been able now and then to explain a few new ideas and views."

People who weren't exasperated by Rafinesque often felt sorry for him. "The wife of the president," a resident recalled, "took a motherly supervision over this lone friendless little creature and saw that he ate his dinner, that the mud from his various expeditions was removed from his garments and his hair was combed and his face washed." It was ungrateful for Rafinesque to put a curse on Mrs. Holley's husband, as he did later.

He came to know Dr. Charles Wilkins Short, a kind of one-man botanical outpost in Kentucky. Rafinesque got specimens from Short, and Short in return got accurate and up-to-date identifications from Rafinesque. Though Short was an accomplished botanist, Rafinesque treated him as a tyro, telling him what plants to look for, how to preserve them and how to classify them. Other botanists accorded Short more deference, impressed by the fact that over the years he sent them some twenty-five thousand plants.

There seemed no end to Rafinesque's energy. By selling stock to interested citizens, including Henry Clay, he raised money to start a botanical garden. Although it was a massive job, Rafinesque built up a garden with forty thousand plant and animal specimens that, on its regional basis, could take its place among some of the best in the world. He founded a journal, called *Western Minerva*, to reflect Lexington's boast that it was "the Athens of the West." The magazine was a marvel of one-man diversity, taking all knowledge as its province and presenting the editor as purveyor of most of it. Almost everything in the first (and only) issue is signed by Rafinesque under his own name or one of his pseudonyms. The subjects include metaphysics, astronomy, meteorology, physics, botany, archaeology, medicine—involving discussions of sidereal spheres, atmospheric dust, the properties of light, botanical finds, and

Rafinesque could be very unflattering not only about his scientific colleagues but also about the ladies of Louisville, whom he taunted in caricatures and catty poems.

some Indian antiquities Rafinesque uncovered in Fayette County. There were also poems in English, French and Italian by the many-tongued editor. Some two hundred subscribers had signed up for *Western Minerva*, but only a few copies of the first issue were distributed. Rafinesque accused "foes of mine" of bribing the printer to suppress it, possibly because of what Rafinesque had written about Lexington and the university.

> There is here, as elsewhere, a set of unfortunate individuals who have two eyes but cannot see; their minds are deprived of the sense of perception. They are astonished at my discoveries and inclined to scoff at them. Here I am like Bacon and Galileo somewhat ahead of the age assailed by a host of revilers and croaking frogs and a target of sophisters, Aristarchs and moles, paltry owls or rather whippoorwills which live in the dark, and now and then utter their lamentable and dismal cries.

Rafinesque's best epithets, it should be noted, were taken from nature.

Discontented at Transylvania, Rafinesque kept nagging Jefferson to get him a post at the proposed University of Virginia, offering to teach not only natural history but French, Italian, geometry, map drawing and political economy—and, as a bonus, promising to bring along his library, herbarium and personal museum containing twenty-seven thousand specimens. The aging Jefferson patiently answered Rafinesque, repeating that the university was not yet ready to open and pointing out that keeping up a correspondence was very difficult for him now. Once, when Rafinesque sent him some locust-tree seeds, he thanked him almost testily by saying he was "too old to plant trees for my own gratification."

Rafinesque's term at Transylvania ended by 1826. As he reported it, he returned from a trip to Washington to find that President Holley "had broken open all my rooms, thrown all my effects, books, and collections in a heap, depriving me of my position as librarian and my board at college. Leaving the college with curses on it and Holley, who were both reached by them soon after, since he died of yellow fever caught at New Orleans, having been driven from Lexington by public opinion, and the college has been burnt with all its contents."

Rafinesque overstated somewhat. Holley was ousted from his job not by public opinion but by his Fundamentalist opponents. As for the fire, it burned down just one building, not the whole college, which has survived its eccentric professor's curse to this day.

Some friends took up a collection to help Rafinesque ship his belongings east. Traveling north to Rochester, he met Amos Eaton escorting a group of students on a cruise down the new Erie Canal. Eaton invited Rafinesque to join his company. "He is a curious Frenchman," he wrote his wife. "I am much pleased with him though he has many queer notions." Bruised and rootless, Rafinesque needed such friendship. "The canal trip was one of the most agreeable journeys I ever performed. I shall always remember this excursion with pleasure." Settling in Philadelphia, Rafinesque published a modest volume, *Medical Flora*, which adopted the old herbalist tradition of cataloging plants that have medical uses. The roots of trillium, he wrote, "are good for rattlesnake bite, uterine hemorrhage, asthma, tumors, putrid ulcers," and he noted that *Collinsonia canadensis*, named for Peter Collinson, was a poultice for men's bruises and horses' sore backs.

Fields other than natural history occupied Rafinesque. He patented his "Divitial Invention," a system of issuing stocks and bonds in divisible units so that they could be easily traded. Finding no market for his invention in the United States—it was prophetic in its concept but too inflexible for practical use—he offered it to the Mexican government. Mexico never responded, even though Rafinesque was willing to throw in another of his inventions: "a new kind of artillery which in a single discharge will destroy one thousand men in arms one mile off or sink a large ship of war." More profitable for Rafinesque was a savings bank he helped found and manage in Philadelphia. One of the earliest institutions of its kind, it was more honest and stable than most. With Rafinesque sometimes working as its actuary, it paid depositors 6 percent interest and shareholders a 9 percent dividend.

But Rafinesque could not limit himself to practical economic matters; he broke out with *The World, or Instability, a Poem in Twenty Parts*. No author was listed on the title page in the first edition, but in the second "Constantine Jobson" was named as author. The reason for this reticence apparently was that the publisher (Rafinesque) wanted to give the editor (Rafinesque) a free hand in praising the author, whose first name gave the whole game away. The poem, said the editor's preface, is "an unusual literary effort seldom expected this side of the Atlantic, difficult to class," comparable to Milton's *Paradise Lost* and Thomson's *The Seasons*. "The great aim is to prove that instability is as much a law of nature as attraction or gravitation. It is as if Newton had explained his laws of attraction and repulsion in a poem instead of a mathematical work." Or as if Rafinesque were making a last gargantuan effort to empty his mind of all it knew. There is hardly a topic that the poem and its hundred learned footnotes do not touch on, from natural philosophy to politics to the evils of "blind faith" to solar spots to the keeping of the Sabbath.

In his last years, Rafinesque wrote a kind of autobiography, *A Life of Travels and Researches in North America and South Europe*, filled with his bitterness, his boasts and his guilelessness in expecting the world to be what he knew it could not be. "I have tried to serve mankind," he wrote, "but have often met with ungrateful returns, with jealous rivals instead of friends." Yet, he said, "I have never despaired long."

Everything soured for him. The wife he had left behind in Sicily believed that he had drowned and went off with a stage comedian. He wanted his daughter, the cast-off mistress of an English nobleman, to visit him but he did not have the fare to send her. His obsession with the new, his outbursts against his colleagues pushed him farther and farther from his contemporaries. Benjamin Silliman, whose *American Journal of Science* was becoming the preeminent scientific publication in America, grew so disturbed by a flood of papers from Rafinesque announcing his discoveries that he bundled them all back. Else, he declared, Rafinesque "alone would have filled the *Journal*."

Had he been less haphazard in publication and more organized in his presentations, Rafinesque would have received more credit during his life and saved other scientists from going over ground that he had already covered. Naturalists since his death have kept rediscovering Rafinesque, sorting out his wild claims from his provable achievements, and finding more and more of the latter. In ichthyology, Rafinesque is now given credit for discovering or first identifying thirty-five genera and thirty species, far more than any other American of the period. In mammalogy, he is credited with six genera and six species; in botany, with some seventy genera and as many species.

The listing of genera and species seems a dry reward for so fruitful a career. Rafinesque himself found other recompense. He described it in a paean to the naturalist's life:

> A life of travels and exertions has its pleasures and its pains, its sudden delights and deep joys mixt with dangers, trials, difficulties, and troubles. The mere fatigue of a pedestrian journey is nothing compared to the gloom of solitary forests, when not a human being is met for many miles, and if met he may be mistrusted. When you must live on corn bread and salt pork, be burnt and steamed by a hot sun at noon or drenched by rain, even with an umbrella in hand, as I always had.
>
> Mosquitoes and flies often annoy you or suck your blood. Ants crawl on you whenever you rest on the ground, wasps will assail you like furies if you touch their nests. You may be lamed in climbing rocks for plants or break your limbs by a fall. You may be overtaken by a storm, the trees fall around you, the thunder roars and strikes before you. You may fall sick on the road and become helpless. Yet many fair days and fair roads are met with, a clear sky or a bracing breeze inspires delight and ease, you breathe the pure air of the country, every rill and brook offers a draught of limpid fluid.

Every step taken into the fields, groves, and hills appears to afford new enjoyments. Here is an old acquaintance seen again; there a novelty, a rare plant, perhaps a new one! greets your view: you hasten to pluck it, examine it, admire, and put it in your book. Then you walk on thinking what it might be, or may be made by you hereafter. You feel an exultation, you are a conquerer, you have made a conquest over Nature, you are going to add a new object, or a page to science. This peaceful conquest has cost no tears, but fills your mind with a proud sensation of not being useless on earth, of having detected another link of the creative power of God.

CHAPTER TWELVE

THE INNOCENT TRAVELER

❦ ❦ ❦ ❦ "MR. NUTTALL WAS A ZEALOUS BOTANIST," WROTE WASHING-
ton Irving in *Astoria*, his account of a famous fur-trading expedition, "and all
his enthusiasm was awakened at beholding a new world, opening upon him
in the boundless prairies, clad in the variegated robe of unknown flowers. Delighted with the treasures, he went groping and stumbling along among a
wilderness of sweets, forgetful of everything but his immediate pursuit. The
Canadian voyageurs used to make merry at his expense, regarding him as some
whimsical kind of madman." In fact, a member of the expedition reported, the
name by which he was commonly known was "*le fou.*"

Thomas Nuttall was indeed, in a metaphorical sense, a fool—a throwback
to that bemused figure of the Middle Ages, the Blessed Fool, who, protected
by his own innocence, wandered unharmed from one peril to the next. As Nuttall walked back and forth across America, lured by the promise of undiscovered plants, he was lost on the unmapped plains, beset by hunger and mortal
thirst, stalked by Indians, left alone and aflame with fever in the hostile land.
Again and again death stretched out to touch him, yet as if some protector had
been hanging over him, he always came away safely, grasping botanical treasures that in the end more than matched the findings of any other naturalist in
America, even the redoubtable John Bartram and the far-ranging André Michaux.

To begin with, Nuttall had no business being with the Astorians, who were
traveling for John Jacob Astor's fur company up the Missouri in the wake of
Lewis and Clark. He was supposed to be somewhere around Winnipeg, picking plants for the eminent Dr. Benjamin Smith Barton, professor at the University of Pennsylvania and author of the first American text on botany. A
printer by trade, Nuttall had determined as a young man in Yorkshire to make
natural history his life and America the place where he would live it. Leaving

England in 1808, when he was twenty-two, he came, as naturalists did, to Philadelphia. His first moments in America laid that indelible mark of the New World on him: "The forests apparently unbroken in their primeval solitude and repose, an air of deep sadness to the wilderness," seemed still to be "the savage landscape as it appeared to the first settlers."

The day after he landed, he was out botanizing. He came upon a woody prickly vine with greenish stems and flowers. "Egad," he said to himself, according to an early biographer, "there is a passionflower." Looking for guidance, he was told to get Professor Barton's *Elements of Botany* and, unable to buy one, he went straightaway to the author to ask him what the flower was. Not a passionflower, said Dr. Barton, but a common greenbrier (an obnoxious pest, the modern botanical manuals call it), and took Nuttall on as a student. A man of learning and influence, Barton was impressed by what he called Nuttall's "ardent attachment to botany," and encouraged him, barely two months after his arrival, to explore the Delaware coast. The aim was to enlarge Nuttall's knowledge and the doctor's plant collections. On his trip, Nuttall was kept awake by the "confused vociferation" of the whippoorwill, a bird new to him, and was so badly bitten around the face by mosquitoes that people would not let him in their homes, thinking he had smallpox. But he found a rare red-bay tree that was not recorded again in the area for more than a century.

Barton next engaged his apt pupil to undertake a two years' journey to the far Northwest: up to the Great Lakes, over to Detroit, northwest to Winnipeg, back down the Missouri and Mississippi. According to a formal contract they signed, Barton would pay Nuttall eight dollars a month plus traveling expenses. Nuttall would look for elk nut at Legonier, pick up a few pounds of Frasera root, look into the salt works at Yellow Creek, inquire about mammoth bones, and so on.

With these instructions, Nuttall packed a gun, powder, paper, scales, Michaux's *Flora Boreali-Americana* and a letter of introduction to General William Henry Harrison—who was then governor of the Northwest Territory—in which Dr. Barton described Nuttall as "a young man distinguished by innocence of character." Only a man so distinguished would, after only a couple of years in America, set out over a route nobody had ever taken, to a place so distant that no one really knew how far away it was. As undaunted as he was unprepared, Nuttall started out, his diary says, on "April 12, 1810. Winter reluctantly yields to the smiling aspect of spring." It was a dull coach trip at the start. He found nothing more exciting than "humble draba and the fetid Pothos" (whitlow grass and skunk cabbage). But he did meet an interesting man on the coach, Manuel Lisa, a famous fur trader. At Pittsburgh, where winter had fully yielded to spring, he found a rare white dogtooth violet and enjoyed visiting

the prosperous glassworks owned by Benjamin Bakewell, whose niece Lucy
was then down at Henderson with her husband, John Audubon. He dispatched
his trunk by river boat to Le Boeuf, then walked down the Monongahela,
finding a whole plain covered with Frasera. Coming upon a new "very elegant
dydinamous plant," he named it *Collinsia* after Zaccheus Collins, a Philadelphia friend. (It is the flower called blue-eyed Mary.) After going more than
a hundred miles to Le Boeuf, he learned that his trunk had never been shipped.
"Brooding on my disastrous journey," he started walking back to get the trunk.
Neither his brooding nor repeated attacks of the ague (probably malaria) could
keep him from making notes on a porcupine, a green moth, a new orchis and an
unfamiliar yellow lady's slipper. Retrieving his baggage, he set out again,
"uncommonly burthened by his trunk and gun." After five days, slowed by
illness and the need to study a fragrant milkweed, he was back again in Le Boeuf.

Nuttall's open ways made friends for him along the way. Farmers lodged
him; their wives nursed him through fits of the ague. A priest lent him books.
When he reached Detroit, he found that the route Dr. Barton had laid out for
him was nonsense. The territory was controlled by the British, who would not
welcome him, and empty except for Indians, who would probably kill him. And
water, not walking, was the only possible means of travel. But he found another
helpful friend. The surveyor general of the new Michigan territory who was going
on to Michilimackinac Island (now called simply Mackinac) offered Nuttall a
place in his canoe.

At Michilimackinac, the wide-eyed Yorkshireman found himself in one of
the rowdiest places in the world, the rendezvous for trappers and voyageurs of
Astor's American Fur Company. "Here," as Washington Irving described it,
"voyageurs frolicked away their wages, fiddling and dancing, parading up and
down like arrant braggarts and coxcombs. They feast, they drink, they frolic
and fight until they are all as mad as so many drunken Indians." While the
voyagers fiddled and fought, Nuttall found *Rubus parviflorus*, the salmonberry,
and made still another friend, Wilson Price Hunt, the boss of Astor's rowdy
bunch. Learning of Nuttall's travel problem, Hunt offered to take him with his fur
brigade up the Missouri into Lewis and Clark territory. That was how Thomas
Nuttall came to be traveling with the Astorians instead of going to Winnipeg.

First they went to St. Louis, and Nuttall passed the winter discovering
Artemisia ludoviciana or western mugwort; *Baptisia leucophaea*, a false indigo;
Psoralea onobrychis, a pea; *Stylophorum diphyllum*, a celandine poppy. When
Hunt's party left St. Louis in March, 1811, Washington Irving noted it included
"two scientific gentlemen: one Mr. John Bradbury, a man of mature age but
great enterprise; the other a Mr. Nuttall, likewise an Englishman, younger in
years."

Bradbury had been sent to America to botanize and particularly to find new sources of cotton for the mills of Lancashire. Calling on Jefferson, who found him "a man stubborn in disposition," he was urged to go north instead of south, which is why he joined Hunt. Bradbury and Nuttall got on very well together, though Bradbury was taken aback by Nuttall's incompetence. When they came to a creek swollen by rains, Bradbury "was now surprised to find that Mr. Nuttall could not swim. I offered to take Nuttall on my back and swim over with him but he declined. About a league farther on, we found a raft of driftwood." In his account of the expedition, *Travels in the Interior of America*, Bradbury told how Nuttall, lost in the prairie after dark, was saved by companions who burned a hollow tree as a beacon for him. And he told of Nuttall's luck when, sitting in his tent in a thunderstorm, he was unharmed by a bolt of lightning that "shivered a tree" a few yards away.

Indian war parties were out, but they were too busy fighting each other to molest the plant hunters. Passing the mouth of the Platte River, Nuttall found a pair of pentstemons, *albidus* and *grandiflorus*; a white evening primrose called *Oenothera caespitosa*; a silvery saltbush called *Atriplex argentea*; a long-leaved artemisia called *Artemisia longifolia*. When he came across a "most splendid plant" of the mustard family, he named the genus *Stanleya* for Lord Stanley, the noble naturalist who got down on his knees to examine Audubon's drawings. There was a new milkweed, a ragwort, an aromatic thorn grass—he seemed to make a discovery a day.

Along the way, Nutall met his friend of the coach ride to Pittsburgh, Manuel Lisa, leading a rival fur-trading party. With Lisa was Charbonneau of the Lewis and Clark expedition with his wife, Sakawajawa, and little Pompey. There was also a young Boston lawyer named Henry Marie Breckinridge, who, in his *Journal of a Voyage up the Missouri*, described Nuttall as engaged in a pursuit

> to which he appears singularly devoted and which seems to engross every thought to the total disregard of his own personal safety and sometimes to the inconvenience of the party he accompanies. When the boat touches shore he leaps out and no sooner is his attention arrested by a plant or flower than everything else is forgotten. The inquiry is made: "Ou est le fou?" Where is the fool? "Il est après ramassée des racines." He is gathering roots. He is a young man of genius and very considerable acquirements but is too much devoted to his favorite pursuit and seems to think that no other study deserves the attention of a man of sense.

Nutall's incompetence was not always a matter for jokes. Checking the firearms against the threat of an Indian raid, the party's leaders found that the barrel of his gun, which he had carried all the way from Philadelphia, was tightly packed with dirt. He had been using it either as a spade to dig up plants or as a safe place to store the seeds he had collected. Far up the river, walking toward what he called "the northern Andes," the Rockies, he ran out of food and water a hundred miles from the post. Turning back too late, he lay exhausted on the ground, unable to go farther. A passing Indian found him and, recognizing him as the addled medicine man who gathered plants that were of no use to ordinary people, he carried Nuttall to the river, loaded him into his canoe, and paddled him down to the post.

Another time, when Nuttall had not returned to the post, the Astorians sent out some Indians to bring him back. The Indians tracked him down, but, fearful of his medicine-making powers, they dared not approach too closely. Seeing them around him, Nuttall concluded that they were out to kill him, whereupon he tried to escape, ducking into ravines, taking cover in the brush, leading his perplexed rescuers in a crazy game of hide-and-seek until, after three days, he staggered back to the post, still herded by the faithful Indians.

They stopped for the summer at Lisa's Missouri River post, which was run by Reuben Lewis, Merriwether's brother. It was a sordid world.

"'It is your own ass,' cried Ellen, the instant she found breath for words; 'your own patient hard-working hack!'"

The absent-minded naturalist, as exemplified by Nuttall, was caricatured by James Fenimore Cooper in The Prairie. *Obed Battius kept getting lost and didn't recognize his own donkey.*

Rambled through the Indian village [wrote Breckinridge] which I found excessively filthy, swarming with dogs and children. Females had become mere articles of traffic. Fathers brought their daughters, husbands their wives, brothers their sisters to be offered for sale. The silly boatmen in a short time disposed of almost every article they possessed. Seeing the chief one day in a thoughtful mood, I asked him what was the matter. "I was wondering," said he, "whether you white people have any women amongst you." I assured him in the affirmative. "Then," said he, "why is it that your people are so fond of our women; one might suppose they never had seen any before."

But it was also a world of unspoiled beauty. In that land the sky was bluer and the birds sang sweeter, wrote Breckinridge. "The sunbeams seemed to have less fierceness. I could almost fancy myself in the midst of enchanted scenes." Bradbury came upon an island "covered with cedar round which is a border in which were innumerable clumps of rose and currant bushes, mixed with grape vines, all in flowers and extremely fragrant. Between the clumps, the buffaloes, elks, and antelopes had made paths which were covered with grass and flowers. I have never seen a place, however embellished by art, equal to this in beauty."

Amid all this, Nuttall worked away collecting—not just plants, but rocks, fossils, many beetles and small animals, including a new species of bat. He shipped them off by river boat, but an old trouble that had long plagued American naturalists now caught up with him. Indians rummaged through his boxes and jars and drank off the alcohol in which he preserved specimens. In the fall, Nuttall sailed down to New Orleans himself, sent his material off to Dr. Barton and left for England, taking duplicate plants, seeds and bulbs to be sold in London. While there he prepared a *Catalogue of New and Interesting Plants Collected in Upper Louisiana and Principally on the River Missouri, North America.* But by the arrangements he agreed to, he got no credit for the plants he had discovered or described. The man who did was Frederick Pursh, then in London. He made as free with the material that Nuttall—and also Bradbury— had found as he had with the Lewis and Clark specimens. It "was not surely honorable" of Pursh, said Nuttall, to "snatch from me the little imaginary credit due my enthusiastic researches made at the most imminent risk of personal safety."

Pursh, incidentally, could not have enjoyed his ill-gained credit very much. Though he was admired in England for his work and took an interesting assignment to straighten out the gardens of Count Orlov in St. Petersburg, he scandalized London by marrying a barmaid. Then, engaged to work for the

Earl of Selkirk, who was settling dispossessed Highland crofters in Manitoba, he died in Canada on the way west.

By 1815, Nuttall was back in Philadelphia and soon went south into the areas combed by Bartram and Michaux. There he came on plants that they had either overlooked or failed to note—a creeping fringed orchis, a flax-leaved gerardia, a long-bristled needle grass, a tall ironweed, a rosy coreopsis. He went into the bogs to collect for a client in Liverpool that eighteenth-century prize the tipitiwichet. Though commercial collecting was never a full-time job for Nuttall, he had to do some to keep going financially.

After another brief stay in Philadelphia, he went back to western Pennsylvania to look for the blue-eyed Mary he had found there and unfortunately lost. He thought highly of this brief-blooming flower: "very elegant—the lower lip is of a bright azure blue which no color can excel." A vain search put him behind schedule but he found some seeds on the way to Cincinnati, where, herbalizing with Dr. Drake, he discovered a handsome mullein foxglove. Down in Lexington, he called on Dr. Short, and came upon a new mountain mint, a slender blue *Aster gracilis* and an uncommon *Magnolia macrophylla* that Michaux had noted. The last especially pleased Nuttall, because he had a client who wanted rare magnolias.

In 1817, he finally settled down in Philadelphia. After barely a decade in America, he was an established member of the natural history community, and the hard-working mainstay of the new generation which was trying to hold on to the eminence that the Bartrams and Wilson had given the city. Of all the Philadelphians, the one closest to Nuttall in friendship and talent was Thomas Say, who had been born into that community and all his life was thoroughly involved in it. Say's great-grandfather was John Bartram, who died before Thomas was born in 1787. Say grew up to work in Bartram's Gardens with his great-uncle William, to know two generations of Peales and to go birding with Alexander Wilson. He probably met Michaux and knew Michaux's son François André.

Though he dutifully worked in his father's prospering apothecary shop, Say much preferred going out to visit his uncle. Encouraged by Bartram and Wilson, Say took on a neglected branch of natural history: entomology. His collections of beetles and butterflies expanded, his hours spent at Peale's Museum increased and his stature in the city's group of amateur naturalists grew. This group included a dentist, a chemist who founded the first alum factory in the United States and a distiller who manufactured oil from the blubber of sperm whales. They took to meeting at Mercer's cake shop on Market Street where, in 1812, they set themselves up as the Academy of Natural Sciences. The Academy was not as imposing as its name. When they elected their officers, the organizers realized they were all chiefs and no Indians. After choosing a president, two vice-presidents, a treasurer, a controller, a conservator and a secretary, they found they had just one plain untitled member left over. Say was appointed curator of the museum, which consisted of insects and shells, some interesting coral, a stuffed monkey and a dried toadfish. In 1817, he began publishing sections of his *American Entomology*, the first descriptive work of its kind in America.

Say and Nuttall, much alike in temperament, enjoyed each other's company. They both spent long hours at Peale's Museum and one or the other often found it handy to bed down under the famous mammoth skeleton and sleep there through the night. They worked together to edit and print the Academy *Journal* on a secondhand press, which was donated by the Academy's president and unquenchable benefactor, William Maclure. A middle-class virtuoso who came into natural history by the usual roundabout way, Maclure used the fortune he had made in English textile mills to satisfy his two enthusiasms: progressive education and geology. Taken with the ideas of the Swiss educator Pestalozzi, who proposed that children learn by doing things for themselves instead of memorizing what others had done, he bought a 10,000-acre estate in Spain to establish a Pestalozzian center, but was thwarted by the Spanish government, which frowned on anything so revolutionary. Geology proved a more satisfying field. "I adopted the idea of rock hunting," he said, "as an amusement in place of deer or partridge hunting." It was not merely an amusement. On behalf of the British government, Maclure made a geological report of the coal strata of Europe and after he settled in the United States, whose democratic ideas were congenial to him, he traveled from the Atlantic to the Mississippi studying the geology. In 1809, he published the first broad American geological survey, *Observations on the Geology of the United States*.

In Philadelphia, where he gave his time, his library and his collections to the Academy of Natural Sciences, Maclure was always arranging other people's businesses and lives. Impressed by a French naturalist, Charles LeSueur, he imported him to Philadelphia, guaranteeing him an annual salary of five hundred dollars so that he could pursue his studies of American fish. Harking back to earlier naturalist days, Maclure set up an expedition to the region that William Bartram had covered. He, Say, George Ord and Titian Peale embarked for Georgia and Florida, Peale carrying a copy of Bartram's *Travels*. Though they saw interesting things, including the estate of a Georgian named Shaw whose four-story home had four-foot-thick walls made entirely of oyster shells, their nostalgic trip added little to natural science. Say found Florida a "promised land not flowing with milk and honey but abounding in insects which are unknown and if they remain unknown I am determined it shall not be my fault"—probably the first time a naturalist in America was ever gratified at the prospect of being beset by bugs.

Nuttall meanwhile had been working on his first significant contribution to American natural science. In 1817, he published the *Genera of North American Plants and a Catalogue of Species*, which was, at the time and for some years after, the best and most complete guide to American plants. There was now a substantial backlog of botanical work to draw on—from Banister and Lawson, through Clayton, the Bartrams, Michaux, Pursh and Rafinesque, along with the work on fungi by Lewis von Schweinitz, on southern flora by William Baldwin and on trees by Gotthilf Henry Ernest Muhlenberg. To these, Nuttall added the many discoveries, identifications and corrections that he himself could make—he was, after all, the first practicing botanist to have explored the new West. The *Genera* differed from existing botanical manuals and went further than all the others. It covered areas never before explored by a competent natural scientist. It was in English, rather than Latin. It explained instead of merely listing. And it set down the observations of one of the sharpest-eyed, most discriminating fieldmen who ever herbalized in the New World.

At the start, Nuttall faced a problem that was troubling all naturalists at the time: whether to stick with the archaic Linnaean system, whose shortcomings grew more and more troublesome with the expansion of biological knowledge, or shift to the more accurate but complicated natural system. He acknowleged the superior merits of the latter. He noted that "the great Linnaeus seldom spared" anyone or anything "that stood in the way of his darling system." He declared that he himself favored the natural "arrangement by affinities." Then he wound up rather sheepishly sticking to the Linnaean system because it was more convenient and widely used.

The *Genera* was an accurate, orderly work. In it, Nuttall presented "new species, the result of personal collections made from 1809 to the present time." He had crammed a lifetime of collecting into this eight-year span. His descriptions are dotted with personal observations. Telling of a pokeweed that grows on "the bare hills around the Arikaree Village on the Missouri," he explains that he gives "this with hesitation, not having seen a perfect flower, merely a flower bud." Dry in most of his notes, he lets go a little when he comes to the *Linnaea borealis*—a plant "unchanged by the vicissitudes of climate, it always apparently presents the same character, stands alone without distinct affinity to any other genus"—as if he were making the plant a parable for the man it was named for. Coming to *Nicotiana*, the tobacco plant, he explodes against "this universal luxury produced at the expense of human liberty and of a soil which could otherwise be employed in augmenting the necessaries of life," let alone the ills it brings. Botanists seem always to have been moralizers. When Nuttall comes to the *Sarracenia*, the insect-catching pitcher plant, he looks down at the dead flies in the pitcher and muses that this provides "a lesson for the incautious."

Nuttall published *Genera* at his own expense and, reverting to his old craft, may have actually set some of the type himself. It got a mixed reception from critics in the United States. Rafinesque, in his review, called it "a more correct account of our genera than has ever been published," and then set out to show how much better it would have been if he himself had done it. Europeans were more impressed by *Genera* than Americans. The famous English botanist William Jackson Hooker declared that it marked "an era in the history of American botany."

Eager to go west again, Nuttall proposed that he and Say be assigned as naturalists to an army expedition that was to explore the Rockies and the Arkansas River region. Say was chosen but Nuttall was not—the expedition's organizers required the botanist to double as physician. Dr. William Baldwin, whom Nuttall considered one of the best-informed botanists he ever met, was given the post. He died just as the expedition was getting under way and was later replaced by Edwin James, a student of Amos Eaton.

Nuttall meanwhile mounted his own private expedition. With the help of four friends, who put up fifty dollars each, he set out for the Southwest.

He told the story of his 18-month trip in *A Journal of Travels into the Arkansa Territory, During the Year 1819*. This time his narrative did not start with a blithe comment on winter reluctantly yielding to spring, but with a travel-hardened look at what lay ahead. "On the morning of the second of October, 1818 I took my departure from Philadelphia," he began. "Though always pleasingly amused by the incidents of traveling and the delightful aspects of rude or rural nature, I could not at this time divert from my mind the most serious reflections on the magnitude and danger of the journey which now lay before me and which was, indeed of very uncertain issue."

At Pittsburgh, he bought a boat, as Wilson had done, and found a young New Englander to help him sail down the Ohio. They camped out on islands, sleeping "with our feet to a warm fire, according to Indian custom." The country seemed poor and the cabins where they stopped could provide "nothing better than mush and milk which though agreeable, is not a sufficiently nourishing diet for a traveler." But he found a new amethyst-colored aster, and a small-flowered false dragonhead. The pawpaws around Steubenville were particularly delicious. Well on down the river he got rid of his companion, whose "insolence rendered our separation absolutely necessary." At Cincinnati he "was again gratified by the company of my friend Dr. Drake, one of the most scientific men west of the Allegheny mountains."

At Shippingport he bought a flatboat, though he knew it was, for an "inexperienced traveler, an act of imprudence." Accompanied now by an elderly gentleman and his son, he rowed swiftly down to the Mississippi into a river of floating ice and an endless succession of troubles. When the boat was stranded on a sandbar, Nuttall plunged into the freezing water to pry it off, but nevertheless after an hour had to pay two boatmen five dollars to get it afloat. At daylight, again grounded on the bar, he paid another eight dollars to get pushed off. They came to a narrow channel

> planted almost across with large and dangerous trunks, some with the tops, and others with the roots uppermost, in a perpendicular posture. The boat grazed on one, and we received a terrific jar. With all our exertions in rowing off, we but narrowly escaped from being drawn into the impassable channel of a sand island. The only course which we had left appeared no less a labyrinth of danger, so horribly filled with black and gigantic trunks of trees, along which the current foamed with terrific velocity—Scylla on one hand, and more than one Charybdis on the other.

They made their way by guess and by luck through the ever-changing channels. The young boy fell overboard. They recovered him but lost their steering oar. For all his own troubles, Nuttall took pity on a lost dog which "perishing with hunger came up to the bank yelling most pitiously." He tried to get it aboard but when he went to get it, "the miserable animal fell back, and yelled until he reluctantly disappeared." Passing an island, "we were accosted by some suspicious characters mimicking distress to draw us to land." But Nuttall had been told about the "gangs of pirates occasionally occupying these solitudes" and went by. His companions left him and, to get up the White River to the Arkansas, he hired a Yankee—"one of the most worthless and drunken scoundrels imaginable"—who refused to do anything more than steer while Nuttall and another hand rowed or towed the clumsy boat against the current.

Spring suddenly came. "The birds commenced their melodies" and he enjoyed a "harvest never before reaped by any botanist" of *Cruciferae*, plants of the mustard family. "With a sort of regret," he parted with his boat and then could get no one to carry his baggage on upriver. "In the meanest garb of a working boat man" he said, "I was no doubt considered one of the canaille. All pride of appearance I willingly sacrificed to promote with frugality and industry the objects of my mission."

Finally getting passage on a skiff, he sailed upriver, botanizing as he went and of course getting lost. Trying a shortcut, he found himself "in a horrid canebrake interlaced with brambles through which I had to make my way as it were by inches." Only the good sense of his companions, who fired three shots to guide him, brought him to the boat "pretty well tired of my excursion."

At one settlement he tried to hire a local man named Childers as a guide—and luckily, as he was to find out later, couldn't get him. At Fort Smith, the main army garrison, he went herbalizing with Dr. Thomas Russell, one of those army physicians who were just beginning to form the network of doctor-botanists that would add so much to American natural history. Almost everything Nuttall picked was new: a poppy mallow, a nemophila, a vervain, a violet variation of the blue-eyed Mary, and a new "species of that interesting plant which my venerable friend William Bartram called *Ixia coelestina*," the celestial lily or prairie iris.

When he found a prairie iris in Arkansas, Nuttall recognized it from this illustration in his copy of Bartram's Travels *as a species of Ixia coelestina.*

A party of soldiers going to put squatters off some Indian lands in what is now Oklahoma offered to take Nuttall along. "Nothing could at this season exceed the beauty of these plains, enameled with such an uncommon variety of flowers of vivid tints, possessing all the brilliancy of tropical productions. I delayed behind the party for the purpose of collecting some of the new and curious plants interspersed over these enchanting prairies." Again, he was lost. Then he lost his horse. When he finally did get back to camp, the soldiers had gone, and since he "dared not venture alone through such a difficult wilderness," he took lodging with a settler. "My botanical acquisitions in the prairies proved so interesting as almost to make me forget my situation, cast away amidst the refuse of society, without money, unprovided with every means of subsistence." He walked over prairies, "gilded with millions of *Rudbeckia amplexicaulis* [a coneflower]" and for the first time in his life "harkened to the inimitable notes of the mockingbird (*Turdus polyglottos*)," whose song brought a touch of Shelley into Nuttall's prose: "Perched on the topmost bough of a spreading elm, it broke forth into a strain of melody the most wild, varied and pathetic that ever I heard from anything less than human, continuing in its note as if overpowered by the sublimest ecstasy."

Like a man marooned on a coral island, Nuttall found it hard to tear himself away from his unsought paradise. But when a party traveling to Fort Smith came by, he went along with them. This time everybody got lost. They kept passing and repassing "terrific ridges over which our horses could scarcely keep their feet." Exhausted, they made it to the garrison, where Nuttall learned of a "horrid circumstance": the man Childers, whom he had tried to hire as a guide, turned out to be a thief and a murderer. He had robbed and shot a local merchant and then scalped him. "Melancholy as were the reflections naturally arising from this," Nuttall mused, "I could not but congratulate myself from having escaped perhaps a similar fate."

He had troubles with the Osage Indians who lived around the post. One of them stole his only penknife. The Indian chief, pressed by Nuttall, delivered a sermon on dishonesty to his braves, which impressed Nuttall with its candor but did not get him back his knife. Another Indian

> wished to exchange a horse with me. I requested to have nothing to say to him, knowing him, by report, to be a consummate thief and rascal; but, as he insisted on the subject, I went to see the animal offered me in exchange, and was truly surprised at the impudence and knavery of the demand. The horse which he proffered was not worth possession, as lean as Rosinante. I rejected his offer, which was nothing better than an insult. I now suspected that he was intent on thievery, and two of us directly fol-

lowed him. By the time we came up with him, he had seized my horse, loaded it with his baggage, and would in a minute or two more, with all the dexterity of an Arab, have carried him off.

Nuttall was "mortified to find that it was necessary, prudentially," not only to let the thief go "but even to bestow a present upon the villain."

Still bent on getting to the Rockies, Nuttall joined up with a trapper named Lee, and headed toward the sources of the Canadian River. It was the dry season and after he "very imprudently drank some very nauseous water," Nuttall was so sick he could barely stay on his horse. Just as imprudently, he was about to bathe when he saw a poisonous water snake lurking a few yards away, and moved off just in time. Then his old affliction, the ague, caught up with him again and his account of the journey became the feverish odyssey of the scientist and the trapper toiling across a hot and oppressive wilderness, the one refusing to give up his search for plants and the other, though hardly comprehending his odd companion, doggedly going along with him.

Stricken with "the remittent fever, attended with delirium," Nuttall wrote,

I was exposed to a temperature of between 90° and 100°. It was with difficulty that I could crawl into the shade, the thin forest being everywhere pervious to the sun, so that I felt ready to burn with heat; by forcibly inciting a vomit, I felt relieved. Mr. Lee, profiting by our delay, began to trap for beaver, and the last night caught four of these animals. At night I again experienced an attack of the fever, and attended with diarrhoea. It continued 36 hours, the paroxysms being only divided for a short space by an intermediate chill. Mr. Lee suggested the propriety of our returning to the Verdigris, before I became so weak as to render it impossible; but the idea of returning filled me with deep regret, and I felt strongly opposed to it whatever might be the consequences.

The next day, Lee, speaking in what Nuttall called "plainer terms," again tried to get Nuttall to be sensible and return to the post. Nuttall agreed "on condition of trying one or two days longer." By then, Lee's horse, his back rubbed raw, could no longer carry the trapper or his baggage. Dependent on Nuttall's horse for doing double duty, he "now said nothing more about returning." The green blowflies filled their blankets, linen and almost everything with maggots, but "to compensate for these disgusting and familiar visitors, we had the advantage of the bee, and obtained abundance of excellent honey, on which, mixed with water, I now almost entirely subsisted."

Proceeding "over stoney hills, with great fatigue," they almost stumbled into an Indian camp. "I need not say how unwelcome this intelligence was to

my cautious companion," who had learned of "the rapacity of the savage hunters" a few months before when some Cherokees robbed and almost killed him.

We delayed not a moment to leave our encampment. I could not possibly walk, and even required assistance to get on and off my horse.
Three days were now elapsed since I had been able to taste any kind of
food, and to add to the miseries of sickness, delirium, and despondence, we
experienced as many days of unremitting gloom, in which the sun was not
visible even for an hour. We now ventured out some distance into the
prairie hills; but, after traveling a few miles my mind became so unac-
countably affected with horror and distraction, that, for a time, it was
impossible to proceed.

Lee must have been a man of saintly patience. In the midst of all the trouble,
he went out and picked for Nuttall a "portulaca, resembling *P. villosa*," which the
naturalist "had seen in a solitary locality." Lee's horse "got into a mirey gulley
and would not be extricated" so he made himself a dugout and paddled down
the river while Nuttall on his horse plodded along the banks. They subsisted for
days on beaver tails, "the flesh of this animal being too lean and musky" to eat.
But the half-dead naturalist collected a

very curious *Gaura*, an undescribed species of *Donia*, of *Eriogonum*, of
Achyranthes, *Arundo*, and *Gentian*. On the sandy beaches grew several
plants, such as the *Uralepsis aristulata* (*Festuca procumbens*, Muhlenberg), and *Uniola* scarcely distinct from *U. spicata* and *Sesuvium sessile*,
which I had never heretofore met with, except on the sands of the sea
coast. We still saw the smoke of the Osage fires in all directions, and hourly
expected a discovery. One of the Indians saw me in the wood, but did not
venture to come up, dodged out of sight, and then ran along with haste
towards his encampment. This wolfish behavior, it may be certain, was
not calculated to give me any very favorable anticipation of our reception.

At this point in his narrative, Nuttall dropped in one of his plaintive understate-
ments. "I could not help indeed reflecting," he wrote, "on the inhospitality of
this pathless desert."

The Indians finally caught up with them. Among them was a blind chief,
whom Lee knew, and

a host of squaws, who were extremely impertinent. An old woman, resembling one of the imaginary witches of *Macbeth*, told me that I must
give her my horse for her daughter to ride on; I could walk. At last, the
blind chief invited us to his camp to eat, but had nothing to offer us but

boiled maize, sweetened with the marmalade of pumpkins. When we were about to depart they held on to the canoe, and endeavored to drag it aground. At length, they got to pilfering our baggage; even the blind chief, who had showed us a commendatory certificate which he had obtained at St. Louis, also turned thief on the occasion.

They left with a pair of Indians slinking after them.

Endeavoring to elude their pursuit, we kept on in the night, amidst the horrors of a thunderstorm, the most gloomy and disagreeable situation I ever experienced in my life. In consequence also of the quicksands and the darkness, it was with the utmost difficulty that I could urge my horse to take the river, which it was necessary repeatedly to cross. In one of these attempts, both myself and it were on the point of being buried before we could extricate ourselves. Dressed in leather, I came out of the water drenched and shivering, almost ready to perish with cold. After some persuasion, I prevailed upon Lee to kindle me a handful of fire, by which I lay alone for two or three hours, amidst the dreary howling of wolves, Mr. Lee not wishing to trust himself near such a beacon. Nothing, however, further molested us, and, after cooking and eating a portion of a fat buck elk, which my companion had contrived to kill in the midst of our flight, we continued our journey by the light of the moon.

They proceeded about twenty miles when, realizing that Nuttall's wearied horse could not keep up with Lee's canoe, they "agreed to part," and Lee went off down the Arkansas River and out of Nuttall's narrative. It is too bad no one ever caught up with the loyal trapper to get his version of the journey with the stubborn collector who was ready to die rather than surrender the hunt.

Making his way alone over sand beaches "as hot and cheerless as the African deserts," through "horrible thickets in which the *Ambrosias* were far higher than my head on horseback," Nuttall finally "arrived at the trading establishment of Mr. Bougie. My feet and legs were so swelled that it was necessary to cut off my pantaloons. I remained about a week with Mr. Bougie, visited by fever, and a kind of horrific delirium, which perpetually dwelt upon the scene of past sufferings."

There was a last bit of sadness to end his dreadful trip. His friend Dr. Russell had died of fever and Nuttall "faintly endeavored to commemorate" his name in *Monarda russeliana*, a bee balm.

Nuttall came back to Philadelphia in a belligerent frame of mind. Writing the introduction to his *Journal*, he attacked its readers even before they had a chance to start reading. He was not, he wrote, addressing his book to those who "vaguely peruse the narratives of travelers for pastime or transitory amusement. Had I solely consulted my own gratification, the present volume would never have been offered to the public. Far from writing for emolument, I have sacrificed both time and fortune to it." Despite his disclaimers, the *Journal* was well received both in America and in Europe. Historians have found it an invaluable source on the American frontier in transition.

Along with the *Journal*, the Arkansas trip produced a fine grab bag of natural history prizes: scores of new and unclassified plants, mineralogical specimens, fossil shells, fish, insects, interesting data on the Indians. Nuttall passed some of his plants and seeds along to friends and customers. He gave his fish to Charles LeSueur and the insects and fossil shells were set aside for Thomas Say, who was not in Philadelphia to receive them. He was out on the army expedition Nuttall had wanted to join.

This expedition was the brainchild of John Calhoun, the Secretary of War, who sent it out to find the sources of the Red River, map the still-uncharted Louisiana Territory, locate suitable places for military posts and protect the American fur trade. In a Jeffersonian bit of farsightedness, Calhoun—an eager gardener who was always cadging new plants in Washington for his garden in Charleston—added a scientific section to explore the area's resources and natural history. The commander, Stephen H. Long, took Say as the party's zoologist and Titian Peale as naturalist and artist.

They left Pittsburgh in May, 1819, with crowds on the bank to cheer them off and see the new wonder of the western rivers, a steamboat named *Western Engineer*. It was like no craft seen in America since, possibly, the days of the Vikings. Designed to impress the Indians, whose lands it would traverse, it also impressed a newspaper reporter. As he watched it depart on its maiden voyage, he set down an awestruck description:

> The bow of the vessel exhibits the form of a huge serpent, black and scaly rising out of the water from under the boat, his head darted forward, his mouth open vomiting smoke and apparently carrying the boat on his back. From under the boat at its stern issues a stream of foaming water, dashing violently along. All the machinery is hid. The boat is ascending the rapid stream at three miles an hour. Neither the wind nor human hands are seen to help her and to the eyes of ignorance the illusion is complete: that a monster of the deep carries her on his back, smoking with fatigue and lashing the waves with violent exertion.

At Cincinnati, the naturalists went ashore to visit Dr. Drake. Audubon, working there at the time, recollected "how Messrs. T. Peale, Thomas Say and others stared at my drawings." Once the expedition started up the Missouri, Say and his fellow naturalists went more by land than by boat. The coarse grass tore their moccasins and leather jackets, poisonous snakes rattled at them, a party of Pawnees stole their horses, game was so scarce that they felt lucky one day when they had wolf for dinner. Wintering at Council Bluffs, Say fished for specimens through the ice and, once he had studied the catch, served it for dinner. Titian Peale was hailed as a hero when he came in with two deer he had brought down with one bullet. Setting out west in the spring, they went through cactus-ridden plains adorned with distracting mirages that lined the horizon with nonexistent cliffs and filled the dry valleys with sparkling lakes through which fanciful herds of bison waded. The naturalists gathered specimens greedily—a scorpionlike spider, a columbine, the beautiful band-tailed pigeon later named *Columba fasciata* Say. Up into the mountains they passed through the Garden of the Gods to the high peak looming near. Edwin James and two others of the party climbed it through a "vast meadow" so full of brilliant alpines that they could not gather all the new varieties. At the top, looking down at the great distances, they saw clouds of migrating grasshoppers far below, the sun glinting on their wings. Major Long named the mountain James Peak, but geographers overruled him and called it Pike's Peak after the man who saw it first but never climbed it.

The way home was hardest of all. Down through the Arkansas region where

Titian Peale, who went on the Long expedition to draw flora and fauna, came home with Wild West souvenirs, including this sketch of an Indian horseman.

Nuttall had traveled the year before, the water dried up in the August heat while the wild grapes remained unripe. Peale's pack mule ran off and he chased it in vain for five miles. Three renegade soldiers robbed them, taking guns and clothes and Say's precious notebooks.

For all the disasters, the naturalists brought back dozens of skins of new or rare mammals, thousands of insects, some five hundred hitherto undescribed plants, new fish, and shells and material for "vocabularies of Indian languages," which Say put together. In his papers, Say acknowledged the help of "Little Black Bear, an Indian of the Otto tribe," who told him about the habits of the insects—the first truly native entomologist in the records of American science.

When Say got back to Philadelphia, he and Nuttall shared woeful accounts of their Arkansas travels and picked up their friendship. Say was a warm and gentle man, easy to approach. Nuttall, shy and reserved, seemed almost morose in company he did not know well—as if, a friend wrote, "he felt a sort of antipathy." Loosened up, he became open and buoyant. Elias Durand, his first biographer, described him as "a remarkable-looking man: his head was very large, bald, his forehead expansive, features diminutive with a small nose, thin lips and round chin, height above middle, person stout with a slight stoop and his walk peculiar and mincing, resembling that of an Indian." At work in the Academy, he would stand for a full hour without moving, in front of a tray of shells or other specimens, only his eyes seeming to move as he looked almost microscopically at the exhibits. When he had his fill of a piece of work and had mastered it, he would let go of it all at once to his friends, talking on and on without stopping.

Nuttall became a good public speaker, sharing the podium with Say at the Academy's lecture series. Expanding his audience, Nuttall went up to New Haven to talk to the students at Yale. All the while, he was busy producing papers on the new plants he had found on his journey, reporting on the mineralogy of the West and anticipating future American geologists with his methods of dating strata by their fossil content.

His friend Say, while teaching in Philadelphia, was also helping prepare Bonaparte's continuation of Wilson's *Ornithology* for publication and putting together the first complete volume of his own *American Entomology*. The final three volumes, whose accuracy and clarity matched any work of its kind published anywhere, not only pioneered American entomological study but also set a standard for it. In 1823, Say went with Long on another expedition, this time up to the north country of Minnesota. When he came back, Nuttall had left Philadelphia for the best academic job an American naturalist could get: instructor in natural history and botany at Harvard and curator of its Botanic Garden.

Thomas Say's American Entomology *was called "the most beautiful publication of its kind" ever printed in America. Charles Le Sueur drew its beguiling frontispiece.*

His predecessor at Harvard, William Dandridge Peck, had come by his interest in natural history in a most romantic way. One day on the beach at Kittery, Maine, he found a tattered copy of Linnaeus that had washed ashore from a wreck. Opening the sodden pages, he became absorbed in the text; he taught himself the Linnaean system and went on to teach it to others. Few teachers in the field had so eminent a roster of students: Thaddeus Harris, a pioneer entomologist; George B. Emerson, compiler of the *Trees of Massachusetts*; William Oakes, who did the first good flora of New England; Charles Pickering, a famous expert on mosses and the most versatile naturalist of his time; Ralph Waldo Emerson, who had a fair knowledge of botany and a lifelong interest in it. Peck's own work in ichthyology is remembered by *Syngnathus peckianus*, or Peck's pipefish.

When Nuttall took over the Harvard post in 1822, after Peck's death, he was made lecturer and curator, not a professor. For all his eminence, he had no academic training, and besides Harvard did not have funds to continue the professorship. Nuttall received five hundred dollars a year, plus fees the college and students paid for his courses. It was a reassuring arrangement. He had always lived on the edge of poverty—in Philadelphia his lodgings were in a basement. Nuttall more than earned his pay. The Botanic Garden improved under his guidance both as a place to enjoy and as a place to study. His botanizing through New England, a new locale for him, produced plants that others had either not known or not bothered with. His own collections, of course, were extraordinary sources for the Garden, and naturalists abroad, always willing to oblige him, sent specimens regularly.

In the classroom, Nuttall proved to be a success. More than forty students enrolled in his first course and, one of them wrote, "a strong attachment sprang up between this teacher and many of his students," who were "often enticed away from the drier studies of the course to a pleasant ramble through the woods and fields in search of their fruits and flowers." Soon he had over a hundred students. Finding no text that suited him, he set about writing one that did: *Introduction to Systematic and Physiological Botany.* Though intended as a text, the book has an attractive air. Nuttall leads the reader up to a flower and examines it with him in a simple but not patronizing step-by-step process, bringing to his explanations some of the wonder he himself always felt when he considered the creations of nature. His descriptions sometimes have an almost epigrammatic ring. The cryptogams (ferns, mosses, algae, fungi) are characterized "by invisible flowers and obscure fruits." It was a useful book, reprinted several times within a few years.

Cambridge society, like Harvard's students, took to Nuttall. When the Boston Society of Natural Science was founded, he was elected president but modestly declined. Faculty wives were delighted to have an interesting bachelor for their gatherings and Nuttall became a particular friend of the widowed Martha Austin and her daughter. A private gate at Nuttall's home opened on the path to Mrs. Austin's house.

Much as he liked Cambridge, Nuttall was restless there. He took a trip to England and went down to Philadelphia to see his old friends and work for a while in his old haunts. On a visit in 1825, he took a rare prize, a white butterfly (*Oeneis semidae*) that lives only around the peak of Mount Washington. It was a gift for Thomas Say, and this meeting seems to have been the last time the two friends saw each other. By the end of the year, Say was off to help William Maclure found a Utopian colony on the banks of the Wabash. He and Nuttall had been the only American naturalists of true first rank left in Philadelphia. With their departure, that city lost its century-old standing as the center of natural science. Mitchill and John Torrey had built up New York. Nuttall and Torrey's collaborator Asa Gray were to do the same for Boston.

Nuttall had become an all-round naturalist, working in mineralogy, zoology and entomology. Now another branch of natural history took his attention. A young friend and field-trip companion named James Brown, then a clerk in a Cambridge bookstore, proposed that Nuttall do a popular bird guide, and Nuttall in 1829 set about preparing his *Manual of Ornithology of the United States and Canada*. Published in 1832, it brought him more readers than any other of his books. Emerson called it "a beautiful book that everyone who lives in the country ought to read." James Brown's publishing firm—Little, Brown—reissued it regularly throughout the century and even into the next.

For a man who seemed so absorbed in botany, Nuttall showed a surprising knowledge of birds and a deep feeling for them. "They play around us like fairy spirits," he wrote in his introduction, "elude approach in an element which defies our pursuit, dart like meteors in the sunshine of summer, glide before us like beings of fancy." Since this was a field manual, it was smaller than Wilson's or Audubon's ornithologies. The drawings were simpler, the organization stricter and the text much more businesslike. Still, it is full of personal touches and admiring remarks. Pointing with pride to the crow, Nuttall declares that it is only "a thousandth part the size of an ox," yet its calls "may be heard as far or farther." He describes his pet kingbird in winter "basking like Diogenes in the feeble rays of the sun," and dubs the owl the "Pluto of the gloomy wilderness." He spins yarns about a bigamous Baltimore oriole who complicated his domestic life at nest-building time by leaving his mate for another female, and about Buffon's pet buzzard who ate with his master at the table and had a haughty way of snatching peasants' hats off their heads.

Nuttall went on at length about birds' songs. Where Wilson, discussing the titmouse, said little more than that it has "remarkable variety in the tones of its voice" and Audubon set down just one call, *tee-tee-tee*, Nuttall went through all the permutations of its songs: whip-tom-killy; day-day-day-day; 'tshica dee dee; day-day-day-day-dait; kai-tee-did did-dit-did; peto-peto-peto-peto-; que-ah, que-ah; 'tsh 'vah, 'tsh 'vay; kerry-kerry-kerry-kerry; pett-peet-a-peet-a-peet; ker-ker-ker-ker-kerry; keeva keeva keeva keeva; leta-leta-leta-leta-lit. Nuttall told about a robin that was taught to pipe Old Hundred, compared the veery's song to the "sound of liquor passing through a funnel into a bottle" and wistfully recalled the notes of the warbling vireo in autumn as "a parting whisper before our vocal woods and fields were left in dreary silence."

In 1832, Nuttall's life in Boston was enlivened by a visit from Audubon, over from England to get more birds. Audubon was relieved to find that Nuttall's *Manual* was no competition for his *Birds*, pleased when Nuttall dismissed the baleful Charles Waterton as a man of no consequence and very much interested when Nuttall told him where he could find an olive-sided flycatcher, a bird

Audubon had never seen. He told the story of their hunt for the bird. Walking out from Boston, they came upon one sitting and singing in a tree. While Audubon stayed to study it, Nuttall went off to borrow a gun from a Mr. Perkins, who lived a mile away.

Audubon knew Nuttall was an experienced wilderness traveler and he could hardly believe what Nuttall brought back: "a large musket, a cow's horn filled with powder and a handful of shot nearly as large as pease; but just as I commenced charging this curious piece, I discovered that it was flintless." So they walked back to Mr. Perkins, borrowed a less antique piece and returned to find the accommodating bird still perched in the tree, waiting, it almost seemed, to be put in an Audubon painting—which it was, as Plate 174 under the title of Cooper's flycatcher. It is now called an olive-sided flycatcher or *Nuttallornis borealis*. Audubon's description of the bird leans heavily on Nuttall's data. Audubon repaid Nuttall later by giving him information on birds he had found in Labrador.

In his decade at Harvard, Nuttall produced two first-class books, considerable research and had an enduring influence on New England naturalists. Appreciating this, Harvard gave him an honorary master of arts degree, doub-

very LONG BILLED CURLEW. *good*

(*Numenius longirostris*, Wilson, viii. p. 23. pl. 64. fig. 4. Bonap. Synops. No. 242. Phil. Museum, No. 3910.)

Sp. Charact.—Crown blackish, with whitish streaks, no medial line; rump uniform in color with the rest of the plumage; long axillary feathers ferruginous, without bars; the bill very long, and much arched.

The Long Billed Curlew is seen in the marshes of New Jersey, about the middle of May, on its way further north: and in September, or the latter end of August on their return from their breeding places. How far south they retire in the course of the winter, has not been ascertained, but a few, no doubt, winter in the marshes of South Carolina, as

bad — THE RUFF. *Never*

(*Tringa pugnax*, Linn. *Pugnax.* Briss. *Philomachus*, Mœhring. *Combattant*, Buff. Ois. vii. p. 521. t. 29. 30. [male.] *T. littorea*, Gmel. i. p. 677. Lath. *T. Grenovicensis*, Ib. *T. equestris*, Ib. *Gambet*, and *Yellow-legged Sandpiper*, Mont. Orn. Dict. *Totanus cinereus*, Briss. v. p. 203. 17. 2. [female and young.] *Ruff and Reeve*, Brit. Zool. ii. No. 192. t. 69. Don. Brit. Birds, t. 19. Bewick, ii. p. 95.)

Sp. Charact.—Bill slightly curved and enlarged towards the point; legs long; tail rounded, the two middle feathers banded, the 3 lateral ones always of a single color.—The colors of individuals extremely variable.—The *male in summer*, furnished with a ruff of long feathers on the occiput and sides of the throat, and with the face naked and warty.—*Female, young*, and *autumnal male*, without the ruff.

The Ruff, no less than the family of Sandpipers, with which it is associated in the systems, is almost equally given to wandering, being found, according to the season, dispersed

Audubon carried a copy of Nuttall's Ornithology *with him and from time to time wrote comments in it. He approved of Nuttall's long-billed curlew, but not his ruff.*

led his salary and, better yet, granted him several leaves of absence, a practice almost unheard of in those days. Nuttall took advantage of them to botanize around New Bern, where John Lawson had been burned to death by the Indians; walk up the Altamaha, where John Bartram had herbalized; go over into west Florida and Alabama, where William Bartram had traveled; and comb the region in between, where Michaux had wandered. Even such trips as these could not satisfy him, and when the chance came to go farther west, through the Rockies—those "northern Andes" which once almost proved his undoing—and to the Pacific, he resigned from Harvard.

This new opportunity came from a young friend, Nathaniel Jarvis Wyeth who had become wealthy working for a flamboyant Bostonian, Frederick Tudor, known as "the ice king." Conceiving the far-fetched idea of cutting ice from New England ponds and selling it in the West Indies, Tudor opened up an immensely profitable market there. But he had trouble with supply. Cutting ice by hand was laborious and expensive, and produced blocks of varying sizes that were difficult to store and ship. In the summer he would run out of ice, and though he persuaded some ships' captains to stop on their northern routes and hack away at the icebergs, this was really no answer. Wyeth came up with a sensible Yankee solution. Fitting a sled with saw-toothed runners, he drove the sled across a frozen pond, cutting parallel grooves into the ice. Having done this in one direction across the ice, he then drove the sled across at right angles to the first cuts, making a neat pattern of equal squares. Then the blocks were sawed out and packed in sawdust.

Wyeth's inventiveness and Tudor's enterprise enriched them both and, by making ice plentiful and cheap, revolutionized the daily lives of Americans. Wyeth then embarked on a grand project, at once speculative and patriotic: he would go into the northwest fur trade, making millions for himself and reinforcing American claims to the disputed Oregon Territory. The Astorian expedition, which Nuttall had joined years before, had been a failure. The British had bought off John Jacob Astor and then tried hard to keep everybody else out. In 1832, with more spirit than know-how, Wyeth led an expedition up the Missouri and over to the Pacific, but through inexperience and disaster— his supply ship was wrecked—his venture failed. Not at all discouraged, Wyeth came back to Boston and prepared another expedition. This time he invited Nuttall to go along.

He had already baited the hook for his friend. The journal of Wyeth's trip noted more than once: "Went out to collect some flowers for friend Nuttall." He sent or brought Nuttall several dozen new plants, including a dwarf sunflower now named *Wyethia helianthoides*. Nuttall not only took Wyeth up on his invitation but asked a friend of his to come along: John Kirk Townsend, a 24-year-old physician and pharmacist of Philadelphia. The American Philosophical

Society and the Academy of Natural History each chipped in a hundred dollars as an advance on birds Townsend was to collect for them. It was a good choice for American ornithology, since Townsend found many new birds and made many useful studies. It was an even happier choice for American history, since Townsend kept a journal, *Narrative of a Journey Across the Rocky Mountains*, that has become—as so many naturalists' journals have—a classic of American western literature.

Townsend had an eye for specific detail and a feeling for the ludicrous. The costumes he and Nuttall fitted themselves out with in St. Louis, where they arrived in 1834, included "several pair of leather pantaloons, enormous overcoats made of green blankets and white wool hats with round crowns, fitting tightly to the head, brims five inches wide and almost hard enough to resist a rifle ball." Their companions at the start of the boat trip included several Indian girls, who spent the time "seeking for vermin in each other's heads and eating them, only suspending their delectable occupation" to take bites out of loaves of bread that "were circulating by being tossed from one to the other."

Leaving the boat to walk, the two found "on the bare prairies thousands of golden plovers, the ground often literally covered with them for acres. They were very fat and we made an excellent meal of them." One evening they were "overtaken by a bluff jolly-looking man," who, on hearing "that we were naturalists, invited us to stop at his house" where he brought forth "three fine-looking daughters. Mr. N. was monopolized by the father, who took a great interest in plants." Townsend devoted himself to the girls.

As they traveled on, they found the inhabitants

> exceedingly inquisitive, propounding question after question in such quick succession as scarcely to allow you breathing time between them. The first question generally asked is "Where do you come from?" We frame our answer somewhat in the style of Dr. Franklin. "We come from Pennsylvania, our names, Nuttall and Townsend; we are traveling to Independence on foot for the purpose of seeing the country to advantage and we intend to proceed from thence across the mountains to the Pacific. Have you any mules to sell?" The last clause generally changes the conversation.

At Independence, Wyeth's brigade was joined by Milton Sublette, a famous fur trader, and a band of missionaries led by Jason Lee going out to convert the Flathead Indians.

> On the 28th of April at 10 o'clock in the morning [Townsend wrote], our caravan consisting of seventy men and two hundred and fifty horses began its march. Captain Wyeth and Milton Sublette took the lead. Mr. N.

and myself rode beside them. The band of missionaries with their horned cattle rode along the flanks. Uproarious bursts of merriment and gay and lively songs were constantly echoing along the line. Ere long difficulties and dangers would assail us but no anticipation of reverses could check the happy exuberance of our spirits.

Townsend's exuberance was not dampened even by a skeptical Indian chief who asked him, "first by pointing with his finger towards the sunset and then raising his hands high over his head, if I was going to the mountains. On answering him in the affirmative, he depressed both his hands and passed them around his head with a very solemn ugh. He meant doubtless that my brain was turned."

Nuttall was enraptured by all he encountered. "The road was very uneven and difficult, winding amongst innumerable mounds six to eight feet in height," wrote Townsend. "Along their bases in the narrow passages, flowers of every hue were growing. Mr. N. was here in his glory. He rode on ahead and cleared the passages with a trembling hand, looking anxiously back at the approaching party as though he feared it would come ere he had finished and tread his lovely prizes underfoot." Townsend himself was overwhelmed.

I never before saw so great a variety of birds in the same space. All were beautiful and many new to me. My game bag was full and I was loathe to leave. None but a naturalist can appreciate a naturalist's feeling —his delight amounting to ecstasy—when a specimen he has never before seen meets his eye, and the sorrow and grief which he feels when he is compelled to tear himself from a spot abounding with all he has anxiously and unremittingly sought for.

Men who have since become legends of the West crossed their way. "We were joined," Townsend notes, "by a Captain Stewart, an English Gentleman of noble family who is traveling for amusement and in search of adventure." This was Captain William Drummond Stewart, a hero of Waterloo who had married beneath him and, leaving his wife and his native land, set out adventuring in the American West. He came first in 1833 and went upriver with fur traders, taking with him Benjamin Harrison, the alcoholic son of the future President, who hoped the trip would cure Benjamin of his failing. (It didn't.) Stewart, a man of talent and temperament, rode at the head of the party clad in a fancy white leather jacket, trousers in green, blue, red and yellow plaid and a Panama hat. His rough companions stopped making fun of him when he proved the best shot of the party, bringing down a grizzly with one try. He was now heading for a fur trader's rendezvous in the Rockies.

Stewart and Wyeth went on to call on Captain Benjamin Louis Eulalie de

Bonneville, a U.S. Army officer whose private ventures into the fur trade
and erratic explorations of the Northwest brought him an uncertain reputation as soldier and geographer—though a huge modern dam is named after
him. Wyeth and Stewart mischievously drank Bonneville out of his stock of
metheglin, a honey-based home brew.

The party had traveled south of the Lewis and Clark route, over what
was to become the Oregon Trail, into lands that no naturalist had ever traversed.
When they left the plains, the going got harder. Returning from a hunting
party, Townsend found that "Mr. N. had become so exceedingly thin that I
should scarcely have known him, and upon my expressing surprise he heaved
a sigh and remarked that I 'would have been as thin as he if I had lived on an
old Ephraim [a grizzly bear] for two weeks and short allowance of that.' "

Townsend wrote that they "traveled over one of the most arid plains we
have seen, covered with jagged masses of lava and twisted wormwood bushes.
We saw not a drop of water and our only food was dried meat. In these regions,
the air feels like a sirocco, the tongue becomes parched and horny, the mouth,
eyes, and nose are incessantly assailed by fine pulverized lava." Even in this
desert Nuttall found new plants. When they lost their way in the 10,000-foot-
high passes, and had to go back through deepest snow, he felt the trouble
worthwhile, for he discovered a couple of new asters and several uncommon
alpines. Old acquaintances of Lewis and Clark were found—Lewis's woodpecker, Clark's nutcracker, the American magpie. Over the mountains and
still short of food, Townsend "strolled along the stream and made a meal of
rosebuds. On returning, I was surprised to find Mr. N. and Capt. T. picking
the last bones of a bird which they had cooked. Upon inquiry I ascertained
that the subject was an unfortunate owl which I had killed and intended to
preserve as a specimen. The temptation was too great to be resisted by the
hungry captain and naturalist and the bird of wisdom lost the immortality
which he might otherwise have acquired."

They went on now in gentler land, but as they rode the last stretch of the
Columbia River in canoes, a storm struck. Nuttall's precious plant collections
were soaked. "He has been constantly engaged in opening and drying them,"
Townsend reported. "In this task he exhibits a degree of patience and persever-
ance which is truly astonishing; sitting on the ground, and steaming over the
enormous fire, for hours together, drying the papers, and rearranging the whole
collection, specimen by specimen, while the great drops of perspiration roll un-
heeded from his brow."

They made their way to Fort Vancouver, headquarters of the Hudson's
Bay Company. Here, half a world away from home, the officials kept up the
appearances of empire. Their Indian servants, dressed in livery, served dinner

An older Nuttall sat for a pensive daguerreotype portrait shortly before he left America to end his years of self-chosen exile in England.

on delicate china and poured wine into crystal glasses. The two naturalists wandered through the land. Townsend shot and prepared several new species of birds and two or three undescribed quadrupeds. "My companion," he wrote, "is of course in his element; the forest, the plain, the rocky hill and the mossy bank yield him a rich and most abundant supply." Fort Vancouver was being overrun by visitors and settlers. One resident complained that "we had an assortment of American missionaries but this is not all. There are more gents as follows; 2 in quest of flowers, 2 killed all the birds on the Columbia and of the United States and you know it would not be good policy not to treat them politely they are a perfect nuisance." Nuttall and Townsend, a pair of those nuisances, went on to Willamette where the Reverend Jason Lee was busy building a village and converting the Indians. There Nuttall ran into some of his old Astorian companions, a group of voyageurs now settled and sedentary, who still remembered their old companion, *le fou.* "Seeing him gathering flowers and plants appeared to the Canadians no less idle and foolish and subject of merriment now than when he accompanied Mr. Hunt up the Missouri River in 1811," wrote an American settler.

Nuttall made a couple of trips to Hawaii, and in 1835 went to California. Townsend stayed in the Northwest for a while as physician at Fort Vancouver, shipping off hundreds of birds and animals to the Philadelphia Academy. Nuttall added to botany a long list of plants, including a dogwood, *Cornus nuttallii*. Audubon used it as background for his painting of the band-tailed pigeon, the bird that Nuttall's friend Thomas Say had found on his trip west. Nuttall also found a whippoorwill, which Audubon named Nuttall's poor-will, and a bivalve now called Nuttall's cockle.

The first American naturalist to visit California, Nuttall found many things "new to my view, an oak with leaves like a holly, a thorny gooseberry clad with pendulous flowers as brilliant as those of a fuchsia. The olive and the vine throve with luxuriance, the prickly pears became small trees and the rare blooming aloe assigned without care to the hedge."

Nuttall had completed the last of his great American journeys. As his biographer Jeannette E. Graustein points out, "No other botanist collected as many new kinds of plants within what is now the United States; no other naturalist saw so much of it in primeval condition. His field knowledge of the natural history of temperate America was unequalled."

At San Diego, having entered as a bumbling hero in one American literary work, *Astoria*, Nuttall now meandered into another classic. On the beach, a former pupil of his at Harvard recognized "a gentleman whom I had known in my better days; and the last person I should have expected to have seen on the coast of California—Professor N. of Cambridge." The former student was Richard Henry Dana, who had gone to sea and wrote of his experiences in *Two Years Before the Mast*, where he described his encounter with Nuttall.

> I had left him quietly seated in the chair of Botany and Ornithology, in Harvard University; and the next I saw of him, was strolling about San Diego beach, in a sailor's pea-jacket, with a wide straw hat, and bare-footed, with his trousers rolled up to his knees, picking up stones and shells. Just as we were about to shove off from the beach, he came down to the boat with his shoes in his hand, and his pockets full of specimens. I knew him at once, though I should not have been more surprised to have seen the Old South steeple shoot up from the hide-house.

Nuttall took passage on the boat and, Dana wrote, "the crew christened Mr. N. 'Old Curious,' from his zeal for curiosities, and some of them said that he was crazy, and that his friends let him go about and amuse himself in this way. Why else a rich man (sailors call every man rich who does not work with his hands, and wears a long coat and cravat) should leave a Christian country, and come to such a place as California, to pick up shells and stones, they could not understand."

For nearly a month, Dana wrote, "Mr. N. had kept in his shell . . . and hardly been seen by anybody." But when they sighted land at Cape Horn, he "came out like a butterfly and was hopping around, bright as a bird. The land was the island of Staten Land and a more desolate looking spot I never wish to set eyes upon, bare, broken and girt with rocks and ice. Mr. N. said he should like to go ashore upon the island and examine a spot which probably no human being had ever set foot upon."

Here on this bare and broken place, Thomas Nuttall had a last chance to shake off whatever guardian angel had been tending him all these years. But, like the passing Indian and the loyal trapper and all the other timely instruments of fate, the ship's captain now stepped in to save Nuttall from his own devices. The captain, wrote Dana, putting it mildly, "said he would see the island, specimens and all, in another place before he would delay the ship one moment. We left the land astern," and the innocent traveler sailed safely home.

CHAPTER THIRTEEN

THE CLOSET BOTANISTS

🌱 🌱 🌱 🌱 🌱 THOUGH HE SEEMED A MILD MAN, THERE WAS NOTHING MEEK about Thomas Nuttall. When his work or his scientific honor was questioned, he would turn on his critics in unmannerly wrath. "Blackguard" he called a captious mineralogist who accused him of making a false claim. "Silent contempt" for "Raffy" was his response when Rafinesque took a stand against him. And scorn was his reflex when he felt he had been wronged by two of his most eminent colleagues, John Torrey and Asa Gray.

He had been helpful to both of them, freely giving his plants to Torrey and his findings to Gray. But when Gray, in a rather petty way, complained that Nuttall had denied him proper credit, Nuttall exploded in a series of letters, defending himself and demanding that his plants be given back to him. He couldn't afford to be so generous any longer, because he had "sold everything I am able to keep out of debt," and had spent his money "and nearly my whole life" without ever getting any real returns. With that off his chest, Nuttall apologized for his angry words and crossed them out—but not so heavily as to make them unreadable. Along the way, he let go with a slap that he didn't cross out. Unlike some scientists, Nuttall wrote, using gratuitous italics, he had done his work *not in the closet* but in the *field*."

That word "closet" was to Nuttall the ultimate botanical put-down. A closet naturalist was one who stayed cozily at his desk using the material that fieldworkers like Nuttall, braving hardship and danger, went out to collect. The description completely fitted John Torrey and Asa Gray. Though both were accomplished fieldmen, they did their major work back in their offices. They directed other collectors to the areas they wanted covered and arranged the specimens sent back in proper order and entered them into the records of science by publishing papers on them.

For all Nuttall's snobbery, there was no disgrace in being a closet botanist. After all, even Linnaeus rarely went out into the field again after his journey through Lapland. What must have galled Nuttall was not just the relatively comfortable life the closet botanists enjoyed, but the fact that they were bringing an era—his era—to its end. The adventurer-naturalist now was being eclipsed by the academic specialist. The self-taught amateur was being shouldered aside by the trained professional. A Bartram or a Michaux or a Nuttall would no longer go where his dream or ambition took him but where a professor told him to go. The Romantic age of American natural history was nearly over.

The two men mostly responsible for this were so close to each other in their work and direction that it sometimes seemed they were one botanical entity. Their collaboration started with Torrey being the patron and the teacher; it wound up with Gray as the leader. Together they moved American botany in many ways: from the field into the study; from Philadelphia to New York and Boston; from old systems into new orders; out of the lingering world of Linnaeus into the world of Charles Darwin.

Temperamentally, they were men of different casts. Torrey was all kindness, helpfulness, dedication, immense patience. Gray, though warm and thoughtful, was more pointed in his ambition and expression, more daring in intellect, blessed with a Linnaean assurance—and a tolerance for difficult truths. Torrey, the elder by fourteen years, was born in New York in 1796. His father was a city alderman and his job of overseeing the city's prisons proved an oddly important matter for American natural history. In prison at the time was Amos Eaton, serving a life sentence on the trumped-up charge of forgery. Young John Torrey, going with his father on prison inspections, met Eaton and impressed him with his already deep interest in botany. The boy showed the prisoner what he had collected in the woods and fields of upper Manhattan. Eaton identified them, sent him out to find more and soon was indoctrinating him in the Linnaean system. John's father was probably helpful in getting Governor Daniel Tompkins—the same man who told Alexander Wilson that he wouldn't buy his birds even if they were alive—to release Eaton from prison, though under pain of exile from the state.

Torrey entered the College of Physicians and Surgeons, where he fell into the benign botanical hands of David Hosack and Samuel Latham Mitchill. He studied under the former at the college and must have haunted the latter's house—for a while his mailing address was "care of Dr. Mitchill." When Mitchill and his friends founded the Lyceum of Natural History, Torrey was made a curator and was sent out with Rafinesque to herbalize in the Hudson Highlands, up past the gardens at Coldengham. While still studying medicine, Torrey wrote a definitive catalog of plants growing within thirty miles of New York.

Graduating in 1818, he set up a practice but was either not very adept at medicine or not interested in it, for he never made much of it. Rafinesque urged him to take a teaching job at Transylvania but he turned it down. The Long expedition offered Torrey a place as mineralogist but there was no pay involved and he couldn't afford it. Still, though he would not go out to see what the West held, the West came to him. When the Long expedition was over, the plants that James and Say collected were sent to Torrey to identify and classify. The role of closet botanist was thus thrust upon Torrey. He filled it so well that the exploring expeditions which soon began to crisscross the West automatically offered their findings to Torrey and, as time went on, to Gray.

It was in working on the plants of the Long expedition that Torrey made a momentous decision for himself and American botany. He discarded the Linnaean system of sexual classification, using in its place the so-called natural system of classification propounded most successfully by the de Jussieu family of Paris and the two de Candolles, father and son, of Switzerland.

The Linnaean method had served its purpose magnificently, bringing a sensible, workable, comprehensible system to natural history. But increasingly, as more and more was learned about the biology of plants, the method of classifying them sexually proved misleading and constricting. The pistil-stamen count, for example, put such disparate plants as the barberry and the rose in the same class. The newer studies of the structure, the form and the functioning of plants on which the natural system was based showed they had no real kinship. The Linnaean system hung on longer in America than in Europe. Its simplicity and efficiency recommended it, especially to beginners in botany. John Torrey was in many ways a traditionalist, cautious about change and reluctant to disrupt established ways. Now he weighed ease against honesty and, influenced by the example of European naturalists, adopted the more complicated, more accurate natural system. His third paper on the Long expedition plants was classified by this new system, the first time an American had made use of it with American plants. Going further, Torrey sponsored the American publication of an English book on the natural system and wrote an introduction for it.

To old-line American botanists, it was as if Torrey were promoting a new version of the Bible written by Satan. His mentor of the jail yard, Amos Eaton, whose popular botanical works clung to Linnaeus, castigated his protégé. "Since Dr. Faustus first exhibited his printed bibles in the year 1463," he stormed, "no book has probably excited such consternation and dismay." Evoking "horrors," Eaton foresaw "an awful catastrophe to all previous learning." Eaton's loyalty to Linnaeus is admirable, but he might have considered the attitude of the great classifier himself. "I do not deny," Linnaeus had written, "that a natural system is preferable not only to my system but to all that have been invented." But until a usable one was devised, he insisted his would have to serve. "Why provoke me to dispute," he wrote a critic; "I ask but peace . . ." for "my harmless sexual system. . . ."

To Eaton, peace meant surrender and his opposition could not be waved off. He had become, by this time, the democratizer of American science, more widely read and respected by students of natural history than anyone before him. Released from jail when he was forty, Eaton had gone on to study at Yale and lecture at Williams. In 1817, he published his *Manual of Botany for the Northern States*, which quickly became the country's botanical best seller. Edition followed edition, eight in twenty years. An evangelist for his science, Eaton lectured from town to town before large and variegated audiences. "I have in my class," he wrote from Northampton, Massachusetts, "55 ladies, four practicing lawyers, 3 students in physics, three other gentlemen from Yale College, one Senator, one representative in Congress, one Common Pleas judge & c." A large and striking man, his strong face dignified by a high forehead, Eaton was an imposing figure on the platform but his approach was plain and homey. "I turn everything in science into common talk," he said. "I illustrate the most abstruse parts by a dish kettle, a bread tray, a tea pot, a soup bowl, or a cheese press." His *Manual*, he boasted wryly, "has merit of a simplifier to be understood by mere urchins and kitchen drabs." But his teaching reached far above that level. Among his many distinguished students was William Cullen Bryant, a devoted botanist. "I showed you the windflower and traced its tender organs," Eaton gracefully wrote the poet. "I affected to be your superior because I knew the names of more weeds than you."

Eaton's influence was extended by a pair of redoubtable ladies. Under his guidance and with his editing, Almira H. Lincoln, sister of the schoolmistress Emma Willard, wrote *Familiar Lectures on Botany*, a text for schoolgirls. Laura Johnson, Eaton's sister-in-law, produced the *Botanical Teacher*, another school text. These simple works became standard texts for beginners, published and republished till the end of the century. Eaton himself went on to produce valuable texts on geology and zoology. Settling in Troy and Albany—"I teach young Trojans and Albanians," he explained—he raised the money that founded Rensselaer Polytechnic Institute.

Despite the opposition of this formidable if fusty antagonist, Torrey quickly gained the support of the new community of naturalists, who followed him away from Linnaeus into the natural system. Meanwhile, seeking a surer livelihood than botany, Torrey became a teacher at West Point and at his alma mater, the College of Physicians and Surgeons in New York City.

In 1830, the other half of the Torrey-Gray partnership appeared. Again it was Edinburgh—the same source of inspiration that directed Colden and Garden and Hosack and so many others into botany—that led Asa Gray into his lifework. But Gray did not have to go to Scotland. In the library of the upstate New York medical school where he was studying, he found an edition of the *Edinburgh Encyclopedia*, reissued by a printer in Utica, and from its three hundred closely printed pages on botany he got his basic knowledge of the subject. From reading, he went into the field, carrying Eaton's *Manual of Botany*. Barely started on the practice of medicine, he gave it up when a chance came to teach botany and mineralogy at a school in Utica. He collected local plants and left a batch of them with Torrey, who praised him and after a while took him on as his botanical assistant.

By 1832, at the age of twenty-three, Gray was settled in New York as part of Torrey's household and the city's circle of naturalists. Following his patron's lead, Gray based his first book, *Elements of Botany*, on the natural system. *Elements* was the first American text to depart from the Linnaean system and the first to offer any kind of challenge to Amos Eaton's manuals. From having been Torrey's assistant, Gray became his collaborator on a *Flora of North America*.

Established as a firm-minded, astute and farseeing scientist, Gray had two promising jobs offered him. One was botanist on a U.S. Navy exploration of the Pacific. President Jackson, who seemed drawn to naturalists—Wilson had visited him in Tennessee and Audubon was a repeated guest at the White House —was enthusiastic about the project. But, for all his efforts, it ran aground in navy politics. Gray accepted the other offer, a post as professor of botany and zoology at the University of Michigan. The only drawback was that the university, though approved by the state, did not really exist. It had a charter, money, trustees, but no buildings, no faculty and no students. Nevertheless Gray was assigned to go to Europe to buy books and equipment for the fledgling institution.

It was a significant trip. Gray had a chance to study the herbariums of Europe, which contained many more American plants than American collections did. In the herbarium of Linnaeus, now in London, he found specimens sent by John Bartram. In Gronovius's herbarium he found the plants on which John Clayton's *Flora Virginica* was based. In Paris, he pored over the specimens André Michaux had collected in America.

That wandering Frenchman, shipwrecked on the way home in 1796, had been washed ashore with most of his plants. After sorting them out and compiling the data on which his *Flora Boreali-Americana* was based, he joined an expedition headed for the South Seas. At his insistence, he was put ashore in Madagascar. There, starting a nursery in this brand-new botanical world, he pushed himself too hard and died of fever at the age of fifty-six.

Among the plants in Paris, Gray came upon a rare perennial Michaux had picked in the Carolina mountains but not named. No botanist had recorded it since. Claiming "the right of a discoverer" Gray gave it a name: *Shortia galacifolia*, after Charles Wilkins Short.

In England, Gray met the leaders of British natural science, and a modest young naturalist, Charles Darwin, just back from his voyage on the *Beagle*. Gray came back home in late 1839, his mind open to the swirling intellectual movements which were to change the bases of Western thought. Europeans, in turn, were now aware that in Torrey and Gray America had two scientists who could measure up to Europe's standards and make America, instead of Europe, the headquarters for its own natural history.

Gray also came home to find that the University of Michigan was still not ready to open. Waiting for something to happen, he worked on the Torrey-Gray *Flora* and managed the longest botanical trip of his career—south into the regions Bartram and Michaux had covered—trying unsuccessfully to find the newly named *Shortia*. But his increasing expertise kept him close to his desk directing field collectors and judging the work of other naturalists. The row with Nuttall came at this time—and both were to regret it. Taking on what he called "a somewhat ungracious task," Gray set out to evaluate Rafinesque and was somewhat less than gracious in his judgments. He harshly called that gullible scientist's passion for finding new things "a complete monomania" and mocked what he called Rafinesque's attempt to classify thunder and lightning by species and genera—which, in actual fact, Rafinesque had never done. As often happened with Gray, he later felt sorry that he had stomped too hard on an easy mark, and his later comments on Rafinesque were more generous.

Tired of waiting for the University of Michigan to manifest itself, Gray took advantage of a new opportunity. Harvard, which had been floundering botanically since Nuttall left, hired Gray as professor of natural history with the understanding that he would be allowed enough time from his teaching to do his own research. A Harvard professor's lot was not an easy one at the time. The students were unruly, and maintaining discipline was as much a problem for a professor as imparting knowledge. Though he was an unsure speaker, Gray did impress his classes by his prestige, by his knowledge and by the fact that he was the author of their textbooks. At Harvard he wrote his *Botanical Textbook* and his enduringly popular *How Plants Grow*—and every new set of readers made a joke out of the way the title was printed: *How Plants Grow Gray*. Over the years, he finished his *Manual of the Botany of the Northern United States*, a landmark in systematic botany, which in its revised editions is still the basic work on the region.

By the late 1840s, the closets of John Torrey and Asa Gray were the acknowledged centers of American natural history. A letter Torrey wrote in 1848 to a friend sounds rather like the letter Linnaeus had written a century before telling of the work and whereabouts of his apostles.

> Our botanists are generally pretty active. Curtis is working at Fungi. Dr. Gray has his hands full of all sorts of work now finishing an account of Fendler's N. Mexico collection with notes on Lindheimer's and Wright's Texan plants. Engelmann is studying his favorites, the Cactaceae. Tuckerman is busy at the Lichens, also working at Potamogetons. Poor Oakes —what a sad end he came to! Dr. Gray & Oakes family try to persuade themselves that he fell overboard accidentally. Mr. Carey is studying Carices and Chenopodiaceae. Sullivant is yet engaged on Musci & Hepaticae.

The names he mentions are an index to the new circle of American naturalists. Moses Ashley Curtis, a New England minister who settled in North Carolina, became a regional authority on fungi. Edward Tuckerman, a young friend of Nuttall's, scoured the White Mountains for lichens (giving his name to a now famous ski-country ravine). "Poor Oakes" had become the preeminent expert on the flora of New England before he fell or jumped off the deck of a ship. William Starling Sullivant was a wealthy Ohio banker who avidly collected and classified mosses. John Carey was a moody Englishman who helped Gray on his *Elements of Botany* and his *Manual* and left some sharp comments on his friend—describing Gray as "given to crusty, snarly, cynical humors" or like a lion "lashing himself with his tail and foaming at the mouth."

The most adventurous men of this network were Fendler, Lindheimer, Wright and Engelmann, the botanical frontiersmen of their time. George Engelmann was the center of their activity, serving as a kind of branch office for Torrey and Gray. He had come to the United States in 1832 to invest some money for a wealthy uncle. But after landing in Philadelphia, where he spent some time with Nuttall, he gave more attention to botany than to business. Settling finally in St. Louis as a physician, he soon was the busiest doctor in that thriving river port. Between patients, he would leave his office and duck into the next room where he kept his ever-enlarging herbarium. His own fieldwork introduced many unknown plants and his researches into grapevines led to the discovery that American vines were immune to phylloxera, the blight that later destroyed the vineyards of France and caused them to be replanted with American stock.

It was as a conduit rather than a collector that Engelmann became most important to American natural history. In 1840 he paid a visit to Gray. From their talk grew a most satisfying botanical arrangement: Engelmann would find collectors to supply plants and Gray would find markets for them. Almost every naturalist traveling west came through St. Louis and called on Dr. Engelmann for help and advice on routes. If they were heading out, Engelmann might give them advances against specimens to be delivered later. If they were back from the field, he would give them down payments on plants which he would transship, more often than not, to Gray or to Torrey. With their own knowledge and access to libraries, the easterners could identify and evaluate what Engelmann sent. With their wide contacts in America and abroad, they could find ready buyers. Knowing who wanted to buy what, they could tell Engelmann where his field collectors should go and what to look for. And they could publish readily, providing what every self-respecting naturalist wanted as much as anything: credit for his work.

When Gray, in 1846, heard that an army expedition was to be sent to New Mexico, he asked Engelmann to look for a good man to go along as naturalist. Engelmann knew a young German named Augustus Fendler, who worked in a refinery but was ready to give the job up for botany. Gray got an advance of fifty dollars from William Starling Sullivant against mosses Fendler would pick up, and wangled a place in the army brigade for Fendler from the War Department. "There is a high mountain right back of Santa Fe," he wrote Engelmann. "Fendler must ravish it."

The mountain, Fendler found when he got to Santa Fe, was disappointingly barren. He instead turned to Santa Fe Creek, where he ran into a bonanza of plants. He came back with seventeen thousand specimens and a classic collector's complaint. "Not the dangers, not the many hardships and privations" made him refuse Gray's proposal that he go right out again. "On the contrary, these botanical excursions make me passionately fond of herbalizing. It is rather the noncompliance with my most fervent requests for money." Gray sent him a small sum and published his finds as *Plantae Fendlerianae*, the first notable paper on the botany of the Southern Rockies.

Fendler was one of the many educated Germans who came to America to escape the political persecutions in their homeland. Two others like him fell into Dr. Engelmann's orbit: Adolph Wislizenus and Ferdinand Jakob Lindheimer. Wislizenus became Engelmann's medical partner, but after a few years he went off collecting in the Southwest. Interned by the Mexicans, who still owned the territory, he kept right on botanizing until the U.S. Army arrived. (Wislizenus never gave up easily. In love with a girl named Lucy Crane, who repeatedly turned him down, he followed her all the way to Constantinople where she finally surrendered.) Wislizenus delighted in the land he explored, a "whole plain so covered with blue sky Tradescantia virginica and light red phlox that it resembled a vast carpet of green interwoven with the most brilliant flowers." Among many other plants, he discovered the unique ocotillo, the coachwhip of the Southwest's deserts.

Ferdinand Lindheimer—whose forebears included a notable Linnaean, the philosopher-poet Goethe—came into Texas as one of Sam Houston's volunteers and stayed in the new republic as a farmer. He engaged himself to Engelmann as a collector, and after fitting himself out with a two-wheeled horse-drawn cart, he trundled across the botanical enclaves that give the state such an astonishing variety of growth—almost untouched territory where, as botanists liked to put it, "plants have no Latin names." He found so many new species that no one has ever counted them all up. There are a dozen or more species named after him; one, *Lindheimera texana*, is the pretty springtime star-daisy. His collections were published as *Plantae Lindheimerianae* by Gray, who kept nagging Engelmann to dispatch Lindheimer into the Rockies, offering to pay ten dollars per hundred plants against the eight dollars paid for Texas specimens. But Lindheimer was a disappointment to Gray. Instead of getting into his cart and going into the mountains, he got married and turned to

Asa Gray directed his adventurous field collectors from his cloistered study at Harvard, for many years a headquarters for American botany.

journalism as editor of the New Braunfels *Zeitung*. Written for the German settlements in Texas, the *Zeitung* was read throughout the country for its scholarly writing about the frontier. "The Indians," Lindheimer once wrote, explaining their raids on cattle ranches, "consider their robbing expeditions great deeds and themselves heroes, like Odysseus and Diomede, who stole the horses of King Rhesus."

Of all the region's collectors, Gray most prized a transplanted Yankee named Charles Wright, a Yale graduate with an interest in botany who settled in Texas where he made a living as a professional hunter and surveyor. For a while, he was a professor at a Methodist college, teaching, as he said, "everything from abecedarianism to the highest branches"—geology and botany. On the side, he gave elocution lessons and temperance sermons. "A helpless odd fellow," Gray called him, "good for nothing but to collect and dry specimens."

After a while, Wright gave himself full-time to herbalizing. Gray got permission for him to accompany an army expedition to El Paso and persuaded the newly formed Smithsonian Institution to advance him $150, the Institution's first cash subsidy to American field botany. Wright walked seven hundred miles across the state on that trip, collecting a thousand specimens, many of them new or rare. The walk wasn't his idea—the officers on the expedition wouldn't let him ride in their wagons and even refused to let him share their rations. "If I were not so full," he told Gray, fuming at the way he had been treated, "I would keep silence. But steam is so high that if I do not blow off, fearful consequences may follow."

In its amiable bickering, the correspondence between Wright and Gray recalls the exchanges between John Bartram and Peter Collinson. The volatile Wright would complain that Gray did not show enough consideration for him. The impatient Gray would retort that Wright didn't show good enough judgment in his job.

GRAY: "It was not well thought of you to send that Texas bundle as they are of no use."

WRIGHT: "I think hard of it that you have not written. Surely you can speak after almost a year's silence."

GRAY: "I have been, am so—busy is not the word for it. Do not growl at me if you can help it."

WRIGHT: "You wrote to me of working like a dog. I know how you live—then call your situation dog paradise and mine hog-and-ass paradise combined."

At some point like this, Gray would find time for a long affectionate letter: "Dear Friend. That I ought to have replied to your letter of the 19th November to say nothing of that of Sept. 21 and June 18 there is no doubt. These letters

I have carried in my pocket a good while hoping to catch a moment somewhere and some time to write you." But his brother had died, the printing of his *Manual* was behind schedule, and "to crown it all I expect to marry in the spring. Forgive my long neglect. I'll see if I can do better hereafter when I have a wife to write letters for me."

The work of the Torrey-Gray-Engelmann group opened up another new world for American naturalists. Others, however, had already explored the region. The first trained botanist to travel the Southwest was a Swiss named Jean Louis Berlandier, who in the 1820s did original but rather erratic work for the Swiss classifier de Candolle. In the early 1830s, Thomas Drummond, an Englishman who had been working up in the Canadian Northwest, came down to Texas and met more than his share of hardships: "the Great Overflow" of 1833, which flooded thousands of square miles; a cholera epidemic, which killed thousands of settlers (Drummond dosed himself heavily with opium and survived the disease); and a Biblical plague. "I am almost like Job," Drummond reported, "smitten with boils from head to foot, unable to lie down for seven nights." Nevertheless he shipped his boss, William Jackson Hooker of Glasgow, 700 species of plants and 150 birds. A collection of mosses sent Hooker into botanical ecstasy. "The whole of North America," he wrote, "has not been known to possess as many mosses as Mr. Drummond has collected in this single journey." Present-day gardeners, to whom mosses are mostly a nuisance, are more grateful to Drummond for having sent back a flower-bed standby, *Phlox drummondii*.

Drummond was only one of many excellent plant hunters sent to America by Hooker and the Horticultural Society of London, which had taken up where the old Temple Coffee House Botany Club had left off. Another was David Douglas, also in the employ of the Society. He had been first sent to the United States in 1825. Douglas met Nuttall, who took him out to Bartram's Gardens. He visited Torrey, who thought him a liar. He lunched with DeWitt Clinton, an Overseas Fellow of the Horticultural Society, who gave him six wild pigeons to take home.

Douglas's next assignment was the American Far West, which up to then had been explored in a hit-and-miss way. In 1786, a French expedition touched at the California coast and sent home seeds of the common little sand verbena, which, as *Abronia umbellata*, was the first California plant to be given a proper botanical name. A few years later, a Bohemian botanist, Thaddeus Haenke, arrived with a Spanish expedition led by an Italian nobleman, Alessandro Malaspina. Haenke had missed the ships' departure from Cádiz and had chased across the ocean after them. Wrecked near Montevideo (all he saved was his copy of Linnaeus), he walked across the pampas and over the Andes to catch up with the ships at Valparaiso. The long chase was worth it: among the many things Haenke collected in California was the redwood tree.

In 1815, a Russian party took back to St. Petersburg a batch of insects and the seeds of the common California poppy, named *Eschscholtzia* after its discoverer, Johann Friedrich Eschscholtz.

In 1827, Paolo Emilio Botta, dispatched by French bankers to report on the natural resources of the Far West, sent home a "running bird to which is attributed the ability to kill snakes for food. It has a long tail which it raises to an almost perpendicular position. It seldom flies but runs almost as fast as a horse." This, of course, was the roadrunner. Botta is less well known for his ornithological discoveries than for the fact that, some years later on the Tigris River, he discovered the ruins of Nineveh and the palace of the Assyrian despot King Sargon.

It was David Douglas who was to bring the Far West into botanical focus. From two long trips he sent back scores of plants that were altogether new to botanists and hundreds that were known but never available to gardeners. At the very start he discovered one of the two peonies native to North America, the purple and yellow *Paeonia brownii*. He kept finding evergreens at such a rate that he wrote home: "You will think I manufacture pines at my pleasure." Coming upon one towering species, he was dismayed to find it destitute of branches for two-thirds of its height, with the cones on the topmost branches, hanging "like small sugar loaves in a grocer's shop." Unable to climb for them, he took his gun and fired at them. He was a fine marksman and the shots brought the cones down. They also brought a band of hostile Indians, but Douglas managed to get away unharmed with three cones of what is now called the Lambert pine. Douglas is credited with finding seven of the seventeen West Coast pines, along with several other evergreens, including the Douglas fir—not really a fir at all and belonging to an entirey different genus, called *Pseudotsuga*.

Traveling up and down the coast over a period of a dozen years, Douglas learned the Chinook language and may have had a love affair with a Chinook princess. The Indians called him the Grass Doctor and thought he was crazy, though not as crazy as that king who sent him out on his strange searches. Douglas was welcomed by the Scottish settlers of western Canada, who were pleased that he brought a suit of the Stuart tartan to wear when he visited them, and by the Spanish friars of California, with whom, since he did not know Spanish, he conversed in Latin. A brave and even reckless man, he lived alone in the woods for months on end, eating berries, ground rats and game. He was "parched like a cinder" by the semidesert heat, almost sucked to an untimely end by a huge whirlpool and blinded repeatedly by sandstorms and the sun's reflection off the snow. Douglas was inclined to call attention to these dangers by belittling them. "On such occasions," he wrote, "I am very liable to become fretful."

In California, Douglas ran into an Irish botanist named Thomas Coulter working for the Swiss de Candolle. Industrious and eccentric, Coulter shipped off some fifty thousand plants and animal specimens while he indulged, de Candolle wrote, "a sort of passion for reptiles, kept them in his pockets and whistled tunes to them to keep them quiet. This passion led him to a strange purpose. He intended to repopulate his native land with snakes," but, de Candolle added, he never got around to carrying out this kind of "herpetological patriotism." The lovely California matilija poppy bears the name *coulteri* and so does the big-cone pine.

Almost as diligent as Coulter, Douglas sent home the seeds of some six hundred California annuals and started something perhaps he shouldn't have: the Victorian vogue for using these many-colored plants in gaudy garden beds to form hearts or squares, or curlicues, or spell out tributes to MOTHER. In Hawaii, he met a horrifying end. Falling into a concealed pit dug to trap wild cattle, he was stomped to death by a maddened bull.

American botanists did not have a wealthy horticultural society to underwrite expensive expeditions, but they did have a public benefactor in the U.S. Army. Along with spectacular efforts like the Lewis and Clark and the Long expeditions, the army provided day-to-day assistance to naturalists. Army doctors out in the field were officially encouraged to work at natural history. Torrey and Gray found them a steady, reliable source of material. The perambulating Dr. Melines Conkling Leavenworth was a special gem. In Alabama he found, among other plants, a striking annual *Leavenworthia torreyi*. In Texas he discovered a fine gooseberry. From Georgia he sent Gray "a rare and very peculiar *Amphianthus pisillus*." Dr. Zina Pitcher kept sending John Torrey plants from the Mississippi valley, including the *Carduus pitcheri*, or Pitcher's thistle, and *Falcata pitcheri*, or Pitcher's hog peanut. Dozens of doctors like Leavenworth and Pitcher, moving from post to post, picked up plants along the way and added to the budding science of plant geography.

Some well-known military men enlisted in the cause of natural history. Captain George B. McClellan, later the Union general, corresponded with Gray about his expedition to the Red River and saw to it that specimens were sent back. Captain David Farragut, the future hero of Mobile Bay, had a fine catch of fish ready for the ichthyologists in Washington but wrote apologetically, as Alexander Garden once had to Linnaeus, that someone in his crew had found other uses for most of them and all he could send on was one toadfish. But of all the military naturalists, the most glamorous and personally most productive was the "pathfinder of the West," John Charles Frémont.

Born out of wedlock to a Virginia belle and an itinerant French school-teacher, Frémont as a young man became the protégé of Joel Poinsett, who had acquired a taste for botany when he studied medicine at the University of Edinburgh. Having taken up government service instead of medicine, Poinsett came back from his post as minister to Mexico with the plant that bears his name. A Secretary of War, he assigned the brilliant young Frémont to two topographical engineers' expeditions to the upper Mississippi, led by a distinguished French scientist named Joseph Nicollet. On these trips, Frémont absorbed a sense of science from Nicollet and the rudiments of botany from a German naturalist named Carl Geyer, who was in the party. Then, having eloped with Jessie Benton, the impetuous daughter of the influential Senator Thomas Hart Benton, Frémont set out in 1842 on the first of four westward expeditions which roused America's imagination about the West and added appreciably to American botanical knowledge.

Like Meriwether Lewis, Frémont was a born naturalist, persistent in searching, sharp in observing, careful in describing. "The artemesia," he noted, "has its small fly accompanying it through every change of elevation and latitude." From his first trip into the Rockies, he produced what John Torrey called "a very interesting contribution to North American botany," sixteen new species and a new genus. He also unfurled a charmingly romantic bit of nature writing. Climbing a 12,000-foot peak, Frémont

> sprang upon the summit. Another step would have precipitated me into an immense snowfield five hundred feet below. Here on the summit, where the stillness was absolute, unbroken by any sound and solitude complete, we thought ourselves beyond the region of animated life; but while we were sitting on the rock, a solitary bee (*bromus*, the bumble bee) came winging his flight from the eastern valley, and lit on the knee of one of the men. It was a strange place, the icy rock and the highest peak of the Rocky Mountains, for a lover of warm sunshine and flowers; and we pleased ourselves with the idea that he was the first of his species to cross the mountain barrier—a solitary pioneer to foretell the advance of civilization. Seizing him immediately, we put him in at least a fit place—in the leaves of a large book among the flowers we had collected on our way.

Impressed by Frémont's haul of new species, Torrey, Gray and Engelmann tried to get him to take a trained botanist on his next trip. But, said Engelmann, Frémont "appears to me rather selfish, disinclined to let anybody share in his discoveries, anxious to reap all the honors as well as undertake all the labor himself." On his second trip, in 1843, out along the crowded emigrant trails, Frémont smelled "the air fragrant with the perfume of *Artemisia filifola*," saw a "whole valley radiant with flowers; blue, yellow, pink, white, scarlet, and purple," vying "with each other in splendor" and came to "a wilderness of flowers, their tall spikes sometimes rising above our heads as we rode among them." Down to earth, he recorded that the leaves of a greasewood he discovered "have a very salty taste," and that the "soil of bare and hot sands supported a varied and exuberant growth of plants."

A reckless midwinter crossing of the Sierras brought Frémont into the Sacramento Valley where, amid "perfumed air," he found the hills "purple and orange with unbroken beds into which each color was separately gathered." Though he collected thousands of plants on that journey, he ran into hard luck. Almost all the specimens collected on the way west were lost when a mule fell over a precipice, and most of the specimens collected in California were damaged by a flash flood. Still, picking through the debris that Frémont sent them, Torrey and Gray found several valuable things.

On his next trip, in 1846, Frémont took no chances. Torrey received a thousand specimens in, as he described it, "tin cases soldered up after being filled with dried plants, then guarded by a strong frame of wood and finally sewed up in a green cowhide." Botanically, this was the most satisfying of Frémont's trips. Personally, it proved a near disaster. In California when the

The Southwest yielded a whole new world of plants to American botany, notably the cactuses which now bear the names of the pioneer plant explorers of the region.

Mexican War broke out, Frémont jumped into the fighting. After a confusion of disregarded orders and unauthorized moves, he was accused of insubordination and found guilty. Resigning his commission, he made a private trip to California, for once taking a professional botanist along, Franz Creutzfeldt. It would have been better for Creutzfeldt if he hadn't gone. Trying to cross the Sierras in winter storms, Frémont lost a third of his men. Creutzfeldt survived in a group that was accused of cannibalism. But good botanists do not give up easily. Creutzfeldt joined a troop of army engineers under Colonel John Gunnison and was killed in 1853 when Paiutes massacred the contingent.

Frémont never again paid much attention to natural history. He made a fortune from the California gold fields, became the Republican Party's first Presidential candidate in 1856, grudgingly gave way to Lincoln in 1860, fought without distinction in the Civil War and lost his fortune. Still, science was enriched by his travels. He was one of the men Asa Gray had in mind when he remarked that before California had been taken over politically, it had already been "annexed botanically."

Another officer, William Hemsley Emory, also of the topographical engineers, all but matched Frémont as a romantic figure and outlasted him as a naturalist. An imposing man with a dramatic bearing and an eloquent way of speaking, "Bold Emory" was a serious scientist, a friend of Asa Gray's and a founding member of the American Association for the Advancement of Science. Sent in 1846 to California with the troops commanded by General Kearny, he passed the time by collecting for John Torrey. The "infinite variety of cacti" boggled him, and he became frustrated because he could not pack and carry them. He did make one botanical find—"a cactus six feet in circumference and so high I could not reach halfway to the top of it with the point of my sabre," a bit of equipment botanists normally didn't carry. The cactus was the unique and picturesque saguaro. When the Americans were surprised by a troop of Mexicans at San Pasqual, Emory used his saber to cut down a Mexican who was about to kill General Kearny.

From his trip, Emory sent back to Torrey eighteen new plant species, including a species of oak now named *Quercus emoryi*. Along the way he made some of the earliest studies in southwestern archaeology and anthropology, writing on the Pecos ruins and the origins of the Pueblo tribes. As the leader of later expeditions that mapped the Mexican boundary, Emory efficiently deployed naturalists through the region. A memorable report on Emory's border surveys listed more than 2,500 species of plants plus some 300 birds, reptiles and mammals.

The navy's counterpart to the army's work in natural history was a four-year Pacific expedition known, after its commander, as the Wilkes expedition.

*The spectacular saguaro cactus was dis-
covered by William Hemsley Emory.
He was astounded by its size and delighted by its fruit—"resembles that
of a fig, of exquisite taste."*

The project had a zany inception, in what was known at the time as "Symmes's hole." John Cleves Symmes, Jr., having retired from the army, set himself to propounding his startling geophysical theory: that the earth was hollow and that a ring of concentric spheres rested in the middle. These could be reached through openings near the North and South Poles. Watching the migrations of purple martins, Symmes concluded that these birds wintered in the subterranean spheres—"a warm and rich land, stocked with thrifty vegetables and animals." His astonishing theory gained remarkable support. Symmes became known as an American Newton and Audubon, then working in Cincinnati where Symmes lived, drew his portrait. When Symmes demanded that the United States send an expedition to find the holes, Congress was pestered with petitions supporting him. One was signed by fifty members of Pennsylvania's legislature.

In a while people lost faith in Symmes's holes, but not in the idea of a grand expedition to explore the oceans and show off American science. In 1828, official work to mount one began. After several years, Charles Wilkes, a navy officer of open ambition and devious ways, who helped keep the project afloat through years of political and scientific maneuvering, wangled the com-

mand for himself. Naturalists were eager to go along. The eminent Thomas
Say offered to serve in any capacity. Titian Peale signed on as naturalist-artist
and Asa Gray as botanist.

Many scientists ridiculed the project. George Ord, taking time out from his
feud with Audubon, harumphed that the whole thing was a farce and the scientists proposed for the trip were "presumptuous and crossgrained animals." When
it was proposed to dump the appointed philologist, Horatio Hale, his mother,
Sarah Josepha Hale, threatened to sink the expedition once and for all—a formidable threat, for she was not only the powerful editor of several women's
magazines but also the hallowed author of "Mary Had a Little Lamb." Hale
went along, and years later became famous as a philological scholar. Gray,
impatient at the delays, resigned his post and the closet claimed him once and
for all.

The expedition sailed in 1838. It took four years to go down along South

*While working as a taxidermist in Cincinnati, Audubon was asked to do a portrait of a
local celebrity, John Cleves Symmes, who argued that the earth had a hole through the middle.*

America, discover antarctic lands, come up through the South Seas and explore the American West Coast. It took another thirty years for American scientists to finish classifying and reporting on its massive cargo of botanical,
zoological, geographical and anthropological data. The age of specialization
had set in. Sullivant had to be called in to do the mosses, Tuckerman the lichens.
Torrey helpfully gave his services, though terribly overworked and woefully
underpaid. Gray was the obvious man to get the job done, but Wilkes looked
on him as a deserter for having resigned his post on the expedition, while Gray
foresaw that it could be an endless job. And so he found it after he reluctantly
agreed to help out. Not until the 1870s were the reports finally finished. Their
content, uneven but often admirable, justified the half-century of planning and
work. And in the course of producing the reports, American scientists hardened
their skills and lost their provincialism.

    All the while, Asa Gray was engaged in a far more portentous matter—
the profound and disruptive debate over Charles Darwin and his theory of
evolution. The account of this battle goes beyond the scope of this book but
it must be touched on.

    Darwin and Gray had met in England in 1838. Later Darwin asked Gray
for data on the geographical distribution of American plants, which Gray provided. He afterward added his pioneer findings on the relationship of Asian
and American plants. At Gray's instance, Charles Wright had sailed with the
navy's second expedition to Japan and astutely collected Asian plants—notably
broad-leaved evergreens—that matched those of eastern North America. Gray
deduced that the plants had once grown in a connected band across the northern
continent and that the connection had been cut off in the West by glaciers.
Though the Asian group and the American group had common ancestry, each
had developed, over the eons of separation, its own distinctive variations. This,
of course, was of enormous interest to Darwin: variation and adaptation were
at the heart of his theory.

    In 1857, two years before he published *Origin of Species*, Darwin wrote
Gray a long letter outlining what he called "the notions" his cataclysmic book
was to introduce. Only two other men, both English (the botanist Hooker
and the geologist Lyell), were in Darwin's confidence. In choosing Gray as
his American confidant, Darwin was concerned that Gray, a devout Christian,
might consider him atheistic. To Gray, however, truth was truth and he recognized it in Darwin's work.

    "Although botany is the amiable science," A. Hunter Dupree remarks in
his definitive biography, *Asa Gray*, "Gray had punctuated his career with
continuous thrust and counter-thrust." He did not back away from the controversy over evolution. As Darwin had hoped, Gray became the leader in

7082

M.S. del. J.N. Fitch lith.

The object of Gray's long botanical quest, the Shortia galacifolia, *blooms for a short season in a small remote section of the Carolina mountains.*

supporting Darwinism in America. In this role, Gray had to win over established thought and all but destroy the reputation of the most charismatic natural scientist in the country—the Swiss-born Harvard professor, Louis Agassiz. Agassiz had once revolutionized science by his work in fossils and glaciers, but he could not accept Darwin's revolution. And Gray had to stand off the harsh attacks of clergymen who tried to make him out to be a heretic. A godly man, Gray saw in evolution—as his botanical forebears had seen in other aspects of nature—a manifestation of God's design. He still kept his engaging sense of humor. "You write in such a captivating manner," he told Darwin. "Almost thou persuadest me to have been a hairy quadruped of arboreal habits, furnished with a tail and pointed ears."

Darwinism finally made obsolete the doctrines on which natural science had for so long rested: that no creature had ever changed its form since it was originally created and that none had ever been added or lost since the Creation. Science's belief in the Fixity of Species and the Great Chain of Being had been eroding. Evolution was their ultimate disproof. The Linnaean age was irrevocably ended. The sexual system had given way to natural systems, which now would have to take evolutionary ancestry into account. Still, one Linnaean bulwark remained—and still does. By a twentieth-century decision of the International Society of Nomenclature, the only way nature's creatures can be scientifically classified is by the binomial system, the two-name device that Linnaeus had decreed.

While Asa Gray marched off into great crusades, John Torrey, still his peer and close collaborator, stuck to his classifying. Both of them, freeing themselves occasionally from office work, took pleasure in going out into the field to see in nature what others had sent them. Torrey went to Florida to look at the *Torreya taxifolia*, a rare yew. He and Gray both made trips to the West where they camped with the mystic naturalist and conservationist John Muir and visited two Colorado mountains of personal interest, Torreys Peak and Gray's Peak. Torrey was too old and fatigued to climb his mountain but Gray went all the way up his.

In the last decade of his life, Gray heard of an event that held a special meaning for him. The *Shortia galacifolia*, the lost mountain plant that André Michaux had found almost a hundred years before and Gray had come upon in the herbarium in Paris, had finally been located again in the Carolina mountains. The many unsuccessful searches for the *Shortia* had made other botanists skeptical, suggesting that Gray had erred in his identification. "Now I will sing my *nunc dimittis*," Gray wrote when he heard about the find: he needed nothing more to content him and he set out to see for himself.

It was like an older day when John Bartram hunted for the balm of Gilead tree or William Bartram for the Franklinia. Up into the hills went the aging master of American botany. On the slopes under the laurels and rhododendrons grew the elusive *Shortia*. Standing there, Gray could again claim his discovery and, looking down at the living counterparts of the dried leaves he had found in André Michaux's herbarium, the closet botanist could now rightfully feel kin to the French wanderer.

CHAPTER FOURTEEN

THE LAST ADVENTURE

❦ ❦ ❦ ❦ ❦ "MY DEAR YOUNG FRIEND," SAID THE VOICE OF ONE GENERATION speaking to the next. "It is now determined that I shall go towards the Rocky Mountains. It has occurred to me that perchance you would like to spare a few months of your life to visit the Great Western Wilderness and perhaps again prefer going in my company in preference to that of any other person."

John James Audubon, now nearing sixty, was inviting a fledgling ornithologist, Spencer Fullerton Baird, barely nineteen, to come along on his last adventure. It was slyly phrased—whose company, after all, could conceivably be preferred to Audubon's? No matter that Baird was not able to go along—the proposal itself had the character of a landmark: a giant of natural history's old guard recognizing the man who would head the new order and do for American ornithology and zoology what Asa Gray was doing for its botany.

There was, by now, little left of that old guard save Audubon, still going on as if he did not hear time whistling so rudely past. Death had dealt with most of the others. Charles Willson Peale had acted as if age could never catch him, traveling up to New York, sample false teeth in pocket, to woo his elderly schoolteacher, and one winter night, when the boat taking him back ran on a shoal, carrying his own trunk the mile to shore. In February, 1827, he took to his bed and, as the family story told it, asked his granddaughter, Sybilla, to feel his pulse.

"I can't find it, Pa," she said.

"I thought so," he replied.

Carriages and mourners stretched through the city's streets at old Mr. Peale's funeral, and his epitaph read: "He participated in the Revolutionary struggle . . . an artist . . . an energetic citizen . . . beloved. . . ."

Samuel Latham Mitchill, according to the diary of the sharp-tongued Philip Hone, died an alcoholic, but this was an exaggeration. The doctor was ill for two years before he died, at sixty-seven, in 1831. His gravestone proclaimed him: "Medicus, Physicus, Civis, Senator, Quantus fuerit"—"Doctor, Scientist, Citizen, Senator. How great a man he was. . . ." A bystander at the cemetery asked who was being buried and was told: "A great character who knew all things on earth and in the waters of the deep."

Amos Eaton kept on teaching the plain and simple facts of science, turning out new editions of his books and defending Linnaeus. When he died in 1842, a student wrote in his copy of *Botanical Exercises:*

> Since no more herbs this world to Eaton yields.
> He's gone a-simpling to the Elysian fields.

Rafinesque died in 1840 in a Philadelphia garret, his body wasted by starvation and cancer, his fortunes so low that the landlord locked his corpse in his room hoping to make up the back rent by selling it to a medical school. A friend came, forced the lock and lowered the body from the window. Rafinesque's books and papers and collections, all the products of his strange and wonderful mind, were shoveled up and, in eight wagonloads, carted off to an auctioneer. After expenses were paid, $22.90 was turned over to his estate, which he had pathetically willed, in part, to a home for orphan girls. His grave was marked only by a board bearing the initials "C.S.R." Many years afterward his remains were taken from that grave and placed in a vault at Transylvania College.

Philadelphia had lost much of its old preeminence. Even George Ord seemed a muted memory of his irascible self—he actually said some admiring things about Audubon in a letter that very much surprised Waterton. Things would have been different for the city if Thomas Say had not deserted it years before to help set up a Utopia far away on the banks of the Wabash. William Maclure and a rich British visionary, Robert Owen, had bought the village of New Harmony, Indiana, and proposed to build an ideal community there. Owen, using his cotton-mill fortune to improve the workingman's lot, had come evangelizing for his beliefs that education and cooperation could solve society's troubles. Everybody paid attention. Congress heard him and let him use its chambers for his lectures. Six Presidents, past, present and future (John Adams, Jefferson, Monroe, John Quincy Adams, Jackson, Harrison), talked with him.

Settlers were quickly recruited for New Harmony. Everybody would work for everybody else, and all needs—physical, intellectual, spiritual—would be satisfied within the community. Maclure, whose main interest was education and science, swept a group together and took them to New Harmony on a keelboat christened *The Philanthropist*, far better known as "The Boatload of Knowledge." Aboard with Say were Charles LeSueur; Gerard Troost, a distinguished geologist; Mme. Marie Fretageot, like Maclure a disciple of Pestalozzi's educational doctrines; Phiquepal d'Arusmont, a noted French educator who later married Frances Wright, the early feminist and advocate of free love; Robert Dale Owen, son of the co-founder, who came all the way from Holland to join the colony, stopping off first at Liverpool to explain things to the Rathbones.

The Boatload of Knowledge left Pittsburgh in December and shortly was marooned in the ice. For four weeks passengers whiled the time away reading philosophical works to each other, or playing whist, or learning from Say how to stuff birds and fish. The children kept falling overboard. When the ice broke, the spring floods almost swept them past Cincinnati, but they managed to land and visit Dr. Drake's famous museum and be lectured on Symmes's hole by Symmes himself.

New Harmony, for a crowded golden decade, was almost what its founders hoped it would be. Under Say and LeSueur it became a focus of American natural history. Foreign scientists came out to the Wabash just to see them and admire the fine library and collections they had built up. Under Mme. Fretageot and Phiquepal d'Arusmont, the schools were so stimulating tthat Mrs. Trollope, the astute and snobbish writer on American manners who was then living in Cincinnati, enrolled her son there. She pulled him out when she discovered that the teachers did not show a proper respect for those in the upper stations of life.

Say finished—and, on New Harmony's presses, printed—his *American Entymology*. He published his *American Conchology*, and eloped with the pretty young lady who made the illustrations for it. LeSueur worked on the first good study of the fishes of the Great Lakes. Doubling as the community's resident artist, he painted sets for amateur theatricals and once, when a play required a thieving magpie, devised a mechanical bird tthat flew down from the rafters, swiped a spoon and flew back up again. Gerard Troost made New Harmony a center for geological study and David Dale Owen carried on his work in geology. Appointed as the federal government's first official geologist, Owen set up his headquarters at New Harmony, where they remained for twenty years. Rafinesque came up from Transylvania to talk about settling in New Harmony. But, he said, "I have made too many enemies" and left after giving a few lectures.

Visitors, impressed by New Harmony, found some contradictions. Earnestly living up to the Utopian doctrines, Say blistered his hands doing fieldwork. Cultured girls fresh from eastern seminaries, caught between the need to promote culture and to do chores, were called away in the middle of their song recitals to milk the cows. Maclure and the elder Owen quarreled and Owen sold out to his partner. The settlers, a mixed lot of idealists and goldbrickers, became discontented. The colony began to fall apart. Say's fine mind and warm manners had helped keep the community together, and when he died in 1834 the spirit went out of New Harmony.

Say's old friend Nuttall was back in Boston "after a perilous passage around Cape Horn," he wrote, "amidst mountains of ice which opposed our progress in unusual array." From then on, his life was one of consolidation and had an air of anticlimax. He sorted out his huge collections. "Mr. Nuttall gave me generously of his ornithological treasures," Audubon said, acknowledging that many of his paintings owe their models to Nuttall and to Townsend. When Nuttall gave a series of lectures on natural science in Boston, twelve thousand people applied for tickets. He revised and added to François André Michaux's *North American Sylva*, a massive catalog of American trees which the younger Michaux had first published in 1810, fulfilling an assignment his father had originally been sent to America to do.

An uncle in England left Nuttall a small estate on condition that he live there for at least six months every year. Tired of his troubles, Nuttall accepted. In 1842, at the age of fifty-six, he settled in Nutgrove, not far from Liverpool, where he became a kind of closet botanist himself. Fascinated by the new rhododendrons that were coming from Asia, he sent a nephew out to collect them for him and in this way introduced many varieties into Europe. He was content at Nutgrove but not happy. "I prefer the wilds of America a thousand times," he wrote a friend. Yet he made only one trip back. It might have been too much to keep coming to the country he had adopted and had left with a reluctance he could not hide. He recalled, in a small farewell passage, how he had enjoyed "those delightful scenes of nature with which I had been so long associated," how he had "rambled through the shade of the Atlantic forests or culled some rare productions of Flora in their native wilds." Then, with a sense of heartbreak, he went on: "But the 'oft told tale' approaches to its close and I must now bid a long adieu to the 'new world,' its sylvan scenes, its mountains, wilds and plains and henceforth, in the evening of my career, I return, almost an exile to the land of my nativity!"

🌷 🌷 🌷 🌷 🌷 AND SO THE AMERICAN WOODSMAN WAS LEFT ALONE. RETURNED from England, he bought twenty-four acres of land along the Hudson River in upper Manhattan. Alexander Garden had passed by it not quite a century before on his way to Coldengham. The family called it Minnie's Land—Minnie was the Scottish nickname they had given Lucy. Audubon built a house and studio, stocked the grounds with wild and barnyard animals and settled down, more or less. There were still two unsold sets of *Birds*, so he went out peddling those. John Jacob Astor bought one, and James Lenox, a founder of the New York Public Library, took the other. Then, carrying a couple of unbound sets to New England, he sailed out to Nantucket and sold them there.

In working on Quadrupeds, *Audubon did separate drawings of Say's chipmunk: the young (top), male and female (center). The lithographer assembled them in the final plate (bottom).*

Meanwhile, a small lithographed octavo edition of *Birds* was being printed. Audubon added some birds that were not in the elephant folios and revised some plates with the help of his son John Woodhouse. The first print order for the octavo, which was issued in installments, was for three hundred sets. Sales were so spectacular that within a year fifteen hundred sets were being printed. Although the number of subscribers fluctuated, it never fell below a thousand. Each set cost a hundred dollars, and the octavo collection proved to be Audubon's largest single source of income.

But birds were the past for Audubon. A new project gripped him: to do for American animals what he had done for its birds. The project was entitled *The Viviparous Quadrupeds of North America*. He already had, as models, 150 skins or stuffed specimens of mammals, and solicited more from everyone. He got the mayor's permission to go down to New York's wharves to shoot rats, and he wrote his young friend Spencer Baird: "Please to collect all the shrews, mice (field or wood), rats, bats, squirrels etc." Like collectors from the days of James Petiver on, he told him exactly what to do with them: "Put them in a jar in common rum, not whiskey, brandy or alcohol. All of the latter spirits are sure to injure their subjects."

Visitors to his studio at Minnie's Land found Audubon working efficiently away in the middle of a zoological mess. "In one corner," wrote a caller, bringing to mind the room at Mill Grove that William Bakewell had described forty years before, "stood a half-finished sketch of a beaver; in the other lay the skin of an American panther. The antlers of elks hung upon the wall. Exquisite drawings of field mice, orioles and woodpeckers were scattered promiscuously." Audubon came in—"a tall thin man with a high arched and serene forehead and a bright penetrating gray eye; his white locks fell in clusters upon his shoulders, his form was erect and his step was as light as that of a deer." There was something about his face that made the caller think of an eagle.

The writer of the text for the *Quadrupeds* was his Charleston friend John Bachman, part of the family now since two of his daughters had married Audubon's sons. Bachman was cocky about the collaboration. "You cannot do without me in this business," he told Audubon, and he was right. The preacher was better informed about American mammals than almost anyone in the land. "It must be no halfway affair," he instructed Audubon. "Don't flatter yourself that this book is child's play—the birds are a mere trifle compared with this." Audubon accepted the warnings amiably. "My hair is gray and I am growing old but what of this—my spirits are as enthusiastical as ever."

In 1842, the first set of *Quadrupeds*, with text by Bachman based heavily on Audubon's notes, was on the presses. Audubon was anxious to be off for more specimens and was determined to go west, where he had never been, to get them. He first went down to Washington to secure introductions from President Tyler, General Winfield Scott, Secretary of State Daniel Webster and the British envoy Lord Ashburton, with whom Webster had just signed the boundary-settling Webster-Ashburton Treaty.

Audubon also did a little *Birds* business, dunning Webster for his still-unpaid subscription. When Webster tried to put him off by offering him a government sinecure, Audubon summarily rejected it—"Humbug," he said. Webster grudgingly paid him a hundred dollars. Audubon hated Washington—the heat, the tedium of waiting on bureaucrats. Even writing with "a miserable iron pen" was an irritation to a man accustomed to quills.

Finally, in the last days of winter, 1843, he was ready to leave. He had four men in his party: Edward Harris, an old friend; John Bell, a taxidermist of Sparkill, New York, whose shop in New York City had become a kind of club for naturalists; Isaac Sprague, an artist who was to become Asa Gray's illustrator; and Lewis Squires, a young neighbor of Audubon. Audubon hoped to recruit William Bakewell, a favorite hunting companion whom he called "the Nimrod of the West," but Bakewell could not leave his business.

On the road, Audubon kept running into his past. In Louisville he called on Dr. William Galt, aged but still botanizing. He had a reunion with John Gwathmey, keeper of the Indian Queen where the Audubons had lived and Alexander Wilson had played his melancholy flute. Mrs. Gwathmey wept when their old lodger left again. Georgiana Keats was still in town—her husband had died a wealthy man and his flighty widow had married a high-living Scot years younger than she. In St. Louis, he met a young man named Heerman—"to whose mother I gave formerly drawing lessons," wrote Audubon, recalling the flirtatious young woman in New Orleans who had cost him a job.

Audubon was lionized in St. Louis. George Engelmann made him an honorary member of the Western Academy of Natural Sciences. Newspaper reporters besieged him and he boasted that he could still walk all day, even though in his now almost toothless state he often subsisted largely on biscuits and molasses. For good measure, he threw in a few insults at Buffon, still the archenemy. The romantic Scottish laird William Stewart, on his way into the Rockies, renewed an offer to include Audubon in his party. Stewart would pay all his expenses and provide a wagon and five mules for his use. Audubon said no.

Audubon's party sailed up the Missouri on a shallow-draft steamer. There were some Indians aboard, and one squaw ran fearfully away when Audubon showed a drawing of some woodchucks. She thought it was alive and its creator a magician. Audubon had a fine stateroom, but the bugs drove him out of it and he slept, as he had done so many years before, on the deck wrapped in his blanket.

His quarry was animals, but as he went up the river Audubon filled the pages of his journals with a delighted catalog of his constant love: "We saw cerulean warblers, hooded flycatchers, Kentucky warblers, Nashville ditto, blue-winged ditto, red-eyed and white-eyed flycatchers, great crested and common peewees, redstarts, towhee buntings, ferruginous thrushes, wood thrush, golden-crowned thrush, blue-gray flycatcher, blue-eyed warbler, blue, yellow-back, chestnut-sided, black-and-white creepers, nuthatch, blue-winged teals, turkey-buzzards, a peregrine falcon," and on and on as if he were not the greatest bird artist in the world but just another bird watcher adding to his life list.

The impression from Audubon's journals is that the trip was not so much an exploration as a meandering. Walking across the muddy river-bottom land toward the prairies, he found himself in "mud up to the very middle, was nearly exhausted which proves that I am no longer as young as I was thirty years ago." The woodsman grew more and more content to sit back and watch, letting others do the strenuous things he once did without thinking.

They settled in at Fort Union, which was presided over by Alexander Culbertson, the chief agent, and his wife, a beautiful Blackfoot princess named Natawista. The first night ashore, a party got going with "clarinets, fiddlers and a drum. We all got up and in a short time were amid the beau monde of these parts. Several squaws attired in their best were present. Mr. Culbertson played the fiddle very fairly, Mr. Guepe the clarinet and Mr. Chouteau the drum as if brought up in the Army of the great Napoleon. Cotillions and reels were danced with much energy."

Work began. The hunters went out daily to bring back antelope, wolves and hares for Audubon and Sprague to sketch and Bell to prepare. Audubon, for a while at least, took his usual scrupulous notes. When he was presented with a western porcupine, "an animal such as I never saw or Bell either," he took twenty-three separate measurements—"from nose to anterior canthus of the eye, 1⅝ in., posterior ditto, 2⅛; conch of ear, 3½; distances from eyes posteriorly, 2¼; forefeet stretched beyond nose, 3½. . . ." To his "delight and astonishment," he saw a new bird he named Sprague's pipit—he had already named a new sparrow for Harris. Up at five in the morning, he worked until midafternoon when, "becoming fatigued," he would go for a "short walk regretting," he said, "that I could no longer draw twelve or fourteen hours a day without a pause or thought of weariness." There was nothing wrong with his eye or hand: "I shot seven Arkansas flycatchers on the wing."

The Culbertsons put on special shows for their visitor, "all mounted on horses with Indian saddles and trappings, Mrs. Culbertson's magnificent black hair floating like a banner behind her. Hither and thither they dashed, and when the whole party had crossed the ravine below, they saw a fine Wolf.

Mr. Culbertson gave it chase, overtook it, his gun flashed, and the Wolf lay dead."

Out on camping trips, Audubon was agreeable to doing chores. He and Harris made themselves useful "carrying buffalo dung to make a fire," Harris reported, "piling on one arm the 'prairie wood' which we had to embrace very closely to prevent its falling and when the capping piece was placed on the pile, clapping our chins upon it and marching off with another lump in our hands." What would the civilized Rathbones of Liverpool or the refined society of London have thought to see their American woodsman trotting across the prairie piled to the chin with buffalo droppings? Or if they had seen him another time, when trying to lure an antelope into shooting range. He lay down on his back "and threw my legs up, kicking first one and then the other. Sure enough the antelope walked towards us. When about sixty yards off I could see his eyes and pulled the trigger without rising from my awkward position." He missed.

The big excitement was buffalo hunting, but Audubon's first venture into it almost ended his hunting days for good. He went after a wounded bull, which

> did not appear to be much exhausted, but he was so stiffened by the shot on the shoulder that he could not turn quickly; as we came near he worked himself slowly round to face us, and then made a lunge at us; we then stopped on one side and commenced discharging our pistols with little or no effect, except to increase his fury with every shot. His appearance was now one to inspire terror. Through my own imprudence, I placed myself directly in front of him, and as he advanced I fired at his head, and then ran ahead of him, instead of veering to one side, not supposing that he was able to overtake me; but turning my head over my shoulder, I saw to my horror, Mr. Bull within three feet of me, prepared to give me a taste of his horns. The next instant I turned sharply off, Bell shot him directly behind the shoulder blade. He tottered for a moment, with an increased jet of blood from the mouth and nostrils, fell forward on his horns, then rolled over on his side, and was dead.

His pleasure was spoiled by the wanton killing—which he joined—of buffalo nobody needed or could use. "What a terrible destruction of life as it were for nothing or next to it, the flesh left to the beasts and birds of prey or to rot. The prairies are literally covered with the skulls of the victims. This cannot last. Even before many years, the buffalo like the Great Auk will have disappeared."

The finest buffalo were saved for Audubon. One of the first he saw was "so full of symmetry and so beautiful" that he could hardly wait to draw it. Another head was lost, "because I forgot to tell Mrs. Culbertson that I wished to save it and the Princess had its skull broken open to enjoy its brains. Handsome and refined in many ways, I cannot reconcile myself to the fact that she partakes of raw animal food with such evident relish."

Audubon no longer attracted young women, but he was taken with the handsome Blackfoot. Her name, Natawista Iksana, meant "Medicine Snake Woman." An admiring artist who came by Fort Union remarked that "she would be an excellent model for a Venus." Culbertson married her not just for her beauty, but because it was good business to have a chief's daughter for a wife. When trouble threatened, she would go along with him to the Blackfoot villages and entertain her tribesmen by telling stories about the funny people who lived in St. Louis.

"Clearly a lady of breeding," Audubon thought her. "We had an arrival of five squaws, who came to see our fort and our ladies. The Princess went out to meet them covered with a fine shawl and the visitors followed her to her own room. These ladies spoke both the French and Cree languages." Natawista had other talents. "She is a most expert and graceful swimmer, besides being capable of being underwater a long time." She dived into the Missouri once after a covey of mallards and brought half a dozen back for Audubon.

In later years, Culbertson became the most powerful agent in the Missouri territory, and, growing rich, took Natawista to Peoria, where he married her in a proper Christian ceremony and installed her in a mansion, with stables for their horses and an English gardener to tend the grounds. Natawista enjoyed it all, but every Indian summer she would have the gardener put up a teepee on the well-tended lawn and, donning her tribal dress, live again for a while like a Blackfoot squaw.

The summer sped away. Audubon made a side trip to the Mauvaises Terres, the Bad Lands—"one constant time of toil, anxiety, fatigue and dangers," he wrote wearily. Then, with their drawings, the skins, some new birds and a live antelope, they started back to Minnie's Land. The wilderness gave him a last salute, "bulls roaring like the continued roll of a hundred drums, elks whistling, wolves howling all around and owls hooting."

On the homeward journey, old troubles plagued Audubon—seasickness on the rough river and "bad dreams about my own Lucy." He hardly had the patience to stop in St. Louis. He was off for home by river, stage and canal. On a canalboat, a young passenger, seeing Audubon sleeping on deck under a stack of furs and blankets, gave him his berth. With his "patriarchal beard and hawk-like eyes," Audubon was to the youth "like one of his old eagles, feathered to the heel." Standing on the boat, Audubon pointed to something on a fence some way off. "See yonder is a fox squirrel," he said, and when his young companion wondered how he could be so sure at such a distance, Audubon replied, "Ah, I have an Indian's eye."

His daughter-in-law wrote of the woodsman's last homecoming. It was a bright day at Minnie's Land,

> and the whole family were on the piazza waiting for the carriage to come. There were two roads and, hearing wheels, some ran one way and some another, each hoping to be the first to see him; but he had left the carriage at the top of the hill and came on foot straight down the steepest part so that those who remained on the piazza had his first kiss. He had on a green blanket coat with fur collar and cuffs; his hair and beard were very long and he made a fine and striking appearance.

For a while, Audubon was able to paint with all his old skill and much of his old energy. But he had actually not brought much back that had not already been described, some by Lewis and Clark. Usually scrupulous in providing data, Audubon now was sloppy. Bachman said he needed material on skunks and hares, not about "a brain-eating, horse-straddling squaw." But the first folios of the *Quadrupeds* were out. "Beautiful, perfectly unique," Bachman called them, and the critics echoed his praise. If his animals did not reflect that profound love and delight that shone from Audubon's *Birds*, they still were the match for them as paintings in their attitudes, illuminating details and sense of aliveness. Two

An aged and toothless Audubon had his photograph taken at Matthew Brady's studio in New York. In her photograph, Lucy looked fragile but was still plainly strong-willed.

hundred subscriptions were already sold, including one to Prince Albert, a highly satisfactory start.

Audubon began to do less and less, his sons more and more. Victor wrote and edited. John painted and collected. Bachman was sadly troubled. Both his daughters who had married Audubon's sons had died and his wife was dying. An old friend visited Audubon in 1846, Thomas Brewer, for whom Audubon had named a blackbird. He found that the "once-piercing gray eyes, though still bright, had already begun to fail him. He seemed to enjoy to the utmost each moment of time, content at last to submit to an inevitable and well-earned leisure."

Spencer Baird, Audubon's protégé, stopped by in the next year. He had first come to Audubon's attention, at the age of seventeen, by sending him a yellow-bellied flycatcher he could not find in any American ornithology. It was a new bird, and seeing promise in the novice naturalist, Audubon recruited him as an animal collector. Audubon was disappointed when a suspected heart ailment kept Baird from going along on the western trip, but kept track of him as he made his way up through natural science circles, became a protégé of Nuttall's and, following an old naturalist tradition, walked everywhere. In a single year, 1842, he logged twenty-one hundred miles on foot. It would have impressed even Alexander Wilson.

An expert classifier, Baird was proposed for a job sorting out the Wilkes expedition's confused haul, but the work went to someone else, who botched it. In 1847, he wrote Audubon asking for his help. The Smithsonian Institution, founded a few years before by a bequest of the Englishman James Smithson (whose grandfather, the Duke of Northumberland, had been one of John Bartram's clients), needed a curator. "I would like the situation amazingly," he wrote Audubon, "and ask you to make out a flaming recommendation." Audubon replied with the impressive formality he could summon up. "I am quite convinced that no one can easily be found so well adapted for such a trust as yourself —your knowledge and high character and industry and your zeal." He expected that the Board would receive the recommendation "as an evidence of my ardent desire for your success," the more readily, he added, "as I have the honor of knowing some of the Board personally."

It was a nice way of understating his influence. Baird got the job, though it took a little while and the help of others. When he took the post as assistant secretary, he brought the Smithsonian his own collection of four thousand bird skins, a few hundred containers of snakes and fish, uncounted cases of eggs and nests. Once installed, he ushered in what has been called the "Bairdian era" of American ornithology, systematizing and renaming, and publishing a thousand-page *Catalogue of North American Birds*. Where Audubon gave American bird watchers images see, Baird gave them lists to keep. All fields of zoology got the Baird treatment. He was not just a superb naturalist but a superlative manager. Working for the Smithsonian and other government departments, he was involved in sending hundreds of expeditions into the field, picking his men and dictating the details of the projects with as much shrewdness and care as Peter Collinson once showed in instructing John Bartram. The enlightened bureaucrat had replaced the virtuoso as the benefactor—and the beneficiary—of American natural science.

By what seems more a stroke of fate than a coincidence, Audubon sealed the connection between an old era and a new in his octavo edition of the *Birds*. "During one of our buffalo hunts," he wrote of his western trip, "we happened to pass along several wet places, closely overgrown by a kind of rushlike grass from which we heard the notes we thought were produced by marsh hens. Harris and Bell immediately went in search. Several times Mr. Bell nearly trod on them before the birds would take to wing. They almost instantaneously realighted, then ran like mice through the grass. I have named this species after my young friend, Spencer F. Baird." He drew Baird's bunting, now called Baird's sparrow, as Plate 500 in the octavo, the last of all his bird plates.

Baird's 1847 visit to Minnie's Land was sad. "Found him much changed," he wrote of his friend. The next year, Bachman came up and, though warned, was shocked at finding Audubon "crabbed, uncontrollable. Alas my poor friend Audubon, the outlines of his countenance and his form are there but his noble mind is all in ruins."

The work went on nevertheless. With Victor as editor, the *Quadrupeds* folios appeared on schedule. John's drawings grew better and better, until today it is hard in some cases to tell which are his and which his father's. Bachman found solace in the success of *Quadrupeds* and, after his wife's death, in marrying Maria Martin, Audubon's devoted friend and assistant.

Audubon lived on until January, 1851. His last days were spent contentedly in other places and other times, in the company of old memories. He listened as his family sang the French rhymes he had heard as a boy and the tunes he had fiddled in the forests for the amused Indians. He fell into long spells of silence, looking, it might have been, at familiar sights—the wood duck wooing with "his silken crest high," the shrill eagles "catitating," the mournful avocet sitting as if in a dream. Lucy's brother William Bakewell, on a farewell visit, broke in on one of these musings, and Audubon, turning his eyes to him, knew him right off as his hunting companion, the Nimrod of the West. "Yes, yes, Billy," he said eagerly, "you go down that side of Long Pond and I'll go this side—and we'll get the ducks."

CHAPTER FIFTEEN

A SPECIES OF ETERNITY

❦ ❦ ❦ ❦ ❦ IT IS HARD, HAVING BEEN SO LONG IN THIS COMMUNITY OF naturalists and been so close to these men, to realize that they are all gone. There was a goes-without-saying defiance of mortality about all of them. They had, in fact, a better reason than most men for their defiance. Linnaeus—naturally, it would be Linnaeus—expressed it with the greatest assurance. "Riches vanish, the mightiest states and most flourishing kingdoms may be overthrown," he wrote, addressing the men whose names he bestowed on plants, "but the whole of nature must be obliterated before the genera of plants disappear. Plants remain and renew their flowers and, with gratitude enduring through the years, they shall always exhale the sweet memory of your names and make them more lasting than marble so that they will outlive those of kings and heroes."

Peter Collinson echoed this, more briefly and with more wit—and with that lovely phrase which has spoken ever since for all the namesakes of nature. When Linnaeus told him that his name had been given to a wild mint which would henceforth be known as *Collinsonia*, he accepted the honor as proper payment for a man who had served science well. He would be remembered now "as long as men and books endure" for—"botanically speaking," he said,—he had been granted "a species of eternity."

1 Linnaeus's description of *Collinsonia*

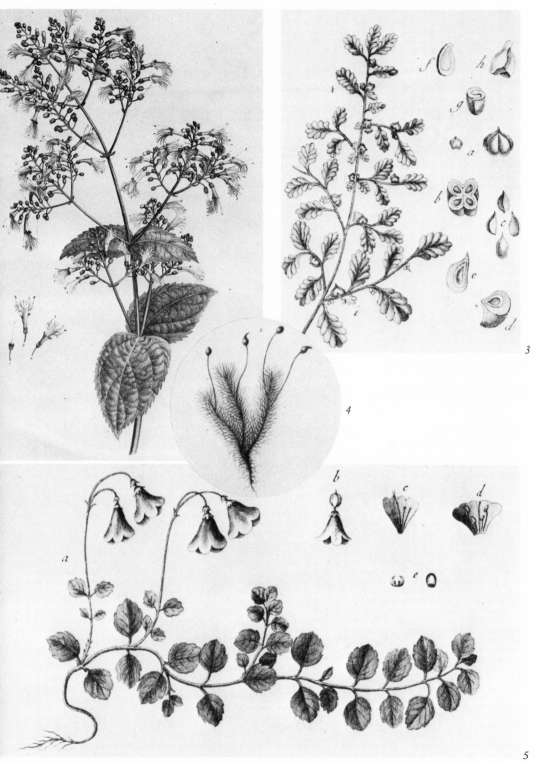

2 *Collinsonia Canadensis* or horse-balm   3 *Coldenia* or wild heliotrope

4 *Bartramia pomiformis* or apple moss   5 *Linnaea borealis* or twinflower

6 Mitchella repens or partridgeberry   *7 Franklinia*
8 Claytonia virginica or spring beauty   *9 Kalmia latifolia* or mountain laurel

10 *Gardenia* or bay jasmine

11 Wilson's plover or *Charadrius wilsonia*   12 *Bartramia longicauda* or upland plover

13 Audubon's shearwater or *Puffinus therminieri*   14 *Rafinesquia californica* or desert chicory
15 *Nuttallornis borealis* or olive-sided flycatcher   16 Say's phoebe or *Sayornis saya*

T.72.

Hellebæns

17

18

17 *Perca mitchilli (Roccus lineatus Bloch)* or striped bass
18 *Rana catesbeiana* or bullfrog (drawn by Catesby)

BIBLIOGRAPHIC NOTES

This is a condensed bibliography, listing books, periodicals and papers most often consulted. It is as much a guide for further reading as an acknowledgment of sources. The very lengthy titles of some books have been conventionally shortened. Reprints are indicated by a second date in the parentheses.

CHAPTER ONE

Primary sources on Cadwallader Colden are *The Letters and Papers of Cadwallader Colden*, 9 vols. (The New York Historical Society, 1917–35); *The History of the Five Indian Nations of Canada* (London, 1727; New York, 1902); and *An Explication of the First Courses of Action in Matter; and the Cause of Gravitation* (New York, 1745). The only biography of Colden is *Cadwallader Colden, a Representative Eighteenth-Century Official*, by Alice Mapelsden Keys (New York, 1906). Two essays flesh out the portrait: "A Colonial Governor's Family: The Coldens of Coldengham," by Brooke Hindle (*New York Historical Society Quarterly*, Vol. 45, No. 3 [July 1961]), and "Cadwallader Colden, Colonial Politician and Imperial Statesman," by Siegfried V. Rolland (unpublished doctoral thesis, University of Wisconsin, 1952). Also informative are *American Philosophy, the Early Schools*, by Isaac Woodbridge Riley (New York, 1907), and *Selections from the Scientific Correspondence of Cadwallader Colden*, arranged by Asa Gray (New Haven, 1843). On Jane Colden: *The Botanic Manuscripts of Jane Colden*, edited by H. W. Rickett and Elizabeth Hall (New York, 1963); *Her Garden Was Her Delight*, by Buckner Hollingsworth (New York, 1962); and "Jane Colden, an Early New World Botanist," by Anne Murray Vail (*Contributions from the New York Botanical Garden*, Vol. 4). For other figures in this chapter: *John Banister and His Natural History of Virginia, 1678–1692*, by Joseph and Nesta Ewan (Urbana, 1970); *A New Voyage to Carolina*, by John Lawson, edited by Hugh Talmadge Lefler (Chapel Hill, 1967); *The Natural History of Carolina, Florida and the Bahama Islands*, by Mark Catesby (London, 1731–48); *Mark Catesby, The Colonial Audubon*, by George Frederick Frick and Raymond Phineas Stearns (Urbana, 1961); and "James Petiver, Promoter of Natural Science," by Raymond Phineas Stearns (*Proceedings of the American Antiquarian Society*, Vol. 62 [1962]). A limited edition portfolio of the *Natural History* has been published by Beehive Press (Savannah, 1975).

On the new world: *A Briefe and True Report on the New Found Land of Virginia*, by Thomas Harriot (London, 1588; Ann Arbor, 1931); *Joyfull Newes Out of the New Founde World*, by Nicolas Bautista Monardes, "Englished" by John Frampton (London, 1577); *An Account of Two Voyages to New England*, by John Josselyn (London, 1674; Boston, 1865), and *New England's Rarities Discovered*, by John Josselyn (London, 1672; Boston, 1860);

New England's Prospect, by William Wood (London, 1634; Boston 1865); *Wildlife in America*, by Peter Matthiessen (New York, 1959); *O Strange New World*, by Howard Mumford Jones (New York, 1964); *Wilderness*, by Rutherford Platt (New York, 1961); *The Eyes of Discovery*, by John Bakeless (Philadelphia, 1950); *Wilderness and the American Mind*, by Roderick Nash (New Haven, 1967); and *The Prairie and the Making of Middle America*, by Dorothy Anne Dondore (Cedar Rapids, 1926).

Several works contain material related to this and later chapters: *Science in the British Colonies of America*, by Raymond Phineas Stearns (Urbana, 1970), a notable scientific history; *The Pursuit of Science in Revolutionary America*, by Brooke Hindle (Chapel Hill, 1956); *The Cultural Life of the American Colonies*, by Louis B. Wright (New York, 1957); *The Americans: The Colonial Experience*, by Daniel J. Boorstin (New York, 1958); *Rebels and Gentlemen*, by Carl and Jessica Bridenbaugh (New York, 1942); *Natural History and the American Mind*, by William Martin Smallwood and Mary Sarah Coon Smallwood (New York, 1941); *Green Laurels*, by Donald Culross Peattie (New York, 1936); *The Plant Hunters*, by Alice B. Coats (New York, 1969); *A History of Science, Technology and Philosophy in the Eighteenth Century*, by A. Wolf (New York, 1952); *History of Botany*, by Julius von Sachs (London, 1890; New York, 1967); and *The Enlightenment, an Interpretation: The Science of Freedom*, by Peter Gay (London, 1969). The *Dictionary of National Biography* and the *Dictionary of American Biography* are wide-ranging sources for all the chapters. So are the *Proceedings* and *Transactions* of the American Philosophical Society (abbreviated here as *Proc.* and *Trans. APS*).

CHAPTER TWO

Primary sources on Linnaeus in English include: *Lapland Journey (Lachesis Lapponica)*, translated by Carl Troilius and edited by James Edward Smith (London, 1792); *A General View of the Writings of Linnaeus*, by Richard Pulteney (London, 1805); and *A Selection of the Correspondence of Linnaeus and Other Naturalists*, edited by James Edward Smith (London, 1821).

Biographies of Linnaeus: *Carl Linnaeus*, by Knut Hagberg (New York, 1953); *The Prince of Botanists*, by Norah Gourlie (London, 1953); *Carl Linnaeus, Pioneer of Modern Botany*, by Alice Dickinson (New York, 1957); *The Compleat Naturalist*, by Wilfred Blunt (New York, 1971); and *Linnaeus*, by B. D. Jackson, based on the biography by Theodor Magnus Fries (London, 1923).

A facsimile of *Species Plantarum*, published by the Ray Society, has a fine explanation of the Linnaean system by William T. Stearn (London, 1957). *Travels in North America*, by Peter Kalm, has been edited by Carl Adolph B. Benson (New York, 1937).

CHAPTER THREE

Published works by John Bartram are: *A Journey From Pennsylvania to Onondaga in 1743* (London, 1751; Barre, 1973); *A Description of East Florida with a Journal kept by John Bartram of Philadelphia, Botanist to His Majesty for the Floridas, upon a journey from St. Augustine up the River St. John's as far as the Lakes* (London, 1766) (the *Description of East Florida* is a report by William Stork which shares the book with Bartram's account); and *Diary of a Journey Through the Carolinas, Georgia and Florida*, annotated by Francis Harper (*Trans. APS*, New Series, Vol. 33, Pt. 1 [December 1942]). The correspondence between Bartram and Peter Collinson is preserved in *Memorials of John Bartram and Humphry Marshall*, compiled by William Darlington, which includes William Bartram's biography of his father and Crèvecoeur's account of his visit to Bartram (Philadelphia, 1848; New York, 1967).

Biographies: *John and William Bartram, Botanists and Explorers*, by Ernest Earnest (Philadelphia, 1940); *New Green World*, by Josephine Herbst (New York, 1954); *The*

Life of Peter Collinson, by Norman G. Brett-James (London, 1925); *John Clayton, Pioneer of American Botany*, by Edmund Berkeley and Dorothy Smith Berkeley (Chapel Hill, 1963); *James Logan and the Culture of Provincial America*, by Frederick B. Tolles (Boston, 1967); "The Scientific Ideas of John Mitchell," by Theodore Hornberger (*Huntington Library Quarterly*, Vol. 10 [1947]); "The Eighth Lord Petre," by James Britten (*Dublin Review*, Vol. 153); *Conrad Weiser*, by Paul A. Wallace (Philadelphia, 1945); and *The Botanists of Philadelphia and Their Work*, by John W. Harshberger (Philadelphia, 1898).

Collateral material: "Scientific Relations Between Europe and America in the Eighteenth Century," by Michael Kraus (*Scientific Monthly*, Vol. 55 [September 1942]); "Traffic in Seeds and Plants from England's Colonies in North America," by Sarah P. Stetson (*William and Mary Quarterly*, Series 3 [July 1946]); *Brothers of the Spade*, by E. G. Swem (Barre, 1957); "Significance of John Bartram's Work to Botanical and Horticultural Knowledge," by John Hendley Barnhart (*Bartonia*, 1931); *Scientists and Amateurs, a History of the Royal Society*, by Dorothy Stimson (New York, 1948); and the *Papers of Benjamin Franklin*, 18 vols. (New Haven, 1959–1974).

CHAPTER FOUR

Alexander Garden wrote what could be regarded as fragments of an autobiography in his letters, found in *A Selection of the Correspondence of Linnaeus and Other Naturalists* and in *The Letters and Papers of Cadwallader Colden*, both works previously cited. The indispensable biography is *Dr. Alexander Garden of Charles Town*, by Edmund Berkeley and Dorothy Smith Berkeley (Chapel Hill, 1969).

CHAPTER FIVE

William Bartram's *Travels Through North and South Carolina, Georgia, East and West Florida* was originally published in Philadelphia in 1791. The best modern edition was prepared by Francis Harper, whose notes and commentary add up to an extensive discussion of Bartram's life and work (New Haven, 1958). Other editions of *Travels* have been edited by Mark van Doren (New York, 1928) and John Livingston Lowes (New York, 1940). Excerpts from the writings of both Bartrams are in *John and William Bartram's America*, edited by Helen Gere Cruickshank (New York, 1957). *Travels in Georgia and Florida 1773–74, a Report to Dr. Fothergill* was edited by Francis Harper (*Trans. APS*, New Series, Vol. 33, Pt. 2 [November 1943]). *William Bartram, Botanical and Zoological Drawings, 1756–1788*, edited by Joseph Ewan (Philadelphia, 1968), is a stunning look at Bartram as an artist.

For biographies and commentaries: previously cited works by Earnest and Herbst; *Billy Bartram and His Green World*, by Marjorie Bartlett Sanger (for younger readers; New York, 1972); *William Bartram, Interpreter of the American Landscape*, by N. Bryllion Fagin (Baltimore, 1933); *The Road to Xanadu*, by John Livingston Lowes (Boston, 1925); *J. and T. Doughty's Cabinet of Natural History and American Rural Sports*, Vol. 2 (Philadelphia, 1822); and *Life, Letters and Papers of William Dunbar*, by Mrs. Dunbar Rowland (Jackson, 1930). Also: "Dennis Rolle and Rollestown," by Carlita Doggett (*Florida Historical Quarterly*, Vol. 7, No. 2 [October, 1928]), and "The Historical Background of the Franklin Tree," by Charles F. Jenkins (*Pennsylvania Magazine of History and Biography*, Vol. 57, No. 227 [July 1933]).

CHAPTER SIX

André Michaux's journals have been published in French with biography and notes by Charles S. Sargent (*Proc. APS*, Vol. 26 [1889]. An English translation of the journals of André Michaux for 1793–1796 may be found in *Early Western Travels*, edited by Ruben Gold Thwaites (Cleveland, 1904–7; New York, 1966). An 1804 biography, "Notice Historique sur André Michaux," was written by J. P. F. Deleuze (*Annales du Musée d'Historie Naturelle*, Vol. 3, 1804). Also: "André and François André Michaux and Their Predecessors," by Gilbert Chinard (*Proc. APS*, Vol. 101, No. 4 [September 1944]); "The Origin of Genet's Projected Attack on Louisiana and the Floridas," by Frederick J. Turner (*American History Review*, Vol. 3 [1898]); "The Activities of Citizen Genet in Kentucky, 1793-1794," by Richard Lowitt (*Filson Club History Quarterly*, Vol. 22, No. 4 [October 1948]); *Jefferson, Friend of France*, by Meade Minnegerode (New York, 1928); and *The Papers of Thomas Jefferson*, edited by Julian P. Boyd (Princeton, 1950-1974). There are two recent editions of Jefferson's *Notes on the State of Virginia*, one edited by Thomas Perkins Abernathy (New York, 1964), the other by William Peden (Chapel Hill, 1954). Jefferson's *Garden Book* (Philadelphia, 1944) and his *Farm Book* (Princeton, 1953) have been reprinted with annotations by Edwin Morris Betts. Jefferson as a naturalist is discussed in *Thomas Jefferson, Scientist*, by Edward T. Martin (New York, 1952); *The Lost World of Thomas Jefferson* (New York, 1948); *Jefferson and His Time*, by Dumas Malone, 5 vols. (Boston, 1948-1976); *The Domestic Life of Thomas Jefferson*, by Sarah N. Randolph (Cambridge, 1939); *The Beginnings of Vertebrate Paleontology in North America*, by George Gaylord Simpson (*Trans. APS*, Vol. 86, No. 1 [September 1942]); and "The Megalonyx, the Megatharium and Thomas Jefferson's Lapse of Memory," by Julian P. Boyd (*Proc. ASP*, Vol. 102, No. 5 [September 1945]). The controversy over a degenerate America is described in "Corneille de Pauw and the Controversy over His *Récherches Philosophiques sur les Americains*," by Henry Ward Church (*Publications of the Modern Language Association of America*, Vol. 51, No. 1 [March 1936]); "Eighteenth-Century Theories on America as a Human Habitat," by Gilbert Chinard (*Proc. APS*, Vol. 91, No. 1 [February 1947]); "Antlers for Jefferson," by Anna Clark Jones (*New England Quarterly*, Vol. 12 [June 1939]); and *Buffon*, by Otis E. Fellows and Stephen F. Millikin (New York, 1972). Also: *The Great Chain of Being* by Arthur O. Lovejoy (Cambridge, 1936).

   History of the Expedition Under the Command of Lewis and Clark, edited by Elliott Coues (New York, 1893), and *Original Journals of the Lewis and Clark Expedition*, edited by Ruben Gold Thwaites (New York, 1904-05), have the explorers' complete reports on the plants and animals they found. The natural-history aspects of the expedition are set out in two invaluable works: *The Natural History of the Lewis and Clark Expedition*, by Raymond Darwin Burroughs (East Lansing, 1961), and *Lewis and Clark: Pioneering Naturalists*, by Paul Russell Cutwright (Urbana, 1969). Also: *Some Neglected Botanical Aspects of the Lewis and Clark Expedition*, by Rodney H. True (*Proc. APS*, Vol. 67, No. 1 [1928]). Original documents pertaining to the expedition appear in the *Letters of the Lewis and Clark Expedition with Related Documents 1785-1854*, which is edited and superbly annotated by Donald Jackson (Urbana, 1962).

   The primary biographies: *Lewis and Clark, Partners in Discovery*, by John Bakeless (New York, 1965); *Meriwether Lewis*, by Richard Dillon (New York, 1947); and *Life of Captain Lewis*, by Thomas Jefferson (Dublin, 1817).

CHAPTER SEVEN

Peale wrote voluminously in diaries, journals, autobiographical notes and letters. It is hardly necessary to go to them for they have been skillfully woven into Charles Coleman Seller's biography, *Charles Willson Peale* (New York, 1965). Other sources for this chapter: "A Box of Old Bones," by Whitfield J. Bell, Jr. (*Proc. APS*, Vol. 93, No. 2 [May 1949]); *A Scientific and Descriptive Catalog of Peale's Museum*, by C. W. Peale and A. F. J. Palisot de Beauvois (Philadelphia, 1796); "Palisot de Beauvois as an Overlooked American Botanist," by E. D. Merrill (*Proc. APS*, Vol. 76 [1936]); *Titian Ramsay Peale, 1779-1885, and His Journals of the Wilkes Expedition*, by Jessie Poesch, Memoirs APS, Vol. 52 (Philadelphia, 1961); *Picture of Philadelphia*, by James Mease (Philadelphia, 1811); "Notes of a Visit to Philadelphia, Made by a Moravian Sister in 1810," with introduction by A. R.

Beck (*Pennsylvania Magazine of History and Biography*, Vol. 36 [1912]); *The Diaries of George Washington* (Boston, 1925); *The Writings of George Washington*, edited by John C. Fitzpatrick (Washington, D.C., 1931–1940); *Museums U.S.A.*, by Herbert and Marjorie Katz (New York, 1965); "The Rise of the Natural History Museum," by Oliver C. Parrington (*Science*, New Series, 42 [August 13, 1915]); and *The Cultural Life of the New Nation*, by Russell Blaine Nye (New York, 1957).

CHAPTER EIGHT

Primary sources for this chapter are: *The American Ornithology* (Philadelphia, 1808–14); *The Poems and Literary Prose of Alexander Wilson*, edited by the Rev. Alexander B. Grosart (Paiseley, 1876). *American Ornithology, or The Natural History of the Birds of the United States* (London, 1832) includes Charles Lucien Bonaparte's supplement to the *Ornithology* and a biography by Sir William Jardine with extensive quotations from Wilson's letters and journals. *Alexander Wilson, Naturalist and Pioneer*, by Robert Cantwell (Philadelphia, 1961), is a work of high literary quality. Also of interest are: *Alexander Wilson, Poet-Naturalist*, by James Southwell Wilson (New York, 1961); *Alexander Wilson, a Founder of Scientific Ornithology*, by Emerson Stringham (Kerrsville, 1958); "Miss Lawson's Recollections of Ornithologists," by J. L. Burns (*Auk*, Vol. 34, [1917]); and "The Memorandum of Ruben Peale and the Words of His Life" (*APS* ms.). Valuable discussions of Wilson appear in "The History of American Ornithology before Audubon," by Elsa Guerdrum Allen (*Trans. APS*, New Series, Vol. 41; Part 3 [1951]), a seed work on the subject; the thoughtful *Birds and Men: American Birds in Science, Art, Literature and Conservation*, by Robert Henry Welker (Cambridge, 1955); and *The World of Washington Irving*, by Van Wyck Brooks (New York, 1944). Also: *The Natural History of Rarer Lepidopterous Insects of Georgia, Collected from the Observations of Mr. John Abbot*, by James Edward Smith (London, 1797), and John Abbot's *Autobiography*, edited by C. L. Remington (*Lepidopterist News*, Vol. 2, No. 3 [March 1948]).

CHAPTER NINE

The voluminous and dispersed writings of Samuel Latham Mitchill can be tracked down in the *Medical Repository* for, among others, his *Sketch of the Mineralogical History of New York* (Vol. 1 [1797–98]); *Collections of the New York Historical Society* for his *Botanical History of North and South America* (Vol. 2 [1814]); and *Transactions of the Literary and Philosophical Society* for his *Fishes of New York* (Vol. 1 [1815]). See also the *American Monthly Magazine* and the *American Journal of Science and Arts*. His legislative speeches are in the *Journals of the Senate and Assembly of New York* and the *Debates and Proceedings of the United States Congress*. His *Letters from Washington* appeared in *Harper's New Monthly Magazine* (Vol. 58 [April 1879]). The only formal biography is *A Scientist in the Early Republic: Samuel Latham Mitchill*, by Courtney Robert Hall (New York, 1934). Brief memoirs are *Eulogy on the Life and Character of the Honorable Samuel Latham Mitchill*, by John W. Francis (New York, 1859), and "A Queen's Country Polymath," by Courtney Robert Hall (*New York History*, Vol. 14, No. 2 [April 1933]).

Collateral material: *Memoirs of John Quincy Adams* (Boston, 1874–77); *Dr. Bard of Hyde Park*, by J. Brett Langstaff (New York, 1942); *The Life and Writings of DeWitt Clinton*, by William W. Campbell (New York, 1949); *Letters on the Natural History and Internal Resources of the State of New York*, by Hibernicus (New York, 1822); *DeWitt Clinton*, by Dorothea Bobbe (New York, 1933); *Life of Robert Fulton*, by Cadwallader D. Colden (New York, 1817); *Memoir at the Celebration of the Completion of the New York Canal*, by Cadwallader D. Colden (New York, 1825); and *A History of the New York Academy of Science*, by H. LeR. Fairchild (New York, 1887).

CHAPTER TEN

Audubon is a major source on himself. *Journal of John James Audubon Made During His Trip to New Orleans in 1820–1821* was edited by Howard Corning (Cambridge, 1929). *Aubudon and His Journals* was edited by Maria R. Audubon, his granddaughter (New York, 1897; Gloucester, 1972). *The 1826 Journal of John James Audubon* was edited by Alice Ford (Norman, 1967), *Journal of John James Audubon Made While Obtaining Subscriptions to His Birds of America 1840–1843*, edited by Howard Corning (Boston, 1929). *Letters of John James Audubon, 1826–1840*, also edited by Corning (Boston, 1930; New York, 1969). The *Ornithological Biography* (Edinburgh, 1831–1839) includes the *Episodes*, stories Audubon told of his life and travels. Maria Audubon's edition of the *Journals* includes the *Episodes* along with *Myself*, an autobiographical sketch that Audubon did not publish in his lifetime. Excerpts from *Ornithological Biography* are in *Delineations of American Scenery and Characters*, edited by Francis Hobart Herrick (New York, 1926), *Audubon by Himself*, edited by Alice Ford (New York, 1969); and *The Bird Biographies of John James Audubon*, edited by Alice Ford (New York, 1957). *The Birds of America* was published by Audubon in the original double-elephant folios and the 1840–44 octavo edition. The octavo *Birds of America*, which included the ornithological biographies but omitted the *Episodes*, has been reprinted with black-and-white reproductions of the engravings, an introduction by Dean Amadon and indexes by John Bull (New York, 1967). The complete engravings are printed in color in *The Birds of America* with text by William Vogt (New York, 1937). About half the engravings, also in color, appear in *The Birds of America* with text by Ludlow Griscom (New York, 1950). A selection of engravings and of Audubon's writings is found in *Audubon's America*, edited by Donald Culross Peattie (Boston, 1940). Audubon's paintings, from which the engravings were made, have been reproduced in color in *The Original Water Color Paintings by John James Audubon for The Birds of America*, with an introduction by Marshall Davidson (New York, 1960).

Biographies: Two authorized biographies were published about a century ago, both unreliable in many instances: *The Life and Adventures of John James Audubon*, by Robert Buchanan (London, 1865), and a revision, with the same title, by Lucy Audubon (New York, 1869). The best modern biographies are *Audubon the Naturalist*, by Francis Hobert Herrick (New York, 1938), the first truly scholarly work on the subject; and *John James Audubon*, by Alice Ford (Norman, 1964), which brings the scholarship up to date. Other useful biographies are *Audubon, an Intimate Life of the American Woodsman*, by Stanley Clisby Arthur (New Orleans, 1937), and *John James Audubon*, by Alexander Adams (New York, 1966). *Singing in the Wilderness*, by Donald Culross Peattie (New York, 1935), and *Audubon*, by Constance Rourke (New York, 1936), are romantic in their approach. *I Who Should Command All*, by Alice Tyler (New Haven, 1937), argues that Audubon was the lost Dauphin. *Audubon, a Vision*, by Robert Penn Warren (New York, 1969), is an evocative poem.

Collateral works include *Fifty Years in Both Hemispheres*, by Vincent Nolte (New York, 1934); *Wanderings in South America*, by Charles Waterton (London, 1825); *The Squire of Walton Hall*, by Philip Gosse (London, 1940); *The Strange Life of Charles Waterton*, by Richard Aldington (London, 1948); *The English Eccentrics*, by Edith Sitwell (New York, 1957); *The Bonaparts in America*, by Clarence E. Macartney (Philadelphia, 1939); "George Ord," by Samuel N. Rhoades (*Cassinia*, XII, 1908); and *Doctors on Horseback*, by James Thomas Flexner (New York, 1937). Also two exhibition catalogs: *Audubon's Watercolors and Drawings* for the Munson-William Proctor Institute and the Pierpont Morgan Library, annotated by Edward H. Dwight (Utica and New York, 1965), and *The World of John James Audubon*, compiled by Howard C. Rice, Jr., for the Princeton University Library (*Princeton University Chronicle*, Vol. 21, Nos. 1 and 2 [1959–60]).

CHAPTER ELEVEN

Published works by Rafinesque include: *A Life of Travel and Adventure in North America* (Philadelphia, 1936); *Icthyologia Ohiensis, or Natural History of the Fishes inhabiting the River Ohio and its Tributary Streams* (Lexington, 1820; Cleveland, 1899); *Medical Flora, or a manual of the Medical Botany of the United States* (Philadelphia, 1825–30); *The World or Instability, a Poem in Twenty Parts* (Philadelphia, 1836; Gainesville, 1956); *Safe Banking* (Philadelphia, 1837); and *Western Minerva or American Annals of Knowledge and Literature* (Lexington, 1821; New York, 1949).

There are two biographies: *Life and Writings of Rafinesque*, by Richard Ellsworth Call (Louisville, 1895); and *Rafinesque, a Sketch of His Life*, by T. J. Fitzpatrick (Des Moines, 1911). Among the commentaries are "Rafinesque, the Errant Naturalist," by S. Gordon Smythe (*Historical Society of Montgomery County, Penna., Historical Sketches*, Vol. 6 [1929]); *Rafinesque in Lexington*, by A. Hunter Dupree (Lexington, 1945); "Transylvania University and Rafinesque, 1819–1826," by A. Hunter Dupree (*Filson Club Historical Quarterly*, Vol. 35, No. 2 [April 1961]); "Rafinesque's Kentucky Friends," by Harry B. Weiss (Orange, 1925); "Rafinesque Memorial Papers," (Transylvania College Bulletin [September 1942]); "The Transylvania Botanic Garden," by Ida Withers Harris (*Journal of American History*, Vol. 7 [1913]); "Notice of the Botanical Writings of the Late C. S. Rafinesque," by Asa Gray (*American Journal of Science and Arts*, Series I, Vol. 40 [April 1841]); "A Generally Overlooked Rafinesque Paper," by E. D. Merrill (*Proc. APS*, Vol. 86 [September 1942]); "Rafinesque's Publications from the Standpoint of World Botany," by E. D. Merrill (*Proc. APS*, Vol. 87 [1943–44]); "The Correspondence Between Constantine Samuel Rafinesque and Thomas Jefferson," by Edwin M. Betts (*Proc. APS*, Vol. 87 [May 1944]); and "Letters by Rafinesque to Dr. Short" (*Filson Club Historical Quarterly*, Vol. 12 [1938]). Also: "Green River, a Poem for Rafinesque," by James Whaler (New York, 1931). Much material on Rafinesque is contained in works by Graustein, Rodgers, McAllister, and Dupree cited in the following chapters.

CHAPTER TWELVE

Nuttall's own writings: *Travels into the Old Northwest*, edited by Jeanette E. Graustein (*Chronica Botanica*, Vol. 14, No. 1–2 [1951]); *Journey of Travels into the Interior of Arkansa Territory During the Year 1819* (London, 1819); *The Genera of North American Plants and a Catalogue of the Species to the Year 1817* (Philadelphia, 1918); *A Manual of the Ornithology of the United States and Canada* (Boston, 1832–34); *An Introduction to Systematic and Physiological Botany* (Boston, 1827); and *North American Sylva of F. André Michaux* (Philadelphia, 1852).

Biographies are: *Thomas Nuttall, Naturalist: Explorations in America 1808–1841*, by Jeanette E. Graustein (Cambridge, 1967), the definitive work; "Biographical Notice of the Late Thomas Nuttall" (*Proc. APS*, Vol. 7 [1860]); "Biographical Sketch of the Late Thomas Nuttall," by Thomas Meehan (*Gardners Monthly*, Vol. 2); and "Some Biographical Sidelights on Thomas Nuttall," by Richard G. Beidleman (*Proc. APS*, Vol. 104, [1960]). Nuttall appears as a character in *Travels in the Interior of North America in the Years 1809, 1810 and 1811*, by John Bradbury (London, 1819); *Journal of a Voyage Up the River Missouri*, by Henry Marie Breckinridge (Baltimore, 1816); and *Narrative of a Journey Across the Rocky Mountains*, by John Kirk Townsend (Philadelphia, 1839). Nuttall's, Bradbury's, Breckinridge's, and Townsend's accounts are all in *Early Western Travels*, edited by Ruben Gold Thwaites (Cleveland, 1904–07; New York, 1966). Additional sources are: *Astoria*, by Washington Irving (Philadelphia, 1836), and *Two Years Before the Mast*, by Richard Henry Dana (Boston, 1840).

Collateral material: *Correspondence and Journals of Captain Nathaniel J. Wyeth*, edited by F. G. Young (Sources of the History of Oregon, I; Portland, 1899); "Natural History at Harvard," by Jeanette E. Graustein (*Cambridge Historical Society Proceedings*, Vol. 38 [1961]); "Frederick Pursh and His Botanical Associates," by Joseph Ewan (*Proc. APS*, Vol. 96, No. 5 [1952]); and "John Bradbury's Exploration in the Missouri Territory," by H. W. Rickett (*Proc. APS*, Vol. 90 [1950]).

Sources on Thomas Say: *Account of an Expedition from Pittsburg to the Rocky Mountains, Performed in the Years 1819 and '20*, by Edwin James (Philadelphia, 1823; Cleveland, 1904–07); *The Complete Writings of Thomas Say on the Entomology of North America*, edited by John L. Leconte (New York, 1859); *American Entomology*, by Thomas Say (Philadelphia, 1824–1828); *Thomas Say, Early American Naturalist*, by Harry B. Weiss and Grace McZeigler (Springfield, 1931).

Collateral works: "William MacLure," by W. H. G. Armitage (*Indiana Magazine of History*, Vol. 48 [1951]); *The New Harmony Movement*, by George B. Lockwood (New York, 1905); *Backwoods Utopias*, by Arthur E. Bestor (Philadelphia, 1950); "Education and Reform at New Harmony," by Arthur E. Bestor (*Indiana Historical Society Publications*, Vol. 15, No. 3 [1945]); *Heavens on Earth*, by Mark Hollaway (London, 1951); and *Indiana as Seen by Early Travelers*, edited by Harlow Lindley (*Indiana Historical Society Collection*, 1916).

CHAPTER THIRTEEN

Sources for this chapter include: *John Torrey, a Story of North American Botany*, by Andrew Denny Rodgers III (Princeton, 1942); *Asa Gray*, by A. Hunter Dupree (Cambridge, 1959), a superb work; *The Letters of Asa Gray*, edited by Jane Loring Gray (Boston, 1893); *Amos Eaton, Scientist and Educator*, by Ethel M. McAllister (Philadelphia, 1941); *Douglas of the Fir*, by Athelson George Harvey (Cambridge, 1947); *Traveler in a Vanished Landscape: David Douglas*, by William Morwood (New York, 1973); *Naturalists of the Frontier*, by Samuel Wood Geiser (Dallas, 1937); *Rocky Mountain Naturalists*, by Joseph Ewan (Denver, 1950); *Freemont, Pathmarker of the West*, by Allan Nevins (New York, 1955); *The Life of an American Sailor: Rear Admiral William Hemsley Emory*, by Albert Gleaves; *Joel R. Poinsett*, by J. Fred Rippy (Durham, 1935); *Ornithologists of the United States Medical Corps*, by Edgar Erskine (Washington, D.C., 1942); *Army Explorations in the American West 1803–1863*, by William H. Goetzmann (New Haven, 1959), and *Exploration and Empire*, by William H. Goetzmann (New York, 1966); *Science in the Federal Government*, by A. Hunter Dupree (Cambridge, 1957); *The Great United States Exploring Expedition of 1838–1842*, by William Stanton (Berkeley, 1975); and *Darwin's Century*, by Loren Eisley (New York, 1958). A special mention must be made of the 1,100-page *Botanical Exploration of the Trans Mississippi West*, by Susan Delano McKelvey (Jamaica Plains, 1955), a one-volume library of the writings of naturalists.

CHAPTER FOURTEEN

In addition to works cited in Chapter 10: *The Viviparous Quadrupeds of North America, Imperial Folio*, by John James Audubon and the Rev. John Bachman (Philadelphia, 1845–1848), consisting of 150 plates without text, and the accompanying royal octavo volumes (New York, 1846–54), consisting only of text. Three other octavo editions, including both plates and text, were published by the Audubons (New York, 1849, 1854, 1856). Additional sources: *Missouri River Journals* (included in Maria Audubon's edition of the *Journals*); *Audubon in the West*, letters edited by John Francis McDermott (Mormon, 1965); *Audubon's Animals*, edited by Alice Ford (New York, 1951); *Up the Missouri with Audubon, the Journal of Edward Harris*, edited by John Francis McDermott (Norman, 1951); *Spencer Fullerton Baird*, by William Healey Dall (New York, 1918); *John Bachman* by C. L. Bachman (Charleston, 1888); and "Fort Benton Journal 1854–56" and "Fort Sarty Journal 1855–56," edited by Ann McDonnell (*Contributions to the Historical Society of Montana*, Vol. 10 [1940]).

ACKNOWLEDGMENTS

My thanks go to many who helped on this book. Mary V. O'Gorman provided perceptive research for several chapters. Dean Amadon, Karl Brooks, Mark Rothenberg and Gordon DeWolf were consulted on the text. Mary Grace read and improved the manuscript. Judith Mara Gutman and Herbert Gutman gave their warm and informed help in shaping this book. I am in debt to the New York Public Library, especially its American history and rare books sections, the New York Historical Society, the New York Botanical Garden, the American Philosophical Society, the American Museum of Natural History and the Nyack Library. I remember gratefully that my personal and professional interest in natural history was stimulated by John Allen, Robert Porter Allen, Roger Tory Peterson, Rutherford Platt—and by Daniel Longwell at *Life*. The astute copy editors at Knopf flagged me down on fact as well as style and Charles Elliott was an essential editor. And my wife, Barbara, affectionately went through it all with me.

ILLUSTRATION CREDITS

Grateful acknowledgment is made to the following for permission to reprint the photographs and drawings in this book on the pages listed.

Haydn Foundation for the Cultural Arts: 126, 131, 152, 167, 184, 194, 222, 230, 234 (left), 273, 309 (bottom)

New York Historical Society: 4, 197, 201, 226 (right) Bella C. Landauer Collection, 234 (right), 249, 301, 321 (center, bottom), 322 (top left, top right, bottom right), 323 (left)

New York Botanical Garden: 19, 23, 33, 65, 298, 303, 319 (top left, top right, bottom), 320 (top left, top right, lower right), 321 (top), 322 (bottom left), 323 (right)

Trustees of the British Museum (Natural History): 13, 92, 93, 96, 101, 320 (bottom left)

General Research and Humanities Division, New York Public Library, Astor, Lenox and Tilden foundations: 61, 74, 75, 235 Science and Technology Research Center, 258

American Philosophical Society: 115, 137, 164 (left), 265, 271, 319 (center)

Princeton University Library: 227, 276, 309 (top and center), 315

Houghton Library, Harvard University: 164 (right), 209

Academy of Natural Sciences: 100, 140

Linnaean Society of London: 28, 29

Gray Herbarium of Harvard University: 281, 292

North Carolina Collection, University of North Carolina Library: 15

British Library Board: 11

National Portrait Gallery, London: 50

Independence National Historical Park Collection: 109

Pennsylvania Academy of the Fine Arts: 147

Collection of the Louisiana State Museum: 213

Collection of the J. B. Speed Art Museum: 215

American Museum of Natural History: 226 (left)

Constantine Rafinesque Collection, Smithsonian Institution Archives: 242

Frances Carrick Thomas Library Collection, Transylvania College: 244

COLOR PLATES

Following page 48: i, ii Rare Book Division, New York Public Library, Astor, Lenox and Tilden foundations; iii–v British Museum (Natural History); vi, vii The Peale Museum, Baltimore (Gift of Mrs. Harry White in memory of her husband); viii (top) Rare Book Division, New York Public Library, Astor, Lenox and Tilden foundations, (bottom) British Museum (Natural History).

Following page 224: i, ii, iii (top and bottom) art copies by Herb Orth, courtesy *Sports Illustrated*; iv New York Historical Society; v (top and bottom) Haydn Foundation for the Cultural Arts; vi (top and bottom) New York Historical Society; vii–viii New York Historical Society.

All photographs from the New York Botanical Garden and the Haydn Foundation for the Cultural Arts are by William W. Swan.

INDEX

Abbot, John
  and Alexander Wilson, 188–9
  painting for *The Natural History of the
    Rarer Lepidopterous Insects of
    Georgia*, 189
Abronia umbellata (sand verbena), 294
Academy of Natural History, 278
Academy of Natural Sciences, 235, 260–1
Adams, Henry, 172, 192
  History of the United States, 172
Adams, John, 124, 306
Adams, John Quincy, 158, 204, 306
Agassiz, Louis, 303
Alston, Charles, 68, 69, 84
America, distorted views by Europeans about
    nature in, 122–4, 126
  refutations of, 124–5
American Association for the Advancement
    of Science, 299
American Journal of Science, 248, 252
American Ornithology (Wilson), 168–92,
    194, 208
  finished by George Ord, 221
  supplement prepared by Charles
    Bonaparte, 221, 272
  see also Wilson, Alexander
American Philosophical Society, 56, 58,
    117–18, 127, 143, 150, 151, 235,
    277–8
Amphianthus pisillus, 296
Amphibians
  frogs, 36, 102–3, 323
  Siren lacertina, 76
  two-toed Congo eel, 76
Anburey, Thomas, 163

Animals
  bears, grizzly, 133–4, *134*
  beaver, 10, 37
  bison (or buffalo), 9, 135, 313
  chipmunks, *309*
  described by Lewis and Clark, 142
  jackrabbit, white-tailed, 131
  mule deer, 131
  opossum, 8, 14, 57
  platypus, duck-billed, 150
  porcupine, 9, 312
  prairie dogs, 130, 143
  pronghorn, 130–1, *131*
  raccoon, 14
  sea elephant, 202
  seals, 238
  sheep, bighorn, 133
  squirrels, flying, 8
  wolf, prairie, 131
  see also Amphibians; Birds; Fish; Insects;
    Reptiles; *Viviparous Quadrupeds of
    North America* (Audubon)
Artemisia filifola, 297–8
Artemisia longifolia, 257
Artemisia ludoviciana (mugwort), 256
Arum (skunkweed), 52–3, 83; *see also*
    Plants, skunk cabbage
Aster gracilis, 260
Astorians, the, 254, 256
Ata-cul-culla ("Little Carpenter"), 105
Atriplex argentea (saltbush), 257
Audubon, John James, 17, 136, 150, 207–39,
    240–2, 270–1, 306, 308–17
  with Alexander Culbertson, 312–14
  and Alexander Wilson, 212, 223

Page numbers in italics indicate illustrations.

Audubon (*cont'd*)
  bad business ventures, 210–11, 214
  Birds of America, see *Birds of America*
  and Charles Lucien Bonaparte, 221
  comparing Wilson and, 222
  and Daniel Boone, 213–14
  death of, 317
  drawing by, for supplement to Wilson's
      Ornithology, 221–2, 222
  early drawings, 209
  experiments in bird-banding, 208
  feud with George Ord, 221, 233, 234–5
  first meeting with Wilson, 177–8, 212
  and Henry Clay, 216, 224
  hoax played on Rafinesque by, 241, 242,
      246
  and John Bachman, 236, 317
  mocking self-portrait of, 230
  and Nuttall, 275–6
  Ornithological Biography, 233, 239
  photograph of, 315
  portraits by, 215, 220, 301
  presenting some of Wilson's birds as his
      own, 234, 234–5
  and Rathbone family, 225–7
  settling down at Minnie's Land, 308
  soliciting subscribers for *Birds of
      America,* 230–2, 235, 237
  and Spencer Baird, 316–17
  travels of, for animal specimens, 310–14
  travels of, to find a publisher, 224–31
  travels of, to paint birds, 216–20, 232,
      235–8, 239
  *Viviparous Quadrupeds of North
      America*, 309, 310–15, 317
  and Walter Scott, 229
  on wanton killing of buffalo, 313
Audubon, Mrs. John James (Lucy
      Bakewell), 208, 211, 214, 220, 223,
      224, 315
Audubon, Victor and James (Audubon's
      sons), 316, 317

Bachman, John, 236, 317
  text for Audubon's *Quadrupeds* written
      by, 310, 315
Baird, Spencer, 316–17
  and Audubon, 316–17
  Catalogue of North American Birds, 316
Bakewell, Lucy, *see* Audubon, Mrs. John
      James
Bakewell, William, 209, 311, 317

Balance of nature, 38
Baldwin, Matthias, 157
Baldwin, William, 262, 263
Banister, John, 10–12, 58
  drawings of plants, 11
  Natural History of Virginia
      (unpublished), 12
Baptisia leucophaea (false indigo), 256
Barbé-Marbois, François de, 121
Bard, Samuel, 195–6, 200
Barton, Benjamin Smith, 128, 254
  Elements of Botany, 129, 255
Bartram, John, 3, 4, 18, 21, 36, 38, 39, 40–67,
      69, 70, 81–2, 84, 86, 91, 106–7
  appointed King's Botanist, 65, 76–7, 81
  and Cadwallader Colden, 56–7
  collecting and shipping specimens to
      European clients, 47–9, 53, 54, 56,
      60–5
  and correspondence with Collinson, 46–7,
      51–6, 62–5, 79, 81–2
  death of, 106–7
  Description of East Florida . . . , A, 66, 81
  and Hans Sloane, 63
  and James Logan, 45–6
  and John Clayton, 58
  *Observations on the Inhabitants, Climate,
      Soil . . . from Pennsylvania to
      Onondaga, Oswego and the Lake
      Ontario in Canada*, 60
  and Philip Miller, 62
  on St. John's River in Florida, 66–7, 81, 91
  sponsored by Benjamin Franklin, 56
  on trip with Evans, Weiser and
      Shickellamy, 40–3, 60
Bartram, John, Jr., 84, 107, 159
Bartram, William (son of John Bartram),
      62, 66, 79–107, 111–13, 115, 128,
      150, 159, 163, 172, 185, 243
  and Alexander Wilson, 160, 162, 164–5,
      176, 187, 192
  death of, 220
  drawings by, 80, 82–3, 92–3, 96, 100, 101
  and George Edwards, 80–1
  and Lionel Chalmers, 85–6, 89, 103
  and Peale's portrait of, 109
  and Thomas Jefferson, 112
  see also *Travels through North and South
      Carolina . . .* (Bartram)
Bartram Gardens, 48, 84, 107, 112, 129,
      260, 294
Bartram (mosses), 63, 319
Bartramia longicauda (upland plover), 321

Bell, John, 311
Berlandier, Jean Louis, 294
Bewick, Thomas
    History of British Birds and General
        History of Quadrupeds, 231
Big Bone Lick, prehistoric bones found at,
    144–5
Binomial system for genus and species,
    31–2, 304
Birch, Thomas, 244
Birds
    blackbirds, 38
    bluebird, 172, 187
    blue jay, 170–1
    Canada jay, 167, *167*, 168
    described by Lewis and Clark, 142
    ducks, diving, 237
    eagle, 14
    flycatchers, 275–6, 316, 322
    gannets, 237
    grackle, 221–2, *222*
    grebes, *209*
    grouse, ruffed, *61*
    heath hen, 193–4, *194*
    hummingbirds, 187
    in Labrador, 237–8
    magpie, 131, 143, 280
    meadowlark, western, 136
    migration of, 17
    mockingbirds, 9, 14, 163, 266
    nutcracker, Clark's, 136, 169, 280
    orioles, 170–1, 172
    parakeet, Carolina, 183–4, *184*, 185
    pelicans, 130
    phoebes, 208, 322
    pigeons, band-tailed, 271
    pigeons, passenger, 8–9, 10, 178–9
    plover, Wilson's, *321*
    plovers, golden, 278
    quail, mountain, *137*, 137–8
    roadrunner, 295
    sandhill cranes, *96*, *97*
    shearwater, Audubon's, 322
    snake birds, 95–6
    snowy owl, 212
    sparrow, Baird's, 317
    swallows, 211
    tanager, Louisiana, *137*
    thrush, wood, 167–8, 190
    titmouse, 275
    turkeys, wild, 8, 9, 40, 91
    upland plover, *321*
    vultures, 234, 235

    whippoorwill, 63, 282
    woodpeckers, 136, 169, 175–6, 190, 280
    wren, winter, 227
    see also Ornithology
Birds of America (Audubon), 219, 228, 308
    completion of, 239
    engravers for, 228, 231
    small octavo edition of, 310
    soliciting subscribers for, 230–2, 235, 237
    travels to paint birds for, 216–20, 232,
        235–8, 239
    see also Audubon, John James
Bird-banding, 208
Birds' songs, 275
Boerhaave, Hermann, 30, 68
Bonaparte, Charles Lucien, 221
    and Audubon, 221
    supplement to Wilson's *Ornithology*
        prepared by, 221, 272
Bones, prehistoric
    found at Big Bone Lick, 144–5
    see also Mastodon
Boone, Daniel, 213–14
Bosc d'Antic, Louis, 116
Botany, 284–304
    American grapevines immune to
        phylloxera, 290
    Botanical Teacher (Johnson), 287
    Botanical Textbook (Gray), 289
    Botany of South Carolina and Georgia
        (Elliot), 176
    Catalogue of New and Interesting Plants
        Collected . . . on the River Missouri,
        North America (Nuttall), 259
    classification system established by
        Linnaeus, 30–2
    Earthly Paradise (Parkinson), 45
    Elements of Botany (Barton), 129, 255
    Elements of Botany (Gray), 288
    English Physician (Culpeper), 45
    Familiar Lectures on Botany (Lincoln),
        287
    Flora Americae Septentrionalis (Pursh),
        201
    Flora Boreali-Americana (Michaux),
        255, 288
    Flora Lapponica (Linnaeus), 30
    Flora of New York, The (Colden), 24
    Flora of North America (Torrey and
        Gray), 288, 289
    Flora Virginica (Clayton), 58, 69, 122,
        288
    Fundamenta Botanica (Linnaeus), 30

Botany (cont'd)
  Gardener's Dictionary (Miller), 62
  *Genera of North American Plants and a
    Catalogue of Species* (Nuttall),
    262–3
  Genera Plantarum (Linnaeus), 7, 51
  Herbal (Turner), 45
  herbariums of Europe, 288
  Historia Plantarum (Ray), 12
  How Plants Grow (Gray), 289
  increase in plants introduced to Europe,
    49
  *Introduction to Systemic and Physiological
    Botany* (Nuttall), 274
  Logan's corn-tassel experiment, 45
  *Manual of Botany for the Northern
    States* (Eaton), 287, 288
  *Manual of the Botany of the Northern
    United States* (Gray), 289
  Medical Flora (Rafinesque), 251
  natural system of classification, 286
  North American Sylva (Michaux), 308
  Plantae Coldenghamiae (Colden), 7, 18
  Plantae Fendlerianae (Fendler), 291
  Trees of Massachusetts (Emerson), 273
  see also Bartram, John; Bartram, William;
    Bartram Gardens; Colden,
    Cadwallader; Collinson, Peter; Eaton,
    Ames; Elgin Gardens; Gray, Asa;
    Hosack, David; Linnaeus, Carl;
    Michaux, André; Mitchill, Samuel
    Latham; Nuttall, Thomas; Plants;
    Torrey, John; Trees and shrubs
Botta, Paolo, 295
Bouquet, Henry, 64, 66, 76
Bradbury, John, 256, 257
  Travels in the Interior of America, 257
Bradford, Samuel, 168, 169
Breckinridge, Henry
  Journal of a Voyage up the Missouri, 257,
    259
Breintnall, Joseph, 46–7
Brooks, Van Wyck, 170
Brown, James, 275
Bryant, William Cullen, 288
Buffon, Comte de (Georges Leclerc), 21,
    172, 190, 311
  arguments with Wilson, 190
  *Histoire Naturelle, Générale et
    Particulière*, 122
  on inferiority of all forms of nature in
    America, 122–3
Bull, William, 18, 69, 71

Burroughs, Raymond Darwin, 139–40
Byrd, William, II, 16, 55, 58

Calhoun, John, 158, 270
Campanula michauxia (Bellflower), 114
Cantwell, Robert, 192
Carduus pitcheri (thistle), 296
Carey, John, 290
Catesby, Mark, 16–18, 35, 53, 58, 163, 223
  correspondence with naturalists, 18
  drawings by, 17, 19
  Natural History of Carolina, Florida . . . ,
    The, 17–18, 63, 189
  and Peter Collinson, 63
Celsius, Olaf, 27
Chalmers, Lionel, 85–6, 89, 103
Charadrius Wilsonia (Wilson's plover), 321
Chemistry, 199–200
Clark, George Rogers, 113, 119, 211
Clark, William, 120, 128, 129, 139, 211;
  see also Lewis and Clark expedition
Classification, natural system of, 286, 304
  used by Torrey, 286
Classification system established by
    Linnaeus, 30–2, 39, 149, 262
  based on sexual characteristics, 31, 286,
    304
  genus and species, 31–2
Class and order, determination of, 31
Clay, Henry, 216, 224, 249
Clayton, John, 18, 30, 57–8, 107
  Flora Virginica, 58, 69, 122, 288
  and John Bartram, 58
Claytonia virginica, 58, 119, 320
Clethra accuminata Michaux (sweet pepper
    bush), 116
Clifford, George, 30
Clinton, DeWitt, 195, 205, 223, 224, 245, 294
  and Samuel Mitchill, 205–6
  writing newspaper column on natural
    history, 205
Colden, Cadwallader, 3, 4, 5–7, 18–22, 36,
    38, 39, 51, 70, 107–8, 195–6
  as authority on American Indians, 20
  correspondence with naturalists, 18–20,
    22, 83
  death of, 108
  *Explication of the First Causes of Action
    in Matter, An*, 20–1
  on formation of waterspouts, 22
  History of the Five Indian Nations, The, 20
  and John Bartram, 56–7

and Linnaeus, 3, 7, 18, 37, 39
Plantae Coldenghamiae, 7, 18
as political leader of New York, 21–2, 108
Treatise on Wounds and Fever, 22
Colden, David, 22, 39
Colden, Jane, 3, 22–5, 77, 80, 108, 195
Flora of New York, The, 24
plant drawings and descriptions by, 22–4
Coldenia (wild heliotrope), 19, *319*
Coleridge, Samuel Taylor
effect of Bartram's *Travels* on works of, 110–11
Collinsia (blue-eyed Mary), 256
Collinson, Peter, 18, 21, 23, 50–7, 81, 83–4, 144
and Benjamin Franklin, 51
and correspondence with John Bartram, 46–7, 51–6, 62–5, 79, 81–2
death of, 83
introducing American plants to European botanists, 50–1, 53
and Linnaeus, 51, 318
and Mark Catesby, 63
portrait of, 50
voluminous correspondence carried on by, 50–3, 83
Collinsonia canadensis (wild mint), 251, 318, *319*
Columba fasciata (band-tailed pigeon), 271
Columbus, Christopher, 8
Colymbus cauda elongata (snake bird), 95
Compton, Henry (Bishop of London), 10, 11, 16, 58
Cornus nuttallii (dogwood), 282
Corps of Discovery, *see* Lewis and Clark Expedition
Coues, Elliott, 192
Coulter, Thomas, 296
Creutzfeldt, Franz, 299
Crèvecoeur, J. Hector St. John
Letters from an American Farmer, 44
Croghan, George, 144
Cruciferae (mustard family), 264
Culbertson, Alexander, 312–14
Indian wife, Natawista, 312, 314
Cupressus disticha (pines), 91
Curtis, Moses Ashley, 290
Custis, John, 18, 55, 58
Cutler, Manassah, 148
Cutright, Paul Russell, 139–40
Lewis and Clark, Pioneering Naturalists, 140
Cuvier, Georges, 127, 153, 232

Dana, Richard Henry
Two Years Before the Mast, 282–3
Darwin, Charles
and Asa Gray, 302–4
Origin of Species, 302
Davis, Jefferson, 247
de Beauvois, Baron Palisot, 150–1
de Candolles, father and son, 286, 294, 296
de Jussieu brothers, 19, 49, 114, 245, 286
de Pauw, Corneille, 123
presenting distorted view of America, 123–4
Recherches Philosophiques sur les Americains, 123
Description of East Florida . . . , A (Bartram), 66, 81
Dillenius, Johann Jakob, 19, 63
Dionaea muscipula (Venus's-flytrap), 64–5, 65, 106, 111
Diphtheria, 85
Dodecatheon (shooting star), *11*, 47
Douglas, David, 294–6
Draba americana, 243
Dracocephalum virginican (dragonhead), 119
Drake, Daniel, 215–16, 246, 263, 270
Drummond, Thomas, 294
Dunbar, William, 105, 184–5, 243
Dupree, A. Hunter
Asa Gray, 302
Durand, Elias, 272
du Simitière, Pierre Eugène, 146

Eaton, Amos, 205–6, 250–1, 285–7, 306
death of, 306
and John Torrey, 285, 286
Manual of Botany for the Northern States, 287, 288
Edwards, George, 80
drawing of ruffed grouse, 61
Gleanings of Natural History, 80
Natural History of Uncommon Birds, A, 80
Elgin Gardens, 200–1, 201
Elliot, Stephen
Botany of South Carolina and Georgia, 176
Ellis, John, 70
and Alexander Garden, 70, 77–8
role of, in naming the gardenia, 78
Ellisia nyctelea (waterleaf), 77
Emerson, George B.
Trees of Massachusetts, 273
Emory, William Hemsley, 299

Engelmann, George, 290–1, 311
Enlightenment, the, 59, 154
Entomology, 260
    American Entomology (Say), 261, 272,
        273, 307
    *Natural History of the Rarer
        Lepidopterous Insects of Georgia,
        The*, 189
    see also Insects
Ephemera (mayflies), 90
Erie Canal, 205–6
Erigon compositus (cut-leaved daisy), 140
Eschscholtz, Johann Friedrich, 295
Eschscholtzia (poppy), 295
Evans, Lewis, 40–3
*Explication of the First Causes of Action in
        Matter, An* (Colden), 20–1
    criticism of, 21

Falcata pitcheri (Pitcher's hog peanut), 296
Farquhar, Mrs. William, *see* Colden, Jane
Farragut, David, 296
Fendler, Augustus, 291
    Plantae Fendlerianae, 291
Fertilization of plant seeds, 45
Fish
    bass, striped, 198, 323
    bubbler, 247, 248
    candlefish, 136–7
    conservation of, 198
    described by Lewis and Clark, 142
    migration by, 36, 37
    mythical, drawn by Audubon, 241, 242
    pipefish, Peck's, 273
    sheepshead, 197, 197, 198
    sunfish, 97
    see also Amphibians; Starfish
Fisher, Miers, 150, 208
Ford, Alice, 217, 224
Fothergill, John
    and Benjamin Franklin, 84, 85
    correspondence of, 85
    and William Bartram, 83, 84, 85, 86, 87,
        89, 103, 106, 109
Fox, George, 50
Franklin, Benjamin, 21, 22, 26, 36, 39, 46,
        58, 65, 69, 70, 76, 79, 84, 107
    on balance of nature, 38
    and Charles Willson Peale, 145
    on herring's migration, 36, 37–8
    as John Bartram's sponsor, 56
    and Peter Collinson, 51

and Peter Kalm, 36, 37–8
on prehistoric bones found at Big Bone
    Lick, 144
refuting Abbé Raynal's theory of
    degeneracy of American animals and
    men, 124
Franklinia, 66, 106, 320
Frederick II, 162
Frémont, John Charles, 296–9
Fretageot, Marie, 306, 307
Fritsch, Catherine, 154–6
Fulton, Robert, 169, 205
Fundamenta Botanica (Linnaeus), 30

Galt, William, 211, 311
Garden, Alexander, 3, 23, 24, 64, 66, 68–78,
        79, 106, 108–9
    banished to England, 109
    correspondence with naturalists, 69–73
    disagreements with Linnaeus, 75–7
    experiments with prickly pear, 73
    gardenia named for, 78
    and John Ellis, 70, 77–8
    shipping specimens to European
        naturalists, 70, 71–2
Gardener's Dictionary (Miller), 62
Gardenia, 78, 321
Gardiner, John L., 188
Genera Plantarum (Linnaeus), 7, 51
Genêt, Edmund Charles Édouard
    ("Citizen"), 118
Genus and species, 31–2
    binomial system for, 31–2, 304
Geology, 199, 261, 307
    Neptunist-Vulcanist controversy, 199
    *Observations on the Geology of the
        United States* (Maclure), 261
    *Sketch of the Mineralogical History of
        New York* (Mitchill), 199
Gillenia trifoliata (Bowman's-root), 11
Glissonière, Marquis de la, 37
Godfrey, Thomas, 45
Goforth, Dr. William, 215
Goldsmith, Oliver
    "Deserted Village, The," 126
    *History of Earth and Animated Matter,
        A*, 126
Gordon, James, 77, 78
Gordonia lasianthus, 77, 98
Graustein, Jeannette E., 282
Gray, Asa, 7, 274, 284–304
    Botanical Textbook, 289

and Charles Darwin, 302–4
and Charles Wright, 293–4
criticizing Rafinesque, 289
disagreement with Nuttall, 284, 289
Elements of Botany, 288
Flora of North America, 288, 289
How Plants Grow, 289
and John Torrey, 287–94, 296, 297–8
*Manual of the Botany of the Northern
    United States*, 289
professor at Harvard, 289
and the *Shortia galacifolia*, 289, 304
Great Chain of Being theory, 126–7, 144,
    303
Great Cypress Swamp, 243
Gronovius, Johann Friedrich, 18, 22, 56–7,
    58, 69
Grus pratensis (sandhill crane), 97

Haenke, Thaddeus, 294–5
Hale, Horatio, 301
Hamilton, Alexander, 150, 200
Harris, Edward, 311, 313
Harris, Thaddeus, 273
Havell, Robert, Jr., 231
Heerman, Mrs., 218
Herbariums, 288
Herrick, Francis Hobart, 217
Hesselius, John, 145
Histoire Naturelle, Générale et Particulière
    (Buffon), 122
History of Earth and Animated Matter, A
    (Goldsmith), 126
Holley, Horace, 246, 247, 248, 250
Hooker, William Jackson, 263, 294, 302
Horticultural Society of London, 294
Hosack, David, 200–1, 245, 285
    Elgin Gardens set up by, 200–1, *201*
Houston, Sam, 239
Hughes, William, 9
Hunt, Wilson Price, 256
Hypericum No. 153, 23, 24

Ichthyology, 244, 247–8, 252, 273, 307
    Fishes of New York, The (Mitchill), 197,
        202
    Ichthyologia ohiensis (Rafinesque), 247–8
    Mitchill's interest in, 196–8
    see also Fish
Illicium floridanum, 98
Imlay, Gilbert, 163

Indians, American
    Cherokees, 104, 105
    Colden, as authority on, 20
    drawing of Seminole chief, *100*
    History of the Five Indian Nations, The
        (Colden), 20
    of the Okefenokee Swamp, 89
    Osages, 266–7
    Tetons, 132
    William Bartram's travels through
        Seminole and Creek country, 99–102
Insects
    ants, 246–7
    flies, 11–12
    mayflies, 90
    Oeneis semidae (white butterfly), 274
    wasps, and their nests, 9, 38, 56
    see also Entomology
Irving, Washington, 238, 254, 256
    Astoria, 254, 282
Ixia coelestina (prairie iris), 265, *265*

Jackson, Andrew, 158, 233, 239, 288, 306
James, Edwin, 271, 286
James, Robert (Lord Petre), 53
Jardine, William, 229
Jefferson, Thomas, 21, 110, 112, 113–14,
    117–18, 119–28, 129, 150, 151,
    243–4, 250, 306
    and Alexander Wilson, 167–8, 169, 174,
        189, 190
    and André Michaux, 114, 117–18, 119
    and Charles Willson Peale, 143, 151, 157–8
    and Great Chain of Being theory, 126–7
    and his Megalonyx, *126*, 126–7, 150
    interested in areas west of the Mississippi,
        113
    interested in natural history, 120–2
    and Lewis and Clark expedition, 120,
        127–8, 139, 143
    and Louisiana Purchase, 203
    on Meriwether Lewis, 128
    Notes on the State of Virginia, 121, 124
    as president of American Philosophical
        Society, 127
    refuting Buffon's comments about
        America's inferiority, 124–5
    and William Bartram, 112
Jeffersonia diphylla (grass), 119
Johnson, Laura
    Botanical Teacher, 287
Josselyn, John, 9

Kalm, Peter, 26, 35–9, 51
  and Linnaeus, 26–7, 35, 39
  Travels in North America, 39, 123
Keats, George, 214
Keats, John, 214
Kemble, Fanny, 237
Kalmia latifolia (mountain laurel), 36, 119,
    320
King George IV, 231–2
King James I, 8

Lafayette, Marquis de, 115, 146
  and Charles Willson Peale, 158
Lamarck, Jean Baptiste, 114
Landscape designs, changes in, 62
La Salle, Sieur de, 9
Latrobe, Benjamin, 174
Laurens, Henry, 82
Lavoisier, Antoine, 199
Lawrence, Thomas, 231
Lawson, Alexander, 164, 168, 221–2
Lawson, Isaac, 19, 58
Lawson, John, 12–16
  burned at stake by Indians, 15, 16
  and James Petiver, 14–16
  New Voyage to Carolina, A, 12–14
Leavenworth, Melines, 296
Leavenworthia torreyi, 296
Leclerc, Georges, *see* Buffon, Comte de
Ledyard, John, 113–14
Lee, Mr. (trapper), 267–9
Lee, Reverend Jason, 281
Lehman, George, 232, 235
Lennox, Charles (Duke of Richmond), 53–4,
    62
Leslie, Charles Robert, 169
LeSueur, Charles, 261, 270, 273
  and New Harmony, Indiana, 306–7
Letters from an American Farmer
    (Crèvecoeur), 44
Lewis, Meriwether, 120, 139
  accomplishments on expedition, 139–40
  and Alexander Wilson, 169
  death of, 176, 181–2
  Jefferson on, 128
  leader of Lewis and Clark expedition,
    127–8
  see also Lewis and Clark expedition
Lewis and Clark, Pioneering Naturalists
    (Cutright), 140
Lewis and Clark expedition, 127–42, 143, 296

  list of species and subspecies that the
    explorers first described, 140–2
  notes from journal of, 129–39
  preparing Lewis for, 128
  specimens from, 143, 154, 200–1
  see also Clark, William; Lewis,
    Meriwether; Sakawajawa
Lincoln, Almira H.
  Familiar Lectures on Botany, 287
Lindheimer, Ferdinand Jakob, 291, 292–3
Lindheimera texana (star daisy), 292
Lining, John, 69, 71
Linnaea borealis, 262, 319
Linnaeus, Carl, 3–5, 24, 26–35, 36, 56, 58,
    69, 75–6, 108, 172, 262, 284, 286
  American plants catalogued by, 30
  approving the name gardenia, 78
  and Cadwallader Colden, 3, 7, 18–19
  classification system established by, 30–2,
    39
  death of, 108
  disagreements with Garden, 75–7
  Flora Lapponica, 30
  Fundamenta Botanica, 30
  Genera Plantarum, 7, 51
  and John Mitchell, 57
  and Peter Collinson, 51, 318
  and Peter Kalm, 26–7, 35, 39
  portrait of, 33
  and Professor Rudbeck, 27
  pupils and admirers of, 35
  sexual approach to botany, 34, 69
  Systema Naturae, 30, 45, 76
  trip through Lapland by, 27, 28–29, 30
Lisa, Manuel, 255, 257
Literary and Philosophical Society, 202
Little Black Bear, 272
Lizars, William, 228, 231
Logan, James, 21, 41
  corn-tassel experiment, 45, 85
  and John Bartram, 45–6
Logan, Martha, 64
Logania (evening trumpet flower), 77
Long, Stephen H., 270
Long expedition, 270–2, 296
  Torrey's identification of plants collected
    on, 286
"Lost plants," *see Franklinia; Shortia
    galacifolia*
Louisiana Purchase, 129, 203
Lucas, Eliza (Mrs. Charles Pinckney), 73
Lyceum of Natural History in New York,
    202, 245, 285

McClellan, George B., 296
MacGillivray, William
  History of British Birds, 233
Maclure, William, 261, 274
  and New Harmony, Indiana, 306–7
  Observations on the Geology of the United States, 261
Madison, James, 174, 204
Magnolia grandiflora, 91
Magnolia macrophylla, 260
Marquette, Jacques, 9
Martin, Maria, 236, 317
Mason, Joseph, 217
Mastodon, *152*
  unearthed, assembled and restored by Peale, 151–3
Mather, Cotton, 15
Medical Repository (scientific journal), 193, 202, 244
Megalonyx, Jefferson's, *126*, 126–7, 150
Meleagris occidentalis (wild turkey), 91
Michaelis, Christian Friedrich, 144–5
Michaux, André, 114–19, 288–9, 304
  Flora Boreali-Americana, 255, 288
  and Jefferson, 114, 117–18, 119
  journal entries, *115*
  travels in America to find plants useful to France, 114–17
Michaux, François André
  North American Sylva, 308
Miller, Philip, 62
  Gardener's Dictionary, 62
Mitchell, John, 57–8, 107
  map drawn by, of British and French settlements in America, 57
Mitchella repens (partridgeberry), 57, 119, 320
Mitchill, Samuel Latham, 193–200, 202–6, 210, 245, 285, 306–7
  and Alexander Wilson, 193–4
  and DeWitt Clinton, 205–6
  death of, 305–6
  doctrine of septon of, 199–200
  Fishes of New York, The, 197, 202
  founder of Lyceum of Natural History in New York, 202
  involved in ichthyology, 196–8
  and the Literary and Philosophical Society, 202
  Medical Repository founded by, 193, 202
  and Neptunist-Vulcanist controversy, 199
  and the New York Historical Society, 202, 203

and phlogiston controversy, 199
in politics, 195, 203–4
provider of botanical data for *United States Pharmacopoeia*, 200
role of, in Louisiana Purchase, 203
Sketch of the Mineralogical History of New York, 199
Monarda russeliana (bee balm), 269
Monroe, James, 158, 306
Morton, Earl of, 229
Morgan, John, 144
Muhlenberg, Gotthilf, 262

Natural History of Carolina, Florida . . . , The (Catesby), 17–18, 63, 189
Neptunist-Vulcanist controversy, 199
New Harmony, Indiana, 306–7
  and "The Boatload of Knowledge," 306–7
Newton, Isaac, 20, 21, 59
New Voyage to Carolina, A (Lawson), 12–14
New York Historical Society, 202, 203
Niagara Falls, 38
Nicotiana (tobacco plant), 262
Nolte, Vincent, 212–13, 224, 225
North, Christopher, 229
Notes on the State of Virginia (Jefferson), 121, 124
Nuttall, Thomas, 112, 254–70, 272–83, 284, 308
  and Audubon, 275–6
  Catalogue of New and Interesting Plants Collected . . . on the River Missouri, North America, 259
  daguerreotype portrait of, 281
  disagreement with Asa Gray, 284, 289
  Genera of North American Plants and a Catalogue of Species, 262–3
  Introduction to Systemic and Physiological Botany, 274
  Journal of Travels into the Arkansa Territory . . . 1819, A, 263–70
  journey by, for Benjamin Barton, 255–9
  journey to the Pacific with Townsend, 277–81
  known as "le fou," 254, 257, 281
  Manual of Ornithology of the United States and Canada, 275
  teaching at Harvard, and curator of its Botanic Garden, 272–7
  and Thomas Say, 260–1, 272, 274
Nuttallornis borealis (flycatcher), 276, 322

Oakes, William, 273
Oeneis semidae (white butterfly), 274
Oenothera caespitosa (primrose), 257
Oglethorpe, James, 18
Okefenokee Swamp and its Indians, 88–9
Ord, George, 186, 192, 220–1, 233, 236, 261,
    301, 306
    feud with Audubon, 221, 233, 234–5
    Wilson's Ornithology finished by, 221
Order, see Class and order
Oregon Trail, 280
Origin of Species (Darwin), 302
Ornithology, 162–3, 278, 316
    American Ornithology, see American
        Ornithology (Wilson)
    bird-banding, 208
    Birds of America, see Birds of America
        (Audubon)
    birds' songs, 275
    Catalogue of North American Birds
        (Baird), 316
    Gleanings of Natural History (Edwards),
        80
    History of British Birds (MacGillivray),
        233
    History of British Birds and General
        History of Quadrupeds (Bewick),
        231
    Manual of Ornithology of the United
        States and Canada (Nuttall), 275
    misconceptions about American birds, 163
    Natural History of the Birds of America
        (Viellot), 163
    Natural History of Uncommon Birds, A
        (Edwards), 80
    Ornithological Biography (Audubon),
        233, 239
    Topographical Description of the
        Western Territory of North America
        (Imlay), 163
    see also Audubon, John James; Birds;
        Nuttall, Thomas; Wilson, Alexander
Oviedo y Valdés, Gonzalo Fernández de, 8
Owen, David Dale, 307
Owen, Robert
    and New Harmony, Indiana, 306, 307

Paeonia brownii (peony), 295
Paine, Tom, 124
Peale, Charles Willson, 143–58, 159, 160,
    202
    and Benjamin Franklin, 145

children of, 149, 156–7
correspondence with naturalists, 150
death of, 305–6
drawing of mountain quail and Louisiana
    tanager, 137
and Jefferson, 143, 151, 157–8
and Lafayette, 158
Linnaean system used by, 149
museum established by, see Peale's
    Museum of Philadelphia
as a portraitist, 109, 145–6, 158
portraits of Washington by, 145–6
self-portrait, 147
sketching bones found at Big Bone Lick,
    145, 146
studying with Benjamin West, 145
unearthing, assembling, and restoring
    mastodon's skeleton, 151–3
and Washington, 149
Peale, Franklin, 157
Peale, Rembrandt, 156, 157
    "Court of Death, The," 157
Peale, Rubens, 157, 159, 162
    and Alexander Wilson, 159, 162
Peale, Titian Ramsay, 157, 216, 221, 261,
    270, 271, 301
Peale's Museum of Philadelphia, 143, 148–57,
    243, 260, 261
    description of exhibits in, 148
    gathering specimens for, 148–9
    restored mastodon displayed in, 153
    specimens from Lewis and Clark
        expedition, 143, 154
    start of, 144–5, 146, 148
    see also Peale, Charles Willson
Peck, William Dandridge, 273
Perca mitchilli (striped bass), 198, 323
Percy, Mrs., at Beech Woods plantation, 220
Petiver, James, 6, 16
    and John Lawson, 14–16
    sources for botanical and zoological
        collections of, 14–16
Philadelphia Academy of Natural Sciences,
    235, 260–1
Phlogiston controversy, 199
Phlox drummondi, 294
Phocaelephantinia (sea elephant), 202
Pickering, Charles, 273
Pike's Peak, 271
Pirrie, Elizabeth, at Oakley Plantation, 218
Pitcher, Zina, 296
Plants
    alpine plants, 271

anemone, double, 159
artemisia, 257, 297–8
aster, 260
aster, China, 53
bee balm, 269
bellflower, 114
blackberries, 36
black-eyed Susan, 27
blue-eyed Mary, 256, 260
bowman's root, *11*
butter-and-eggs, 62
cacti, *298, 299, 300*
chickweed, 62
chicory, desert, 322
coneflower, 266
coreopsis, rosy, 260
daisy, cut-leaved, *140*
dandelion, 62
described by Lewis and Clark, 141–2
docks, 62
dogtooth violet, white, 255
Draba americana, 243
dragonhead, 119
evening primrose, white, 257
Franklinia, 66, 106, *320*
fungi, 290
gardenia, 78, *321*
gerardia, flax-leaved, 260
grass, 119
heliotrope, wild, 19, *319*
hog peanut, Pitcher's, 296
Hypericum No. 153, 23, 24
Indian corn (or maize), 14, *15*
Indian pink, 69
indigo, 73
indigo, false, 256
jimson weed, 14
lady's slippers, 52, 53
laurel, mountain, 36, 119, *320*
lichens, 290, 302
marigolds, 34
mint, wild, 251, 318, *319*
mosses, 63, 273, 290, 294, 302, *319*
mountain cranberry, 116
mugwort, western, 256
mullein foxglove, 260
of mustard family, 257, 264
orchis, creeping fringed, 260
partridgeberry, 57, *320*
pentstemons, 257
peonies, 295
phlox, 294
pitcher plant, 18, 263

plantain, 38
poison ivy and poison sumac, 36, 54
pokeweed, 20, 36
poppies, 295, 296
poppy, celandine, 256
prairie iris, 265, *265*
prickly pear, 18, 73, 135, 136
primrose, 117
primrose, evening, 257
purslane, 62
salmonberry, 256
saponaria, 62
shooting star, *11*, 47
Shortia galacifolia, 116, 289, *303, 304*
skunk cabbage, 18, *19*, 38
skunkweed, 52–3, 83
snakeroot, 57
sorrel, 62
spring beauty, 58, 119, *320*
sunflower, dwarf, 277
sweet pepper bush, 116
thistle, Pitcher's, 296
tobacco, 8, 11, 262
trumpet flower evening, 77
twinleaf, *319*
Venus's-flytrap, 64–5, *65*, 106, 111
verbena, sand, 294
waterleaf, American, 77
see also Trees and shrubs
Poinsett, Joel, 297
Port Folio (literary magazine), 166
Prehistoric bones, found at Big Bone Lick,
  144–5; *see also* Mastodon
Primula mistassinica (primrose), 117
Pseudotsuga (Douglas fir), 295
Psoralea onobrychis (pea), 256
Puffinus therminieri (Audubon's
  shearwater), 322
Pursh, Frederick, 201, 259
  Flora Americae Septentrionalis, 201

Quercus emoryi (oak), 299

Rafinesque, Constantine, 240–53, 263, 284,
  285, 289, 306, 307
  botanical garden of, 249
  and Charles Short, 248–9
  criticized by Asa Gray, 289
  death of, 306
  genera and species discovered or
    identified by, 252

Rafinesque (*cont'd*)
  hoax played on, by Audubon, 241, 242,
    246
  Ichthyologia Ohiensis, 247
  journeys in America, 245
  *Life of Travels and Researches in North
    America and South Europe, A*, 251–2
  Medical Flora, 251
  miniature portrait of, 244
  and Mitchill, 245
  teaching at University of Transylvania in
    Kentucky, 246–50
  Western Minerva, 249–50
  World, or Instability, a Poem . . . , The,
    251
Rafinesquia californica, 322
Ramsay, Nathaniel, 145, 174
Rana catesbeiana (bullfrog), 323
Rathbone family and Audubon, 225–7
Rattlesnakes, 16–17, 40, 55, 80, *101*, 101–2
  on being bitten by, 46
  myth about, 10
Ray, John, 12, 16
  Historia Plantarum, 12
Raynal, the Abbé
  Benjamin Franklin's refutation of the
    Abbé's theory of degeneracy of
    American animals and men, 124
Reptiles
  alligators, 91–4, *92–3*, 95, 116
  described by Lewis and Clark, 142
  mud iguana, 76
  snakes, *see* Snakes
  turtles, newly hatched, 56
Rider, Alexander, 169
Rittenhouse, David, 150
Rothschild, Baron, 238
Royal Society, 51, 55, 63
Rozier, Ferdinand, 177–8, 210–11
  partnership with Audubon, 210–12
Rubus parviflorus (salmonberry), 256
Rudbeck, Professor, 27
Rudbeckia (black-eyed Susan), 27
Rudbeckia amplexicaulis (coneflower), 266
Russell, Dr. Thomas, 265, 269

St. John's River in Florida
  John Bartram's voyage on, 66–7, 81
  William Bartram's voyage on, 86, 90–9
Sakawajawa, 132, 136, 139, 257; *see also*
  Lewis and Clark expedition

Say, Thomas, 112, 216, 260, 261, 263, 270–1,
    272, 301
  American Conchology, 307
  American Entomology, 261, 272, 273, 307
  death of, 307
  and New Harmony, Indiana, 306–7
  and Thomas Nuttall, 260–1, 272, 274
Sayornis saya (Say's phoebe), 322
Schweinitz, Lewis von, 262
Scott, Walter, 229
Sellers, Charles Coleman, 153
Sarracenia (pitcher plant), 263
Shickellamy (Indian chief), 41, 60
Short, Charles Wilkins, 248–9, 289
Shortia galacifolia, 116, 289, 303, 304
Siegesbeck, Johann, 34
Silliman, Benjamin, 248, 252
Siren lacertina (amphibian), 76
Slaughter of birds and animals, 238, 313
Sloane, Hans, 19, 63
  Natural History of Jamaica, 63
Smith, James E., 189
Smithsonian Institution, 293, 316
Snakes, 9, 296
  blacksnakes, 38, 39
  coachwhip snake, 102, 116
  described by Lewis and Clark, 142
  rattlesnakes, 10, 16–17, 40, 46, 55, 80,
    101, *101–2*
  see also Reptiles
Society of Natural Science, Boston, 274
Species, *see* Genus and species
Sprague, Isaac, 311
Stanley, Lord, 227, 257
Stanleya (mustard family), 257
Starfish, 9
Stewart, William Drummond, 279, 311
Strachey, William, 8
Stuart, Gilbert, 156
Stylophorum diphyllum (celandine poppy),
    256
Sublette, Milton, 278
Sullivan, John, 125
Sullivant, William Starling, 290, 302
Symmes, John Cleves, Jr., 300
  Audubon's portrait of, *301*
  and "Symme's holes" theory, 300
Syngnathus peckianus (pipefish), 273
Systema Naturae (Linnaeus), 30, 45, 76

Temple Coffee House Botany Club, 10, 11,
    63, 294

Teton Indians, 132
Thomson, Charles, 79
Tipitiwichet, *see* Plants, Venus's-flytrap
Tompkins, Daniel, 172, 205, 285
Torrey, John, 245, 246, 274, 284–9, 291,
    297, 302, 304
  and Amos Eaton, 285, 286
  and Asa Gray, 287–94, 296–8
  discarding Linnaen system of classification
    286
  Flora of North America, 288, 289
  identifying plants collected by others, 286
Torreya taxifolia (yew), 304
Townsend, John Kirk, 277–8
  and westward journey with Nuttall,
    277–81
Travels in North America (Kalm), 39, 123
*Travels through North and South
    Carolina . . .* (Bartram), 86, 87–106,
    109–11, 236, 261
  effect of, on works of Coleridge and
    Wordsworth, 110–11
  European popularity of, 110
  excerpts
    alligators, 91–4, 92–3, 95
    Cherokee Indian girls, 104, 111
    coachwhip snake, 102
    Florida fountains, 98–9, 110
    frogs, 102–3
    Gordonia lasianthus, 98
    looking for *Franklinia*, 106
    Okefenokee Swamp and its Indians,
      88–9
    St. John's River, 86, 90–9
    sandhill (or savanna) cranes, 96, 97
    Seminole and Creek country, 99–102
    snake birds, 95–6
    yellow bream (or sunfish), 97
  Trees and shrubs
    andromeda, 34, 89
    azalea, 103
    balsam (or balm of Gilead) firs, 60–2, 82
    catalpa, 66
    described by Lewis and Clark, 141–2
    dogwood, 282
    Douglas fir, 295
    evergreens, 91, 295, 305
    Franklinia, 66, 106
    magnolia, 91, 260
    oaks, 66, 89, 299
    orange, Osage, 129
    persimmon, 10, 38
    pines, 295

red-bay tree, 255
redwood tree, 295
rhododendrons, 308
sassafras, 8, 36
sweet-bay tree, 36
tallow nut tree, 66
tupeloe, 66
see also Plants
Troost, Gerard, 306, 307
Tuckerman, Edward, 290, 302
Tudor, Frederick, 277
Turdus polyglottos (mockingbird), 266

U.S. Army
  providing assistance to naturalists, 296
  see also Lewis and Clark expedition; Long
    expedition
U.S. Navy, 299–300
  and Wilkes expedition, 300–2
United States Pharmacopoeia, 200

Vaccinium erythrocarpum Michaux
    (mountain cranberry), 116
*Viviparous Quadrupeds of North America,
    The* (Audubon), 309, 310, 315, 317
  Audubon's travels for, 310–14
  text for, written by John Bachman, 310

Washington, George, 73, 110, 112, 115, 196
  portraits of, by the Peales, 145–6, 156
Washington, Martha, 55
Waterspouts, formation of, 22
Waterton, Charles, 233, 275
  Wanderings in South America, 233–4
Webster, Daniel, 237, 311
Weiser, Conrad, 41, 60
Wernerian Society, 229
Wesley, John, 84
West, Benjamin, 169
  and Charles Willson Peale, 145
Western Academy of Natural Sciences, 311
Western Minerva (journal), 249–50
Whitaker, Alexander, 8
Whytt, Robert, 24
Wilkes, Charles, 300, 302
  expedition led by, 300–2
Wilkinson, James, 176, 184–5
Wilson, Alexander, 17, 112, 150, 159–94,
    223, 236

Wilson (cont'd)
   American Ornithology, 168–92, 194, 208
   arguments with Buffon about American
      birds, 190–1
   and Audubon, 177–8, 212, 223
   chance first meeting with Audubon,
      177–8, 212
   comparing Audubon and, 222
   correspondents of, 186–90
   death of, 221
   on death of Meriwether Lewis, 181–3
   drawing by, 164
   as editor of Ree's Cyclopedia, 168
   first American journey, 166–7
   and Jefferson, 167–8, 169, 174, 189–90
   and John Abbot, 188–90
   journeys by, to peddle his Ornithology,
      171–86
   learning to draw birds, 165, 168
   and Meriwether Lewis, 169
   and Mitchill, 193–4

   poetry by, 161, 165–6
   Rembrandt Peale's portrait of, 164
   and Rubens Peale, 159, 162
   and William Bartram, 160, 162, 164–5,
      176, 187, 192
Wislizenus, Adolph, 291–2
Wistar, Caspar, 128, 150
Witt, Christopher, 44–5
Wood, William, 8–9
Wordsworth, William
   effect of Bartram's Travels on works of,
      110, 111
Wright, Charles, 293, 302
   and Asa Gray, 293–4
Wyeth, Nathaniel Jarvis, 277
Wyethia helianthoides (dwarf sunflower),
   277

Zoology, see Amphibians; Animals; Birds;
   Fish; Reptiles

Joseph Kastner is a former editor
of *Life* magazine and the author of a number of articles
on natural history and horticulture.
He lives in Grandview, New York, and has
a summer home on Block Island.

A NOTE ON THE TYPE

This book was set in Monticello, a Linotype revival
of the original Roman No. 1 cut by Archibald Binny
and cast in 1796 by the Philadelphia type foundry Binny & Ronaldson.
The face was named Monticello in honor of its use
in the monumental fifty-volume *Papers of Thomas Jefferson*,
published by Princeton University Press.
Monticello is a transitional type design,
embodying certain features of Bulmer and Baskerville,
but it is a distinguished face in its own right.

This book was composed, printed and bound
by The Haddon Craftsmen, Inc., Scranton, Pennsylvania.

Four-color separations were prepared
by the Offset Separations Corporation,
New York, New York, and Milan, Italy.
The color inserts were printed
by Creative Lithography, New York, New York.

Typography and binding design by Camilla Filancia